Agents of Fortune

The Blue Öyster Cult Story

Martin Popoff

Agents of Fortune

The Blue Öyster Cult Story

Martin Popoff

WYMER
PUBLISHING
Bedford, England

First published in Canada in 2004
This revised edition published 2016 by Wymer Publishing
Bedford, England
www.wymerpublishing.co.uk
Tel: 01234 326691
Wymer Publishing is a trading name of Wymer (UK) Ltd

ISBN 978-1-908724-41-0

Edited by Jerry Bloom.

Every effort has been made to trace the copyright holders of the
photographs in this book but some were unreachable. We would
be grateful if the photographers concerned would contact us.

Front and back cover images © Richard Galbraith.

Printed and bound by
CMP (UK) Ltd, Poole, Dorset, England

A catalogue record for this book is available from the British Library.

Cover design by Andy Bishop.

Contents

Introduction

I've always been fascinated with The Blue Öyster Cult. Here was a veritable, compact army of creative beings brought together in worship under Marshall stacks, sending forth tales that balanced pathos, humour and the paranormal, to great digestible rock 'n' roll effect. Through 12 studio records and five live shootouts (depending on how ya count) over four decades, Eric Bloom, Donald "Buck Dharma" Roeser, Al Bouchard, Joe Bouchard and Allen Lanier (plus eventual and residual replacements) have deliberately carved a niche that has yet to be cohabitated by any other sonic assemblage.

Agents Of Fortune is an attempt to examine the many facets of the band's creative pathways, and for that reason, is quite specifically focused on the band's records, both the music and the lyrics, and the motivations thereof. For above all, Blue Öyster Cult is a study in the creative process, the band combining musical skills, studio craft and exquisite story-telling in construction of some of the most timeless, mysterious and beautiful recorded music ever to wear a Godzilla head. The book's a fan thing and by no means a complete biography. It's the art that matters, and not the people. Or at least that's the focus here, and indeed in most interviews I do with any band, not to mention the journalism that falls out of those talks. I can hear the reviews now... "he makes no mention whatsoever of (insert a thousand factoids here)"... "but what of the band itself, their home life, their wives?"... "where's the dirt?" Believe me, I have plenty of dirt, but it's staying locked up in my computer. I respect these guys too much, not to mention what they've done with their lives in the realm of art.

So following this central thrust, you will find little in the way of pre-record band history here, or sordid personal stories throughout the band's moderately-to-considerably turbulent trip. Also, the detailed discussions of live gig setlists, equipment, exhaustive discographies that often clog rock biographies is left brief and breezy. It has always been my belief that bands are made up of real, only semi-remarkable people making what is hopefully quite remarkable art, and therefore really what matters is the work. Because, plain and simple, the work has seen work (a painter paints; writing is rewriting etc.). And that is especially the case with this band, much blood sweat and tears going into the many amazing songs that we will discuss. The art, in this case and in most, is more compelling than the artist, Blue Öyster Cult records being collaborations of teams of creative souls, quite collaborative and painstakingly built achievements that deserve our appreciation.

So above all, this book is an appreciation of a body of work, in no way designed to supplant the only other lengthy piece of journalism (in English) on the band, "Don't Report This": The Saga Of Blue Öyster Cult, by Steve Roeser and Bolle Gregmar, which appeared in Goldmine magazine, June 7, 1996. Steve is a cousin of Donald's, and Bolle, well, as he quite accurately states, is the Blue Öyster Cult, a qualification that makes perfect sense when you realize that on any subject related to the band, he most likely knows more of the angles, facts and figures than any one member of the band. He would kill any of the actual Oyster boys in a round of BÖC jeopardy. Dead.

Also much credit goes to John Schwartz, who is (or was, at the time of writing the brunt of this book), the keeper of the Blue Öyster Cult FAQ on the Internet, not to mention a pretty cool site on the band. John also figured intelligently, and frequently on many discussions of the band on the net. Not only does John know reams of stuff on the boys, but also he is packed with razor-sharp opinions.

This brings up a point I must make. I don't know if all of what I just said still stands. Fact is, I wrote the first edition of this book pretty much in '96 through '98, issued it first in 2004, offered a new and improved version to you in 2009, and now am back in 2016 with more nuggets of goodness added. But yeah, for years it sat, in my computer, doing nothing. Loads of people kept asking me about it because I would mention its existence at my site www.martinpopoff.com, where I also posted what is essentially the Cultösaurus Erectus chapter of my *Ye Olde Metal* concept (six books in the series and counting!), years ago. I figured it was time it saw the light of day, and so I soldiered through and yeah, in 2004, we all got our first book on the Cultsters.

So why does this book exist? Two reasons. First, no other book on the band currently exists and it's quite likely none besides this one ever will, as it takes a guy with no commercial aspirations or worries for such a tome's success to make it happen. Yet, there is no doubt in my mind that if (or when) Bolle eventually puts one together, it will become the definitive work on the band, rendering this one pretty much obsolete, a quaint stab at understanding a band of enormous complexity, sitting on your shelf as a cute collectible with some weird rock criticism and interesting interview segments, but uh, damn near redundant.

But by the same token, the book Bolle would do would be 700 pages long, and even more commercially unviable than what you see here. Unless the band suddenly sells shiny discs in numbers known by Metallica, or warms hockey barn seats in the manner of Kiss and Aerosmith teamed-up and touring, or Journey with the Philippine firecracker (love that guy). We are not talking about a currently popular band here. Which brings me to the crux of my first point. This book exists because I spent hundreds of hours writing it with no real thoughts of ever finding a commercial publisher for the project. And yet first it came out through Metal Blade, and now, through the fine folks at Wymer. Still, this book is simply the product of a fan, believing in promoting the works of a great, vastly under-rated band, nothing more.

So why does this book exist? Well, it exists because any given author on any given subject is going to have different hot buttons. And mine is, as I say, the body of work, and little of the peripheral codswallop that is the lives of what are essentially, uh, people. Towards that end, what will follow will be a brief prerecording history, and then a bunch of chapters dealing in a very demarcated way with Blue Öyster Cult's recorded output, plodded and plotted song by song, stroke of mischievous brilliance by stroke of luck. It may not fit the standard description of a rock bio, but deal with it. And in essence, it isn't so much deeply written, by me, but more of an oral history (and then, as I say, mostly about the albums)—much of what you'll be witnessing are explanations in the band's own words, with little window-dressing or second guessing.

Plus, this book is all you're going to get until Bolle builds his Book of the Cult, and like I say, more importantly, convinces someone to print it! Oh yeah, one thing, if you'd like to get a sense of Bolle's hilarious insights into this admittedly unhealthy obsession of his, have no fear. His halting, often poetic commentary has been respectfully recorded throughout this book, as if he was the sixth wheel of the band—that he pretty much is.

In addition to my own critical (critically injured?) commentary, and the fruits of my many interviews with Cult members and honorary members, band quotes were used from what unfortunately was only a handful of articles that have appeared in rock mags over the years, when my own interviews failed to unearth the appropriate nugget of truth. These folks have been duly credited in the back, and their work exposing the depth and brilliance of BÖC is much appreciated. Yes, thanks to all who had the good taste to speak to the band.

So, yeah, what you get here is a combination of me spoutin' off, and a whole lot of explanatory, contextual, anecdotal reminiscing on the part of the members of the band and their immediate orbit. And I hope, like I say, that I've succeeded in keeping it fairly focused on the records themselves. Bolle: you do the rest. I'll be the first in line to buy it.

So kick back, pour something red or perhaps black, and read about where in damnation Buck and his army of enablers get this stuff. And one more thing: if you don't already own all the Blue Öyster Cult albums, please, get out there and buy them. Now. As you will read in the following pages, it is a catalogue of intense quality, musically, lyrically, with respect to arrangement and production. In its eye-winked, expertly sequenced, smart, pert totality, it is a body of work that is (or should be) a staple of any thinking rock fan's album collection.

Martin Popoff
martinp@inforamp.net

Öyster Sea Legs!

"Do you got a van?"

As I mentioned in my intro piece, this pre-deal history of the rock animal that is The Blue Öyster Cult is going to be brief and hopefully painless. I've read a million rock bios and I usually can't wait until I crawl my way through those first 30 pages about favourite public school subjects, dad's job, pageboy haircuts, broken vans (usually "lorries"), first hits of acid, and pimply bands with names like The Pedestrians, The Lemonswabs, or Dirk Windbag and the Devlintones (although, sorry, there's some of this boy band stuff!). Suffice to say that The Blue Öyster Cult sort of fell together like any of these sorry ragamuffin pop combos. Let's just pick it up as the ball seemed to get rolling. First, we'll go with drummer Al Bouchard's version of events, Al of course being a pivotal songwriting piece of the puzzle and drummer for the band until his ouster in 1982 (more on that later)...

"The band as Blue Öyster Cult... we actually had the concept before we had the band. Of course I had played with all of these guys in different configurations and concepts before BÖC, concepts that maybe didn't work, or had served their purpose and were discarded at a certain point. And of course my brother Joe and I had The Regal Tones, a cover band where we just developed our musical vocabulary in terms of rock." Joe had played both keyboards and guitar in this surf-style band, while Albert contributed organ; a cousin Ted was also part of the line-up. The band actually lasted ten years, including a stint in Beatle wigs. Albert had also been part of The Clansmen.

"Then I had two bands with Donald," continues Albert, who first met guitarist and vocalist Donald "Buck Dharma" Roeser in '65 at college in Pottsdam, NY, "first The Disciples (note: including Skip O'Donnell on vocals, Bruce Abbott on bass, who had been in Donald's band Eve of Destruction, and Jeff Latham on guitar), then The Travesty. They were the same sort of deal, although The Travesty developed to the point where we were a blues/jazz type band, more improvising than we had ever done before. And it was all the same people except that we switched instruments. I mean I was still on drums and Donald was still on guitar but the other guys switched."

It is of note that Donald took up the guitar as a form of physical therapy after breaking his wrist playing basketball. Roeser started on the accordion, and had switched to drums, but the injury had him switch to guitar, a $16 Stella, on which he learned the licks of surf greats like the Surfaris and the Ventures, as well as Carl Wilson and Chuck Berry. More direct influence and technique came from

The Blues Project's Danny Kalb. Axe-wise, he progressed through a Premier, a Univox, a Fender Jaguar (with Bandmaster) and a Hagstrom until settling upon a 1961 Gibson SG which he would use through 1975, followed by a mix of guitars anchored by a Les Paul and a Stratocaster.

"When I got the Strat," Buck told Steve Rosen in 1975, "there was something about the body, the way it was cut away in the back for comfort, and the way the neck was that made it very orthopedic in my hands. I'd never taken any lessons on guitar, so I developed a lot of bad habits through the years from just playing Gibsons. Also, I didn't have a lot of strength in my hands. My ear wanted me to play something, and I'd just play it any way I could, but I didn't have any established hand technique that would really enable me to be free. I knew that would take years to develop, so I decided I might as well get on the stick. Playing a Fender guitar helped spark these realizations."

"I had a lot of ideas, but I just couldn't play," continued Donald, intimating to Rosen that his breakthrough didn't come until work on the band's second album. "I was very frustrated. I would overdub leads, and go over it again and again and again until I got what I wanted. Finally, I said, 'There's got to be an easier way.' I was 25, and I realised then that I was a professional musician, and this was what I was going to do for a living. Now I'm dedicated to being a musician. I don't think I'll ever do anything else. But I don't really know where my music is headed. I'd like to get involved in my own style—that's what I'd like to do—not play like anybody else, but draw from a lot of influences. It's about time people started listening to me; that's the way I look at it. I've put a lot of work in."

"Drums were my first instrument but I did study piano formally first," adds Albert, on his own particular path. "I wanted to play the drums after I saw a parade and the drummers in action. Influence-wise, Gene Krupa was first, then Joe Morrello, then the Ventures' drummer (Mel Taylor) and all the rock guys. Then Elvin Jones, Joe Jones and Rufus Jones. But my first album was *Hey Let's Twist* by Joey Dee and the Starlighters and after that I bought all the records of the Ventures, Beach Boys and Beatles.

"Albert and I grew up in a large family," adds Joe, citing a few Canuck connections. "Six boys and one girl, in Clayton, NY on a farm on the edge of the St. Lawrence River. My father's early ancestors were from Montreal and Ottawa, but his family moved south to upstate NY a couple of generations back. Most of the radio that my brother and I listened to was from Kingston, Ontario. They had the Canadian content law where a good percentage of the artists played on the radio had to be Canadian. We listened to Ian and Sylvia and a lot of British stuff like Cliff Richard and The Shadows. Actually we heard the Beatles' Canadian releases months before they was ever played in the US. The Canadian DJs were flipping out for the Beatles, but my first impression was that they weren't as good as The Shadows. There is a line in 'P.S. I Love You' where Paul sings exactly like Cliff Richard!"

"When I was in high school I was deep into the music scene of the sixties," continues Joe. "The Beatles and Beach Boys/Brian Wilson were my heroes, but I loved the Paul Butterfield Blues band and the Stones and the instrumentals of the Ventures. I did a wide variety of music too and I sang in the choirs and played trumpet in the school band. It was all good for me. I decided to study music in college, but in 1966 there were almost no colleges where you could study guitar, so I decided to become a piano major. The only problem with that was I sucked on piano, I had very little piano skills outside of playing Jerry Lee Lewis boogies. So my first years at Ithaca were a big struggle, doing mostly scales and arpeggios three, four hours a day, to try to catch up to my peers who were amazing classical piano players. But I loved it all. I would fall asleep in my repertory classes every afternoon. Those were classes where a pianist would play their classical pieces. It was all really mellow stuff. The only problem is I'd start snoring in class and somebody had to shake me cause the noise was so bad! I got to sing with the Ithaca Chorus at Carnegie Hall with Leopold Stokowski conducting. I was being groomed for a career as a high school vocal teacher, but I was never a strong singer. If I didn't go into rock I'd probably be teaching in a high school somewhere with a choir and chorus and doing music for the local school musical.

"In 1968 I joined a band at Ithaca College called Que Pasa. We were a Latin jazz/rock group in the mould of Sergio Mendes and his popular group Brazil 66. Que Pasa was an amazing band of experienced older players who needed a bass player. I was their man even though I had not played a bass at all. The leader of the band, Steve Brown, who also taught guitar at Ithaca, bought me my first bass. We had charts for everything and I learned a lot about music from that band. With two years of playing jazz and rock on bass, I was all set to slip into the Soft White Underbelly in their waning days. Soon we modified our style and changed our name to Blue Öyster Cult."

Once Donald and Albert had dropped out of college, they proceeded to kick around upstate New York playing music and working odd jobs, with Albert embarking on a brief side-stint to Chicago to be in another band with Jeff Latham. Albert continues the tale. "Then we had the Soft White Underbelly (note: reportedly a reference to Nazi-controlled Italy from a Winston Churchill speech), which was some of the same people. Towards the end of the band, Eric Bloom had joined, and that was more of a Grateful Dead-type thing, developing our improvisational skills and songwriting abilities, although really it was just Allen and myself who were writing the songs, Allen, myself, Sandy and Meltzer. Those were the four songwriters. And the bass player, who is now a nutritionist, was Andy Winters; he was the only other person who did any writing. And then when Eric joined we went through a bunch of different names, a bunch of different concepts, first with Andy Winters in the group. Then my brother had joined and Andy was let go. We were still fooling around with different ideas, and actually took a step backwards and started doing a lot of non-original material, copy material, just trying to survive as a band, playing bar mitzvahs and anything we could get our hands on."

"My degree is in classical piano," reflects Joe, "so I was exposed to a lot of stuff early on, but I knew those guys from when I was just graduating from high school. Albert was working with Donald and they were doing Soft White Underbelly and I followed that really closely the whole time. If anything, I found my spot. Soft White Underbelly never really broke through. When I came in I thought that if I played my cards right, it could break through. I am not saying I was the reason for it, but I think the chemistry just gave us a chance. I was surprised. Soft White Underbelly had a great writing team. We had Sandy and

Richard Meltzer and Albert and Donald, and later Allen was writing a lot. They had a great team and I was able to jump in."

At times the resident band at "the house on the hill" also included saxophonist Jeff Richards, and early on, pre-Albert even, the drummer involved was named Joe Dick. Eventually keyboard player John Wiesenthal would be out to pursue a career in film. The Meltzer of which Albert speaks is one Richard Meltzer, penner of the first rock criticism tome ever, *The Aesthetics of Rock*. Released in 1970 on Something Else Press, the book was actually written in late 1965. Meltzer would, as Albert noted, figure as one of the early writers of the band's lyrics. Richard now lives in Portland, and has contributed continually if sparingly to the Brain Surgeons (Albert's band with his third wife Deborah Frost, now converted to third ex-wife!), and Al's and Joe's solo projects mostly through Albert's use of a substantial Meltzer backlog that Al's had on hand for some years now. Richard was a philosophy major with an art minor at Stony Brook in the mid-'60s, also DJing at WUSB. He later went on to graduate work at Yale.

The late Helen Wheels, penner of 'Tattoo Vampire', had this to say about Richard. "He's a wild, brilliant guy, undisciplined except for his writing. I would say he's kind of charming, and very, very smart. He sent me two copies of his new book. But I was very good friends with his girlfriend at the time. They were good cats, but it was a very wild house to live in. We ended up living in a big house in a part of Great Neck. Richard and Ronnie lived with us for a number of years."

And Joe Bouchard's take on Meltzer? "Richard's a really great guy. I don't think I really ever spent that much time with Richard, but he and Sandy were of a similar mind. They knew what they were doing, what they wanted to do artistically. I think they took a lot of aesthetics courses. I think Sandy was a philosophy major. When I was taking my master's degree, I had to take some philosophy courses, so I know where they're coming from now. *The Aesthetics of Rock* was Richard's book, and I was showing it to my aesthetics teacher, and he goes wow, this is really amazing. This is where they were coming from. He's got a new book out now. His time is yet to come. But *The Aesthetic of Rock* is a great book. It's about 500 pages. And it's totally believable if you've studied any aesthetics. It's wild. He was one of those writers that would sucker you into, 'Oh this is bullshit bullshit bullshit,' then all of a sudden he'd hit this amazing truth, like whoa! Then he would wander off and talk about all kinds of trivialities, then come back and hit you hard. He's a good writer."

Meltzer recalls the tale of his friendship with Sandy "Memphis Sam" Pearlman (Sam or Samuel was his real name), the man who would become a *Crawdaddy* writer at the beginning in 1966, the band's manager, and more importantly visionary for the Cultsters on the literary side of this literary band.

"My relationship to him is that I met him when I was 11. We went to junior high together, high school and college. He was my best friend for a while. We both majored in philosophy. We'd stay up and work on these papers together. When we first started thinking about 'Let's write about rock 'n' roll,' this would have been '62 or '63, a long time ago. We had to do a paper about... we had this art teacher named Alan Capro, who did environments and happenings. He was kind of an important historical figure who happened to be stuck at this dinky little school that didn't appreciate him. We had to do a paper on comparing

German Expressionism and fauvism. Pearlman said as a joke, you know, I really think the link is the Beach Boys, surf music. Then we talked about, let's think about how would we verbalize that. I mean, how would we even come up with the fake case for that? We would have all these hypothetical discussions about how we could shuffle rock content into these papers we were doing. And he didn't have the inclination to do it himself so I did it. But he certainly was a co-conspirator at first. And I would start putting it in papers, no later than '64. Anyway, we were friends. Then time marches on, and he becomes an entrepreneur and he really became a creep, you know? Somebody who cheated most people he ever did business with in those days out of substantial monies."

"Before I met Sandy, I had no burning ambition to be a rock star," mused Buck Dharma back in 1982. "I just played for bar band-like enjoyment; I never thought that was what I would do seriously. We would never have surfaced as even a Bob Seger-type of band, or even at all, if it wasn't for Sandy."

Al recounts the tale of meeting Eric Bloom, future front man for the BÖC, for the first time. "John Trivers was one of my links to Eric. What happened was when I came home from college in the summer, to Clayton in upstate New York, there was a band, and I taught the drummer how to play, giving him lessons when I was in high school. Then I went away to college, and played in college with Donald and some other things. I came back during the summer, and this drummer who I had taught to play was moving out of town. His band had all these gigs for the summer, so they asked me to join, to replace my student. I said okay, and we played all over, Cape Vincent, Alexandria Bay, the whole Thousand Islands area. The lead guitar player and sometimes lead singer was this guy Peter Havilland. Havilland said, 'Oh yeah, I've got a really good band.' I said, 'Where'd you learn all these blues songs?' He said 'I have a really good band back at my school, that I play with during the year, called the Lost and Found. I said, oh, the Lost and Found, I've heard of you guys. So anyway, he was always talking about the Lost and Found, and Eric Bloom and the other singer, and the bass player John Trivers who was really good. Then I played with Donald in college. About two years later I was in New York City, and I was in the Sam Ash music store and I saw a picture of Peter Havilland. I said, 'I know these guys; this is the Lost and Found, Peter's group.' There was this guy standing right next to me who said, 'Oh, you know Peter? That's my group!' I turned around and it was Eric Bloom. He was working in Sam Ash and he put a picture of his band up on the wall. We got to talking and he said, 'Do you guys need anybody to work for you?' I said, 'Well, I don't know; do you have a van?' And he says yeah. So he started driving us around, and that's how I met Eric."

As singer for the Lost and Found, Eric was deemed "Rock King of the Finger Lakes." After trying to re-ignite the band back in Geneva, he had finally called it quits in the summer of '68. That's when he got the job at Sam Ash.

Donald "Buck Dharma" Roeser (Sandy, as many good Svengali types do, had aliases for everybody, but only Donald's stuck) offers his slant on Eric's initial Cult status: "Working at Sam Ash was Eric's first gig, and he had a truck. Eric came to work for the band as a road manager while we were making the first Elektra record, which of course was never released. But after the whole thing fizzled out, he was tapped to be the singer because we knew he had rock experience. Also he had amps and two PA columns. So he was just the guy we were looking for. Not only that, he had a set of pipes too. Les had talent, but he's just never been able to get it together."

Buck is speaking of original front man Les Braunstein who was figured to be not hard-edged enough, for the band. Donald recalls how at one early gig, they had the new guy, Eric, up there singing with a 12-string guitar that they didn't bother to plug in.

"Eric and Les had both gone to Hobart College, university, whatever it's called, in New York State, near Geneva," offers Meltzer, filling in some of the blanks on Eric's hiring. "Les had a VW van; they needed his van, and the van got repossessed. He wasn't making his payments. And who shows up then, but his college buddy Eric with, not only a van, all paid for, but a PA! That's why he was the singer. And even after he was the singer, they would have these meetings. They lived in this house in Great Neck, New York, this decaying mansion, four stories, and Eric slept all the way on the top. He was also allegedly a drug dealer (note: Eric strongly disputes this, and knowing mischievous Richard…). But anyway, it was one night after he was already the singer, possibly even after they had recorded the Stalk-Forrest stuff… I'm trying to remember the sequence. But in that neck of the woods, where they made sure he was asleep all the way at the top of the house, and they actually auditioned me and Pearlman to sing. And we were terrible. And it was like, okay, we'll stick with… he was called Manny then. We'll stick with Manny. His position with them was always very tenuous."

"I went to Hobart College in upstate New York," says Eric, offering his version of events. "At the same time, Albert and Donald were at the Clarkson University. We didn't know each other, but they're both in upstate New York. Allen Lanier was going to the University of North Carolina. We were all sort of contemporaries. I'm the oldest by a couple of years. I graduated from college in '67. At around the same time, a guy I went to school with—this is all coincidence—got into Soft White Underbelly with Albert, Donald, and Allen. I stayed up there to keep my college band going, and this other guy moved to Long Island to be part of what was Soft White Underbelly, and they got a record deal with Elektra. I moved back to New York in the fall of '68 to become a booking agent with Premier Talent, which was the premier booking agent at the time, after William Morris. I didn't think I'd ever be in a band again, having been in several during my school days. The tour I was supposed to become a trainee on fell through—The Crazy World of Arthur Brown. Brian Auger and Julie Driscoll were the opening act. There was visa trouble and my trainee job collapsed."

"I had moved back to New York City to go to work, and the job fell through," continues Bloom, offering a slightly different telling of the story than Albert. "So I had to scramble. I took a job at a music store. It was the time of the draft also; it was a bizarre time in American history. The punch line of the story is Buck, before he was called Buck, and I think Allen and some others, walked into the music store I was working in and saw a picture of my college bar band. As a lark, I put an 8" x 10" (photo) of my band on the wall, next to The Who and the Rolling Stones. The bass player in those days was Andrew Winters. He was replaced by Joe Bouchard later. Anyway, Andrew noticed the picture and said, 'I know that band. Our lead singer went to school with their lead singer.' We started talking.

It was around Thanksgiving Day '68. Then I got a call from the guy I went to school with—he was the lead singer in Soft White Underbelly. He said, 'We're playing the Electric Circus and the PA isn't very good. Can you bring your PA down?' So, I had a van and a PA and did sound for them. We proceeded to get very '60s-ish in a smoke-filled way. I met Pearlman for the first time. I met Richard Meltzer for the first time. Helen Robbins was Albert's girlfriend; she became Helen Wheels later. We all just had a great time together. Pearlman asked me on the spot: 'Would you like to work for the band? They have a record deal. You have a van, you have a PA. They need somebody.' At the time, I was living at a relative's house, and I said, sure. I moved into the band house on Christmas Day '68 and by April of '69 I was the lead vocalist. They had a falling out with their singer and Allen had heard some tapes of my previous bands and told the other guys they should give me a shot. I had never played guitar much before. I could play a couple of chords. It hasn't changed much. I know four chords instead of three."

Curiously, Meltzer actually got to sing with the band at an actual gig, at the Café Au Go Go in the East Village, where the bill included James Cotton. Other spots known to take the band included The Electric Circus (which Eric mentions), The Anderson Yiddish Theatre and Generation. And what is the source of Eric's nickname Manny? "He worked at a music supply place," notes Meltzer. "He was The Man, Manny, the man. He could expedite things for your band! He can get you your amps. Somehow it came out of his job. Sandy wanted Manny to be called Roy Mucilage, and Manny wanted no part of that. Basically Eric was, 'Don't call me Manny!' He was known as Eric "Don't call me Manny" Bloom. Another one for Eric was going to be Jesse Python. That didn't take either." Sandy's aliases for the other guys included Andy Panda for Andy Winters, Prince Omega for Al Bouchard and La Verne for Allen Lanier.

Along the way, two records were actually made (sort of—there's some overlap) for the band's fragile deal with Elektra (none other than Jac Holzman being the band's initial booster, after being out to see the band at The Diplomat), but neither was released at the time. The Stalk-Forrest sessions (the band name was inspired by Chinese food) saw CD reissue in 2001 as *St. Cecilia: The Elektra Recordings* in a limited run of 5000.

The second batch of songs was actually completed product, the band piling up and heading across the country to California to record, to add to a larger amount of material from some New York sessions. But relations turned sour, with the label getting the idea that the band was, as Donald says, "just jerking them around for a lot of money," Roeser admitting that, "We soaked about 70 grand by that time." After tweaking the tapes back at The Hit Factory in New York, Donald recounts that, "By this time, Elektra were really disgusted. They got the tapes and they didn't like it, and they said to hell with it; we're writing it off for taxes. You guys are off the label, forget it, bye-bye."

"Sandy got one last-ditch attempt to patch things up with Elektra," continues Buck, "and he got Don Galucci to come out and produce a single. He came out from California and the bass player said, 'Well, I gotta go work in the bakery; I gotta leave.' He couldn't believe it. He came all the way from California and the guy goes off. This was the last straw. The guy went back to Elektra and said, 'Look, these guys are just a bunch of assholes, forget it.'"

"They did an entire album for Elektra as Soft White Underbelly, that they never mixed because Les Braunstein basically destroyed it," explains Meltzer, referring to the first full-length, the one that remains unreleased. "They had a song called 'Buddha's Knee;' that was a Buck song, and maybe Pearlman wrote the lyrics, 'Sitting on the Buddha's knee.' It was a big psychedelic jam number, and Les Braunstein doesn't tell anybody—they were taking solos, just going all over the place, playing collective improv—and Les Braunstein bangs a gong that nobody knew he brought in there. He found any way he could to destroy what they were doing because he was a fool."

Reportedly tensions with Les grew, Braunstein taking too much time recording his vocals and pushing too hard for the band to record his compositions. His days alas, were numbered. Of note, various studio sessions took place during this time, including jingle work, bits for Jerry Ragavoy and producer Peter Siegel, and a drum session for Albert on Tom Paxton's 'Bishop Cody's Last Request'. With respect to the second "record," after Les's ouster and Eric joining the band, Pearlman persuaded Jac Holzman to let them take another crack at it. As mentioned above (as Oaxaca this time), they recorded first, ten tracks in New York, and then in early '70, seven more in California, creating what they called the California album. The new sessions were co-produced by Sandy and Dennis Murphy. Three tracks (not part of then ten submitted and rejected) from the earlier New York sessions were combined with these six to comprise the new version of the album, which again, never happened.

Disputes with Don Galucci arose over the psychedelic nature of the proposed single (he then suggested they go with 'Gil Blanco County'). As alluded to by Donald above, Winters' not showing up for a make-peace meeting with Galucci is another point cited as to when he was fired and Joe was brought in. The Galucci problem could indeed be part of the reason relations broke down with Elektra, but one must also factor in a justified loss of patience and the fact that the label liked Braunstein a heck of a lot more than the guys in the band did. In addition, Sandy didn't want the album to come out in the dead of summer (this is 1970), so he kept delaying, giving Holzman a proper track sequence, which no doubt perturbed the label brass no end. Pearlman volleys back with an opinion that he didn't think the label liked the album anyway, and that tacitly, they were all preoccupied with the sale of Elektra to Warner.

With respect to the Stalk-Forrest songs, most of them are discussed, or at least mentioned, elsewhere in this book, as befits the time travel this band's material has seen. Three are not, to the best of my recollection, and I mention them now. 'Ragamuffin Dumplin'' occurs on the *St. Cecilia* CD twice, in original version and "final." They are quite similar, revealing a track that is a swirl of psych, occasionally sinister chords, a definite Byrdsy flourish, and a lyric from Meltzer that sounds like a bad trip. The song indeed has punch, and it would be a joy to hear the modern version of the band, with all their weapons, trot this one out. 'Bonomo's Turkish Taffy' is a funky psych track with a tight drum groove and lots of Hammond sounds from Allen Lanier. Buck sings this collaboration between (an absurd) Meltzer and Al Bouchard, while adding a clean, wandering solo that reveals the man's effortless sense of melody. Finally, 'St. Cecilia' is offered in two versions. Almost seven minutes long, the song is pure mellow, ethereal psych, the band yet again going to their Grateful Dead-derived bag of tricks, Buck again demonstrating sophistication beyond rock standards at the time.

Back to the chronology at hand, Al makes the link to the early Columbia years. "Then Murray Krugman, okay, let's give credit where credit is due, stepped into the picture. He was a product manager for Columbia and said Warner Brothers has Black Sabbath, and London has the Rolling Stones. Columbia said we have our Rolling Stones, we have Bob Dylan, but we have nothing like Black Sabbath. We need a band that's going to be like Black Sabbath. There's no beating around the bush. This is what they wanted: Columbia's answer to Black Sabbath. So he said if you guys can work up a repertoire that is ominous, that is scary like Black Sabbath, you will get signed to our label. I guarantee it. To make sure that it happened, of course he had originally approached Sandy with this idea, and Sandy approached us and said, 'You know, there's this guy Krugman, and he's got this idea blah blah blah.' Sandy and Murray rehearsed with us for about a month to get our material up to the proper ominous fulfillment (laughs) or whatever. Then we auditioned and we got the contract. So we were basically Columbia's answer to Black Sabbath in a quantity and a product kind of way. Murray had already rejected us twice before, but Sandy and him figured out this way to make it work, basically turning us into a metal band."

"So yeah, what happened was we were presented to them as being a hard rock band that could be their answer to Black Sabbath, and the person who sold them on that idea was Murray Krugman, who was a project manager and became our producer, and his main job was to make us heavier and more mysterious and darker. And he did that. He worked with us on that first record and every song, he tried to make it dark and heavy and mysterious."

Was this the tenor of the times? Was heavy viewed as commercial? "Yeah, what was that trio from the Midwest? Grand Funk Railroad—they were having success, and Alice Cooper was big back then around that time. So there were some heavy-ish kind of groups although it wasn't heavy like it is now. That kind of music didn't really exist before Metallica and those groups. One of the different things was that we were less blues-oriented, and more just strange. And after we met the Alice Cooper guys, then we really started developing our own sound. In the late '60s, there was Jefferson Airplane, Dylan and all the folk rock, but people started getting a little cynical as the drugs got harder."

"They had a bunch of name changes," recalls Richard, corroborating Albert's recollection of nefarious calculation with respect to locating a sense of purpose. "Pearlman was nuts. You know, they did one show at the Fillmore East as Soft White Underbelly and they were third bill behind Jeff Beck and Jethro Tull on a hot Fourth of July and nobody paid any attention to them. So Pearlman insisted, our name is mud in this town! You know, we have to change our name. That's when they became Stalk-Forrest, and they were also called Oaxaca (mystical, very old Mexican city). They had a bunch of dumb names. The Santos Sisters. So at some point, Pearlman tried to sell... tried to get Al Kooper to be his man inside Columbia and they did a session with him. I think some of that stuff is on one of the expanded Sony CD versions. But Al Kooper hated them and he hated Pearlman. So finally, just on their own, they had to decide, what are we going to do? They had a meeting, and it was brought up, can we go metal? Can we do that? They said no, we can't do that. Could we be pseudo-metal? Let's try. So I would say that through the early '70s, they were comedy metal. You could laugh at their sets. They were just terrifically like… it was like Spinal Tap. And they would smile at each other, like, hey wasn't that fun? Then they became, when they went to Columbia, and the die was cast, they became, just Pearlman's automatons. He would dress them in lederhosen and silver hot pants."

Donald supports Al's contention that Murray, an A&R rep for Columbia at the time, was initially unimpressed. "Murray had prevented the group from being signed at CBS a couple of times before. We did a couple of demos for Columbia and Murray said, 'Well, these guys are jerk-offs from Stony Brook. I know these guys. They're no good.' But Sandy convinced Murray that together they could fashion a commercially viable rock 'n' roll band. We still didn't really have a name at that time."

"The band existed before I joined," explains Eric, providing a further distilled history leading up to the amusing story of the Columbia audition. "Different people were in it than were in Blue Öyster Cult. There was a different singer than me and there was a different bass player before the initial Blue Öyster Cult album in 1972. I joined the band in April 1969. We had a couple of different names. When I joined it was Soft White Underbelly then it became Stalk-Forrest Group then Oaxaca. We had a few different names and we kicked around and wrote songs and tried to get accepted. Eventually, we did an audition with Columbia Records in 1971. It was an interesting audition because it was in a conference room in the CBS building in New York City. They took the tables and the chairs out, and we lined up against one wall and faced the other wall and just played. Clive Davis was the president of Columbia Records at the time. He liked what he heard and signed us. In the audition, Patti Smith was there. Harry Nilsson was there; he should rest in peace. The drummer of Blood Sweat & Tears was there, along with people from the A&R department. We played five songs and they left the room. Our manager came back in and said, 'They're going to sign you.'"

Al's brother and bassist for the band, Joe Bouchard adds to the Clive Davis signing saga. "Yeah, well about two or three years ago I was reading a book on Led Zeppelin. And I didn't realize that they had gone through this whole routine with Columbia, and that they were courted by Columbia, and that then all of a sudden their manager Peter Grant signed with Atlantic. And I don't think that Clive Davis ever got over that, and that signing Blue Öyster Cult (in the fall of 1971) was part of his revenge (laughs). But I think it had something to do with that, because about a year and a half later we signed with Columbia. But I think he was still stinging. You know, he took things pretty personally. And that's the reason we had very Zeppelin-y, Sabbath kinds of stuff. We needed to fill the bill for a label that had no outlet for that kind of music. So, I'm thinking that this must have happened maybe six months before we did our audition, and of course Peter Grant all of a sudden snatched Led Zeppelin away from Clive Davis and took it to Atlantic. I think that Clive was pissed-off. Plus Atlantic had done a really good job promoting Led Zeppelin, so I think one of the reasons he signed us— because we are not his style at all—was that he was still mad (laughs). He was still mad about losing Zeppelin. That's just my guess after reading this decades later. Nobody said anything at the time but it is pretty well common knowledge that Peter Grant was flirting with Clive Davis to get a deal with Columbia. At the same time Sandy had connections at Atlantic and he shopped us around to them and I forget who else. Luckily Clive was still pissed-off enough to sign us (laughs)."

"It was really wild," recalls Joe, of the audition process itself. "I didn't think we played that good for the audition. We played everything way too fast; it was almost like speed metal. We were all very nervous. We had five songs that we were allowed to play. Clive had been clued in that we had something happening and he kind of liked 'Last Days of May' which made it to our first album. I was surprised that he went for it. We performed right in the conference room. Harry Nilsson was there, as was Bobby Colomby from Blood, Sweat & Tears. They were nice and friendly. I was a big Harry Nilsson fan. It was really a blur. We were like, 'Wow, here we are in the conference room at Columbia Records.' We really couldn't believe it. We had all of our equipment in the room, which took up most of the conference room, and we were blasting out these songs as loud as we could. For some reason, they said, 'We like you guys. But Clive is a good enough businessman and trend follows a lot of trends, and he knew he had to get into it. And for us, I think because the Elektra deal fell apart so tragically, everybody wanted to stay in the business. So we were ready to make a change and Sandy is very persuasive. If you've ever talked to Sandy Pearlman, he's a very persuasive guy. He just knew that the hippie jam band stuff was dying, and heavy metal was coming in. 1969 peaked with Woodstock, and then Altamont came along, and the first song that we did in Blue Öyster Cult referred to Altamont. So Altamont was the nail in the coffin for the hippie peace and love generation. The writing was on the wall, so that didn't bother us at all. That was okay. I think some of the more pretentious parts of metal were never what we could do. There was always tongue-in-cheek when we'd do our metal riffs and stuff like that. The show was definitely a high-energy show, so I don't know if we would have gotten more mileage out of concentrating on the whole package, like contriving the package. Instead, it really kind of happened randomly."

Further on the connection to a Sabbath sort of sound, Joe recalls that, "Even before we did the first album Sandy said you've got to see this band. And he drove us down to a theatre in Staten Island in New York to see Sabbath. I remember seeing them for the first time. It was loud, 'England's Loudest Band' (laughs), and I remember I was in the back row of this proscenium theatre, an old vaudeville theatre, standing next to the back wall, and the sound was like so loud, it was pushing me up against the wall. They did 'Paranoid' and stuff. It was good. But I don't think they ever put on a really entertaining show like Alice or Aerosmith. Their show was kind of a disappointment considering how great their music was."

"But Sandy was excited about it, and he mentioned it would be great if you guys could do more music like this. So later on after that, we started working on our demos for Columbia and I know that Murray Krugman and Sandy definitely wanted heavy. And I think that it made sense. It was the turn of the decade, '70, '71. And I was ready to do anything (laughs). I was right out of college, I had really not ever played a lot of professional shows, so that seemed like a good idea to me—start over fresh. Moved on from Soft White Underbelly, started over fresh with a sort of heavier attitude."

Donald has his own view of the Sabbath connection. "We had all decided that we definitely wanted to be a heavy band, in the Sabbath mould, although we would never sound like Sabbath, never had and never would. Actually we had no similarity to Sabbath at all. I think the Cult's always been a light metal band rather than heavy metal, but actually we just redefined heavy metal."

Joe continues, offering a few words on his early musical development, as we circle back on the circumstances of him winding up in the Blue Öyster Cult. "I never claimed to be a great bass player. To tell you the truth, I have a degree in music, and I was actually a classical pianist in Ithaca College back in the '60s. While those guys were in New York, I was studying classical music in upstate New York. I've been a guitar player for many years, and the bass is really an afterthought. It's happened to me more than once, that there was an opening, and you need a player, so I end up playing. Whatever the instrument, I would adapt to it. So I started playing the bass when I was I guess a junior in college, and I took a few bass lessons. But I probably started studying it a little more seriously, probably not until after I left the group in the mid-'80s! I don't think that I was ever a fanatic about it. I did realize, even from the Soft White Underbelly recordings that there was one great virtuoso in the band, and that's Donald Roeser. Donald is not a studied player, but he has a tremendous amount of natural ability on the guitar. He's phenomenal. If he was ambitious he'd be a superstar today (clears throat, laughs). But I just got my master's degree in music composition, so now I'm a studied guy (laughs)."

"They were a bunch of hicks," muses Meltzer, when asked for a psychological profile of the band as they formed. "They were basically Long Island and upstate New York hicks, except for Lanier. His real name is Allen Glover Lanier, and the Glover plantation was one of the biggest plantations in pre-Civil War Alabama, so he was from money. His father went to Annapolis and was somehow involved in publishing in New York. And he was the only one in the band who ever read a book and we got along very well until he became a junkie, which would be in the '70s. We had a falling out, because somewhere in the '80s, I sent him some stuff I wrote, and he said something to the effect that this is all well and good, but it's not informed by the miracle of heroin addiction. Like the writing of his dear friend Jim Carroll. So we never spoke again."

In fact, Allen had most recently arrived in New York from North Carolina (he grew up in Atlanta), in hopes of working in the film editing field. Originally starting on rhythm guitar, Allen gradually shifted towards keyboards, actually learning much of his technique on the job. Richard goes on to confirm the events leading up to Joe Bouchard joining the Cult, filling in a few more details. "My original best buddy in the band was the original bass player Andy Winters, who is also a good friend of David Roter (now deceased, Roter will feature later in the tale, also as one of many lyricists for the band). I went to Stony Brook with Roter and Pearlman, and Pearlman, in '66, '67, started thinking that he would like to manage a band. His father had a drugstore in Smithtown, New York, Long Island, near Stony Brook. Andy Winters was the delivery boy for his father's drugstore, and he was like a finger-picking folk guitarist and Pearlman asked him, 'Do you think you can play bass?' Sure! So he became the bass player. And his line was always, in later years, 'You punk! I hated Pearlman, before you were born.'"

"It's funny," continues Richard, "this guy Andy Winters, was the first one to quit the band. One of the reasons he quit the band was that Helen (again, Robbins, later Wheels and yet another band lyricist—we'll meet her later) was selling drugs. It was a band that did so little drugs in the early stages. Maybe they would smoke pot once in a while and maybe each member of the band took acid once. In any case, all of a sudden in the fall or winter of '69, suddenly Helen was selling mescaline; without telling anybody, she started this business. And she worked part-time at a liquor store. She'd tell these kids, 'If you like gin, I know something that will really get you high.' So like, 11 PM, knock on the door, in a suburban neighbourhood, a bunch of rich people, like a very upscale suburban neighbourhood, and two strangers knock on the door, 'Where's the mescaline?' What? Oh that's for me! Helen. What? What? And you know, Helen, this is a bad idea, selling drugs to strangers in this neighbourhood, come on. She wouldn't give it up."

"So Andy quit," says Meltzer. "It was like, fuck this. You'd hear a siren in the distance, and it was like, this is it, they're going to lock us up and throw away the key. It was only a matter of time. So one Sunday morning, Andy says to me, help me put the bass amp in the car, I'm leaving. He was talked back, and he's on the Stalk-Forrest album, but by the summer of '70, he was gone. He hated Pearlman. He didn't get along with anybody too well by then. Like I said, he's the one I was closest to originally and then it was Lanier. But Andy became good friends with Roter, and they had a moving company together called Half Starving Graduate Students. He was a guy who dropped out of high school and over the course of the years that I knew him he got his high school equivalency diploma, went to college and was going to graduate school in public health."

"Worried about being arrested? Well, everybody was like that in those days," laughs Albert, who takes more of a swingin' '60s view of the band house situation. "Things were illegal, and people were doing a lot of drugs, and I don't know, I think that's maybe Richard's way... I think Richard didn't really do any of that stuff, so it probably affected him more than other people. I know Helen worked at a pharmacy for a number of years, and she would get stuff—just, take it (laughs). She would just take it from the back, you know? Like prescription drugs, all kinds of uppers and downers, stuff like that. And I remember we would get mescaline. I don't remember actually selling it; I remember taking it. But I don't remember any kind of quantity where we could actually sell it and make any money. Maybe she got some for her friends and split it up or something, but it wasn't like a dealing situation, ever."

"But in any case, suddenly Joe shows up," continues Richard. "It was when it was getting really iffy. Does Andy really want to play with us? I went with Albert; we took a ride to the airport to JFK, and his brother was flying in from wherever the hell he lived, Clayton, New York, somewhere near the Canadian border. I imagine there is some actual French Canadian blood there. So anyway, he picks up his brother, and his brother was wearing patent leather shoes. His brother was like a real square-and-a-half. The first thing he says to Albert is, 'Hey, have you listened to the new Laura Nyro album? It's great!' *Eli and the Thirteenth Confession*. Albert says, 'We don't really listen to that kind of music. You'll see.'

Then within a couple of days, they're trying him out as the bass player. Andy comes back and says 'What's going on here?' I mean, there was another guy they had for awhile called John Trivers, and he was the bass player for about ten minutes, and I think he probably knew Eric and Les. But in any case, Andy would show up. But then finally when Joe was there, it was too late for Andy to come back. But Joe always seemed like the biggest hick in the bunch. Likeable guy, but never knew who he was. Albert was more... more was given. And more was presented. So anyway, years later I got to know Mike Watt from the Minutemen and Firehose, and he basically liked to talk about E. Bloom and J. Bouchard. So, when I told him Joe wore patent leather shoes, he thought that was amazing. He really liked that."

"I started out in high school as a guitar player," reiterates Joe. "My brother Albert and I had a very successful band in high school. A situation came up where they—the future Blue Öyster Cult members—were playing as Soft White Underbelly and they were in desperate need of a bass player. I said, 'Oh sure, I can play the bass.' I had been a big fan of Soft White Underbelly and I would go to Long Island where they had a house and actually jam with them for weeks on end during my college breaks. Three months after I graduated college, my brother call up and asks, 'Do you want to join the band?' I ended up joining up with them and was the bass player for 16 years."

"The big pluses were that we understood each other," Joe answers, upon being asked what it was like having a brother in his band. "We could develop our tracks just by knowing each other. I would know exactly how he would play a fill and I knew what bass line I had to play underneath his beat. That was all pretty easy. I played my first gig with my brother when I was ten years old. We played on the streets in front of my uncle's house for tips and we made 35 cents! That was like a fortune to us. On the negative side, he is my older brother so he is kind of domineering when it comes to making musical decisions. Most of the time I would defer to him but we would have some pretty good fights over little musical things."

To summarize the formative years, gigging began as early as 1967 with various configurations from a cast of characters that included Andrew Winters on bass and Les Braunstein as vocalist as we move into 1968. Eric's first gig with the band, at a debutante's 16th birthday party, takes place in May of '69, followed by his first gig proper at the Fillmore east, in support of Jethro Tull and Jeff Beck. First gig for the classic line-up takes place when Joe joins on bass for a show on a flatbed truck in Great Neck Park on Long Island in September of 1970, followed quickly by the two days of shows at a nudist retreat at Camp Swan Lake. Back to Columbia, the label that would be home to the band through the glory years and beyond. It is Murray Krugman that is widely credited as the guy who got the band signed, Krugman hailed as the insider, the catalyst to bring these weird kids into a commercial, unit-shifting world. He would go on to be the band's co-producer and business manager for years to come, somewhat acrimoniously leaving the scene as pressures mounted for more and more out of BÖC in the late '70s. After some nasty lawsuit stuff with the boys, Murray settled in rural Vermont, running a small folk music label called Silverwolf Records, established in 1991.

Murray offers his take on those early days. "Well, let's see. I was working at

CBS at the time in the marketing department, but I was doing some producing and I had just had a lot of success with a Johnny Winter live record. Sandy had brought me the band twice before, once as the Soft White Underbelly and once as Stalk-Forrest Group. They were sort of a west coast kind of band, you know like Jefferson Airplane, and I was looking for something more immediate, more harder-edged. So he brought the latest configuration and I liked that song 'Last Days of May'. They had a demo, I think, with 'Redeemed', 'Last Days of May' and 'The Red & the Black'. I felt that 'Last Days of May' was great. I had the leverage to sign them, so I did."

I ask Joe about one of the more enduring mysteries with respect to the band, the name "Blue Öyster Cult." "The true story is that Sandy wrote a poem (*The Soft Doctrines of The Imaginos*) that was part of the *Imaginos* song cycle. I guess he wrote it back when he was going to graduate school, Brown University. He had dreamt up this whole *Imaginos* thing, and that was one of the songs. So it's nothing to do with the anagram story."

What Joe is referring to there is this idea that Blue Öyster Cult came to them because it was an anagram of Cully Stout Beer, a crappy beer Meltzer and Pearlman used to drink at Richard's in Greenwich Village. Playing with anagrams of the name, they came up with Stout Belly Cure, Trolleybus Cue, Trycolute Blues, and finally... but it is alas, of no (or perhaps little?) significance.

"What happened was that I joined the group in 1970," continues Joe, "and they were known as the Stalk-Forrest Group. It was an interim name because it looked like Soft White Underbelly had run its time, so they were trying to re-conceive the notion of what they were going to do, although I would have been perfectly happy to have kept the name. So we had this interim name, and nobody really liked that. So we were about two weeks away; we knew we were getting signed to Columbia Records. This was in the summer of 1971, and so we spent months arguing about names. It was the worst! We had these fierce arguments, and I don't remember arguing about any good names. Everybody would just come up with an even more stupid name (laughs); you know, how stupid can it get? So finally we said to Sandy and his partner Murray Krugman, we're going to lock you in a room, and we did, a room next to our practice room, and said, 'You're not coming out until you have the name of the band! We've had it. We're not going to talk about it anymore.' So they came out of the room and said, 'Here it is—Blue Öyster Cult!' We went whoa! That was the first of the 'cult' names. I don't think there was ever a group called Cult. And since then there's been several." It is of note that Murray recalls that Sandy had the name on a list of possibilities, and that Murray had picked the name from the list as his favourite.

Donald tells his version of the event: "We got a contract, we did the first Cult album, and we decided on the Cult name about a week later. We had about eight names. We couldn't agree. But that was par for the course. We're not really the same kind of guys at all. We never agree on anything. So a couple of the names we were considering were Big Bullet, The Santos Sisters, The Night Wailing; Scumbags was proposed. We had to sign the contract the next day, so we said to Sandy, 'Okay, pick something.' 'The Blue Öyster Cult.' The what? It turned out to be the name of one of Sandy's songs, which eventually became 'Subhuman.'" And if you're asking, one other theory is that the name derives from a recipe for Blue

Point oysters. But back to the band's music, if Black Sabbath was a big influence in turning the band onto the evils of heavy metal, so was a young upstart named Alice Cooper.

"Yep, that made a big difference," says Joe. "That sort of put the nail in the coffin for the Soft White Underbelly. You know the hippie guys in jeans just sort of doing 25-minute freak-out jams. We saw Alice Cooper decimate an audience in 45 minutes. The crowd was never the same after (laughs). That's true, you know. We didn't know what we were going to do. The day before we went out on our first tour, Eric and I went down and saw Alice Cooper at the Academy of Music. I remember sitting in the audience and being just terribly frightened! Somebody came by from the first show and said you won't believe what he's going to do. That was freaking me out! Then we saw the first show and said wait a minute, these guys are not virtuoso players, but they certainly had their act together. It was stunning, it was rock 'n' roll, it was heavy, but it was still entertaining, you know? And that influence still is out there."

"I talk to Dennis Dunaway a lot about those days," laughs Joe. "Alice Cooper had such a wild reputation but Dennis has told me that they just worked their butts off to get their show to be the tightest it could be. We first met them when they were touring *Killer*. I didn't expect that it was going to be that good, but it was really amazing. It was totally different and I had never seen anything like it before. It was encouraging to us. Playing with the Byrds was a disaster because we were not the right kind of band to play with the Byrds. But then when we actually played with Alice Cooper, back in 1972, it all turned around for us. We grew up on their music, and they know ours well too. My favourite track is 'Under My Wheels'. 'Ballad of Dwight Frye' is a close second, but it's very difficult to perform. You can't beat the hits, 'Eighteen' and 'School's Out'. Surefire rock songs as you will ever get to play."

Eric seconds that emotion. "You're always influenced by people you see. I'd say one of the bigger, earlier contributions to what I do would be Alice Cooper. We opened for him in '72, and I mean, I was a huge Alice Cooper fan. Then when we got that tour, it just blew me away, to get to go on tour with the guy. I was such a fan. He not only impressed me, but he was very bright and very creative. Anybody who is 20-something today and doesn't know what Alice's contribution was has really missed a lot, because he's the first. How can you describe this to people who have never seen him in his heyday? It's like, I have an 18-year-old son who doesn't get the Beatles. It's hard to explain to people. But rock 'n' roll before Alice was different. He was an innovator. He was the first rock group that used creative stage lighting. Now you take it as a given, that it's already there already. You go to a rock show today and there's a lighting designer and there's lights and there's things going on on the stage and you take it as a given. But before Alice Cooper there was nothing like that. He had all these specials and spotlights. It was amazing. If you went to an Alice Cooper show it was like Vegas. He took show biz and put it in rock 'n' roll."

"That was kind of kismet," explains Eric, on the situation of the Cultsters getting onto that bill with Alice. "We were signed to a booking agency called ABC. Alice Cooper was their biggest act. Alice Cooper was on a tour and Redbone was opening. They had one hit called 'The Witch Queen of New Orleans'. I don't want to tell stories out of school, but what filtered back to us, so it is sort of hearsay… there was some sort of problem between their management or between Alice Cooper the band and their band or something. Up to this day, I can't really tell you; it's still a foggy story. Anyway, our first album wasn't even out yet. Our agent came to us and said, 'If you do one show with Alice Cooper and they like you, I'll get you the remainder of the tour.' I remember it very well because we had just finished a tour with the Byrds and the Mahavishnu Orchestra (ed. November and December of 1971). That was our first tour. Very, very interesting experience. We didn't go over very well. It was a great learning experience. We had to change everything we were doing. We changed what we wore, we changed what we played, we changed everything in that six-month period. Then we got this Alice gig. It was at Worcester, Massachusetts and we went over. Alice Cooper was happy, we were happy, and we got 15 shows with Alice! It was the *Killer* tour; there were some great songs."

The instructive dates with Alice Cooper took place in April and May 1972, up and down the Eastern seaboard and as far away as Texas. Other bands sharing the stage—mostly one-offs—included Spirit, Chase, Tom Rush, Edgar Winter's White Trash and The Chambers Brothers. The Worcester show Eric refers too was in fact an audition of sorts, taking place at the Harrington Auditorium on March 3rd.

Eric relays that he soaked up a wealth of influence from Alice in terms of showmanship. "Everything. I played in many other bands before BÖC. They were college bar bands or fraternity bands, things like that. I was semi-pro. It wasn't like I walked into this band being a dishwasher or something! But when I walked onto the stage at the Fillmore East on July 3, 1969, and went 1-2-3 into the microphone, I said, 'Wow, this sure is different!' We bumped and stumbled for quite a while. The Alice Cooper tour was like a big strong cup of coffee on what we had to do."

"It goes back to that first Alice Cooper tour," replies Joe, when asked when it looked like the band had the ambition to actually make it. "That got us onto a big stage. It was the first time that we were successful on a big stage. We knew that we had to get on as opening acts for happening groups who were drawing a lot of people. We had been a bar band before that. Soft White Underbelly had been an opening act for a lot of classic '60s bands like Jefferson Airplane, The Grateful Dead and Quicksilver Messenger Service. That was when they were back at Stony Brook. I'd say we had the idea that we wanted to play on the big stage. Things started taking off. Earlier, we went out with the Byrds; I am a big Byrds fan. The opening act was the Mahavishnu Orchestra. It was a weird concert that our manager Sandy Pearlman put together. The Byrds fans didn't like our brand of heavy metal. After that tour we were pretty disillusioned. If the Alice Cooper tour had not happened next we might have gone back to our day jobs."

Back on a creative tack, one would have to say that the most profound catalyst for the building of the BÖC beast was an internal virus, namely Pearlman himself, as stated, a close college friend whose mind was on fire with the intellectual, creative, and fascist possibilities inherent in this new, leaden, serious form of rock 'n' roll called heavy metal. Bolle Gregmar (see introduction for more on this cat), keeper of the Museum Of the Cult in Hollywood, is a good friend of

Sandy's.

"He's a really well-read person. But also according to Albert he's like a Jewish wannabe Nazi, so that's kind of like strange too. He's really totally into occult ways of dealing with things. Which makes me think that he's a Jewish pagan. The combination does not exist. But in his mind he's very fascinated by the old druids and all that stuff. But he wants to put it in context with the future rather than going backwards. So he thinks about the whole thing with the world wars and stuff as something in the future, that, well, we've lived through two of them right now, and we're expecting a third one. But that third one's not going to be a war, it's just going to be a confrontation between minds. This is all perpetrated by his reading H.P. Lovecraft and Richard Chambers' *The King in Yellow* from 1895 and other books that he's been reading about the righteousness of believing what you read."

Joe, when asked what reading shaped Sandy's thinking, offers the following. "You know, everything that you've heard is probably what I've heard, probably through the same sources, places like the internet. I get out there and say, 'Oh, this is where that came from!' He would never tell us what his sources were. Never! He would just say, 'Oh, it's just something I thought up.' Now everybody is sort of like figuring the puzzle out. He's a pretty crafty guy. He knew his place. He had to protect his sources because everybody else would go and rip him off (laughs). All I knew of Sandy was that he was one of those brilliant merit scholars, who had too much time on his hands, and read too many books. You know, even when we were making an album, Sandy would be reading these very difficult, technical books on warfare (laughs). We're making an album, he's reading books on warfare (laughs)."

Sandy sheds some illumination on the psychological make-up of the band and himself. "Things that shaped the whole philosophy of the band were first of all, the entire young scientist atmosphere of the early '70s. I had thought I was going to be doing that. I wound up not doing it, but I still had this entire young scientist mindset. So there was the entire sort of can-do science fair attitude. Then whatever was the current, hot, leading edge research of the time of the early '70s was really important. On top of that you can overlay a tremendous amount of reading in original alchemical source texts. Then you can add on top of that an education in the history of ideas, a degree in philosophy and sociology. And then you can add on top of that a life-long fascination with H.P. Lovecraft and other writers of that ilk, although I don't think there's anybody nearly close to Lovecraft. So those are probably the main sources. I can remember pretty closely where all the things from *Workshop of the Telescopes* (a two CD compilation out at the time of my first interview with Sandy) come from. They come from the various pits that I've just referenced for you."

Such a philosophy, presumably, could only be set to the musical form and formula known as heavy metal...

"Yes, well, it's the vocabulary with which to communicate with a very large audience," explains Professor Pearlman. "A lot of the songs were by me—and they had very specific intentions. And even if the guys in the band don't want to talk about the intentions—which some of them are very reluctant to talk about— heavy metal was the best vocab with which to communicate the intentions of these songs. Most of the songs, or many of the songs, or at least the plurality, I guess, through *Agents of Fortune*, up until then, half the songs or more were written by me, and I was the producer, and this vocabulary was a great musical vocab with which to project and communicate the intentions of the lyrics."

"Because most of these songs started with the lyrics, which was the case with Meltzer's songs as well. And Meltzer's songs were susceptible to that vocabulary as well. I mean Meltzer really was not communicating the same intentions that I was. But having said that, his lyrics were workable within this sort of musical vocabulary. They worked very well with it, and a song like 'Harvester of Eyes' which is a really old song, obviously worked fantastically well with this vocabulary. And even 'Astronomy' with Soft White Underbelly was a pretty heavy song, only to become heavier with Blue Öyster Cult."

Sandy closes our opening chapter with a bit of a counter to the tale of the band's signing. "They weren't resentful," he says, of Columbia. "They were never going to get Sabbath or Zeppelin. They maybe could have gotten Sabbath because their partner in Europe was Phillips. I believe that Sabbath came out on a Phillips label, Vertigo. So I don't actually think it was an attempt to equalize the situation, you know, and get a shot at this burgeoning heavy metal universe. They just liked the demo. The demo was great. And the band did a good audition for Clive Davis and that was that."

So with this coterie of minds, and an urge to twist rock into metal (-light?), Blue Öyster Cult was born. What transpired is some of the most intelligentsia-friendly hard rock ever to be created. Right on. Read on…

Blue Öyster Cult

"He lived alone in a little garret"

So after much Spinal Tapped hoopla, false starts, rethinks and revolves, the newly minted Blue Öyster Cult finally had their debut record. Released in January of 1972, *Blue Öyster Cult* was a creepy, uncoloured smudge of what ifs, inviting all cliff-lurched detritus of '60s society to muse at new (and uneasily old) mysterious worlds.

A half page ad in *Circus* at the time contained the following superlatives. Legendary, pioneering rock critic Robert Christgau: "The tightest and most musical hard rock record since—dare I say it—*Who's Next.*" *Rolling Stone*: "Parents and priests used to warn of the dangers inherent in rock and roll. Maybe this is it." *The New York Herald*: "This is no Led Zeppelin, it's no helium zeppelin, it's hydrogen zeppelin all the way, the real thing, the one and only." *Circus*: "It could well be the album of the '70s." And finally, the classic *Creem* magazine warned us to "*Get behind the Blue Öyster Cult before they get behind you.*" The ad closed forebodingly with the tagline: "*A panorama of violence and suffering on Columbia Records and Tapes.*" The hype was justified. *Creem* magazine, in '72, voted the Cultsters the year's Best New Band.

Who better to graphically depict such a curious record than clearly bonkers school chum Bill Gawlik? Sandy retells the story of the enigmatic draftsman: "Gawlik had gone to the Rhode Island School of Design, and he had left there and transferred to Stony Brook. He was living in the dorms, and I had ran into him, quite literally on the day when he was unfurling the huge scroll on which he had all of his architectural designs. He was sort of like the Albert Speer of H Quad at Stony Brook. You know, Speer was commissioned by Hitler to design all of future Europe. Bill Gawlik was designing all of future America, although he was not being commissioned by Hitler or anyone else. So a lot of the cover art really is on those original scrolls, which were so long that they would go the entire length of the building. It was like 4:00 in the morning when we were unfurling these things, and anybody who was up and moving around at 4:00 in the morning didn't seem to mind (laughs). Anyway, that's where I first ran into the stuff."

"He was sort of eccentric to say the least," continues Sandy. "He lived alone in a little garret when he got out of Stony Brook on 14th Street above a children's clothing store that catered to Hispanics. His neighbour across the hall, I believe, was Wayne County, or one or another of those Warholoids or something like that, some person who was famous at The Factory not for 15 minutes, maybe for years. He was a cab driver; that's how he paid his bills when he left Stony Brook. When *Taxi Driver* came out, I really thought that Scorsese must have ridden around with Bill Gawlik, you know, talked to him and got the idea for the film from him! So all of these things came out of his stint at the Rhode Island School of Design. He was probably there when the Talking Heads were there. It was about the same time. Now you should understand, since there's no such thing as coincidence, the Rhode Island School of Design is located in the historic district of Providence, Rhode Island. Just down the hill from what they call the RISD hill, where the school is, is the intersection of Benefit and Angell Street where Lovecraft lived. So you can sort of roll down the hill, or sled down on a snowy day, and you would arrive at H. P. Lovecraft central. I don't know if he knew this. I was talking to some people from Providence the other day, and we were talking about all that. But yeah, there's something there."

As Sandy is wont to do, another connection has taken place: "I also, as it turns out, not knowing it until I read some biography of Lovecraft, grew up in Lovecraft country, Arkham and Dunwich. I grew up in one of the towns that actually was Arkham and Dunwich in the Berkshires in western Massachusetts. I think it was Arkham that I grew up in (laughs). I didn't know that at the time. My family had a lot of property up there. They had 200 acres on the Connecticut River, which Lovecraft called the Miskatonic River. I would walk around there, like at night, and it always seemed kind of strange to me; this place seemed weird. I read Sprague DeCamp's biography of Lovecraft and realised, well, it felt weird for a reason. Anyway, all of those architectural structures and patterns come off the scroll; he had a colour monitor in his head (laughs) and he added colour and it made it more self-consciously structural as in the structure of a building."

"There's two things he did for us that essentially came off the scrolls," Sandy recounts with respect to Gawlik. "He also came up with the name *Tyranny and Mutation*. He said that this is the way he worked; he would lock himself in this garret. He didn't have any money for heat, and he didn't have much money for food. So he would basically lock himself in a cold garret and not eat much and just work on his stuff. I remember we had to get that second cover from him about an hour before the absolute deadline that would have thrown the record back by at least two or three months. And the band had a tour to go out on so we really needed that cover. You know, he just couldn't get it done. We just had to grab it from his frozen fingers and say that's it, we're going to go with this. But his theory was that we should lock the doors to the studio, turn off the heat—of course we were recording in the winter—and that's the way we would get the best result. That was his working method, so he thought that we would—we should— follow that working method also, and you should call the record *Tyranny and Mutation*. I'd like to claim it for my own. In fact, *Secret Treaties* was mine, *Blue Öyster Cult* was mine; most of them were mine, but not that one." Lenny Kaye, in the liner notes to *Tyranny*, suggests that Gawlik saw the band's rehearsal space ("Columbia's studio in an old church on E. 30th Street"), and the atmosphere of the band working furtively in it, and deemed the situation tyranny and mutation. One final (fanciful?) tale has Gawlik deeming the record so after listening to it for 24 hours straight.

Al Bouchard corroborates the tale, save for the naming of the album! "I still think that was a brilliant cover. Sandy just said, 'I found this guy Gawlik,' a crazy architecture student, and Sandy had found that bit in his City of the Future and we were very happy with it. This was part of his project, and Pearlman picked out things he thought were cool and he more or less sat on him until he modified it in such a way that it was good for us. After the second one, Pearlman said that's it, this is too much torture. As a matter of fact, he had told Murray, this is like tyranny and mutation, and that's where the album title came from. Just the pain of getting the work out of him, because Sandy never liked what he did. I mean, he liked the basic idea but he wanted changes which was very difficult, because this guy was very neurotic. I don't know that he ever did get his graduate degree. I think he ended up as a cab driver or something. He got 500$ for each cover."

Another important Gawlik contribution to saga Öf the Cult is the mesmerizing, all-pervading band logo, the cross with dot and hook, the inverted question mark, symbol for Saturn, the sign of Chronos or Kronos (Greek) or Cronus (in Webster's)... who really knows for sure? It apparently appeared on Gawlik's architecture school Master's thesis.

"That was a gift," says Buck. "I think the graphic of the first album cover pretty much sprung whole from Gawlik's mind. As for the logo, that was a great gift. We can't take credit for creating it. It was Gawlik's thing. That came fully realised into our lap." Bolle assigns credit to Allen Lanier for the two dots, or "umlauts" above the "Ö" in Öyster, to add mystery, a flair of the European, or the "Ger-magic," as Lenny Kaye's liner note to the reissue of the debut album attest.

But mystery surrounds the exact origins of the band's distinct logo. "This is another sort of Sandy Pearlman-ism," says Bolle. "He would make up a lot of long stories to try to build up the image. So I thought he was just making this up, that this was an ancient, alchemistic symbol for heavy metal. I thought, that would be perfect; how appropriate, it's got to be a made-up story. So about ten years later, after all the albums came out, somebody had this book of symbols, and there's this symbol for white lead that looks very similar to this symbol, except it's got a sharper point on the hook. So it's actually there and it's true. So some of the other connotations are a bit more dubious, like Saturn or Kronos or Chaos or energy. But anything that would fit into that bag would be good. But the actual symbol was done by Gawlik, who was a friend of Sandy's at school. So who knows what they talked about back in the dorm? (laughs)."

Richard Meltzer offers his recollection of the enigma that was Gawlik. "Well, a seminal figure with the Cult was a guy named John Weisenthal, who was a friend of Roter's. Roter, me and John hung out a lot together at Stony Brook. Weisenthal is now teaching classical guitar in Rochester, NY. But he was a charter member of the Soft White Underbelly. He played keyboards, guitar; he would get them to practice when they didn't feel like it. Basically, in a certain moment, Pearlman decided this guy must go; he's disruptive. Because he could think and had some ideas, and they conflicted with Pearlman's. So anyway, in the course of him being eased out and forced away, he brought Gawlik over; he knew Gawlik. And Gawlik was kind of an annoying, one of these guys who was an ear-bender, one of these guys who would start talking and never leave you alone. Pearlman was that way too. So he and Pearlman hit it off. When he saw Gawlik's art, he was like, 'I'm going to give this guy a lifetime contract.'

"I tried to tell him," continues Meltzer, "no, this guy's stuff is really not that good. Look at the draughtsmanship here; these lines aren't parallel, blah blah blah. At a certain point Gawlik was in Connecticut or upstate New York. He was just driving through somewhere, and he had stopped. Some cops had pulled some people over. He stopped just to take a look and it was like, 'Well, what are you doing here?' They took down his name; they weren't quite sure about him, because they were investigating a murder. Somehow they thought his interest was a little too acute, and so there was the thought. He had been told not to leave town, and Pearlman thought, oh oh, we're going to have to get him a lawyer; this is going to cost money. It got to the point where Pearlman decided that Gawlik wasn't essential. I never saw much more than those two covers. I mean, I saw the original versions of those two covers, and I liked the originals better. Pearlman didn't want to hear that either. He said the originals looked too much like R. Crumb. The kind of line he had was more freehand. I liked the originals better."

Joe recalls specifically the invention of the band's iconoclastic logo as a mystical experience, at least for its shadowy creator... "He spent a lot of time on it, several weeks, and he had pasted it on the wall in our living room. He would stare at it for hours and hours, and he was so concerned about getting the curve of the logo just right. I remember him debating how that should go for a long time. I wasn't really in on when he was doing the album, but I do remember him actually working on the album cover in our living room for like weeks on end. It seemed like he was really obsessed with getting the logo just right. And then he was a lot of fun. One of the reasons I wrote 'Hot Rails to Hell' was because he asked me if I wanted to go to a concert in New York. We were so poor we couldn't afford to park the car in the city, so we would park the car on the street in Brooklyn and then we would take the subway in to the concert; it was this jazz concert with Lena Horne and one of these really radical sax players. So we went to the concert, and it was very intense, but coming back on the subway, I got this whole vibe that... you know, Phil King had just been shot, who was our agent at the time. They get that wrong on the Internet. 'Phil King was a member of the band.' No, he was actually just a guy who was sort of our agent in the early days. So I'm riding back on the subway with Bill Gawlik and it was just one of the more bizarre nights of my life. I was thinking about Phil King who was living with us in the same house with Gawlik, and we were rehearsing in the living room, and Bill Gawlik is doing the logo on the living room wall, and it just came together."

Where did Gawlik end up?

"He was a taxi driver in New York, and you know, I haven't heard from him since. I do not know. He certainly was a character though. So I lived in the house with him and Phil King was there, and I think Eric Bloom was there. The other guys, I think they were living in other places. Actually I think Allen Lanier was there too. We had a big house in Long Island. It was a rehearsal place, and it was our place when we were not touring. I mean, touring back in those days, it was like any kind of club, anything we could get. Yeah, that's my knowledge of Bill Gawlik, but I haven't seen him since."

The sounds on this first BÖC opus reflected Columbia's obsession in getting their own version of Black Sabbath, even if already, their concept of the great Sabbath was stuck three records back into the Sabs' debut, what with Blue Öyster Cult's acid casualty psychedelia, timid rhythms and slightly jazzy overtones. Buck concurs: "In a lot of ways, the production values were not as polished as some of the Elektra stuff was. But I think what we were going for was pretty well realised. I don't have a problem with it."

Blue Öyster Cult also marked the band's longtime association with engineer David Lucas, who the band met at a classic '60s swingers party at a summer camp in the Catskills, at which the band played. Albert: "He hung out with us and got us stoned on hash, I remember. He was really into the blend of our voices, and he liked a lot of other things about the band. He says, 'You know, I have a studio (ed. an eight-track jingle-churning set-up called The Wherehouse, on 46th in Manhattan). You should come over and we'll make a little demo'." Joe explains that the first set of demos fizzled commercially, and Lucas was gracious enough to have the band back for a second go, many of the tracks being used for the first LP, with Lucas being instrumental in working the band's harmonies into something useable.

Continues Albert, filling in a few blanks, "This crazy swingers party… his friend had put it together. He was there with his family, and of course, he doesn't know it was going to be a swingers party, so he was not totally thrilled. I'm sure his wife at the time was totally un-thrilled. So he kind of stayed away from all the people. But the second night… it was like a boys and girls summer camp that was closed for the winter, right? The season was over, and they had this party up there. In a place called Swan Lake, on Route 17 in upstate New York. We were supposed to be the entertainment. We had a friend, a booking agent. We had two or three different people who would get us gigs so we wouldn't starve while Sandy Pearlman was trying to get us another record deal after we had been dropped from Elektra. So we went to this party, we played the first night, it was pretty crazy, people getting weird and taking all kinds of drugs, and then the second night, we played inside this... it was like a tent that was blown up with air, okay? It was very cool, it was fun."

"But David came up to us that night and said, 'You know, I really like the sound of your voices. I like how you blend together. It's just really unique how you've got the two brothers, and then these two other guys that have radically different voices, and it all comes together with this nice sound. I'd really like to see what I can do with you in my studio.' We said, 'Really?! Okay.' And so we went to his studio, like a few weeks later, and we cut four songs, and one of them was 'Last Days of May', and when we did the rounds of auditions, Sandy brought the demos around, and they really liked them. The version of 'Last Days of May' on that record is the demo, the thing that we did. We did four songs in one night."

Al continues wistfully, "Yeah, the first album was just a total riot; it was a lot of fun. We made it like, at the end of the day, when all the jingle people would go home. Next door to the studio was a church. We would come in and play our rock 'n' roll and drive the priest nuts. And that was of course the source for the big quote that they used for that first album: 'Parents and priests warned us against the dangers.' Because the priest would call up and say, 'I have to get up for mass tomorrow morning. Could you please turn it down?' So that was the first record."

"Great record," adds Buck. "Obviously any band's first record is like a pretty complete statement of where they are because usually they've had their whole creative time to work on it. It's not like the second record or the third record, you know what I'm saying? So as an out-of-the-box thing for us, I thought it was a fine example."

The inaugural track of the band's first record was to set the tone for Blue Öyster Cult's lyrical terrain for many years to come, 'Transmaniacon MC' supercharged with many of the themes to which the band would return gyre-like over time. "It was a good song," says Sandy. "It was certainly highly distilled. But that had originally been written for a kind of book that I was writing called *The History of Los Angeles*, which was going to be a history of Los Angeles music, which got partially published in one of the Jonathan Eisen anthologies. I had created a paranoid explanation for a conspiracy theory, or a proto-conspiracy theory explanation for the events at Altamont. This was to be like the drinking song, or club song, or whatever, the Mickey Mouse song of the people who were really responsible for Altamont, who were indeed the Transmaniacon MC, the club at the secret core at the heart of the Angels. So that's there, that's their life."

Altamont was of course, the true-life rock festival which is forever etched in time as the evil underbelly of Woodstock. Headlined by The Rolling Stones, things turned ugly when a concertgoer was beaten and knifed to death in the crowded section right in front of Mick and the boys, by one of the Hells Angels, the legendary motorcycle club who were hired by the Stones as security for the gig. It is said that a bounty still exists on Mick's head for his distancing himself from the Angels and indeed any responsibility for the killing after the incident. It is also alleged that a few attempted hits have been made on Jagger. So Sandy's lyric dug beneath the incident (which was basically a spontaneous, mob-psychographic brawl turned serious), positing that some sort of planning had taken place by a secret inner sanctum of the club, as some sort of conspiracy to kill rock 'n' roll, or conversely strengthen it through the cachet of evil. The band's musical soundtrack reinforced the story splendidly, mixing a sort of smothered, paranoid, skirmished sort of rhythm with the darker sounds of '60s icons like Jefferson Airplane and The Doors. Also worming its way through the track is a palpable "secret agent man" sort of vibe, adding to the intrigue of Sandy's tale. Sympathy for the devil, indeed.

Bolle adds an interesting footnote to the analysis of this song. "'Transmaniacon MC' is basically the same scene as 'Golden Age of Leather.' Transmaniacon is basically a motorcycle gang that dies because of their way of thinking. They live only through that song. They are conceived and forgotten as that song ends. It's a really great science fiction story as such, because it begins and ends before the song is finished (laughs)." Albert has claimed that Sandy actually imagined his "motorcycle club" as the "Los Maniacos Bus Boy Club," which was supposed to conjure an image of insane Mexican waiters that form a musical group.

Track No.2 was a strange one, another Pearlman lyric, music credits to Al Bouchard and Eric Bloom, Al also in effect co-writer of the lyrics. What's odd about 'I'm on the Lamb But I Ain't no Sheep' of course is that it was reworked, whipped and lathered (or would that be frothed?) into the much more popular

'The Red & the Black' for the band's second record. This lower octane version utilizes the same lyric, while musically being arranged more like a psychedelic blues lollygag. Bloom modestly admits that song credits in the early days treated him kindly. "Essentially, I'd just sing the songs, come up with a melody to fit the lyrics. I was not hired as a writer. I was hired to be the front man and the singer. So my contribution as a writer in the really early days was very small, because the other guys were doing all the writing. I had never tried to write a song before."

The "Lamb" lyric is of course a scream, Al and Sandy mixing images of Canada's Royal Canadian Mounted Police to sadomasochistic sexual effect. Al explains, "I had this dream once; it was during this period when I was trying to get out of the draft. Vietnam was going on and I did not want to go. I had already lost one of my friends and I didn't want to lose myself, okay, to the war, which I believed then and still do, was a total exercise in futility and stupidity. But anyway, I was trying to get out of the draft and I had a dream one night that all of these draft board people were going through my papers. I already had tried conscientious objection, and I went before the draft board and they refused me. I was pretty close to becoming an ex-patriot in Canada, and so I wrote a song called 'I Saw You'. I woke up from the dream and I picked up a guitar and I figured out the lick, the melody, the whole thing, and I wrote this song. It became a very popular Soft White Underbelly tune. Sandy said, 'This is a good song but it needs better lyrics,' and he proceeded to rewrite the lyrics. So, it's all about being an expatriate, a Canadian refugee basically, and the government trying to hunt you down, using the mounted police."

"'I'm on the Lamb', of course, came to light again with the unearthing and issuing of the Stalk-Forrest Group sessions as *St. Cecilia*. It is included on the CD twice, having been captured on tape at both the New York and the California sessions. Expectedly more laid-back and Grateful Dead-like, the California version nevertheless establishes many of the traits and tones that would remain on the version used here. The New York version is considerably more progressive and jazzy.

Following was one of the band's most enduring, mysterious and even mystical ballads, a masterpiece of shade, future shock, heat and hazy possibility. 'Then Came the Last Days of May' was left pretty much intact from the demo version (the four-track demo, with this title, was the calling card that first got Clive Davis interested in the band), and is said to be the first full song Donald had ever written.

"There was this news story, basically that three kids from Long Island, college kids that were middle class smart guys, got into dope-dealing at Stony Brook U," recalls Buck. "They sold mescaline and marijuana, mostly. Anyway, they went out to Arizona to buy marijuana and got ripped off. I don't know who their contact was. But it was two brothers, some notorious family in Tucson or somewhere that were known rip-off artists or whatever. They just took these kids out, shot 'em, and took their money. One of the guys didn't die, and crawled out to the highway and was rescued, and lived. He testified against these two desperadoes; they went to jail for about ten years, then got out. But it was a big story on Long Island, because it was probably the first time that 'good kids' were involved in this stuff. One of the guys who died, we knew. He went to Stony Brook. So the story was basically factual, from the news accounts. Some of the description was fanciful, but it basically happened."

"Donald came up with 'Last Days of May,'" affirms Joe, "and both the music and lyrics are his. He tends to write them both at the same time. He shapes the music, and then finds the right words, and then shapes the music some more. I think that is the way he did that one."

Next up was a curious little ditty called 'Stairway to the Star', which was a mischievous piece of work, musically somewhat metallic with a hooky chorus. Not one of the band's more popular numbers, the song was nevertheless still in the band's live setlist as of at least 2002. It marked the official recorded debut of Richard Meltzer as BÖC lyricist (granted, he's all over the pre-BÖC stuff), Meltzer, as discussed, possibly as important as Krugman and Pearlman in the band's inception and subsequent intellectualization. In any event, Richard's "Stairway" lyric splices a witty commentary on the act of signing autographs with a few bizarre lines about uh, autos. "Well, that's the one that Lou Reed insisted I lifted from him," recalls Richard, "because I have a line there, 'You can have my autograph.' And on the Velvet Underground *Loaded* album, there's a line, 'Can I have your autograph?' So Lou insisted that that was plagiarism."

"Richard and Sandy Pearlman went to college and they were the smart guys in the class," laughs Joe. "They basically founded Blue Öyster Cult. They were around before BÖC back when it was Soft White Underbelly. Sandy would write half of the lyrics and Richard would write half the lyrics. I think they both would have liked to be performers but when it came down to it, they left the performing to the guys and just came up with the lyrics. In the old band house, there would always be a stack of typed-up lyrics. We would go through those when it came time to put an album together. Albert still has some of that stuff and I think he will put it together one day."

The album's next track was one of those slightly Sabbath send-ups, containing much of Albert's stated jazziness, but fraught with doom tones, not to mention the sinister clown music break that adds splendidly to the record's enigma. Lyrically, Sandy taps into a rich amalgam of personal interests, weaving a tale with links to the other tunes from all eras of the BÖC catalogue, a strong sense of magic, bikers and intrigue pervading the scene.

"'Before the Kiss' is another of your pre-classic conspiracy theory takes on the way things work," pontificates Pearlman. "I posited that there was a secret organization called The Motif of the Rose, sort of like one of those French or Belgian fascist organizations, something right wing. So they sort of ran this place, this bar on Long Island called Conry's Bar, where Blue Öyster Cult actually used to play all the time. They would induct people into their cult by transferring a drug from the tip of their tongues to the tip of the tongue of the inductee. Hence the line about the tongues extending and retracting and the redcap before the kiss. So the drug was the redcap. They delivered this pill, and then you're a made humanoid." Curiously, Eric has stated that something resembling this story actually happened, to Sandy himself, in the Conry's Bar washroom, at the hands—or tongue—of a burly biker. Also of note: the line about gin glowing in the dark refers to another incident where a scuffle broke out in Conry's, and a gin and tonic was spilled onto Sandy's table, where it proceeded to glow in the dark.

Albert has said that there were in fact a Conry's East and a Conry's West, both having been closed down some 20 years ago. Blue Öyster Cult were the house band at Conry's West for several months in 1969-'70, and had played Conry's East on New Year's Eve, 1970-'71, playing an 'Auld Lange Syne'/'In-A-Gadda-Da-Vida' medley at midnight.

'Screams' is as much an odd-man-out as ever there was on a BÖC record, Joe writing a progressive rock nightmare with a strong Doorsy grey. "I thought that Joe's songs had an incredibly strung-out quality when they were very good," points out Sandy. "So I thought 'Screams' for example, was really you know, like King Crimson the day after a three-day methamphetamine binge. That's the kind of mind state I think that song represents. I think that's great."

Buck underscores the Doors-like quality of the band's early work. Speaking of an Elektra exec, Jac Holzman, who had hopes for the band, Buck relates that, "I guess Jac thought that we were kind of the east coast Doors, or maybe the next 'Doors vibe.' Of course, the Doors were a heavy influence for us; that first Doors record just totally blew our minds." Sandy: "Jac thought they were amazing. He, as well as the entire company, thought Les (original BÖC front man) was the second coming of Jim Morrison, who was still alive but due to die pretty soon!"

Joe relates the tale on this first recorded BÖC tune for the bass man, written by Joe and Joe alone. "'Screams' was about when we used to drive into the city late at night to go to a club, or for Chinese food, and there were these buildings with lights on in them. All the lights on even though nobody was working, and red lights on top. So that image just stuck in my mind, driving along the Long Island Expressway, small town boy being blown away by all these lights. So it was like, well, let's see if I can write a heavy song, and it just popped in. It was like an overnight thing. The music probably took me a day to write, and the lyrics probably about two hours. When I wrote the music, we were thinking in terms of changing from the Soft White Underbelly sort of pseudo-hippie/Grateful Dead/endless jam thing to a more hard-edged, Black Sabbath kind of thing. And I felt I could do some music like that."

Joe puts in perspective his place in the band. "Most of the time, I didn't want to write the lyrics. Then again, you didn't have too much choice. I think early on, see, when I came into the situation, they had already had a pretty well-defined working relationship with Sandy Pearlman and Richard Meltzer as lyricists, and Albert and Donald, and sometimes Allen, mostly those three, as music writers. So I came into that situation, and I had to do a song, because that seemed like the right thing to do. It was like a Beatles-type situation where everybody could sing, and everybody could write songs. There might be people that might do more that others, but it was certainly that type of democratic group, which is certainly a rarity these days."

'Screams' builds to a roar and finally a drum fill from Albert that collapses into the sublime, eastern recline of 'She's as Beautiful as a Foot', Rick Meltzer's veiled jab at pre-Bloom front man Les Braunstein. Joe called this strange transition "a Beatles-type thing to do," and "one of the great moments on the record." But "Foot" is stranger still than this transition, the lyrics betraying little of Meltzer's stated intention, sounding more like a macabre but nonchalant treatise on cannibalism. Any intended humour becomes soured by the band's delivery which is both dated and deadpanned, psychedelic and Spinal Tapped. "Yeah, that's an early one," says Richard. "That's from the early days when Les Braunstein was the singer. I wrote it as 'I'm as Beautiful as a Foot.' And I don't know if he actually ever sang that. But they worked it up. They worked up an arrangement, the song, for him to sing: 'I'm as Beautiful as a Foot.'"

One final note from Albert: "I remember that Paul McCartney had written a song called 'Scrambled Eggs'. I was fooling around on piano and I started singing 'Scrambled Eggs' or maybe it was 'Yesterday'. Anyway, I started playing this piano riff which was the music for 'She's as Beautiful as a Foot', and I thought oh, this is really bizarre, I think this Meltzer song would fit, and of course it did."

Following "Foot", we get the long-revered, travel-weary BÖC classic better known as 'Cities on Flame with Rock and Roll', a song with an intriguing family tree indeed. Musically, Albert, Donald, and anybody else in the band who is asked, readily admit that much of its structure is lifted directly from Black Sabbath's 'The Wizard'. This becomes hilariously obvious with a little metallic split-screening. Not so obvious or convincing is the talk of comparisons to King Crimson's '21st Century Schizoid Man', given that the staccato licks compared to this classic, are to my mind the very same ones borrowed from Sabbath, rather than Fripp and crew.

Al remembers the song's germination. "Patti Smith was loft-sitting for Johnny Winter. I don't know if she had anything going on with him or just taking care of his loft. Anyway, she was there, and that was the first time I met her. I think that was the first time for all of us, and we rehearsed there in Johnny Winter's loft. That first day, we wrote 'Cities on Flame with Rock and Roll.' That was our first attempt at imitating Black Sabbath. And of course we stole the lick from 'The Wizard;' it's well-documented. We stole the first part from 'The Wizard' and the second part from '21st Century Schizoid Man'. So, two of our favourite licks."

In any event, the track is a heck of a heavy highlight live, with its many climactic moments, warm boogie chorus and end-jam potential. This version is of course as subdued, muddy, grey and psychedelic as the rest of the record. Look elsewhere for explosions. Lyrically, the song borrows most overtly from MC5's 'Motor City's Burning', while also fitting quite snugly into Pearlman's whole idea of rock 'n' roll as a potentially fascist, evil, political, corrupting force, the song imagining a war between three thousand guitars polarized into camps of Marshalls and Fenders. This track also arcs the orbit of Sandy's whole *History of Los Angeles* motif, even possessing hints of *Imaginos*, biker themes and of course conspiracy. It may also remind one a bit of what Rush addressed with 'The Trees', this allegorical battle between inanimate objects.

Al compares early BÖC with the great MC5. "I've been listening to the MC5 a lot lately, and I've noticed some parallels with BÖC's second record. Both sound very trebly and light, but with BÖC, the aggression still came through. There was a train of thought in those days that this trebly sound was good. And there wasn't so much concern with, 'How is this going to translate to a home system?'"

Posited Sandy Pearlman, speaking with the *NME* in 1974, "The function of art in general and the reason these records are the way they are and say the things they say specifically is that you should provide people with transcendental models, so they'll find themselves reaching out to realms of imagination they wouldn't have ever dreamed of, and maybe some of that can seep over into the conduct of their lives. It may be calls for violence, or it may be calls for other transcendental exercises, and that's what it's all about. In 'Cities on Flame with Rock and Roll' for example, I tried to write a sleazy epic, using tawdry language that would express unfocused teenage anarchistic antiauthoritarian rebellion. It's a real teenage anarchistic epic anthem. I think I succeeded lyrically, and the music the group wrote definitely succeeded."

"The first song I ever heard of ours on the radio," remembers Albert, was 'Last Days of May,' when the first record came out. And that was on a small FM station in Long Island. But then the day that we were going to see Alice Cooper for the first time, we'd never seen him live. We were talking about doing some gigs with him and we were going to meet the band and all this stuff, and they were playing in New Jersey. We drove over the George Washington Bridge, Manhattan into New Jersey, and as we were going over the bridge WABC AM, Cousin Brucie was playing on the radio. All of a sudden 'Cities on Flame' came on the air, and we went nuts. Whoa! I couldn't believe that I was hearing my song on the radio. This was my dream. Not just on the radio but on WABC AM. You know, Cousin Brucie's like, 'Hey, that was a groovy cut by a group called Blue Öyster Cult,' and I'm like whoa! But it sounded so different from everything else."

Agrees Joe, "We bent over backwards trying to sound different in the early days. We didn't want to be your typical rock band. I was all for it, as I was very excited to be recording music. We ended up recording something like 17 records for Columbia—what an exciting time that was. In the early days, we were really excited because we really didn't think we could ever come up with anything that anybody would ever like. We really were just trying to entertain ourselves. 'Cities on Flame' was totally done differently. It started out as a song called 'Siren Singalong'. I said to Albert, 'I like that song; you should start working on it.' He decided to take it in a different direction and that is where the music for 'Cities on Flame' came from. Albert had some of Sandy's lyrics and I really think he just grabbed a few lines from the poem. 'My heart is black and my lips are cold' was not originally the opening line, it was in the middle. That song was a real collaboration between Sandy, Albert and Donald."

Second to last track 'Workshop of the Telescopes' is a typical BÖC trip musically, the band working their miniature vampire-like sound, vaguely psychedelic, vaguely bluesy, like old Black Sabbath on brown-out. But the lyric is quite the nugget, Sandy fishing out an assortment of references to alchemy, the philosopher's science which Pearlman found illustrative and inspirational and otherwise useful as a metaphor for heavy metal.

"Well, that song incorporates every single one of the alchemical themes," reflects Pearlman. "Silverfish Imperetrix is this alchemical creature sort of like the salamander. There are these signature concepts and creatures in alchemy, embodiments of certain alchemical principles, for example the principle of transformation, which is embodied in several of these alchemical creatures, one being a salamander, which reduces everything into an ash. Jung adopted this kind of analytical grid. He thought that everything had to be reduced to negrito, the black state, the burnt-out state, to an ash, before it could flourish again in a new and improved, enhanced, more evolved partaking of a higher archival state or form. So Silverfish Imperetrix is a kind of alchemical creature that I thought up, as an embodiment of an alchemical format, or alchemical and transformational principles. So once you have received the wisdom of the Imperial Silverfish, your vision then is pretty much perfect, and you can see through the lives, not only the lives of appearance, but also through the lives of social structure and political formatting. So you can see through the lives of doctors and their wives. It becomes clear once you know exactly what it's about."

Discussing Patti Smith, with further elucidations on "Workshop" Sandy notes that, "Silverfish Imperetrix—Patti really loved that. I used to read all this stuff to her as I was writing it. She was like, wow. She loved 'Subhuman' the most. She thought the line about ladies, fish and gentleman was very amusing. The thing about 'Workshop of the Telescopes,' it's really what I call a gothic technology song. We understand that better now than we used to, because we've had 75 generations of technology in the last 20 years (laughs). So a lot of stuff that really isn't all that old looks gothic now. So it really was a song about gothic technology, the old plumbing and hardware kind of thing, which comes at the dawn of the age of the IC, which had been invented, but nobody knew about it at the time, i.e. in '72 and '73. So it has a kind of Frankenstein's laboratory techno-gothic take on how things would be transformed, and what the transformative mechanism would be. It would be brought by a technology and it would be a physically intensive technology as opposed to the far west physically intense technology that we see today."

Closing the record was a sinister, but deceptively light-hearted and small-ish tale called 'Redeemed'. Musically it's a rare sort of acoustic southern rock for this staunchly northern band. Great lyric too, but it's willfully obtuse. Buck offers a glimpse into the tune's origins. "'Redeemed' might have been or might not have been part of Sandy's *Imaginos* song cycle. And when we did it, I think we were thinking about the way The Grateful Dead would do stuff around the 'Uncle John's Band' era. Certainly as an album closer, it seemed like a really appropriate thing."

Positioning and promotion for *Blue Öyster Cult* got off on the right (beautiful) foot with a lively and entertaining record company bio (with slight changes made to song titles. etc., for consistency) that strikes the author as very much the professorial work of Pearlman himself: "*During a rather bizarre gig in Oaxaca, while the Blue Öyster Cult was in the midst of 'Transmaniacon MC,' two (not one, count 'em) eclipses occurred within minutes of each other. The experience was so jarring to the boys that when asked about their omnipresent dark glasses, they usually reply, 'Ah... it's the light'.*"

"*The Blue Öyster Cult is composed of five leatheroid men. Several members of the group were in the famed Soft White Underbelly, while other joined forces with the short-lived Stalk Forrest Group. Donald Roeser/Buck Dharma has two very definitive sides, but is, nevertheless, one of the great guitarists in the history of mankind (or rock 'n' roll, anyway), and has been called such in the likes of* Rolling Stone, Crawdaddy, The Voice, The Herald, *et. al. Donald's Snydly Wiplash mustachio has been known to tickle the twine of pre-teens and sub- humans inhabiting the front rows. Vocalist Eric (Jesse Python) Bloom is often referred to as The Rock King of the Finger Lakes, and was the most affected by the incident* at Oaxaca. Allen (LaVern) Lanier handles keyboards and rhythm for the BÖC, and generally holds things together. A scholar/athlete at heart, Allen's greatest influences have been Baudelaire and Bryant (Emmette, that is). The rhythm is covered in a most macho manner by the Bouchard Brothers: Albert (Prince Omega) on drums, and Joe on bass. Albert has the Derek Sanderson moustache, Joe, the Mel Schachter moves."

"Since the eclipses at Oaxaca, 'Transmaniacon' (' across all madness)' has become the group's theme. If their vision was somewhat darkened by the experience, so were their musical concepts: the first eight songs on their debut Columbia album, Blue Öyster Cult, deal primarily with violence and murder. 'Transmaniacon MC' is about bikers (MC = Motorcycle Club), whose hogs were jostled, the results being the chaos that followed. 'I'm on the Lamb but I Ain't No Sheep' has a well-defined political connotation inborn, and concerns scandals within the storied halls of Columbia University, which fleeced a number of parents and students during the mid-'50s. 'Then Came the Last Days of May' is the resurrection ballad inspired by four Stoney Brook drug dealers who were bumped off in Arizona before they could stash the loot."

"'Stairway to the Stars' deals with the milieu of hit-and-run violence, while 'Before the Kiss, a Redcap' is a tortured story set in the city of Babylon. It's about Conray's Bar in Babylon, New York. 'Screams' talks of the ominosoid, while 'She's as Beautiful as a Foot' is an R. Meltzer special describing the violent dangers of foot fetishism. 'Cities on Flame with Rock and Roll' is the Blue Öyster Cult anthem, and although the crowd is not required to stand throughout, the band's logo is usually saluted. The concept is broken at this point to give the vinyl a break, Ozzie. 'Workshop of the Telescopes' is a supernatural epic song with eyes closed, behind dark glass. The album ends on a mildly optimistic note, as 'Redeemed' describes the redemption of Sir Rastus Bear by a song. The theme throughout is clearly osirification. Lyrics were written in large part by rock critics Sandy Pearlman and R. Meltzer, while the music stems from the guts of the boys and their production crew. Seventeen murders occurred within 12 blocks of the studio during the production of Blue Öyster Cult."

It is of note that the 2001 reissue of *Blue Öyster Cult* includes four bonus tracks that provide elucidation as to the band's pre-BÖC beginnings. 'Betty Lou's Got a New Pair of Shoes' is a Bobby Freeman cover and an old Chuck Berry-styled rock 'n' roller tracked during the Soft White Underbelly demo session of July 21, 1969, the same one that yielded band original 'What is Quicksand? ', a Buck-sung soft rock lopester in the style of The Grateful Dead or Bob Dylan, despite the garish psychedelic lyric.

"'What Is Quicksand?' is one of my favourites," says Richard, who, repeatedly, emphasizes that the psych incarnation of the band was indeed the good band, making what is perhaps their only good record, save for the "awful" drum mix. "Basically, I think I wrote that with Lanier. Elektra actually put out a single of 'What Is Quicksand?' and 'Arthur Comics,' and they pressed about 50 copies (ed. other sources say 200 and even 300; these were radio station promos). But anyway, I was very proud of that. A British punk band from around '79 was actually called Arthur Comics."

Emphasizing this predilection for the boys as quality psychsters, Richard, in

1982, said that, "They were a good psychedelic band. They used to play the Hotel Diplomat. They'd change their sound every few months. Pearlman's original hype on the Underbelly, which was not too inaccurate, was that they were like a cross between the Jefferson Airplane and the Doors. Pearlman and I went to college together at Stony Brook out on Long Island. It was the Summer of Love; we went out to the Monterey Pop Festival, hung out in Haight-Ashbury, there were bands galore, and when we got back, Pearlman wanted a band and put out the call."

Richard, in the same interview, adds that, as the band took shape, "Watching them was like looking at this chess game where everything was total calculation. It had a high degree of comedy attached to it, because you could tell they were somewhat resistant to the notion of being heavy metal; they would be ironic about it and make reference to it rather than just be it. Little by little, the will to resist went away. They didn't calculate a goddamn thing until they became the Cult. They knew certain aspects of show for its own sake, but their musical ideas were much more independent of the march to success. I came in maybe 15 minutes after they came into being and started writing songs for them too. At first they were very reluctant to sing. The lyrics didn't really take hold of their total identity until they took responsibility for singing them. The way they are to this day is as an expression of Pearlman, Pearlman's whole riff that life is an illusion."

The other two bonus tracks added to the reissue of the debut are from a separate Soft White Underbelly demo session, September 11, 1969. 'Donovan's Monkey' is quite a commendable track, housing psych, prog and hard rock, all with adequate inky darkness to have made it a potential strong moment on the band's debut album. 'A Fact About Sneakers' is similarly sophisticated in terms of changes, rhythms and chord progressions, but again, helps to illustrate the fact that the band were psychedelic, not that heavy, certainly different from what the stated direction would be a couple years later. This version is more powerful than the one that ended up on *St. Cecilia*, by/as Stalk-Forrest Group.

With respect to 'Donovan's Monkey', Meltzer says that, "It was also recorded for the first Soft White Underbelly record that never happened, with Les Braunstein singing. And that's one where I mention Killer Kowalski, who was my favourite wrestler. He's actually Canadian, from somewhere in Ontario. And he actually has a degree in philosophy from some small Ontario school. His name was Wladek 'Killer' Kowalski; I think he's still alive. He's one of the few wrestlers I ever saw in a hairpiece; he actually was fighting with a hairpiece, and he would jump on people's heads or whatever. I think 'Donovan's Monkey'... just the title... there's a movie *Donovan's Brain*, so I think I got it from there. 'A Fact About Sneakers' was something about football kickers. Living with that band... they were basically beer and *Wide World of Sports*. I mean, when I say a bunch of Long Island hicks, you know, Saturday would be, let's get some beer and watch an auto race, let's watch football, let's watch the New York Mets. And whatever there is in there about football kickers, I'm sure I wrote while watching a game."

"In terms of the bonus tracks, 'Donovan's Monkey'—great song," mentions Buck, looking back. "It was a classic Underbelly repertoire piece, recorded as a demo for Columbia. We didn't get signed off the demo, by the way. I think by the time Clive Davis signed us we weren't doing 'Donovan's Monkey' anymore. 'What is Quicksand?' we recorded for the Elektra sessions, and they're out on Rhino now. That was the first single for the Elektra sessions. That was on the *Nuggets* record too. This version indicates demo, so it probably was. That was probably a version that we did on the Columbia demo. 'A Fact About Sneakers'—great song. You know, it's funny; I would like to compare these versions with the versions that are on the Rhino Handmade record. 'Betty Lou's Got a New Pair of Shoes' was a cover that we'd done. An odd choice you might think, but then again we made lots of odd choices."

As the notes explain and as we've discussed, the band then changed their name to Stalk-Forrest Group, signed to Elektra and re-recorded 'What Is Quicksand?' for that two-track single Meltzer correctly recalls (EKM45693 – mono), all alas, to no avail. Quickly, the band "calculated" their way toward Blue Öyster Cult and were off on Sandy's trip, no looking back.

Blue Öyster Cult's dance card for 1972 filled in nicely after the release of the debut album and the milestone shows with Alice Cooper in April, first for some Illinois shows with Big Brother & the Holding Company, followed by multiple shows with the Allman Brothers, Black Sabbath and Jeff Beck, and one-offs with the likes of Quicksilver Messenger Service, Spirit, Cactus, Hydra, Rare Earth, James Gang, Flash, Camel, Wishbone Ash, REO Speedwagon and ELP. This would be the year of the band's first extensive spate of tour dates, with BÖC blanketing, essentially, the eastern half of the US. The pronounced uptick in tour dates versus 1971, along with the release of the debut album right at the start of the year, essentially argues for 1972 as the inaugural year of the band—especially given the complicated naming and personnel history going back fully five years previous. In 1972 we have focus, even if Buck will always lament that lack of focus is what doomed the band to a glass ceiling of the band's own choosing.

Tyranny and Mutation

"And then Phil was in the morgue"

Now that the band had a record under their belts, it was felt they'd better look the part live. Much gigging ensued, the band slowly learning the ropes, discovering what it takes to play bigger halls and concert stages as opposed to basement dives. *Tyranny and Mutation*, recorded in late '72 and released in February '73, would be blessed and cursed by Blue Öyster Cult's tireless road slogs. The main detriment turned out to be not having enough time to write. The advantage turned out to be a marked increase in musicianship. Indeed a rare, live promo EP (known as *Bootleg EP* or *Live Bootleg*) was released in the interim. This bare-bones 12" release (Columbia AS 40) is without a doubt some of the greatest live BÖC material in existence, many citing this 'Cities on Flame' as the best the band ever performed it (note the tracks can be collected by getting the '01 reissue of *Tyranny and Mutation* plus the two CD compilation *Workshop of the Telescopes*). "It's a four song EP," notes Eric. "It was actually made in a bar in Rochester, NY. It was just a stereo recording, in other words, a reel-to-reel stereo machine. Just left and right—that's all there was."

But back to the main attraction, Albert concurs with the second album's hurried feel. "I think that in our contract, it said that we were supposed to produce a new record every 12 months. And I can't say I really prefer that second record to the first. It was written almost entirely on the road. We'd rehearse in motel rooms and stuff, with acoustic guitars, cardboard boxes and overturned waste paper baskets, to try to get a sound. So it was very organic."

"The first three albums were like one long album to me," adds Albert. "I can't even think of them as separate entities. That whole concept was just like descriptions of hell. That was our take on Black Sabbath. 'Well, we won't write about any quasi-religious stuff; we'll just try and describe hell as best we can'."

"Plus a lot of what we were creating at the time were songs that would translate well for a live show. We were following Alice Cooper's lead on that. They had the best show in the world at that time and we were trying to compete with that. I have always been a big fan of underground comic books so that's where my interest was. Eric liked sci-fi so that's his thing. Pearlman was always reading every kind of esoteric book imaginable so that had a lot to do with our subject matter. There was more harmony in the beginning. After awhile, later, I decided that I just wanted to support the other guys. Eric was particularly bothered by all the other guys taking the leads on the songs."

One small consolation of all this humbling touring turned out to be the complete reworking of the debut's 'I'm on the Lamb But I Ain't no Sheep' into *Tyranny*'s signature track 'The Red & The Black'. Albert explains. "I'm on the Lamb' was not really going over well live. This guy Richard Dostel, the guy who had actually booked us at the swingers party, said, 'The ending of that song is really good. You should have the whole song be fast like that.' The Blood, Sweat and Tears' drummer had also suggested that the song had too many parts. 'Any one of the parts was great. Why don't you guys settle down into a groove?' And being a drummer, I was thinking about that."

Buck: "When we started playing stuff live, as opposed to the studio versions, we routinely would evolve and change the arrangement. And we thought we had so much improved the arrangement of 'Lamb' from the first album, that we'd record it again."

Albert continues, "And I was also thinking that the Blues Project had always opened their shows with 'Goin' Down to Louisiana', which was a real up-tempo, double-time song. So we redid it and took out the part that was based on Hendrix's 'Hey Joe' riff. But we wanted it up-tempo so we could use it at the beginning of the set and just knock everybody over. Between the first record if you listen to my drumming, you'll notice a change. We did about 12 gigs with Mahavishnu Orchestra. They opened the show and blew us off the stage. I mean, talk about humiliation! And they weren't even trying to humiliate us. They were just playing their asses off. So for years we opened with that song, because we wanted something that was just really tight and fast, and lots of notes, just a mind-blower." The song definitely demonstrates a jazzy, busy, textural Albert, and is probably the rawest and energetic vibe the band has ever achieved.

"*Tyranny* was made kind of in a hurry," relates Joe, "and 'Red & The Black' was, of course, a remake of 'Lamb.' We were doing a version on stage that heavied everything up, and that was one of the first songs we picked for *Tyranny*. At the time, it was kind of odd to redo a song that you had done on a previous album. But nowadays re-doing, remixing and tossing something out again is pretty common."

It is of note that the new title 'Red & The Black' borrows from a line in the original lyric, but is also the name of a Stendhal novel, although the connection to the novel from the lyric is pretty much non-existent, none of the band members ever admitting to the influence of the book on the song. The words were also used to demarcate the sides of the original vinyl, side one being "the black" and side two being "the red." Facetiously, I'd have to add that while side two's tunes struggled to push the band into the red, side one's songs over the years, have helped keep them in the black! Sandy has also said that red symbolizes Quaaludes and black symbolizes methedrine.

Next up—to continue that train of thought!—was a negative and mopey blues called 'O.D.'d on Life Itself', a strange combination of T.Rex's 'Bang a Gong', ludes and carnival choruses. Albert recalls the song's conception. "I remember, Sandy Pearlman was riding with us. We were driving around and he just came up with that line. I think we'd just come from an Allman Brothers concert and we were passing by the medical tent, and somebody said, 'I wonder if anybody OD'd?'

Sandy came up with that, and then of course he built a song around it. I don't pretend to know what he's talking about!"

Track three; Joe Bouchard's 'Hot Rails to Hell' was to become a band classic on par with 'Cities on Flame'. The tune is a complex metal showcase, flipping from as sinister a riff BÖC could muster for the verse to a warm boogie chorus. Joe reveals the motivation. "'Hot Rails to Hell' and 'Wings Wetted Down' came very quickly. They sort of fit that notion of, 'Well, it's gotta be heavy.' So I used chords that would be harder-edged than some sort of flower power/hippie stuff. When I joined the band, I think they were a little reluctant to do metal songs. But right out of the gate I was ready to go for it. So a song like 'Screams' was definitely nothing like Soft White Underbelly. Then 'Hot Rails to Hell' was also nothing like the Soft White Underbelly, and it was kind of a little definitive metal excursion, although it had a lot of rock 'n' roll in it too."

Albert underlines the song's immediacy. "The second record was a blur. We did it in about two or three days. And I remember I screwed up a drum fill in 'Hot Rails to Hell.' So I overdubbed the whole drum track from start to finish, and of course I didn't have my old drums to listen to either, just the guitar. It's a wild track. It's really loose, and it was like one take."

When asked about his vocal performances, Joe adds this note. "Well there aren't many (laughs). 'Hot Rails to Hell' is the main one. But whenever I think of Blue Öyster Cult songs I never think of 'Hot Rails to Hell'. For some reason, it just seems like a different band (laughs). But I probably sung that song more than any other tune. I wrote the lyrics for that as well as the music. It has to do with this agent friend of ours Phil King who was murdered back in the early days of the band over gambling debts or something like that. We never really knew, but supposedly it was by somebody who owed him money. All of a sudden Phil was booking shows, and then Phil was in the morgue. So 'Hot Rails to Hell'... I just knew, I've got to get this song out, and it just sort of came in a flash. We played it a lot live, but every time I think of the Blue Öyster Cult catalogue, I always leave that song out."

The track's lyric is demonstrative of Joe's macabre themes sent deep within the belly of the big city, the subway as conduit to hell, a motif revived on *Agents of Fortune's* 'Morning Final'.

Joe touches upon the Phil King story with the line about the king not knowing (for more on Phil, see our discussion on the less cryptic Phil King song, 'Deadline'). Joe says that, "Phil was a compulsive gambler. I guess he just got in with the wrong crowd and was trying to shake down people who owed him money, and this one time, he shook down the wrong guy and that was it. But yeah, 'Hot Rails to Hell' was one of those things where I wanted to write an up-tempo rock song. As I say, Phil King came to an untimely end. I used to live with Phil and he was our agent and promoter in the early days. The weird part is, I was hanging out with the guy who did the album cover, Bill Gawlik. Which, by the way, that was a really strange cover—very futuristic, definitely other-worldly. I think it fit the kind of music we were doing, our futuristic science fiction-leaning thing. Anyway, Bill and I took the subway because he was too cheap to pay for a parking space in New York. We would drive to Queens and then we would get on the subway and go to New York. We went to a jazz concert in the city and then we took the subway back to Queens. On the way back to Queens, on the subway, the whole idea for 'Hot Rails to Hell' came to me. The guys liked it and it was the right song for our second album. It was put out as a single. It is a great song and it has survived the test of time. I sang it for years in BÖC shows, but I don't feel as connected to it as some of the others, I don't know why. I wished I had written more songs for BÖC, but I'd get so pissed-off when a song got dropped from the album at the final sequencing, I'd hesitate writing more for future albums."

'7 Screaming Diz-Busters' was another hard-hitting construct soon to become a live classic. Sandy, when asked about Blue Öyster Cult's music still sounding relevant today, recounts a funny story revolving around this pioneering "speed metal" track.

"I think *Tyranny and Mutation*, and to a lesser extent, *Secret Treaties* are like records that could have been made yesterday. And there is no doubt that those records and their attitude influenced a tremendous number of people. You know I used to say—and this is not an insult—that *Master of Puppets* was the best Blue Öyster Cult record of the mid-'80s (laughs). Like, if you didn't know who it was, you'd think it was them. So to answer your question, yes, I think they hold up. And they probably are, except for *Master of Puppets*, especially *Tyranny and Mutation*, the best take on fast but heavy metal, and the best take on music as abrasion, as astringent. They really have a surface, or an abrasive grain on them that is very hard to achieve. Even *Master of Puppets* is a little too civilized."

"I remember Bruce Springsteen coming up to the 12th floor of CBS," continues Pearlman, "when Columbia Records was still part of CBS, and hearing '7 Screaming Diz-Busters' through the door of one of the product manager's office, and saying, 'Who was that?!' 'Blue Öyster Cult.' And he said, 'I can't believe anybody can play that fast' (laughs). Who, by the way, turned out to be a major Dictators fan!'"

Musically, the track really held back, in comparison to the live version from *On Your Feet*. The band's inherent jazziness, in particular Albert's painterly drumming, dampened the rock-out quotient of the fast part, lending the song a progressive, enigmatic quality. Like 'Hot Rails to Hell' and 'Cities on Flame', it too had many divergent sections, building to crescendos, leaving respites for furtive jams and future crowd participation.

Joe recounts the song's germination. "I remember I got the lyrics from Sandy. And I spent quite a bit of time twisting it around, to make it a little more musical. I ended up throwing a lot of things out. Sandy would put in these big literary things and I thought, 'This is not going to sing very well.' So I spent several days rewriting the lyrics. By that time we had moved out to a house in Dix Hills, and we had a big Hammond organ in the living room. And I remember most of it was written just bashing away on this big organ, and making it fit with Sandy's lyrics."

Albert has revealed that "diz" refers to the cleft of the penis, and that "duster's dust" refers to sperm. But the concept of diz-buster is left ambiguous. The definition of "something that can make one ejaculate" most plausibly applies to a reading that these seven diz-busters are evil, paranormal sex sirens, woman beings without a conscious, the number seven bringing in a biblical element to the lyric as well. But this track could also be one of Sandy's biker songs, diz-buster referring to the result of a long, vibrating Harley ride (and then, mamas and old ladies often joke about the orgasmic qualities of a good ride). Indeed, many lines in the song could have one believe that the diz-buster is a bike (there is mention of cast iron, the mirror's face, rigid arms, routes, all suggesting this interpretation), especially in light of the fact that females, female pronouns, or sexual ideas are never mentioned in the song.

Joe sheds more light on his approach to this track's lyric. "I had a tendency where I would take a Sandy Pearlman lyric and shape it. Those guys would use a Sandy Pearlman or Richard Meltzer lyric just the way they wrote it. But I always felt that structure was important in music, the structure of the lyric. So I ended up changing around the lines, not changing any of the words per se, but changing the order of the lines, which I also definitely did in 'Astronomy'. The same with '7 Screaming Diz-Busters'. Like I say, I wrote pretty much most of the music on our organ, which was in the living room of the house we rented. I would just get up in the morning and start banging on the organ, and came up with that, while Donald and Albert added in sort of the jam section."

First track, side two marked the lyrical debut of a then 23-year-old Patti Smith on a Blue Öyster Cult record, 'Baby Ice Dog' indeed predating Patti's own first solo release *Horses* by two years. "With respect to 'Baby Ice Dog'," recalls Albert, "that's another song Patti gave me after I failed with her first tune. She said, 'Well here's another one—use this one.' I'm not exactly sure what the story's about. As you've seen on other BÖC albums, there's all kinds of things it could be. But I think that's one of the things about Patti is that she can be very deep."

Band expert Bolle finds a lesbian undercurrent to the tune. "Patti Smith is very difficult to read. She has this sexual fetish with, number one, lesbianism. All of her lyrics have some clue towards lesbianism, and it's very strange because sometimes I don't know whether she's really describing her sister Kimberley, her brother Todd, or herself. But I know that she's that deep and that poetic, that her licence as a writer will give her the creative moment where you can explain other people's sexual fantasies in totally different words. You can make up Disney characters if you want to. I think that's what Patti Smith always did, because she wanted her meanings, the actual interpretations, to be thrown out at the media. But she knew she couldn't do it in an obvious way because of the times. Remember, these are times when the band itself had to change the lyrics of their single 'Career of Evil' from doing it to your daughter to 'do it like you oughta,' which actually isn't two different vocals. It's just finesse engineering. They took the 'd' out. Oughta is the same as daughter. You just don't hear the 'd'."

Albert responds, "I think that's definitely the image that she was trying to encourage. But I actually don't think that's what it's about."

"Okay, basically, I was the one who brought her to the band," recounts Meltzer. "She was my friend. In the summer of 1970, my dentist was around the corner from the bookstore where she worked, Scribner's Books on 5th Avenue in the 40s. And I stopped in there and we became great friends. And somewhere down the line I brought her to the band. Pearlman wanted to fuck her and that was his interest. And I don't know if he did or didn't, but once it was clear that she was with Allen, it got to be that there was a lot of tension between Pearlman and Allen. Allen was very anti-Semitic without any irony whatsoever. You know, fuck the Jews, all that kind of stuff. And so there was a lot of anti-Pearlman wrath from both of them. I lived with this woman Ronnie and we would hang out with Allen and Patti a lot, through the mid '70s. And essentially what made the relationship viable was we didn't mind his anti-Semitism. But the point is that Allen thought the faux-Nazi stuff was a joke. I mean, everybody took it as a joke."

It is of note that spacing between songs on *Tyranny and Mutation* is virtually non-existent, each track winding up with the next starting immediately, or each track linked to the next with a sound effect of some sort. 'Baby Ice Dog' begins with a lupine howl, and ends the same way, segueing into the opening chords of Joe's sinister 'Wings Wetted Down'. Joe sets the scene: "Now 'Wings Wetted Down' is another thing I sort of adapted. When I first moved into the Blue Öyster Cult house, we had a couple of boarders that actually lived there, and one of them worked in a bookstore. He gave me a book of Pablo Neruda's poems, or more specifically, translations of his poems. He's actually gotten a lot of press these days with that new movie about him. Then I got into the whole thing. I mean, I'm not a political guy, but the song has tinges of the end of the Vietnam War which was happening just about the time I wrote that song. So I just threw a bunch of images together. I don't remember the song much. But people ask me about it a lot. I just found some nice phrases and connected them with my own phrases."

A stellar job, given that on the surface, the lyric reads like an arch-vampire tale, lots of blackness, motion and fantastic flight imagery. Bolle has a particular favourite line. "The fun thing in the lyric is that that he doesn't sing 'echoes of vampires'—it's empires. But it sounds like vampires and Joe thought that was just excellent. That's his favourite thing about the lyric."

Essentially all of side two of this record is a bit of a wasteland, none of these chilling, creepy tracks becoming stars of the band's catalogue. The final two tracks are perhaps the most anonymous, least talked about of the four. 'Teen Archer' is a sort of funky, lop-sided black metal, psychedelic, damp and just plain dark. "Meltzer lyric," notes Buck, "as a writer, I was just starting to write. I did 'The Last Days of May' and then basically that was my second song, and as a vocalist too, I was finding my voice. It's a funny song."

Richard's lyric almost abstains from existing, Meltzer offering a kind of ancient blues lack of literacy, flippant nonsense unworthy of the Cult, really. Richard, however, calls it "one of my favourite BÖC lyrics," adding that he "felt it was the best recording they did of anything of mine." Musically speaking, there's a nice jazzy, Doorsy climax to the tune. And again there's practically no space between its whipped wind-up and the record's closer 'Mistress of the Salmon Salt'.

Bolle figures the "Mistress" lyric is about, "Love. I guess it's a groupie song, sex." "Super dark," adds Buck. "We were going for a Rolling Stones kind of evil on that one." Albert offers a few words on this characteristically weird tune. "Well, that was actually a song that I had written called 'Checkout Girl' (laughs), and it wasn't much of a song. Sandy said 'I re-wrote the lyrics for 'Checkout Girl' and he gave me this 'Quicklime Girl'. Of course I was like, 'Okay this we can use, but we're going to have to make it more scary' (laughs). These lyrics are really bizarre, you know, the famous story of the person that kills people, or actually I don't think she kills people, but she performs a service. She would bury the murdered dead, and use them as fertilizer for her plants."

As far as touring *Tyranny and Mutation* went, 1973's itinerary looked a lot like that of 1972, with the band concentrating in the eastern half of the US, on a bewildering array of multi-band bills in gyms and theatres and auditoriums. Playing with over 100 different bands, BÖC nonetheless made it to California for the first time, as well as into Canada where they played Winnipeg plus the storied Massey Hall in Toronto, between opener Aerosmith and headliner Mott the Hoople.

"Great record, a lot of angst in it," mused Buck, 30 years later, looking back on the band's important sophomore step. "We were certainly feeling a lot of pressure to come up with the second installment in our saga. It was written around touring and all the pressures of that. That was our first exposure to the actual nuts and bolts of what it was like to be recording artists. Once you've actually made a record and have had it released, there's a lot of angst there and I think that's reflected in the music—there's a lot of tension."

Secret Treaties

"The transit point that moves us from old history to new history"

The last of the "black and white" records, *Secret Treaties* is widely considered one of the best of the entire catalogue, even if Richard Meltzer, if forced to pick even one he actually finds listenable, goes with *Tyranny*. *Secret Treaties* is the third and last from the band before transformation, the most mature of the harsh, monochromatic buffets of badness that mark the "black and white" era.

There's no real change in approach or technique yet, the band still feeling somewhat rushed and frazzled, as Eric puts it, caught in "an endless cycle of write the album, record the album, tour the album." Also in deference to its predecessor, *Secret Treaties* rattled on insistently like a coal car through hell, each track separated by nary a breath of silence, effects like a ticking clock, a German musical box (Al: "that's my mothers favourite part of the album!"), and a synthesizer swirl used as segues between twisted tales.

The record's Ron Lesser cover art depicted the band posing in front of an ME 262, a World War II fighter jet, pilot's seat filled with the figure of Death. Eric is dramatically caped, holding the reigns of four German shepherds, which, on the back sleeve are shown mysteriously (ritualistically?) slaughtered. The band is gone and the plane seems to be in motion, although this is not clear. Another quirk of the cover art is the shadowy background scene, which appears to depict Mexican farmers, or perhaps images from another time, something like time warpage circa *Imaginos*.

The inner sleeve contained two slight variations of the outer front and back. The band shot is distinguished by a clearer background of an older city scene, something akin to Washington, D.C. The "slaughtered dogs" shot depicts the jet parked on what looks like a desolate and dusty, urban Mexican street. Albert, on the credit for the concept says, "*Secret Treaties* was created by the Columbia Records art department, because they really wanted to get involved. We wanted to keep control of the artwork, but after the first two records, which they thought were really great, they wanted a shot at it. So we let them do it and we didn't like it. The original cover was what was on the inner sleeve. They thought it was too graphic and so did we, so we ended up with this other thing that they did. They did two versions, the inside and the outside. How it ended up was that Sandy's idea was the front cover and Murray's idea was the back cover, with the dogs being slaughtered. But all in all, *Secret Treaties* was mostly Sandy's idea." Another complication is that the European release of the record sported red lettering; while stateside the text was green.

The inner sleeve adds this cryptic note. "Rossignol's curious, albeit simply titled book, the Origins of a World War, spoke in terms of secret treaties, drawn up between the Ambassadors from Plutonia and Desdinova the foreign minister. These treaties founded a secret science from the stars. Astronomy. The career of evil." As is well-documented, the book does not exist. But the notation ties nicely the band's (most notably Pearlman's) recurring theme of conspirators (be they Rosicrucians, Illuminati, Masons, Gnostics, Hermetics, or secret divisions of the CIA, FBI and Yale!) causing wars and other human upheaval (i.e. Altamont), in addition to the link with beings from other planets and possibly other times.

Opener 'Career of Evil' is another early Patti Smith collaboration with Al Bouchard, again a very dark and Doorsy track, propelled by Lanier's keyboards, aged, crusty and gothic. The tune (and for that matter the whole record) perpetuates the band's compressed, claustrophobic sound to this point—Krugman and Pearlman still not exactly succeeding with taming the crude equipment at CBS studios. An interesting line in the song with respect to surgeons and picking your brain perhaps had something to do with Al and Deb Frost calling their band The Brain Surgeons years later. Another line, the aforementioned one about doing it to your daughter, was later censored for the *Don't Fear the Reaper* cassette-only release and the *On Flame with Rock and Roll* compilation album, which features on the track a completely redone vocal by Eric.

"'Career of Evil' was a nice collaboration between Patti Smith and my brother," says the bassist Bouchard. "And pulls no punches... except when they did the single version. I think we had 'do it like ya oughta,' not 'do it to your daughter'— oh my God. But that was Patti Smith, so you could get away with it. Not meant to be a hit single, but on the other hand, a very good song, and it kind of sets the tone for the whole heaviness of the album."

"We put out 'Hot Rails to Hell;' that got some traction in radio but oddly 'Career of Evil' didn't do so well. I think maybe it was too controversial in terms of lyrics. And we put out that edited version because we thought 'do it to your daughter' might sound paedophile. So we changed that, but it didn't do any good. It was just too abrasive a lyric."

Track two was 'Subhuman', a tune that would be revived 14 years later on *Imaginos* as signature track 'Blue Öyster Cult', rightly so as it seems to encapsulate Sandy's complex concept of the band, the character Imaginos, and the intertwining of the two. A type of literal translation of the band's name occurs, similar to graphic artist Greg Scott's approach to the *Fire of Unknown Origin* artwork, with talk of oyster boys, the sea and the "blue sky bag." Overtones of Lovecraft's Cthulhu or "old ones" can also be spotted in terms of death-like creatures who inhabit the seas. In any event, the occurrences in this lyric seem to mark a traumatic, transformational moment for Imaginos, a character who could change form and traverse time (more on this in the *Imaginos* chapter).

Musically the track is perhaps the mellowest and jazziest on the record, although there's a number of parts to the tune, one being decisively heavy metal, but arranged timidly to blend into the Doorsy fabric of the whole, very 'Riders on the Storm'. 'Subhuman' also marks a rare solo Eric Bloom credit for music. Eric indeed participated much more on this record than the previous two, chalking up his increased contribution to the fact that much of the band were acquiring wives and girlfriends at this point (Buck and Albert had been married in '73; Allen was living with Patti Smith), and that he had a goodly amount of time alone at the latest Blue Öyster Cult house to write music.

Track three, 'Dominance and Submission', marks another great Pearlman lyric, draped over an immediate chord progression that turned out to work splendidly live. Sandy explains, "That is a metaphorical morality play, having to do with the unleashing of the dark forces of rock 'n' roll, by—even though it seems weird now—the Beatles, on New Year's Eve in 1963. You remember when those records began to be played in North America? It was like nothing can stop this process. It's all preordained. And furthermore, whatever has been preordained is unknown to us, and things are going to wind up a lot more chaotic than we ever dreamed they would. So I just picked that transit point of '63 to '64 as the movement, the transit point that moves us from old history to new history. I think that's pretty supportable actually. This teenager who's hanging out in Times Square on New Year's Eve, he's listening to the Beatles, which is now being pumped, whether we want it or not, into our consciousness, you know, over WABC on a transistor radio. He's picked up by these characters, this brother and sister team, who are being driven around on New Year's Eve in a large black limousine, and they initiate him into all sorts of undreamed of sexual experiences. That's what it's about. Charles the laughing boy."

So the lyric fits enigmatically with Sandy's whole idea that rock 'n' roll possesses untapped power... his *History of Los Angeles* project, Altamont, the interweaving of heavy metal and conspiracy, the sounds of heavy metal as sonic metaphor for the pseudo-science of alchemy, indeed the whole philosophical construction of the Blue Öyster Cult itself. Perhaps this is why the title *Power in the Hands of Fools* was considered for *Secret Treaties*, both presupposing a sort of paranormal or at least fascistic weight to this gathering of rock guys making loud sounds.

There is also the resonance of this power being concentrated amongst the puppeteers, i.e. Sandy, Murray and even Meltzer. The latter quite viably enters the mix both as lyricist for the band and pioneering art critic, the man being perhaps the first that argued successfully that rock is culture worthy of higher academic consideration, the idea that this explosive new phenomenon is true art, and thus possessive of a power beyond age or the lower reaches of the IQ scale. To be sure, Meltzer wasn't involved in the blood and guts, day-to-day operation of the band, but his bullshit detector (like Albert's), and perhaps merely just his presence, must have been valued, overtly or at least subconsciously.

A more sinister and global reading of 'Dominance and Submission' would also have to include the Kennedy assassination. One very conspiratorial and intriguing theory of this event posits that the assassination was part two of a trinity of events set in motion by the secret society known as the Illuminati. Alchemy is also an important piece of the puzzle, given that the first event was the transformation of matter that occurred with the atomic bomb tests at the Trinity site in New Mexico. The Kennedy portion, or 'The Killing of the Divine King' was designed to vanquish American spirit and will, not so much a political motivation, but one of mass psychological destruction, of mass evaporation of moral centres. And indeed, culture-watchers decried the almost immediate acceleration of harder, faster, crazier sex, drugs and rock 'n' roll... more killings, a willful extermination of innocence. So as Sandy relates, the Beatles' invasion (mere months after the Kennedy assassination) could be considered a turning point in history, or, as conspiracy theorists suggest, a result (celebration?) of the main event succeeding to the secret society's satisfaction. With this in mind, the actual 'Dominance and Submission' story sounds somewhat like the Illuminati plan itself, the destruction of morals and beliefs, if on a merely humourous, rock 'n' roll level.

As mentioned, 'Dominance and Submission' turned into one of the band's most enduring live classics, still trotted out 20 and 30 and 40 years after the fact. Eric reflects on the question of favourite songs he likes to sing. "There are songs I like better than others but it's cyclical. There are songs you do for a couple of years, then you get tired of it, drop the song, then you get another song. I probably prefer to sing my own tunes rather than other people's tunes, like 'Dominance and Submission' which I wrote some music to, not the lyrics, but the chords. But that's a fun song to sing, because of the shout and reply, audience participation part of it."

Next came the rollicking muscle boogie classic 'ME 262', a song which perhaps got the band in more hot water than any other, really cementing this idea that the band were a bunch of Nazis, quite a leap, given that many in Blue Öyster Cult's orbit were Jewish! Helen Wheels, future writer for the band, was Albert's girlfriend, and designer of the band's costumes at the time. She feels that this Nazi image thing was an amalgamation of many smaller cues: "It was things like the leather costumes, and those big flags that Sandy designed. There were big Blue Öyster Cult logo flags on, I guess, the band's first tour. There were two huge ones, one on each side. I guess they were the Cult logo, but they were red on black. It just looked a little... and by '75 they had 'ME 262' and that kind of material. But I also got branded in the punk era. I have a couple of books that say, 'Oh, she wore Nazi regalia and this or that.' I mean I did have one thing that was like an American Indian reverse swastika. They've been using that symbol for thousands of years. I don't know, I think it was just a lot of people trying to pin bad stuff on them, like it was 'devil music.' I never thought much of it. To me, 'ME 262' and those flags was the extent of it. And they were one of the first bands to be wearing black leather and studs."

Allen, during the launch of *Spectres*, looked back on the controversy with Tony Parsons from *NME*, saying that the Nazi imagery was, "a metaphor for negative imagery. Rock 'n' roll lives off false imagery. We've dropped all that simply because it wasn't amusing anymore. It was just an in-joke that had run its course. I'm a very conservative person when it comes to rock 'n' roll."

"'ME262' is spectacular!" laughs Joe. "The lyric is spectacular, the approach to the music is incredible, and the performance Eric Bloom does is just off the hook."

The 'ME262' lyric is a colourful one, name-calling many of Hitler's top operatives, telling the story of a World War II air battle from the point of view of the Germans, closing with the memorable refrain over which the German fighter muses with respect to how his English enemy has to die, for he himself to survive.

Just for the record, BÖC fan Jon Jarrett has pointed out a few technical errors with the song's lyric: "Errors, for the pedants (like me!): 1) the 262 didn't fly at night, except a very few two-seater versions: but Von Ondine is alone surely. 2) The British didn't use Fortresses except for ECM work this late in the war, and the Americans only flew them in daytime. 3) No 262 carried both cannon (gray-silver slugs) and R4M rocket installation in the 'snout,' and those with that installation never tested in combat because of the blinding effect of 24 rockets firing off from right before the pilot's eyes. Not to say Von Ondine couldn't be flying an experimental one for an emergency mission, but special pleading required, I think."

Side two of *Secret Treaties* opens with a sinister, alien Meltzer/Bouchard composition called 'Cagey Cretins' (Meltzer: "that was another one of those I wrote in five minutes"), adding to the strong argument that *Secret Treaties* has the best set of song titles of any BÖC record, or quite possibly any record out there, period (read 'em in sequence: it's quite the picture.).

Bolle offers this scenario with respect to 'Cagey Cretins': "That's another funny one. When I deciphered this lyric, I thought well, Richard Meltzer is sitting at the Blue Öyster Cult house where they all lived, bored out of his mind. He reads the newspaper or sees something on television about some weird guy who escaped an insane asylum and he's out there killing people, and Meltzer just conjures up ideas about these cagey cretins. Because when they speak to the perpetrator, he has weird fantasies and strange ideas. This thing about being chased around by the cat and being lonely in the state of Maine... I think this is all possible, but there's no real truth to this story. It's just fiction."

Albert supports this reading of the tune's origins: "Richard had written that when he had stayed at his girlfriend's house in Shirley, New York, which is in the middle of Long Island. There's absolutely nothing to do there, and he felt like it was the most boring place in the universe, and he came up with this lyric."

"'Cagey Cretins' was okay, but I think it was a little on the light side," figures Joe. "It was probably a song that today, a metal band doing it now, would come up with something heavier. They would do an 'ME 262' on it, rather than a 'Cagey Cretins'. But, that being said, it's still a good track."

The next tune was a sort of stuttering, heavy rocker, 'Harvester of Eyes' sporting a queer, almost comical but macabre lyric from Meltzer over a Roeser/Bloom funked metal musical bed. Once again, it's a great riff, but the delivery is subdued, allowing breathing room for Bloom's histrionic vocal. Again, the Sabbatherian does battle with the Doorsy, hard verse and chorus collapsing into barroom breaks and solo jams. The lyric is quite directly about a harvester of eyes, a guy who goes around collecting and subsequently cherishing eyes.

"Well, 'Harvester of Eyes' I wrote much, much, much earlier, like '67, for Soft White Underbelly," recalls Meltzer. "I'm not sure if they already worked that up. But the lick they use in that song is lifted from The Grateful Dead, on *Anthem of the Sun*, 'That's it for the Other One' (sings it). Straight from the Dead. And they were using a less metal version of the lick in the '60s. But I'm not quite sure whether that lick went with those lyrics. But when they finally presented it as a BÖC tune, I really thought, this was great. I thought it was a great arrangement, great production, and the lyrics I got, I think I probably said it somewhere... there was this guy Abe Fortas, who had been one of Lyndon Johnson's Texas cronies, who apparently started out as a lawyer. Lyndon Johnson, when he was running for Congress, some legislative position in Texas... there's this famous election where 270 dead people voted. The election was contested and Abe Fortas, his lawyer, got him the seat. So from that point forward, Abe Fortas... LBJ would always have something for him. And then he made him a Supreme Court Justice when he was President, and then somehow after when LBJ was out, maybe it was the late days of LBJ, Abe Fortas was involved in some corruption and had to resign. When they printed his bio, it said that he had ocular tuberculosis, tuberculosis of the eye (laughs). Something I'd never heard of. So I wrote the song, after reading this bio of Abe Fortas."

"That's a song that was actually written about some confirmation hearing that Richard watched, the Senate confirmation hearing for the Supreme Court Justice, Abe Fortas," recalls Buck, filling in some blanks. "He somehow mentioned something about ocular TB and that's how that ended up there. I think the whole tune took off from that moment, and Richard created the whole story."

Secret Treaties, unlike its two withering, waning predecessors, ended on a triumphant note, the one-two punch of 'Flaming Telepaths' and 'Astronomy' offering two live and lyric signatures, cornerstones of the band's reason to be, emotional uplifts of any Blue Öyster Cult concert from many a Blue Öyster Cult era. 'Flaming Telepaths' is a musically dynamic piece, punctuated by rhythmic shifts and moody respites, even pumping in pieces of the band's recurring boogie woogie. The lyric certainly contains alchemical themes, but goes further than rote textbook perusal, entering the mind of the alchemist, perhaps the torment of working within a frustrating discipline that either isn't working scientifically, but working on a psychological level—or a paranormal level. The line about the joke being on you can be seen as omnipotent forces taunting the alchemist, or in a live setting, a wry Bloom admonishment that the band is not to be taken so seriously as fans might desire. Of note also is that Allen had discovered an early generation Moog synthesizer tucked away at Columbia's studio and used it for lather and leather on this track.

"Another really sort of epic track," figures Joe. "Unfortunately we stole a lick from Jimi Hendrix, on that, but we changed it enough so it doesn't sound anything like Jimi Hendrix, really, in reality. And you have to have that lick in there."

"On the new album there's the song called 'Flaming Telepaths'," explained Sandy, in conversation with *NME*'s Dan Nooger circa spring of '74, "which deals with the same sort of theme (as 'Cities on Flame') but in a scientific way. It's about an attempt to create a mutation, to mutate consciousness. The first lines are, 'I will have opened my veins too many times, poison's in my mind, poison's in my bloodstream, poison's in my pride,' and that's the key line, 'poison's in my pride.' It's about this scientist who attempts to mutate consciousness and he just can't do it; he's failed too many times. But the scientist has this poisonous pride and he's got to keep on trying, beating his head against this barrier. And just because he's doing it, that's good enough. It's a very, very noble song. What I've always wanted to get across is that the purpose of everything is to provide models. Artists provide the models and motivation for history. I think it's undeniable that rock 'n roll has provided the dynamics for a great many of the events of the last ten years. You see, I may be wrong, but I believe you can read history just like you read events in a book. If are going to do something like this, you've got to believe that."

Added producer Murray Krugman, "'Telepath' was the one song on the album the tape operator was moved by. Originally, Eric set out to do a vocal, and the song begins with this big flourish of an introduction, and in the middle of it, Eric said, 'Hi, I'm Eric Bloom of the Blue Öyster Cult. Kids, don't take drugs,' and it was one of the five funniest moments in the history of the universe. So it's on the tape, and we're trying to decide whether or not to keep it. It's completely déclassé compared to how noble the song is."

Closing this vibrantly written—but perhaps weakly recorded—album is arguably the band's most revered single track, 'Astronomy'. Undeniably, the song is one of the band's epics. Indeed, Blue Öyster Cult rarely exploited the concept of the epic in full prog rock fashion, preferring to wade in at the short end, having a song approach epic proportions at the less indulgent end of the spectrum, stretching to six or seven minutes but little more, retaining the logic of song by limiting the numbers of parts or passages. 'Astronomy' certainly fits this bill, being a concise epic, but one with grand intentions.

Explains Joe, "That's another song where I got the lyrics from Sandy, and I felt pretty good about it. At that time, we moved our house again, out to Eaton's Neck (ed. a small cottage, rented for the writing of the album—Eaton's Neck is near Northport). We were like 50 yards from the beach. And it's corny, but it's actually true: I used to walk down the beach, and one time walking down the beach, I started thinking up that melody. So it came from one of those rehearsals there. My version was a little 'ballad,' and Albert's contribution was to put the rock in it. That was a pretty good collaboration. I was feeling stronger about being a songwriter at that time, and that turned out to be one of my most popular songs."

"So yeah, it is a classic and it just doesn't go away," continues Joe. "Again, how did that song happen? I went for a walk on the beach; it was a simple as that. We were rehearsing in this little house on the beach on the North Shore of Long Island. Sandy had given me the lyrics and I had been pushing some things around, like I moved the third line which was, "When the clock strikes 12." I was like, "No, that should be the first line." I had to work all of that stuff out and I went for a walk on the beach. When I came back I had the song. I quickly played it for the guys and the next day Albert said, 'We are going to do this on the arrangement for it.' There was not a lot of thought to it. It just happened. I am very, very happy that song has had such longevity. Albert came up with that classic riff. He is a great arranger."

"But basically, yeah, Sandy gave me those lyrics. The line, 'The clock strikes 12" was not the opening line of the poem; it was in the middle. I knew that line had to be the start of the song because it is such a magical hour. We had a house that was on the beach and I went out for a walk and as I was walking along the beach, I had this idea for a melody. The song came pretty fast. I brought it back and we were rehearsing in the living room of the house that we had rented. I told the guys that I had this song and I started playing it for them. Albert said, 'Let me work on that overnight.' The next day he came back with an arrangement. So a lot of the connecting riffs in 'Astronomy' are Albert's while I wrote the music and Sandy wrote the lyrics. It was a really good collaboration. We were really lucky when Metallica covered that song (ed. on 1998's *Garage Inc.*). It is every songwriter's dream to be on an album that sells five million. We didn't have to do anything. It was sitting out there for 20 years and then one of the biggest bands in the world comes along and covers it."

When I asked Albert about the extent of his lyrical contributions to the band, these two closing tracks came to mind... "I don't think I wrote very many lyrics at all, but the most lyrics I wrote on was 'Flaming Telepaths', where I wrote about half the chorus, and Sandy wrote almost all the verses. I think I might have contributed one line on a verse, and then Eric and Donald contributed a line apiece in the chorus. I'm proud of that song; I think it's a very good song. But I must say, I'm prouder of 'Astronomy', although I probably did less lyrically on that. Of course, I'd only written half the music because my brother had already started it and he got stumped and left it. I grabbed a hold of it and used what he had done and expanded it. Basically he did the slow part and I did the fast part plus the transition between the two. That's one of my favourite songs. It's very simple. There's not much to it. But I really dig it. I think it has a quality that's really enduring. The Cult fans really like it too."

Helen Wheels, long-time friend, poet and lyric writer for the band (now deceased; more on her later), figured 'Astronomy' was pretty much her favourite Cult composition. "Gee, I loved so much of their stuff, but 'Astronomy' was one of the ones I always felt jealous that I didn't write. I don't know why. It's not that I analysed the lyrics and thought they were great or anything. It's just that the song is a union of words and music, and it makes its own entity. And the way I judge a song is, 'Do I like to sing it real loud in my living room to the record?' And there was a lot of Blue Öyster Cult I liked to sing really loud in my living room to the record (laughs)."

Albert, on Eric becoming the vocalist on 'Astronomy' figures, "In the beginning I sang both 'Dominance and Submission' and 'Astronomy' live. I had planned to record them that way and when I got into the studio, I sang 'Dominance' first and that came out great, and then I tried 'Astronomy' about a hundred times and got worse and worse each time. Finally Sandy asked Eric to sing it and he did it perfectly in one take. After that I think Joe took a crack at singing the verses, which he wrote the music for, to get a warmer tone than Eric, but Eric still sang it the best. I believe the definitive version of 'Astronomy' is yet to be done. And I eventually stopped singing 'Dominance and Submission' live because it was hard for me to sing and play at the same time."

As it turned out, the band was none to happy with the final mixes of *Secret Treaties*. "As always, we tried to make the best album possible," says Albert. "We tried to write simpler, with more emotional impact, not trying to do the complicated egocentric songs we had been writing until then. Good songs, but the final mixes were, I dunno, stiff. It was a bit of a surprise because we were on the road while it was being done. So we learned our lesson. After fighting with Murray about it, we vowed to always be there when mixing happened, which was always the case while I was in the band. There was also a lot of tension at the time. In fact I was almost turfed a couple times because of my behaviour."

Joe speaks to his brother Albert's (ahem) erratic tendencies, which Albert admits were beginning to get him in trouble around this time. "Well, Albert was at the top of the volatile list, as most drummers are. But also, Albert's creative input was complete, you know? He had the most energy, the most creative ideas. Most of the arrangement ideas on the first ten albums were Albert's. He did most of the arranging. I was definitely the other side of the coin, yin and yang. I was the guy that kept everybody from punching out Albert (laughs). I was basically the calming influence. We'd have arguments, and I'd be the guy that would argue, 'Well it's gotta be this way or that way, but wait a minute!—there's probably a third way!' So we'd always look for a third answer to the question that was driving us nuts. That was my role in the band, but I'd wish I'd taken a harder stance and pushed it. But of course we didn't have 20 Top Ten hits either."

Albert embarked upon some additional reflection with respect to his place in Blue Öyster Cult history, some of it triggered by his reading of the first edition of the book you now hold in your hands...

"I remember reading the book and hearing all these things about after I wasn't there anymore, after I got kicked out, that made me feel like... strange. You know, that Joe was saying, 'Oh, it's like a breath of fresh air right now, now that Al isn't here.' And I'd never heard that before—until I read your book. Of course, it's a long time ago, and Joe and I... I was pretty mad at him at the time, but it's water under the bridge now. He's my brother and I love him, and there's nobody I would rather play with than him, in a band. But, it made me think about my role in Blue Öyster Cult, because I always saw myself as this style or taste 'policeman.' It was like, I did not want something to come out that wasn't a really top-quality thing, and I think that maybe... I think I have a very positive work ethic, in that I would never ever criticize what somebody was doing, and just say, 'Oh, that sucks,' or anything like that. It was always, 'Hey, maybe if you did this it would be better.' That was my approach. I think that—I'm trying to be subtle and diplomatic—it was the fact that they could just count on me to come up with something that 'helped' them, that maybe it was a little overbearing for some of them. Especially for people who were a little quieter. At the time, Joe was quieter, and I think that I might've stepped on his toes a bit. Allen too, you know?"

In the obscuring sands of time, *Secret Treaties* has held up well, the record somewhat considered a watershed for the boys, a well from which many a live set has been assembled. The record was well received at the time, Britain's *Melody Maker* Critics' Poll rating it "the best rock album of all time," although the band took the honour lightly and suspiciously at the time.

Melody Maker also posited the following, in an early days round-up of heavy metal bands circa the summer of 1974, calling Blue Öyster Cult, "*The challengers, but have they got the stamina to take the world title from Black Sabbath? We'll have to wait and see until they come to Britain, but with three fine albums under their belt, it's going to be a great fight. Like recent Black Sabbath, they made a subtle switch away from the dead simple riffs to more sophisticated ones. But then sophistication's the Cult's middle name; with a former rock writer as éminence grise and songwriting collaborator, they've come up with numbers like 'I'm on the Lamb but I Ain't no Sheep,' 'Cities on Flame with Rock 'n' Roll,' '7 Screaming Diz-Busters' and so on. They're almost barred from the simple, anyway, by virtue of their three guitar line-up (live, the other two in the band join in on guitars too, which must make one hell of a climax). But that basic dominant riff, without which there'd be no heavy metal, is there all the time. Book your tickets for the big fight now."*

As mentioned, fans appreciate the record's hard, heartless exterior, most deep BÖC ponderers now pretty much calling it the band's heaviest album, perhaps a peak within the band's least contrived, most purposeful era. The record's been a slow but steady seller over the years, finally going gold in the U.S. in 1994, 20 years after release.

Looking back after 40 years since the record's arrival on the scene, Albert agrees that, "A lot of people like *Secret Treaties* and say it's the best BÖC record. I actually kept a journal during the recording of that, you know, for the entire process, because it took several months. It started in the fall, when we were still on the road, and we would do some gigs, and we would come back to the house, work on the songs, then we would go to do some more gigs and come back. Somewhere around February or March or something, we started going into the studio and recording it. It's amazing how, even though it would say 'Dominance and Submission,' Eric Bloom, Albert Bouchard, Sandy Pearlman, everybody in the band helped arrange that song. That was the case for every song, and the only reason why we split it up. I mean, it really could have been five names on every song. There was no one song that was like a 'Reaper' or 'Divine Wind' where one person wrote everything. It just wasn't like that; it was really a lot of collaboration. It was just whoever had the main idea with the song, got their name on it."

So why does Albert think that record resonates with so many fans?

"I think it has the dark mood, but it also has the full gamut of what Blue Öyster Cult is, or was capable of. Kind of a dark thing, but then a humorous side, but a lot more dark than the other stuff. Personally, I find the sound a little thin on that record, and I wish it sounded fatter. But you know, I guess that's what makes it unique too."

Significantly, the 2001 reissue of the album contains a wealth of bonus tracks. A turgid, phase-shifted, gutted and reworked studio version of 'Born to Be Wild' (single version b-side) just barely edges out a shorter single version of 'Career of Evil' in treasure-ability. Higher up the scale, there is a punky boogie bonus original called 'Boorman the Chauffer', penned by Joe and Murray Krugman. 'Mes Dames Sarat' is an Allen Lanier number that moves briskly like 'The Red & The Black'," while '60s R&B rocker 'Mommy' offers music courtesy of Eric, lyrics from Meltzer.

"'Mommy' was just an attempt to be as misogynistic as I could possibly be," chuckles Meltzer. "It was just a totally stupid piece of misogyny. The fact that they didn't do it was, it's kind of like... they asked for excess! They wanted stuff that would appear to be savage or severe, but they decided they didn't want it. There is one I did that had anti-Christian lyrics, that I did very, very early on that had some literal anti-Jesus words that Albert was going to work up, but then he thought his mother wouldn't like it. He never even used it with Brain Surgeons. I think it was called 'JC,' or 'JC, Son of a Gun'."

"It started out as a song called 'The Limo Man'," recalls Joe, with respect to 'Boorman the Chauffer', credited to Murray Krugman and himself. "And it relates to a show that we did in Nashville, Tennessee. We were opening the show for Freddie King and Lynyrd Skynyrd. One of the first times I'd never seen Lynyrd Skynyrd on stage, and it was a wild show! I guess we played and then Freddie King came out and stirred up the crowd, and of course when the Skynyrd boys— the original Skynyrd band—hit the stage, the place went nuts! So we were just leaving the show. It was an outdoor show, and we were leaving in a limousine, and it was the most bizarre day of my life (laughs). So that's why it says, 'The limo driver kept on driving' (laughs). Most of the lyrics are complete nonsense and they were never finished. Then we had cut a track that wasn't great, but it was okay. Murray said, 'Why don't we make the chauffeur, you know, a Germanic figure?' Oh, that makes a lot of sense! It completely destroyed the idea of my song (laughs)."

In closing, Buck comments on these bonus tracks, beginning with a very positive appraisal of *Secret Treaties* as a whole. "Probably the quintessential BÖC record as far as what BÖC was in its formative period. I see the first three studio albums as sort of a piece, chapters of a book, and that's the last chapter. After that we did *On Your Feet or on Your Knees*, then *Agents of Fortune* where the band shifted gears, became more popular, had some success. My voice emerged as the radio voice of the band, so a lot of things happened. But if you want to know what Blue Öyster Cult began as, *Secret Treaties* is probably the place to go. In terms of the bonus tracks, 'Boorman the Chauffer' was kind of funny, and I hope the humour comes through on it. You can see that we were trying to craft our image a little bit and you can see why we might have left that one off. 'Mommy', that was a Richard Meltzer lyric and we thought it just sounded too mean-spirited so we elected not to put it on. But for the completist, why not? 'Mes Dames Sarat,' now there's an Allen song that is actually pretty good. I don't know why that didn't make it. It was just one of those things that, especially in those days, you could only get a certain amount of minutes on a vinyl record. So you had to cut somewhere. 'Sarat' probably should have made the record."

On Your Feet or on Your Knees

"People still talk about the church there"

So it was deemed time to trot out a live record. Perhaps this was a little early in the band's career, but this was also the '70s, and this was also the Blue Öyster Cult, a better than average live band, and one with a catalogue that really sucked for sound so to date.

The band had become a well-oiled machine, touring 1974 hard, including lots of dates with Kiss, Nazareth, Manfred Mann's Earth Band and T. Rex, but also one-off bills, like 1973, with over 100 different bands. California got a little more attention and there was a small Western Canada campaign, but once more, the band attacked repeatedly that time honoured bread-and butter-territory for hard rock known loosely as the Midwest—BÖC also paying greater than average attention to the Deep South. Most of the recordings used for *On Your Feet or on Your Knees* would hail from T-Rex dates in October, meaning that the *Secret Treaties* songs would have been worked in nicely.

The biggest leap forward was this record's stunning cover image, featuring a foreboding limo with funereal Cult symbol flag parked in front of an even more foreboding church. "Yeah, Sandy had found this church on Long Island, you know, equating the idea of a cult with a church," explains Al. "He had a few other covers that we rejected. One was a picture of somebody bowling in a bowling alley except the bowling ball was somebody's head. We decided that's not for us!"

"That was pretty much done by the Columbia art department," recalls brother Joe. "They just did a great job. The only thing that we did was pose for the centrefold. Sandy Pearlman had a lot to do with that. We knew it was really bizarre. We're all standing up there like rock stars, in front of that wall of amplifiers. That was classic (laughs). I love the cover. People still talk about the church there. It's down in... not very far from me, but I've never been by. But I know exactly where it is. I've talked to fans and they say, 'That church! Wow!' It's certainly one of my favourite covers, and it certainly has this sort of church of occult reference to it. I think it's a pretty outrageous-looking cover, to have our limousine in front of this church. Even the promotion for that album was going to be more radical. There was a very controversial ad. You may have seen it—the preacher at a pulpit in bondage gear; it was pretty radical."

The steely silver rendering of the band's name would also make an impression, showing up on many rock t-shirts throughout the '70s. The original vinyl included a gatefold featuring a cut-and-paste rendition of the band's five guitar assault, a back cover with album credits listed in a Bible-like book (this image also graced the label centres), and two inner sleeves full of psychedelic, time-lapse live shots. The album's CD reissue fits the entire double set (12 tracks, three per side, three from each LP thus far, plus three extras!) on one tidy, 76 minute disc, with much of the artwork retained, albeit economized.

Eric looks particularly resplendent on his gatefold shot, establishing the persona of the mirror-shaded front man so integral to the band's live persona. Eric: "Where did that come from? I'd say it goes back to I guess my wannabe beatnik era, which is pre-hippie. I mean, you have to be from a certain age group to understand what I'm talking about. But when I was in junior high or even high school, I used to go into the city. I'm from Long Island and Queens, and I used to take the bus and the subway into Manhattan, and put on shades and hang around the village and try to be cool. So I would say I've been doing that since I was about 14, much the way kids today would go to the mall and hang."

The music enclosed played to the band's obvious strengths, containing a barely controlled mayhem, offering many improvements and frills over original studio tracks, also offering a few fairly uninspired covers and an unveiling of 'Buck's Boogie', the liner note indicating: 'Dedicated to Ron McCoy', an L.A. disc jockey who let Buck guest-DJ his show one day.

The record's production is... interesting, perhaps quite good for the time, quite enigmatically mixed, but not altogether lusty with bass or treble. "We had a horrible time recording it," explains Bloom. "It left a bitter taste in our mouths. The sound system we had was no good, and the monitors were not great, far from it. Trying to make a record when you can't hear yourself is an arduous task. We were not happy with the sounds, and it could have been done better. But from the perspective of other people listening to it, it's obviously gotten a lot of critical acclaim, from fans and the like. People were saying that's what they liked about it, that it sounds raw, it sounds live. So looking back, I guess it was fine."

"Yeah, I like that," agrees Joe. "I like the fact that Jack Douglas worked on it. You know, Jack did all that great work for Aerosmith at the time, so I felt like we had a real pro in the driver's seat there. The album is kind of crude in spots, because we didn't fix up anything. That's all really live. There's no overdubs or 'fake live.' But it caught the energy of the time. That's my favourite live one, I think. But we were just young, and didn't have our hands on the technology like they do today. We were playing way loud (laughs), and that record, to me, was saved by Jack Douglas. Jack Douglas mixed it, and his touch on the mixer is an incredible one. He pulled a lot of things out that made that record sound pretty good."

Albert: "That was the one bad thing about *On Your Feet*, was that the PA company we had was horrible. And our monitors were horrible. There was so much feedback. So that was the problem, although the mixes were excellent. We had Jack Douglas, who was a very good producer and engineer. He mixed that for us, as a favour to Sandy. He did an excellent job."

I asked Murray Krugman, of all the albums, with which was he the least pleased... "Well, I didn't like *On Your Feet or on Your Knees* particularly much, because I don't like double albums. I talked Johnny Winter out of a two record set. I just didn't feel the band warranted it. You know, I did the bootleg record myself, the legal bootleg with four cuts (referring to the rare promo boot from '72), I don't know if you've ever heard that. You should try and get a hold of it. It's really a great record. It's only four songs, mastered at ludicrously hot levels. But you know, a two record set, at the time... what was that, 80 minutes of music? I don't think there's 80 minutes of Blue Öyster Cult music that's arresting, cherry-picking the whole catalogue. It's like that Humphrey Bogart story, *The Harder They Fall*, where the guy playing Primo Carnera goes, 'Well what about all these headlines?' Humphrey Bogart goes, 'I wrote those headlines.' When you start to believe your own press releases, there you go."

Murray continues, questioning the direction the band was pursuing, providing a glimpse into his impression of things as the years progressed. "I just don't think they... Sandy kept pushing them out on the road, and I guess my attitude was they need time off to write songs."

Albert, conversely, when asked which is his favourite of the three live records, speaks fondly of *On Your Feet*. "Well, I think the original is still the greatest. As a matter of fact, depending on my mood, I usually say it's my favourite Blue Öyster Cult record. It's the one with the least disappointments. I mean, at the time I remember doing an interview for *Punk* magazine with John Holmstrom, and going on about how all these gigs they recorded were just all screwed up, and the monitor people were idiots. But actually in retrospect it stood up very well. I like the sound of it."

"It had very little fixing," he continues. "I will say though (laughs) that we did take... I mean, we really had a great audience track, but because Murray had produced Johnny Winter's live album, he just couldn't resist slipping some of that audience into our audience, so that's the main thing that was fixed up. On *Some Enchanted Evening* I don't think there were any overdubs whatsoever. And I have no idea about *ETL*. Even the two tracks I'm on, I didn't even know about until it was done."

In terms of interesting curios, *On Your Feet* offered an acceptable amount for the times. One was the aforementioned 'Buck's Boogie', a blistering instrumental track that finds Buck blazing a silky smooth pathway, soloing, texturising and tenderizing like the closet jazz guitarist that he is. Allen also figures prominently, soloing Hammond-style not unlike Jon Lord. 'Buck's Boogie' was also included on the four track *Bootleg EP* (see Murray's previous comment), but few ever heard it at the time. It also saw release on the *Guitars that Destroyed the World* compilation from '73: This version eventually showing up on '95's two-CD compilation *Workshop of the Telescopes*. Credit for the track originally included Eric and Sandy along with Buck. Eric's contributions are unknown, and apparently Sandy's credit is based merely on his naming the track, although the original title was 'Boogie For Buck'. Albert may also deserve some credit for the tune, which bears resemblance to unreleased Stalk-Forrest Group track 'Arthur Comics'. Credit indeed arrived with the release of *Workshop of the Telescopes*. Further on the title, Buck has commented that it merely salutes guitar legend Jeff Beck and his track, 'Beck's Boogie'.

The record closes with a couple of covers, the first being a nine-minute rendition of Yardbirds classic 'I Ain't Got You', somewhat frenzied, jammed-out, not to mention pre-ambled with a touch of 'L.A. Woman'. Oddly enough, northern label rivals Aerosmith also included this song in their live sets at the time, recording a '73 take for their '78 *Live Bootleg* double spread. Here the tune is remonikered as 'Maserati GT (I Ain't Got You) ', in deference to Pearlman's favourite car fantasy of the day.

Last track was the also lengthy 'Born to be Wild', originally recorded by Steppenwolf. Even though it is the last track on the album, the tune is prefaced with a hilariously cheesy band introduction, including barking like a dog, and the famous incantation, "On your feet or on your knees for the Blue Öyster Cult!" This intro line also occurs at the beginning of track two 'Harvester of Eyes', while the actual start of the record merely offers an ominous, almost muttered 'The Subhuman', before lounging into the subdued, reptilian, and mellow track, oddly placed, given that this is a double live record by a supposed heavy metal act.

The live set was essentially toured like a studio album, in that it was issued at the start of the year with the band hitting the road for the balance. Preambling the album's February release, BÖC played a half dozen Eastern dates with The Faces, quickly transitioning west where they played multiple shows with REO Speedwagon and Man, and then into the south with Strawbs, Trapeze and Bloodrock. Summer featured multiple dates with ZZ Top, Journey and Uriah Heep, while the fall had them playing mostly with Uriah Heep. Most significantly, the band made it to Europe for the first time, spending October and November hitting a number of countries, including a concluding leg in the UK supported by Birth Control.

All told, *On Your Feet or on Your Knees*—as well as the European campaign—seemed to signal an arrival of sorts, this previously black and white, no photos mystery of a band finally opening the doors, boldly announcing that the concept of launching a double live record so early into one's career does not intimidate in the least. And as with most double live records from the '70s, *On Your Feet* also signalled closure, with Blue Öyster Cult indeed getting ready to make bold creative advancements one short year hence.

Agents of Fortune

"It's not impossible to have a hit with death"

L ike so many bands in the '70s, Blue Öyster Cult, whether through foresight
or hindsight, punctuated their eras with live records. *On Your Feet or on
Your Knees* was effectively utilized to close one chapter—the black and
white era, as Donald and many others call it—and open another. Towards that
end, the band was looking to make big changes, reversing the cold and grim
metal lite of their previous three studio albums with stronger, braver songwriting
that would stylistically go where no Cult had gone before. Producer Murray
Krugman opines that, "The live record was the culmination of the first stage, and
Agents of Fortune definitely marked a second stage. The live record was a good
one, even though I don't think double records really work. You just cannot sustain
enough interest over four sides. It always ends up as a situation where you wish
you could edit out and keep the best single record's worth of material."

Years later, Murray places events in context. "The group wanted more, or was
more interested in the high fidelity nature of the records, and was craving
commercial success, and (sighs), there was a lot of money pressure from the
seven individuals—Sandy and I and the five of them—who were all making a
living from it, to achieve that commercial success. You know, I was never blind
to the weaknesses of the group. When I first encountered them, I felt that Donald
had all the talent in the world. You know, having worked with him over the years,
I felt that Albert was really the core of the group, and was the one person with
that really special gestalt if you will. But there were a lot of people in that group
who talent-wise didn't pull their weight. So going onto commercial success there's
a lot of norms that have to be conceded to. I felt that from the word go, that if
they did everything right, which they pretty much did, and had a lot of luck,
which they certainly did, they would make it. Which in the short term they did.
So I wasn't disappointed. You know, Eric Bloom is not Robert Plant. Albert won't
be confused with John Bonham a hundred years from now as a rock drummer,
presuming anyone's heard of John Bonham in a hundred years. But yes, for the
most part it worked."

Murray continues, expressing a palpable dissatisfaction with the band's
growth or lack thereof. "Well, when I first signed them, they were really an
underground sort of a critic's band. We made each record and each record sold
100,000 more than the last record. So between the group and the record label,

there were increasing levels of commercial demands put on the project. I never liked that sort of thing. I sort of like art to evolve out of what it wants to be, rather than what radio wants it to be. But you know, we started to work at the Record Plant, with Record Plant engineers, who get a much more colourful sound than the CBS studios that we had done the first three records at. It was what the band wanted, and I didn't want to stand in the way. It was kind of a nice change, working in a more hi-tech studio. So that was sort of interesting. Although I felt that each time it came time to do a record, and we'd sit down and hear the songs, it would be more of a stretch turning to each other and going, 'Yeah, there's a record's worth of songs here.' I always found my standards higher than Sandy's. For me, it fell off after the first record. I mean, 'The Reaper''s obviously a great song, and there are scattered good songs here and there. But I've always been into whole albums. As a whole album, the first one's always been special to me."

Probably the main difference in the construction of the record was the fact that the band were given four-track recording machines to create their own personal visions at home, to bring them along and coddle them into songs before those sometimes tense meetings where the band would critique, disassemble and reassemble material individually furnished. Buck said at the time, "We've all got tape machines now where we can do our own demos. We can present a whole arrangement of a song to the group, rather than trying to convince the group that if you play it this way, it will be good. You can try things and it becomes obvious what works and what doesn't. As far as the future goes, I think we'll always work this way. You really get a lot of very different sounding tunes this way."

Setting the scene, Albert says that at this point, the band "were headlining and playing national tours and doing a lot of gigs. We played 200, 250 gigs a year, each year. And that was for the four or five years before that. We just gigged constantly. We would play like a medium-sized club and would be able to headline down south. We'd do those Agora clubs; there was a whole chain of them—we headlined those. There was a lot of 500-600 seaters that we could fill. We'd already gone a couple times around the country supporting the James Gang and Jo Jo Gunne and Alice Cooper and Edgar Winter and all these people. We opened the show for Stevie Wonder and Billy Preston, all of these acts you wouldn't think, Rare Earth, Ike and Tina Turner, all these weird bills, you know?"

"I would have to say that the Midwest is where we really got established. That's where we started headlining, in the Midwest—Ohio, Indiana, Pennsylvania. The coasts and those places are trendier. Like I mean, we were headlining Chicago, but not the coasts. As a matter of fact, we didn't really go to the west coast until we had a hit, and then all of a sudden we were huge out there. But before that we couldn't even get a gig. It wasn't worth it for us to go out there and play.

"You're going to think this is really crazy," laughs Albert, "but the band collectively just hated how *Secret Treaties* came out. Not the songs. We were very happy with the material and we were happy with the arrangements and we felt like we had done a great job recording that record, but then what happened was we went out on the road right after we got the record done. We were touring... I think we were playing the Agora, in Michigan and Ohio. We were playing all around the Midwest, and Murray and Sandy mixed the record while we were away, and when we heard the mixes, we just thought it sounded like somebody had thrown a blanket over the sound. That's what it sounded like to us. It sounded really lifeless and dead compared to what we heard in the studio."

"So at that point we decided we were going to get much more involved in the sound of the records. Sandy had been working with this engineer Tim Geelan, and we just felt Tim just didn't have what it took. That was around the time when Aerosmith was coming out. We heard Jack Douglas and Aerosmith's sound, and we said, well, we have to get Jack Douglas to mix the next record, which was *On Your Feet or on Your Knees.* I don't know if you can tell, but the sound actually changed at that point. The material changed for *Agents*, and the reason why the songs changed was because the band had got these four-track tape recorders and we started doing much more preliminary work."

"Before that, I don't know if any of the guys ever even did any demos of the songs. I was the only one that ever did demos of songs to present to people, and what I would do would just be live. I'd be singing my song to the mic and playing the guitar, and that would be it, you know? I'd try and show them what to do and they'd do their own thing and we'd come up with a record. But that one, you know, Donald came in with 'Reaper' fully arranged. When he came up with 'The Reaper,' he had the whole middle section. I mean basically we just played what was on his demo. He didn't have a real drum kit, he was just banging on a box or something and slapping his knee. But what we ended up playing was basically what he did on his original demo. There was no bass, so Joe was the only guy to do anything different, really. But I know that I played the drums exactly how Donald had it."

"As a matter of fact, some folks who now of course deny it vehemently, but a certain lead singer, shall we say, was adamant that we not put 'Reaper' on the record because he felt it was too soft. So anyway, yeah, he'll deny it now, but I remember. He was like, 'If this goes on, I'm quitting the band.' We said, 'Well, don't be a stranger, because it's going on' (laughs)."

Joe confirms the positive creative situation all around. "One good thing was that we had put out the live record, so we actually had two years to write the material. It was well worth it. It allowed us to really find some new stuff. Donald turned a corner with his writing. But we had all bought tape machines, four-track and eight-track tape machines for home use, which made it easier to present your songs to the band, because they're the toughest critics. They're the worst. You've got to convince them that this song actually has a life (laughs). So when we got tape machines it was like, cool, there was a little less sweat, a little less cold sweat on that first meeting. You could actually play them a bit of a fleshed-out song on a tape recorder rather than sit there with an acoustic guitar, or just sort of trying to describe what's in your mind."

Allen Lanier, doing the press rounds post-release explained that, "We'd always been pushing in one direction since we started, and I hope this record gives our albums a bit more validity. On our earlier records, we went through a lot of conceptualizing. Look, we were trying to make it in a tough business and we took as obvious and as brash an approach as we could. It's cool, we dig all those records, we've got some tremendous and loyal fans, and we have no qualms about what we've done before. But we reached a point where we had a great backlog of material—some 30 songs over the past few years—and we demanded the freedom to be able to pick out what we wanted and record it just as we wanted. Everyone had songs, so we all said to each other, 'Hey, go to town and check it out; do what you want to do and we'll all stand together by it.'"

"One thing the band really wanted to do was make a real studio record," continued Lanier. "Our other records were mainly performance records. We didn't do all that much overdubbing and we were always concerned with transferring the songs to the stage act so everything was as powerful and live-sounding as possible. This time we really wanted to make a record that you could really listen to."

"It was two years between *Secret Treaties* and *Agents*," explained Allen, in a second UK chat, this time with Ian Birch from *Melody Maker*, shortly after the release of *Spectres*. "So in some ways our songwriting styles has changed somewhat, our playing styles have progressed and certainly our studio technique was much improved. The biggest ones were called time and money. The time we took on *Agents* was much more than we'd ever taken on a studio album before. Normally we'd come off the road for about a month, do an album in Colombia's studio, then go back on the road while someone mixed it. But we didn't see it as a radical shift. I've said this again and again. We have always, when it's time to do an album, simply looked at each other and said, 'What have you got?' We see what we have, and see what lyrics Sandy has, and throw the lot together. It was no different."

Continues Allen, still looking at the shift from the "black and white" albums to *Agents*, "It was more commercial and presumably more accessible maybe, because we were a bit tired of dealing with some of the past subjects in our songwriting. I think we had stated our case—*Tyranny and Mutation* and *Secret Treaties* were put together in terms of the metaphor of politics and rock 'n' roll, the image of illusion and delusion and that's a subject you can't dwell on. We were writing too much about rock 'n' roll rather than simply rock 'n' roll as just another part of the normal experience of living. That realization has partly motivated the way we have written since. The more you work on the process of being a songwriter, the more you want to write the type of songs that most people will relate to. Good songs deal with common phenomena; writing a song doesn't make much sense unless there's you and an audience. So it's a natural temptation to move in that direction."

"The early image was just too restrictive, too overwhelming after a while," figures Allen. "It was a joke. We've always been susceptible to images, but then I've always seen the band as people in a group. It took us a long time to become what I consider good songwriters, to know what the hell we were doing. I think we were hiding behind that early image to a large degree, hiding the fact that we were limited in communicating ourselves. We are perfectionists. Maybe there were other ideas, but we just couldn't seem to put them together, so we banded together more. Now I think the band has broken up into individuals, but it took a lot of effort, and years on the road. Our early image got us a lot of press, but it was mainly a gimmick. Think of how absurdly related the idea of a Hitler and a Mick Jagger are in the sense of power, control, and decadence, and knowing it only through the media."

"This album was the most fun for us," said Albert at the time. "Even though our past albums have had a lot of humour, we found this one much more effective because there are a lot of very serious, very sad songs. So the tongue-in-cheek things bounce off the other songs." Eric chirps in, "The record's like Abe Lincoln, man. Before we were pleasing some of the people most of the time. Now we can please all of the people all of the time."

"We told Sandy that we had no more interest in this leather foolishness," said Eric, looking back a few years later. "We enjoyed it up to a point, but then we started seeing ads for us with, like, S&M leather and zippers over the mouths preaching on pulpits and stuff, and we said, 'What the fuck?' So we started taking more of a hand in lyric-writing and image-or non-image-making."

Another very cool album cover this time around, and the first actual colour one, save for the live record the previous year. But the somber colours used matched the sinister music inside, with the cover featuring a depiction of a tuxedoed man holding a set of four tarot cards surrounded in a dreamy sea of blue and grey. "With *Agents of Fortune*, the band had checked out a lot of different art, and we voted on this guy John Berg to do it," says Albert. "We came up with the concept and he did it, so that was a real band idea. Basically the title, *Agents of Fortune* was Murray Krugman's idea, and that's because he used to play cards with this guy who used to call the cards 'agents of fortune.' So we wanted to capture the idea of gambling, of taking a chance, and that the idea of chance was the agent of fortune. So that's the significance, to lend some conceptual weight to the title." It is also reported that the cards derive from an actual Tarot reading on the band, these in particular representing the King, Queen, Sun and Death.

"That was kind of fun," adds Joe. "We got Lynn Curlee (note: to clarify, John Berg and Andy Engel are credited with album design, Lynn Curlee, with cover painting, with special thanks to Peter Robbins). Great artist; we went to his loft in New York City for the unveiling of the cover, and it was stunning. First of all, it's about 8' x 8', quite large, and he had lit it so that the moon would just glow. I mean, just walking in the room it took your breath away. Wow! This is amazing. That was great. Unfortunately the original art has disappeared; we don't know where it is. Yeah, somebody's got it. But the original art, the purple in the tuxedo just had a glow to it, and that sort of reflected off the moon; it was unbelievable. An awesome cover."

"I saw it before it was done," remarks Albert. "I saw it when he was working on it, because Peter Robbins was Helen's brother. So he would say, 'Oh, why don't you come over to and take a look and see what you think?' Sandy Pearlman was consulted as well. So yeah, I thought it was a good idea and a pretty good painting. It was also... Gawlik disappeared, so we didn't have Gawlik to do another Gawlik. Sandy didn't want to do it anyway; he said, 'Oh I can't work with him anymore. He's crazy.' But we would've been happy to have had another Gawlik."

"We do everything and just deliver the package to CBS, who shrink-wrap it," said Allen, with respect to being very hands-on in the cover art department. "We've always aimed to make each album a coordinated thing. With *Agents*, we realised in the studio that we had an album that had more sales potential than any previous one. So we wanted to put a title on it that had a reference on it to the idea of taking a risk and coming through. We found this artist, Lynn Curlee, who was like a super-realist painter. He had a fixation with dirigibles and zeppelins, but we couldn't use them because of the obvious reference to Led Zeppelin. So we commissioned him to do it with the tarot cards in reference to the fortune idea. We had someone cast a reading on the cards for us and it was an incredible reading for overcoming obstacles and having great success!"

Concerning the gatefold image, Allen says that he had "worked out that design. I guess we've never completely gone away from the alchemical/mystical, scientific/technological connections. It's a NASA space probe, a shot of the Earth taken from the moon. That was like a nostalgic deference to all the sensibilities that we had."

The music inside definitely took the cover's overt theme of chance to heart, Blue Öyster Cult trying a half dozen completely new things, in construction of what would become their most commercially successful record ever.

Agents of Fortune lurched into view with a sinister little metal riff, 'This Ain't the Summer of Love' exploding into one of the band's smartest anthems, an inversion of good that definitely connected with mentors Black Sabbath and that band's original premise of being the antithesis of the hippie generation. Albert traces the strange origins of the tune's memorable chorus lyric. "Basically, I gotta be honest, I really didn't have much to do with that song. I wrote the melody. A guy named Don Waller wrote some of the lyrics. He had actually just sent the lyrics to Murray Krugman and Murray said, 'Well, this sucks, but it's a great idea.' He had the first line about the garden of Eden. I don't think he even had the part about no angels above. Murray said this is a great idea and he came to me and said we should use this, and we should use the chord progression of this song by this Irish group that nobody had ever heard of. It was this Irish Republic Army group and they were very radical. You know, in the beginning days of punk, and it had some line like 'You be pulling your grenade pin, I'll be pulling mine' and it was a real tough kind of thing. I took that and filled out the chords to make it a whole song. Murray really wrote all the lyrics, and I mean, he had a lot to do with that song. But it wasn't his riff, and it wasn't mine either. Legally you can take a riff from somebody as long as when it goes to the chord change, you don't go to the same chord change."

Next on plate was a typically New York-ish solo effort from Allen called 'True Confessions', which combined R&B and pop with Allen's slightly unsettling, slightly squalid demeanor. It was definitely a shock to fans of the band, containing by far the most pleasant sounds BÖC had ever attempted, even including a sunny sax solo from the one and only Randy Brecker (Brecker's brother Michael had recorded a flugelhorn part for '(Don't Fear) The Reaper' which was omitted from the final mix). It is of note that this is Allen Lanier's only lead vocal of the entire BÖC catalogue, Allen once remarking on his terrible pitch and the months it took him to get his singing acceptable. But all in all, Allen was pleased. "It was really gratifying to me that the track came out like it did. It was the first time we went in and were able to pump out a wham-bam, good ol' drums-and-piano rock 'n' roll basics song."

"Pretty straight-ahead the way it was recorded," seconds Joe. "It was meant to be old rock 'n' roll, so we played old rock 'n' roll, and it's kind of cute in its own way."

The record's third track, ' (Don't Fear) The Reaper' would keep them talking for years, turning waves of newcomers onto the band, setting the guys up for a lifetime of residual cheques as the song established itself as a radio classic, probably for eternity everlasting.

'(Don't Fear) The Reaper' would indeed find Donald "turning a corner." Al had this to say about Mr. Buck Dharma. "Donald, I would have to say is not very generous as a person but he can surprise you sometimes. But he's incredibly talented. Anything he does seems to be without any effort whatsoever, and he can be very funny. He's very witty, he has a great sense of humour and that's it. He's a pretty interesting person, I would have to say, and yes, '(Don't Fear) The Reaper' was a pretty interesting piece of work. It was a folk song, the most un-BÖC-like thing we had ever done. It felt profound and touched something. We each spend most of our lives trying not to fear the end, and 'Reaper' addressed that fear. But yes, 'Reaper' marked a better sense of, 'Yeah, okay, we really are doing this. We are professionals'."

Extrapolating this concept of fear, Albert relates the following. "There was this book I lost some years ago that best describes our fans' fascination with us. Best translated, it means 'pleasure from fear.' If you know that you can return to a normal world, there's a pleasure that comes from playing with darkness. It's part escapism, part survival from confrontation. To stare at evil somehow makes it safer."

Joe echoes Albert's opinion of the song. "Well, okay, even though it's the most popular song, I love 'The Reaper.' It is a tremendous collage. It's too artsy to be a big hit. But it's a song that still mystifies me. 'Reaper' is a pretty good track period. With incredible 'legs' as they say in the biz. I knew it was a hit song when I first heard it, but in my wildest dreams I can't believe what it's become. The song is a legend in the music world. Quite quirky, it is a little off-base to be a big song per se, but many people can't stop playing it. Then there is the rest of the BÖC catalogue. Many gems, many experiments for the hardcore fans, a few misses, but I'm pretty proud of it all. At this perspective it's an amazing achievement just the bulk of it."

On the most superficial level, the song was extremely "Byrds-like" in that it was carried with an incredibly memorable and breezy pop riff that sounded like an amalgam of Roger McGuinn signatures. Besides a majestic, almost apocalyptic passage that elevates the tension of the tune, the whole thing just floats with a sort of rarified and icy, macabre forward mass.

"I knew from Donald's demo—which you can hear on the remasters—that it was going to be a big hit," reiterates Joe. "I called up our accountant and told him, 'Bet the farm on this one. It's going to be a big hit!' It is hard for a band as different as Blue Öyster Cult to actually have a single. A lot of bands like Black Sabbath never had a single or not a single as big as 'The Reaper.' It had the magic. When we cut that and I heard the mix for the first time I thought it was great. It took off and made us headliners. It filled a lot of stadiums and arenas all over the world."

"Allen did an incredible clavinet part on 'The Reaper,'" continues Joe, adding some cool trivia to the tale. "Eric Bloom plays the Hammond organ on 'The

Reaper.' It was all five of us in the studio. Allen was playing the clavinet, Eric was on the Hammond organ, I was on the bass, Albert on the drums of course, Donald on the guitar. So a couple weeks later we had a really nice version of '(Don't Fear) The Reaper,' which is still here, all the time. But it is all five of us playing live in the studio."

"It's a strange kind of hit, and it has that death vibe about it," reflects Joe. "Not too many songs can get away with that. I mean a few. We go back to some of the songs from the 1950s, the car crash songs and stuff like that, so it's not impossible to have a hit with death, but it was really difficult. Donald put together an incredible demo at home, and when he brought it in, like I say, certainly in my mind it was a smash. It just pulled the right strings at the right time. My biggest worry was that we wouldn't record it properly, so David Lucas came in and helped us with the harmony singing. I just ran into a guy who was a friend of Shelly Yakus, and I was saying we probably wouldn't have had a career if it wasn't for Shelly Yakus. Shelly did the mix on 'Reaper,' and it's a really classic and classy mix."

And was the band being pressured to come up with a hit?

"Only internally," dismisses Joe. "I think we could have probably made a few more records that were more like our early records, but we had a little time off because we had the extra advantage of putting out the live record. That gave us almost two years between *Secret Treaties* and *Agents of Fortune*, so we had time to think about making better songs. I think we wanted a little bit more of a refined sound. We could afford it, for one thing. Before that we had gone in and made records in a month—in and out, the whole thing. Maybe less than a month. In a couple of weeks we did *Secret Treaties*. There was more time spent on *Agents of Fortune*."

"Plus Buck is definitely a pop kind of guy, pop sensibility—Beatles. Actually Albert and I, we'd been listening to The Byrds a lot. And a lot of Blue Öyster Cult is based around those... not so much the early Byrds but the sort of middle period Byrds, which was, you know, *Notorious Byrd Brothers*. There were a lot of strange things on those Byrds records, so we definitely emulated that. I think the overall kind of thing was that you got a bunch of singers that don't mind singing harmonies, a lot of sort of eccentric parts. Donald was a virtuoso on the guitar, so we definitely wanted to feature that. But those records were played constantly in our band house: *Sweetheart of the Rodeo*, *Notorious Byrd Brothers*, *Younger than Yesterday*. Those records are real band records, you know? Of course they changed personnel in the middle of all that, but still managed to retain their sort of Byrds-isms. So you know, we, of any group, if we could get a little bit of Sabbath in there and a little bit of Byrds, you'd have a pretty strong combination."

Sandy in his days as pioneer rock writer, posited that The Byrds were really the originators of heavy metal. "Yeah, well there's a present-day interview I did with Roger McGuinn a few years ago for *Mondo 2000*, and so he got to understand what I was thinking. He didn't appreciate it, and was rather appalled, being a born-again Christian, that I had felt that Byrds had actually been quite responsible for the genesis of heavy metal. That artificial energy was one of the sources, self-consciously or not one of the sources of heavy metal. He then told Columbia Records that they couldn't use my liner notes that I had written for him because he didn't want to be associated with that kind of stuff! So Donald was actually reading my stuff. He had actually written a couple of articles for *Crawdaddy* and was reading all this stuff. What was there to read? It was 1970-'71. There were two things to read and I'm sure all these theories had some sort of impact, and I'm sure they were behind a lot of the production directions, the arrangement directions, whatever, songwriting directions that we took. For the most part, from the first record through *Some Enchanted Evening*, I really had the most influence on the way most things worked out. My theories would be heavily influential. So yeah, whether he was adhering to the theory of the Byrds as vortex for heavy metal or not, he was aware of it, and so it probably has had some impact."

Looking back further, toward Bob Dylan and his possible influence on the band, Joe says, "I remember those days. It kick-started the Byrds, and it affected the Beatles, and if you're going to affect the Beatles, that's a pretty big influence that you have. For some reason I think when we were making all those Blue Öyster Cult records, the idea of being Dylan-esque never occurred to us. I don't think those were his strongest days, his early recordings. He was kind of a recluse. I mean he does a lot more now than back then. His reputation was a little more quaint than it is now. Now it's sort of God-like. So it didn't really affect us. I mean we had determined that we were… we were more influenced by someone like Paul Butterfield Blues Band than Bob Dylan, you know? Or The Band. I admit, the way The Band made records, that was discussed. Patti Smith had worked at The Band's studio in Woodstock, and so Allen would say, 'Well here's what Patti said about working with The Band.' But never much Bob Dylan. We wouldn't try to do a typical Bob Dylan lyric on any of our stuff. I mean we covered the Jimi Hendrix version of 'All Along the Watchtower' but that's about as close as we ever came to doing anything Dylan-esque."

Albert, when asked if ' (Don't Fear) The Reaper' happens because of Buck's love of pop, he says, "Oh, no. I mean, I think he had no idea why it happened. It's just one of those things. He got a really good riff, he couldn't get enough of it, he kept playing it over and over, and if you analyse the really huge hits, they tend to be extremely simple. Slight variation that goes slightly away from the norm but then it just makes it better when you come back. I don't think the Byrds influence was a conscious thing. That was one of the groups we toured with originally and that was basically because Sandy wanted us on this bill, and they were our label-mates on Columbia. That was actually our first big tour, and that was definitely a schooling. But even before that we played a lot of Byrds. We played Byrds all the time. That was the staple of our set when we would play the clubs and when we were basically a cover band."

Similarly playing down any Bob Dylan influence, Albert concedes that, "Joe and I actually had a group with some of our friends and our relatives. I don't remember what we were called but we played folk rock. We just played guitars and we sang folk songs, and we sang Bob Dylan songs, and then when he went electric we played Bob Dylan on electric. We were really into it. It was an exciting moment. But I don't think Bob Dylan is very heavy. I lumped him right in with the Beach Boys and the Beatles, you know? It was just good music."

"I remember after 'Reaper' was a hit," continues Albert, "we played a headlining show with Boston as our opening act, and the press, whoever was writing, they said, 'Yeah, they've got a hit with ' (Don't Fear) The Reaper' but you know, they're really a one-shot. I don't think they'll ever have another one and I don't know why they're headlining over Boston. Boston is going to have millions of hits.' So it was like, 'Oh, well, fuck you.' Then I was like, uh, but we *do* only have one hit. Maybe we better get some more hits (laughs). That was probably one of the deciding things to where we tried to have hits, which was probably not our best career move. Or one time we played in Buffalo and it was hysterical. The guy said Blue Öyster Cult was great but they didn't play a lot of their old hits like 'Cities on Flame.' It was the only show that we didn't play 'Cities on Flame.'"

"The band thought they could get bigger and better by writing and recording more pop-ish kinds of songs," notes Pearlman. "Again I don't mean that bad, but more radio-oriented songs. You know, 'The Reaper' was both an incredible opportunity and a snare and a delusion. It showed them they could have a really big hit, but they had a really big hit with a metaphysical masterpiece. 'Goin' Through the Motions' was not going to have the same results 'The Reaper' had, and all the other songs that were written as radio hits, of which there are a large number. There's really only one heavy song on *Agent of Fortune* and all the rest is pop. I don't regard 'The Reaper' as pop. I know exactly where 'The Reaper' came from. Don't forget, these guys grew up with The Byrds and the Grateful Dead. If you listen to *St. Cecilia*, which I have not listened to since it was made, I've never been sent a copy by anybody (laughs). Although I think in my parent's house there is a tape that I took away, a quarter-inch copy of the master, whatever the master was, but I would have to bake it in… put it in olive oil before I dare play it."

The creator of ' (Don't Fear) The Reaper', Buck Dharma, seemed to understand that magic was near when the song was conjured. "Yes, certainly, that was a point where I said we've hit it. 'The Reaper' was the first song I wrote on a multi-track home recorder, a Teac, and I played it back and said, wow, this is really good. I had no idea it was going to be as big as it really was, but certainly, when it came off the demo tape, I said wow, I've got something here."

Bolle speaks wistfully about Buck's original idea. "On rare, rare occasions, I will play a personal demo for someone visiting. I think Buck's original 1975 'Reaper' demo, made by himself on a four-track, is a necessity to hear. Sounds great. It's really cool to track the evolution. It gives you a totally different grip and perspective on music. That's part of what's missing with final product from any band. You only see the compromise aspect of something that is sellable product. It has nothing to do with the band, nothing to do with the producer, nothing to do with the record company. It's a compromise of all three." This demo was indeed added to the '01 reissue of the album, and to my mind, is just a lesser version of the song, made all the more annoying by the mic-tapped rhythm track.

'(Don't Fear) The Reaper', of course, ended up being a smash hit, but in the process, landed the band in a bit of hot water for its wry, sly, elusive invitation not to fear the Reaper. Many felt the line is crossed with the characters of Romeo and Juliet, possibly suggesting a suicide pact and the ultimate romance thereof. After renewed interest in the song amongst fans on the Internet, the author himself wrote in to explain his provocative lyric. Donald: "Guess I gotta jump in here. 'The Reaper' is specifically about two concepts: 1) A powerful enough romantic love can transcend physical death and endure in the hereafter; 2) Death is inevitable whenever it happens to us, and we should know that and face it without fear, having some confidence in the universality of the human spirit, but having no proof until we actually die."

"I wrote this tune at a time in my life when I was thinking about dying early (in my 20s)," continues Buck. "So I'm thinking (first verse) 'I'm dead, now what?' So I sing this song to my love (kiss for Sandy here) saying 'It looks like it's all over for us, but I'm on the other side now, and that's not the only way it can be.' Turns out that if love is strong enough, spiritual things are possible that wouldn't make it to CNN or the Congressional record. There is a way to be reunited on another plane of consciousness."

Buck figures, "The part about we being like they are could be my favourite line in the tune, implying that there are entities that are doing stuff way different than you and me here on earth. The second verse is the one that's caused all the trouble all these years; valentine as metaphor for mortal/love stuff, done now. I had used Romeo and Juliet as an example of a couple who had the faith to take their love elsewhere given that in their case, they weren't permitted the freedom to love here and now. What I meant was, they're in eternity, because they had the faith to believe in the possibility. It frankly never occurred to me that the suicide aspect of their story would be plugged in (like images in a rock video?) to people's take on 'Reaper,' making it an advert for suicide. The 40,000 number was pulled from the air as a guess about how many people died every day worldwide," Buck clarifies, "not how many people committed suicide."

Buck's verse by verse analysis continues. "The idea with the third verse is that a critical mass of emotional and mental intensity is necessary to create this event. What if the remaining partner just can't stand being alone? What if by dint of sheer will, lovers can reunite again after death? In my vision, 'permission' of the event has to come from the 'other' side, the afterlife. The event transpires when there is enough faith and belief to make it happen. Not really so different than any other afterlife system. It never bothered me that 'Reaper' was embraced as a horror icon (i.e. its use in *Halloween* and *The Stand*) or allegedly enjoyed by Gary Gilmore (mass murderer portrayed in *Executioner's Song*). It would bother me to know 'Reaper' gave someone an excuse to commit suicide. I never would have come anywhere close to really wanting to commit suicide. I'm gonna live until I die. On the other hand, when I go, I don't want 'Amazing Grace' as the musical centrepiece at my funeral. I want '(Don't Fear) The Reaper'." Enough said.

So 'The Reaper' quite deservedly became the centrepiece of the Blue Öyster Cult catalogue. It is intriguing to note however that its inclusion on the record almost didn't happen. But this premise is cloaked in confusion. As mentioned, Al insists that Eric threatened to leave the band if 'Reaper' made the record. Sandy says it was Al that threatened to quit. In any event, strong emotions all around.

But other hits—or at least concert favourites—emerged from this breakthrough record. 'E.T.I. (Extra Terrestrial Intelligence)' turned out to be both. The tune was a sort of funky mid-metal, with a lope that was both unwieldy and infectious. Murray, after I mention that Albert figures Krugman probably was a bit shortchanged in the credits department, offers, "Well, you can thank Albert for me for saying that," Murray going on to imply that "E.T.I." could indeed fit such a sentiment. "Yes, that was the normal, customary thing to do. I'll tell you this. It was time to do the *Agents of Fortune* record, and Donald came in with this fantastic riff and chorus and he had this track all worked out. Just great. It was probably the third or fourth best thing they had ever done. There were no lyrics for it. Sandy tried to put some S&M lyrics on top of it called 'Punishment Park.' Joe Bouchard had a really stupid set of lyrics called 'No Traffic Can Bore Me on My Way.' Then one night Sandy came over with this absolutely garbled set of phrases to an extra-terrestrial, or satellite kind of song. We were living about a half hour from him, out on the eastern shore of Long Island. And we spent the night going over all these phrases and I threw them together for him into a singable set of lyrics. Those lyrics virtually are the 'E.T.I.' lyrics on the record."

Going on to express his unarguably crucial role within the workings of the band, Murray offers this observation. "If you look at the heights that they attained when they had reached the top of the mountain, and you look at how far they've fallen, and how fast they've fallen... because, you know, they weren't that much smaller than say Aerosmith, who opened a lot of their shows. They started at the same time, they reached the top of the mountain at the same time, and Aerosmith gets $30 million for their next five records on CBS and Blue Öyster Cult doesn't have a deal. You know, my theory is that they killed the golden goose. You're talking to him. I'm perfectly open to other theories. I just haven't heard one that's particularly persuasive. They also killed the minor golden goose when they threw Albert out, who literally wrote three-quarters of the material, and who was the one of the five of them who was not just penultimately bourgeois."

Sandy's "E.T.I." lyric is a classic, cryptic Blue Öyster Cult UFO tale, the main thrust being the concept of the "Men in Black," stiff, starchy black-suited FBI types who are said to show up after a UFO sighting with a warning that essentially implores the frightened earthling, "Don't report this." The mention of a king in yellow and a queen in red references the pioneering science fiction/fantasy volume written by Robert W. Chambers in 1895 called *The King in Yellow*, Chambers being a worthy precursor to H.P. Lovecraft, one of Sandy's literary mentors. Chambers uses a literary device often employed by Lovecraft, that of creating fictional books within stories. *The Encyclopedia of Science Fiction* states, "The eponymous *King in Yellow* is not a person, but a verse play in book form, which drives its readers to despair, madness, and even suicide."

The band itself of course was guilty of "making up" literature, within the liner notes of *Secret Treaties* referring to Rossignol's *The Origins of a World War*, which does not exist. Another interesting twist in the tale is the mention of Balthazar, one of three wise men who visited Jesus upon His birth. This may prompt one to suppose the band is suggesting Jesus was delivered to the earth by aliens. The story gets more intriguing with the fact that the inner spread to the fold-out of the Stranglers' *Meninblack* album, shows a man in black edited in just over the shoulder of Jesus, in a classical painting of The Last Supper.

Other lyrical elucidations (brought to light by Dan Clore), include the origin of the term "daylight disk" which derives from J. Allen Hynek's classification system for UFO sightings, daylight disk referring to an object sighted during the day (as opposed to nocturnal light), an object too distant to be considered a "close encounter." "Fairy rings" may be used a number of ways. First there's the mushroom talk: either referring to a fungus that kills the grass above in a distinct ring pattern or one that produces a very green ring of grass above it. The term is also used in discussions of fairies, or "little people" dancing in ritual circles, leaving odd ring patterns deep in the woods. Finally, there is the link with UFOs, which perhaps is the most plausible, many UFO stories including burnt or dead rings of grass or vegetation where the supposed craft touched down or hovered. The idea of dead leaves giving up motion is also a UFO reference, referring to the "dead leaf motion" or "falling leaf motion" UFOs supposedly mimic when visiting us poor sods here on earth, swinging back and forth, pausing and finally touching down. Eric later quipped that, "It has a lot to do with extraterrestrials having a lot to do, perhaps, with religious myth in western civilization. People seem to get upset about it."

Next on *Agents of Fortune* was the sparse but chilling 'The Revenge of Vera Gemini', music by Al Bouchard, lyrics by Patti Smith, who performs a sinister spoken word intro to the tune. Sandy on Patti's cameo: "Murray did a marvelous job of putting together Patti's discourse in the beginning of 'Vera Gemini' which never sounded as good to me as when one day the piano player from the classic San Francisco punk band Crime dragged me out of the blue across the street to an exotic dancer place, where his girlfriend was performing. And he gave her a signal and she stripped to 'Vera Gemini' followed by 'E.T.I.' I said, 'Wow, she's taking it all off to Patti Smith.' So anyway, while recording, Patti had come in and done many raps, and we were trying to get something that wasn't going to be all that long, but would be really great. We were having a hard time, so we went out to eat, and came back and Krugman had put it all together. I thought that was great. But after awhile Murray wasn't doing that much. He was gone from '78... I take that back, he was gone from '77 on. The last record he really worked on was *Spectres*. So everything post-*Spectres* for better or worse did not involve him at all."

"That was the first song that Patti Smith ever gave to me, for my 25th birthday, May 24, 1972," recalls Al, concerning 'Vera Gemini'. "She gave me this lyric and said, 'This is for you.' She actually gave it to me; we had a little birthday party for me at our band house in Dix Hills. We even had people from the record company come out, and we served them hash brownies. Everyone got so stoned. It was a total disaster. So she gave it to me on my birthday and said, 'You should make it into a song. Chop it up, do whatever you want!' I said, 'Oh, is this about me?' She said, 'No, Bob Dylan has the same birthday as you.' I said, 'You're kidding.' I didn't know that at the time. She had actually written it about Bob Dylan, something about getting snubbed by him at a party. It was about how she was going to get her revenge. So I wrote music to it, the next day, actually. I played it for Donald and he said, 'You got a lot of nerve, just stealing this song of Bob's, 'Positively 4th Street'. Actually he didn't say it, he sang it (singing like Bob Dylan), 'You've got a lot of nerve, to steal his song!' Anyway, I said, 'Oh, sounds like that, huh?' Yep. So I went back to the drawing board, pulling it out every six months or so, trying to make it not sound like 'Positively 4th Street.' Anyway, it took me pretty much four years to write it!'

'But I got the idea for that piece of music the night after we played the Jacksonville, Florida coliseum which was this big barn. I don't even know if it's still there. It was a big round room where there's about a ten-minute echo. You clap your hands and it just goes and goes and goes. Every note just ran into each other. So I was trying to figure out a song that you could play that would have some impact in a room like that. It was really just a drone kind of thing, where you just went low, high, and things wouldn't cancel each other out, and you would get a cumulative kind of drone thing. Then of course I had to mess it all up and throw in the chromatic changes. But, I like it a lot!' Al recalls that the band actually performed the tune at least twice with Patti, once at the Kingdome in Seattle and once at the convention centre in Asbury Park.

Joe offers additional information as to Patti's involvement with the track. "'Vera Gemini'—awesome. Patti came into the studio, and she was going to sing on it, and so David Lucas was coaching her on the singing, and she totally freaked out. Couldn't get two notes out of her. She just tightened up and couldn't get anything, and I think he said, 'This is awful. What are we going to do?!' Then I guess probably Sandy Pearlman persisted, 'Well, we gotta do something. How about if she just, like, reads some poetry?' That's how that came about. I think it's really magical. Not only that, I love the way the bass and the drums are on that one."

So how much was Patti supposed to sing?

"I don't know. I just remember, David, being like the old Broadway pro, jingle man and all of that, he expected a singer, when she came into the studio, to at least give it a try, and she had like freaked out and couldn't do anything at all. Who would believe that she's had such a fabulous career since then? That was her first recording with us. I mean, she had a couple of those punk records before that, I think."

Not quite so, counters Albert… "No, I don't remember that; I remember it went pretty quickly. I think we tried to get her to sing some stuff, and she didn't want to. She just wanted to speak. So David said, 'Well, I think she should sing it. It's going to be better if she can sing it.' We're like, 'It's fine, it's fine, it's fine.' So Patti actually came up and said, 'Well, maybe if I do a little introduction.' He said, 'Like what?' She said, 'Boned like a saint.' We went wow, that's cool. So she recorded that, and we positioned it in the front of the song, edited it there, and it goes right into the song. She did it on a separate piece of paper. Of course, that set up the kind of rap thing that she was doing."

Opening track on side two of the original *Agents of Fortune* was a taut, psychological number with a patented sinister pop mass. 'Sinful Love' marked the introduction, creatively, of Helen Robbins (a.k.a. Helen Wheels) as an integral addition to the band's arsenal of poet-lyricists. Helen was an incurable artist/poet/publisher who was friends of the band since their infamous "band house" days, later becoming Albert's girlfriend, later still, playing matchmaker between Al and Deb Frost, Al's (now ex-) wife and collaborator in The Brain Surgeons, now necessarily retired for obvious reasons.

Notes Joe, "Helen was Albert's first girlfriend. When he moved to New York, right after he left college, he met Helen and she became his girlfriend. Helen was a multi-talented lady. She was a bodybuilder, she wrote lyrics, she was a fine artist, she raised snakes and she was in a punk band. I would be writing for Blue Öyster Cult and Albert said that I should ask Helen for some lyrics. I did and she wrote two really good ones that went with my songs on the next album in 'Celestial the Queen' and 'Nosferatu'.

"Well, she was a student at Stony Brook College," explains Al, "and she was my girlfriend for awhile, and she lived at the band house, and she was friendly with everybody basically. After we weren't an item, we were still friends, and we still are to this day (ed. Helen was still alive at the time of this interview. She died on January 17, 2000, due to infection-related complications after surgery). She lives about two blocks away from us. She still writes with Deborah and myself. She actually introduced Deborah to me. Helen worked out at the same gym as Deborah, and Helen had said to Deborah and me as well, 'Boy have I got somebody for you to meet.' So she was our yenta. She set it up. This was 1984, although I was not in a position to... I was in an unhappy marriage with Caryn Bouchard, who is now Caryn Schlesinger, so there we go!"

"I have a piece about Helen in my book, *Autumn Rhythm*," explains Richard Meltzer. "It's the third piece in the book, and it's called 'Dust'. When she died, I wrote this. It was basically just that she went from being... when I met her, she was probably 18 or 19. She was Albert's girlfriend, and she was just a sweet, little, soft person; maybe you could think of her as a hippie girl. She was just sweet and soft. She ended up hard as nails. That was also to me, how the BÖC school of rock 'n' roll worked. It's like, The Dictators tried it and she tried it. One of her goals was to be more kick-ass than the Cult; that was her terminology. I didn't care for any of that music she did at that point. But she would send me these photos, body building photos, or a photo with a big snake, motorcycles, and the whole letter would be, 'Do they play my record where you are?! I just got a new python for Christmas! Ain't that cool?' I thought there was something tragic about her going in that direction, because it was just so mindless. It was even a misreading of what the cultural weather was like in New York at the time. When real punk was happening, the Ramones and so forth, she just went to this ersatz sort of metal-ish hard rock thing that just had no specificity to it."

"I knew them from Stony Brook, from pre-Soft White Underbelly," explained Helen, in an interview I conducted with her a few years prior to her death. "They had a bunch of names in the early days. Albert was my boyfriend at the end of the '60s. I was a poet; I was always a good writer, and Al had asked me in 1975 for some poems for lyrics, and those two songs, 'Sinful Love' and 'Tattoo Vampire' are part of my first submission. Actually, I gave them three lyrics for that record, the two that made it and one called 'St. Vitus Dance' which the Brain Surgeons have just recorded (laughs). So I was really lucky, two out of my first three lyrics. But yeah, I had a scholarship to be a marine biologist, and then I sort of switched to poetry. I had made the dean's honour list in biology, but I switched to poetry and left Stony Brook and got a regent scholarship to go to an experimental state school. They said, 'Oh poet, that's great, come on!' They loved the work."

"I never really got involved beyond lyrics," Helen states, "but I did get to hang out in the studio, which to me was just like a magic place, where the sound got layered through machines. I mean I was used to seeing the band rehearse, because they rehearsed every single day in the basement of the house. They built this little studio with all this insulation and egg boxes on the wall and stuff. They taught me all about music. They were fantastic musicians, really interesting writers, affable people. There were earlier fights that occurred, but they were with earlier members that are no longer there (laughs). I went through a couple of those ones. But it was always a pretty neat experience. I was 18, a freshman in college, and I moved in with the band, and it was like, whoa!"

Helen sets the record straight on her new, nifty nickname. "Yeah, that came about because I was hanging out with Hells Angels and stuff. It was in the early days. I had met The Dictators when they first started and it was Handsome Dick who gave me that nickname. I was doing Blue Öyster Cult's costumes in the early days, and when The Dictators started, I did theirs too. Sandy had hired me, so I did a lot of the early leather costumes. I mean in the '60s it was just like crazy stuff. So that name came from Handsome Dick. I guess it was for Blue Öyster Cult's first European tour, that I needed an official business name, so I used The Amazing Helen Wheels, and that was the beginning of that. It was amazing for me doing the costumes, because a very expensive top that I had made for Albert with 300 studs in it, a very fancy top, was stolen twice, and I got hired to make it three times (laughs). I can think of some pretty wild costumes I made for them. I made one that was based on sort of the look of a wet suit? It was for Buck Dharma. But it was made out of shiny, white stretch stuff and it was like a custom, white, shiny wet suit. He wore it for an entire tour. I have pictures! I used to pull photographs out of *Creem* and *Rolling Stone*. Oh yeah, they wore all the outfits I made for them."

"'Sinful Love' was sort of an ode to Patti Smith actually. She was a big influence on me at the time. It was sort of my personal declaration that I wasn't going to be influenced by her anymore, that I was on my own, that I was making my own songs. But when she had started writing for the Cult, two albums before that, I was very struck with her work. I thought that she was a very good artist. I went to see the band and she was also there, when they were rehearsing at the now defunct Fillmore East. They had rented it as a rehearsal studio and I remember being there two rows behind Patti and she just had done 'Baby Ice Dog'—I think it was her first thing with them—and they were playing it on stage and it was like wow, maybe I can write something (laughs)."

Al offers a few thoughts on the nervous pop energy of 'Sinful Love'. "See, that one I thought was going to be really heavy (laughs). It was supposed to be kind of like a heavy metal James Brown tune, but for some reason it didn't come out that way. It came out very melodic, and I'm not sure exactly why. I have demos that I did where I had used Ross the Boss from The Dictators, and he really played it the way that I felt that it should have been played. And Donald could never play it that way. None of them could. Even I dropped the ball because I changed the beat. I mean inadvertently; I didn't mean to do it. But a few years later I went, 'What went wrong with this song?' People like it and it's good but I still feel that my demo… you know, if we had ADATs, we would have just put the demo on the record. It didn't really sound that good, but I had done a really nice number with Ross."

Hot on the heels of 'Sinful Love' was yet another Robbins number, 'Tattoo Vampire' which is perhaps the band's most ripping, heavy metal number ever; a masterpiece of the genre indeed.

"It's actually an amazing story," laughs Helen. "It was inspired by a real event. There was this guy, Erik Emerson from The Magic Tramps, an early glitter rock band from the New York Dolls era. He was also in some of the Warhol movies, and I acted as an assistant to a tattooist known as Ernesto Tattoo that had tattooed Eric and his girlfriend, who Erik had us tattoo at knifepoint later (laughs). That was pretty crazy. We were all partying hearty into the night and Erik was reaching a new manic level of behaviour, insisting with a big kitchen knife that now it was his girlfriend's turn, even though she was unconscious and Ernie was all sails to the wind, high and drunk. Ernie protested that he couldn't even draw a straight line, but before you know it, Erik had him at knifepoint, rolling B's lifeless body onto the table, stripping her clothes off and tattooing "ERIK" in six, seven inch letters across her side, hips and tush. She lay there snoring like a beached whale, never waking as the huge tattoo proceeded in thick, wavy red letters. Ernie looked about to cry, knowing he could hardly keep it together. Erik's glee mounted as the square inches of bloody red letters scarred across B's backside. Then it was done, the knife put down, B's butt bandaged up, and still snoring, she was rolled to another location."

"Erik has long since died; rode his bicycle into a truck in New York traffic. But yeah, I wrote that song in the Cafe Figaro on MacDougall Street on a paper bag, and boy, it made me the most money of all my stuff. The song was written from that experience. And it's before I had tattoos. It's interesting. I mean I was sort of like boiling the water for needles and stuff. I have a good number of tattoos from the '70s and one from the '90s, but this was before all that, so it was quite a long time ago. It was the first song I'd ever done for the band, churned out over cups of espresso on a scrap of paper in a cafe. The tune was also used as the b-side to '(Don't Fear) The Reaper,' so that was cool."

Getting more candid and specific, Helen recounts in her journal the inspiration behind the wicked first couple of verses. "Ernie was illustrated up and down and all around his body. One night he and I ended up bunkin' together. The minute Ernie fell into a fitful sleep, evil, inhuman, oriental fantasy creatures came to life, heaving and twitching. I watched them all night as if they'd bite or jump or walk over onto my body without Ernie's conscious mind to restrain them! It was Ernie's chest that inspired the beginning of that song."

Bolle notes that Helen's original lyric was, "I went down last night with a tattoo man," which of course this tough band couldn't sing. Another original line went, "Wrapped in hair, I lost my breath," which Bolle says Eric found "too wimpy, too female-ish," subsequently changing hair to hell.

Summing up, Helen offers, "Well, I'll say one thing about 'Tattoo Vampire'. When they did it, I thought it was really Las Vegas-style, and it helped push me into becoming a singer and starting a band. Because I felt misinterpreted. I saw it as a much rougher, cruder thing. It seemed really polished to me at the time, and my punk band did a much rougher version of it."

vHelen's opinion of the Cultsters as creative people remained high 'til the end. "Among the Cults, Sandy was pretty much my lyrical influence, I would say. But they all did songs I thought were very interesting. That was the wonderful thing about that band, that all the musicians were the writers. Albert was a really big writer, but Donald was a fantastic writer. Joe was a wonderful writer."

Albert says the heaviness of 'Tattoo Vampire' was a mistake, envisioning something even less rocking than the final take. "This just goes to show that things never come out the way you think they do (laughs). Because I really thought I was going to make like one of those uptempo Chuck Berry song like 'Maybelline' or 'Memphis'. It wasn't originally going to be so heavy. But with the lyric I really couldn't have the major Chuck Berry key kind of stuff so I just shifted it to a minor key and I put some tri-tones in there and all of a sudden it came out really heavy and ominous. It's wild."

"Lots of funny sounds on 'Tattoo Vampire'," adds Joe. "Like the carnival sounds—they had one of those masks that had this really goofy laugh. You pull the string, and this goofy mask would give you this really horrendous laugh, and that ended up on 'Tattoo Vampire.' That's in the bridge section; I always loved that song, especially the lyric. The beginning, that's just muting the strings on the guitar. We wanted to have sort of a buildup at the beginning of the song."

Next, the record enters a bit of a black hole, a morbid grey area marked by two fairly anonymous tracks, 'Morning Final' (later adopted as the name of the fine and definitive Blue Öyster Cult fan club newsletter), and 'Tenderloin'. 'Morning Final' is one of those spooky, reflective, melancholic tunes, solo-composed and sung by Joe Bouchard. The lyric mixes murder with Joe's familiar subway theme, poetically echoing Joe's other stomping ground, the world of vampires, the tune rife with images demarcating above ground from underground, with all the attendant moral implications thereof.

When asked about his reliance on the rails, Joe laughs. "Well, I came from Clayton, a small town in upstate New York, which is really idyllic, a place for fishing and stuff. So we used to listen to Kingston Radio. We were influenced by that Canadian scene. So I moved to New York and I was freaked-out (laughs). I was honestly freaked-out. I didn't know what to expect, so that's where those subway songs come from. I never rode the subway that much, and I actually never lived in New York for any more than like five days, but that was enough. Also I had felt that we had taken on a concept that would not allow sentimentality—that was definitely anti- the love generation. So I didn't mind experimenting with styles that were more like horror and science fiction. I probably didn't know what I was doing at the time, so I just did it."

Allen Lanier's 'Tenderloin' is the record's second to last track, somewhat previewing 'Searching for Celine', both songs rolling with decadent disco pop ennui, the 'Tenderloin' walking bass line chafing against a reverberating percussion pattern from Albert. The song is vaguely and cryptically about the Tenderloin district of San Francisco, and the whole disintegration of hippie ideals into bad drugs and soul-destroying promiscuity, an idea the Grateful Dead very much felt but rarely wrote about. The time imagery is particularly potent, begging the question of how long man can thrive on fumes. "Allen's song," notes Buck simply. "Don't know too much about motivation there; we just liked the spooky mood of it."

"Another Allen Lanier thing," adds Joe, with respect to 'Tenderloin'. "Allen played bass on 'Morning Final' and I played piano—that's how it worked. And then I really like it, because it fades into 'Tenderloin,' and then you hear me playing bass on 'Tenderloin,' and Allen doing the keyboards. And it's really kind of a nice shock, feel-wise, right at that moment, where you hear this really strong bass line come in. That's another one Allen wrote about our trips around the world in the rock 'n' roll days."

"I think Joe wanted to play the keyboards more," comments Albert, on the curious situation of having so many talented multi-instrumentalists in the band. "Allen didn't really like to play keyboards that much. I mean, Allen loves to play guitar, and whenever he picked up the bass, for instance on 'Morning Final,' he does a fantastic job. Allen played bass on a couple of songs, while Joe was playing keyboards, and it worked out really well. It was fine. I guess if all of us were still there, he would still be doing that, and Joe would be playing more keyboards."

"'Tenderloin','" says Lanier, was "one of those instances where I had a picture in my mind when I was writing it where I felt as if I was there. I'm not going to tell you the details of where it exactly came from. That's the way I like to write. Put down the clues and let other people fill in the spaces as opposed to taking care of all the details. I don't like to be too detailed because songs tend to end up being soundtracks to your own life."

Adds Allen, on his reduced output over the years, "I stopped writing because I got self-conscious about my abilities as a musician, so I sat down and concentrated on them for several years. I co-wrote with people, but I didn't spend a lot of time on songwriting. I just came back to it. I don't know why. I would have to say that my material isn't as applicable to BÖC as perhaps some of the others. I really don't know why. Also I'm terribly lazy! I tend to get bored easily. I get three-quarters through something and then give it up. On *Agents*, there was a sense of, 'This is Donald's song, this is Albert's song, this is my song,' and I wondered if we would come up with five short little solo albums. But it didn't turn out like that because we have been together so long that our styles are very much influenced by one another. We steal from each other more than anyone. People put as much—if not more—effort into someone else's song if they have a certain feeling about it. It all trades off that way. Donald is a narrative writer; he likes to tell stories. I'm not such a great narrative writer; I tend to go purely for mood. Atmosphere is so important, making the song sound like what it's about."

Finally, closing out the record was an innocent little pop slice called 'Debbie Denise'. BÖC expert Bolle considers this the biggest mistake the band ever made, and many fans agreed, souring at the thought of this black leather battalion branching so far out toward easy listening. Albert defends this mushy pile of lush: "I think it's kind of a funny song. I think it's actually heart-felt. I don't feel like it's a mistake. I know I've taken some heat that this is a sappy kind of tune and all of that. But to me it was honest. It was honest and humourous at the same time. I still don't fell bad about it."

Some Cult watchers figure that Patti Smith's lyric is a veiled flirtation with lesbianism. It was never ascertained who Debbie Denise was, but a couple of gals by the names of Debbie and Denise were known to hang with members of the band for a short time in the mid-'70s.

Joe sheds a bit more light on the track. "'Debbie Denise' was very difficult to record. We couldn't seem to get it nailed down. Finally, David Lucas, always a good one for ideas, came out to the studio and sang the bass part to me. He said,

'Do this here; put a little McCartney in the song.' And he sang the bass part and I just copied what he was singing, and that made all the difference, and then we were able to cut a track that we thought was acceptable. And I like that, you know, because I love the 12-string guitars. I think Albert's vocal is a riot (laughs). He was getting divorced from his wife Denise, at the time, so that even put more reality into the song. There is more reality in that song than a lot of songs. Nobody knows that; they just think, oh, this is pretty light."

An interesting side note: 'Debbie Denise' was included in place of 'Fire of Unknown Origin', sung by Albert, a track even mentioned in interviews at the time. This version of 'Fire of Unknown Origin' was added to the '01 reissue of *Agents of Fortune* and is a much different, more subdued, almost murky song than the potential hit version that was on the album of the same name. The chord patterns are baffling, Albert's vocal more fragile than usual, and the time changes unsettling. Better left off, I say.

"'Fire' was actually written twice," explains Buck, "both times mainly by Albert, from a Patti lyric. It didn't make the cut the first time and then it was recreated for the *Fire of Unknown Origin* record. We actually spent a lot of time trying to get a version we were happy with. The lyric is very morose and dark."

Also best left scattered to the four winds are two additional originals added to the '01 reissue, 'Sally' being a bouncy, psychedelic Albert Bouchard composition more suited to the black and white period of the band and even earlier (Donald says this is Albert utilizing a Patti Smith lyric), and 'Dance the Night Away' being an Iggy Pop-styled under-achiever (think *Kill City* era) of a Lanier/Jim Carroll track picked up for recording by Carroll, but left untouched by the Cult. It had potential as a BÖC tune, but perhaps more so as a deep album track three sides into *Exile on Main Street*.

"'Sally' I remember we worked on a lot," comments Joe. "Albert re-recorded it with The Brain Surgeons. I always liked that. I don't know if it could've made it as part of the whole album, because that was a good album, and we had a lot of good stuff to choose from. That was one of the strengths of that, that the writing team had two years of great material. 'Dance the Night Away', Allen sat down in the studio said, 'I want to play you this song.' He did a version of 'Dance the Night Away' and for some reason we lost that tape, and then he did it again, but it was never quite as good. I had a good feeling about that song, but for some reason, we lost the tape with the good demo on it. So what you hear is not quite the version that I thought had the horses. But since we had Allen singing 'True Confessions', his only real vocal on an album, I think we decided that we didn't need 'Dance the Night Away'. It never really was finished. Allen had a hard time finishing songs. He would come up with a pretty good idea, but he would never be able to finish the arrangement, polish it off. Whereas Donald is great about that and Albert was great about that."

"Oh, I was very surprised that they include that," exclaims Albert, with respect to 'Sally' making an appearance on the reissue. "I forgot that we'd even recorded it. My story with 'Sally' is that we were out on the road, and we had come back, had a week off, and I'd been working on some demos, and one night I am working on my demos, and I think I just recorded 'Sally,' and I get a phone call, and it's Donald. He says, 'Hey man, I just wrote a new song—wanna hear it?' I said sure.

So he played me this guitar riff (sings it). I'm like, 'Man, that's pretty cool; that sounds like the song that I just wrote!' I mean, in a different key. I played him mine, and he says, 'Yeah, that's cool; yeah, it's the same thing.' That's funny, that we both came up with the same thing at the same time. Anyway, his song was 'Reaper,' mine was 'Sally', same pattern, and I think maybe we thought that mine sounded too much like 'Reaper'. We did a vocal with Donald singing it, and you know, now listening to it, it doesn't sound that much like 'Reaper' at all. But I guess that was part of the reason we didn't put it on."

"But the other thing was, the guys were getting a little bit concerned that it was like, Donald with two songs, and my seven songs, that I was going to dominate the record, writing-wise, which, I said, 'Well, what do I care? Put your name on the song. I don't care. It's not about the money.' It wasn't about the money. It was about, 'No, we just want our stuff on there.' So the major fighting that went on was about whose songs were going to be on there. It wasn't me. It was the producers that wanted my songs on the album. It was Murray, Sandy and David. There was a huge fight about 'Fire of Unknown Origin' that Eric didn't want it on the record. 'If it goes on the record, then I'm quitting.' But he already said if 'Reaper' goes on the record, he's quitting. I said, 'Well, don't be a stranger (laughs). Because that's going on!'"

Rolling Stone, unsurprising, given their disdain for all things metal, was quite encouraged by the band's jaunty new direction. "Agents of Fortune *is a startlingly excellent album,*" begins scribe Ken Tucker, "*startling because one does not expect Blue Öyster Cult to sound like this: loud but calm, manic but confident, melodic but rocking. Every song on the first side is commercially accessible without compromising the band's malevolent stance. One area of clear improvement is in the matter of the lyrics; for the first time, there is less emphasis on absurd, crypto-intellectual ramblings and more of a coherent attack on a variety of subjects. The former had become simply tiresome; the latter opens up whole new areas for Cult investigation. By dropping the S&M angle and by inserting slivers of genuine rock 'n' roll like 'True Confessions,' their best song ever, the Cult is easing into maturity with integrity.* Agents of Fortune's *comparative slickness even serves to enhance their dark image: the ominous villainy conveyed by Buck Dharma's agile guitar lines on 'Tenderloin' is far more effective than his heretofore standard thudding meanness.*"

In terms of touring *Agents of Fortune*, the band hit the road in May '76 and stayed there until December 31st. Once more, myriad bands shared stages with the Cultsters, but multiple dates were logged with the likes of Angel, Starz, Rush, Mahogany Rush, Montrose, ZZ Top and late in the year, Bob Seger. The theme this year was America only—all of it, with only a couple of Canadian dates and no return trek overseas. As a comical exercise in contrasts, the band's two encore numbers were '(Don't Fear) The Reaper' and 'Hot Rails to Hell' with a little 'I Ain't Got You' to further confound.

Succumbing to a seductive hit song, people bought *Agents of Fortune* in droves, Blue Öyster Cult finally ringing up the numbers they'd deserved for so long. This rollercoaster record of creative risks eventually went platinum, again, on the strength of 'Reaper' but also concert staples like 'E.T.I.' and 'This Ain't the Summer of Love'. Now years later, 'The Reaper' still fascinates (and who can forget *Saturday Night Live*'s "more cowbell" sketch?). Lore has it that it is one of the top ten most played classic rock songs of all time (I don't believe it—I can think of dozens that I hear more often), and as recent of 1996, the tune's been used yet again in a major motion picture, Wes Craven's *Scream* (albeit an acoustic version played by Gus), with previous flicks exhibiting good taste being *The Frighteners*, and as Buck has mentioned, *Halloween*, and Stephen King's *The Stand*. I believe there's been an insurance commercial as well. But the bottom line is, *Agents of Fortune* was a deep record that went past the singles, rapidly becoming both a considerable critical and commercial hit. Profits, pressures and petty jealousies escalated.

Spectres

"The new religion would be born in the stars"

*A*gents of Fortune had altered Blue Öyster Cult's destiny forever. On the surface and well beneath, the band had discovered colour, dynamic, hue, and a previously foreign capability to straddle pop to metal and all points in between. Plus there was the bewildering matter of a hit single. Now they owned one, and it sat there taunting them, scythe in hand, potential damnation to the band if the lure of commerce would be too strong to resist.

So big expectations were in store for the record's follow-up, with *Spectres*—one working title was *The Big Hurt*—being issued in November 1977, a year claimed by punk but owned by Fleetwood Mac. Telegraphing the band's return was the record's flashy cover art.

"*Spectres* was pretty much Sandy Pearlman's concept," begins Albert. "We were just about to embark on the laser experience. Ronnie Hoffman, who was Richard Meltzer's girlfriend, at the time was the art director. She just brought us a whole bunch of stuff to play with and we came up with the idea." Eric explains further, "Someone at CBS had helped us go to a costume place on Broadway and we all picked out this archaic clothing to wear. We had brought our concert laserist along to run the lasers for the session (ed. more on the band's experiences with lasers in the *Some Enchanted Evening* chapter). It was a juxtaposition of old and new; the clothes, the laser light and all the creepy symbols like the cat and the clock. As photo sessions go, it was fun." The band's hook symbol this time, always somewhere on the band's covers, was a trick to locate, showing up in the lower left hand corner within the crystal ball on the floor, a portion of the photo that was carelessly cropped out of the first CD reissue, but restored on the definitive 2007 package.

"That was simply a question of trying to take pictures with lasers," explained Allen Lanier back in '78, "to see if we could capture lasers through photography. It's the age of the laser, after all. Also I thought it would be nice to make time references. That's why we specifically picked the clothing, which I suppose is turn-of-the-century, but it's also a movie reference. It comes from my influences, like Fritz Lang and the film *M*. You know, spectres in the night and a mysterious atmosphere. And you have the cut 'Nosferatu' there too on the album. I get a kick out of historical references like that. In a way, that could hurt us, because there are so many different references to grasp. It ain't Fleetwood Mac. But you can't really help what you do. I admit on *Spectres* that we tried to be as commercial as we could. In the sense of good, clean arrangements, straightforward songs played well, strong harmonies and so forth. No matter what we decide to do, we always come out doing what we do, if you get what I mean. Also I think there's a nocturnal feeling. Most of the subjects, through no particular design, refer to the night. One of the album titles we considered was *Unfinished Nights.*"

So yes, the band's sixth record was wrapped in a stunner of a cover. But what of the contents? *Spectres* was the second record for which the band wrote and recorded their demos at home and submitted them for approval, or for competitive, manly and/or jocular ridicule. It was also the second where Sandy Pearlman was conspicuously absent from the writing credits, in part due to his move across the country to San Francisco. Again Krugman and Pearlman produced, with invaluable assistance from David Lucas (his last for the band), using the trusty Record Plant in New York.

Although, says Krugman, for the first time, the band used a different engineer for each instrument... "We always knew certain engineers got a particular drum sound that we liked for example, and another would get a great guitar sound but his drum sound was no good, So we got the idea to use separate engineers to record each sound we wanted." This all culminated in what would be, up until that point, the band's most expensive record to make, at one point commanding all four rooms at The Record Plant. Adding to the complexity of the thing, was growing tension between the triumvirate of technicians. Albert: "Yeah, making the record was all-out war. All three of them—Murray, Sandy and David Lucas—all hated each other, kept denigrating the others' work. So it was kind of a schizophrenic record."

"You know, I was just thinking about him yesterday," adds Albert, asked for a profile of David Lucas. "Because I was having a particularly bad day, and I was walking down the street with a sour look on my face. I thought, 'I bet I look just like David Lucas.' No, he's a guy who was extremely talented, very successful; he really knew how to create something that would please the public. Yet, I always thought that he didn't seem that happy, that he was kind of like... you know, he had two or three marriages, and there was always a problem with women and I don't know, it seemed like, I can identify with him, you know (laughs)? Anyway, David, in the studio, can be very upbeat. It was only outside of work, he would kind of get a little down or cynical or whatever. But when it was time to make music, he was extremely enthusiastic. He would always be having some new toy or new sound that he found, 'Check this out!' He was a genius at harmonies. Just a genius, I mean, not just the notes that fit together, but how the tone of the notes worked, and how they would fit together."

Perhaps, emphasizing what would become a quickening shift away from Pearlman, Al had stated, back in the day, back in context, "At this point we feel really comfortable in the studio and our writing reflects that. Everybody keeps coming up with stronger and stronger material. At first it didn't seem like the songs were going to be as good as *Agents,* so we went back to work. Now everyone agrees the stuff's tremendous, and I can tell you, it's pretty hard to get us all to agree on the same thing."

Sandy pulls no punches about the growing rift between him and the band, a rift that really gathered steam with the subsequent year's live record. "Well, they were sick of me! You know, sick of being sort of like the philosophical Kiss. You know, Kiss got sick of it also, but that was all they could do. The truth is, this is probably all Blue Öyster Cult could do. I don't mean that badly, because they did it really well. There was a future in it, I think. Other bands doing the same thing had become very, very big. Obviously it wasn't something the public had become sick of, or more to the point it was something the public was interested in. There is a large audience for this kind of stuff. But, yeah, they just got sick of me."

Kiss was often brought up as something comparison- and contrast-worthy to the Blue Öyster Cult. Eric once commented that, "Gene Simmons once said to me, 'The kids are not interested in poetry.' Up to a point he's right. If you compare our career with theirs—Gene and Paul came up with the idea of the type of band Kiss would be; it was the whole package. At the same time, Pearlman and Krugman came up with the idea, along with the band members, of what Blue Öyster Cult should be. It's a very different attack on what the listening public would be buying."

Joe, 20 years later, looked back on the construction of *Spectres*, figuring, "The rumour that these songs were leftovers from the wealth of material going into *Agents* is totally untrue. If anything, it could have been recorded better, maybe mixed better. But material-wise, that's all new stuff. We ended up doing *Spectres* in two sections. It might have been a different album if we did it all at one time. But we did the first part of the album, then we went out on tour for about two months. What happened is that we were in Canada, and we were about to take the railway over to Vancouver through the Rockies—I was really looking forward to this—then we found out our Vancouver show and our Victoria show were cancelled. So we flew back home, kind of dejected. It wasn't bad for me because I made the best of my time and wrote two songs that eventually got on the album, 'Celestial the Queen' and 'Nosferatu'."

"What happened is we came in with ten songs totally unrelated, and then we dropped four of them," said Albert, doing press duties at the time. "Then we went on tour for several weeks in July. The four new ones we came back were the ones that we used to fill in the gaps. From the original six, there was no killer, fast rock 'n' roll, and we needed some of that, which is what we added. One is what you might expect from Steve Miller and the other is what you might expect from Queen."

The band had grown fond of being stars. Sandy had said in an *NME* piece, "*Spectres* is a deliberate attempt to make an album that would sell three million units and beat Fleetwood Mac."

Albert echoed this sentiment somewhat pragmatically. "What we're trying to do is please everybody all the time. We're trying to keep a balance between having enough smooth pop stuff so that people will buy the album and enough heavy stuff we can do in our live show."

"I think this album is more commercial just because we're getting better," mused Donald. "That's part of the Cult's maturation process, that we become more integrated into the mainstream of pop music. The longer we go on, we're not going farther out. The fact is, we're getting closer to the mainstream. We can't afford to be strictly a cult group. We have such a big show with the lasers and everything, that we can't make a living as an underground band. We have to have a large rabid following. It's all entertainment basically." Going a little deeper, he theorizes that, "The idea of night crops up a lot. The common theme of the songs, I would say, is the soul on the other side of the Earth."

Patti Smith, Allen's girlfriend at the time and privy to the recording process chuckled, "It's going to be a good record because I'm doing Allen's laundry. Every day he goes into the studio with clean socks and shirts. He likes to translate his energy into hard work, and he's really doing it on this album; it's a very masculine album." Then going along with the interviewer's joke, she quips, "You could say it's that too—a masculine/mescaline album."

Incidentally, Patti wouldn't be Allen's girlfriend for much longer. "What were the years?" thinks Joe. "'71 to '78, maybe? Until she married Fred Smith. They had an apartment together in New York, a beautiful apartment, a corner apartment right on One Fifth Ave., which is right there by Washington Square, down in the village. An incredible apartment that they bought together. Allen had two things in the apartment, a pool table and our grand piano (laughs).
So, he had a Steinway grand right over by the window, so he could play any time. You know, 'Allen, turn off the TV, get off the thing, start writing some songs!' He was the first guy I knew who had a remote control on his TV (laughs). So I guess it was kind of domestic life, with Allen and Patti. And they had a lot of rock 'n' roll friends. They have a lot of stories of all kinds of people, artsy people from New York, pretenders, a lot of people who are not with us now. Luckily Patti and Allen are still with us, but a lot of people, Robert Mapplethorpe, and a lot of that sort of downtown artsy crowd, were part of Patti and Allen's scene. One Fifth Ave... in fact, *Saturday Night Live*, the original cast, had their cast party downstairs in the restaurant of the hotel. So every Saturday, if they were around, after rehearsals, that was the hang-out for *Saturday Night Live*, in their building. So they were friends with John Belushi. Yeah, I was not part of that thing. I was out in the suburbs with my wife, and rarely did the New York thing. But this is what I heard from Allen—a pretty cool time. Then it all went to... you know, they broke up, and Patti married Fred Smith from the MC5."

"I remember what it was like, but I don't remember any parties, ever," muses Albert. "But I heard about parties. They had this huge living room, and in the middle of the living room was a pool table. He told me one time that he had Dennis Hopper up there playing pool with him, and Jim Carroll would come up there all the time. I would see Jim Carroll and Tom Verlaine up at their apartment, playing some music, and I was told that William Burroughs came up there, but I never saw him. But it was right in the middle of the city, really. I mean, One Fifth Ave. I guess it would be sort of the east side of the West Village, right in the middle of Manhattan. Very central location, and I remember looking out the window towards the back, and you could see the Washington Muse there, this cool little street which looks kind like the *Strange Days* album cover; I think they might've taken the picture there. The Doors thing with the midgets and all of that."

"I was probably not that close to Allen," continues Joe. "Eric and Donald were definitely closer to Allen than I was. We had a nice kind of interesting situation when he was Patti Smith's boyfriend though, that went on for those seven years.

There was always that, 'Well, you know, the lyrics have got to be as good as what Patti would come up with' (laughs). So there was definitely a, 'You know, we've got some of the best poets in the world, influencing the band' (laughs). If not adding a direct influence, at least an indirect influence. Allen was a lot of fun. He certainly believed in the Keith Richards rock 'n' roll... you know, it had to be like that. The drugs? Let me tell you. I had no idea that he had a bad habit. I mean, as bad as it was. I didn't even realize it until after I left the band. He kept his habit to himself."

Eric's view of Patti Smith's background with the band?

"Before she was Allen's girlfriend, we'd go see her, before she had a band; she was doing poetry readings. She was going out with Sam Shepard before she met Allen. When we met her, there was a New York underground scene going on. No one had a record deal. Patti was trying to get a deal and we were trying to get a deal. We just got a deal first, that's all. It was inevitable that Patti was on her way. I used to go see her play with just Lenny Kaye on guitar. It was great, in a little bar."

Adds Buck, "When we first met Patti she was just about to make the transition from poet to performing artist. There was actually some talk of having Blue Öyster Cult be her band. Now obviously that didn't happen and she began to work with Lenny Kaye and the band that she has developed out of that. We never actually wrote songs together as an intentional project. What we would do is Patti would give us a lyric or we would go in her book of writings and take a section of something and create songs from it. Later, when I wrote 'Shooting Shark', I hadn't seen Patti in seven, eight years, after she left Allen and married Fred 'Sonic' Smith. I came across the typewritten sheet ands went, 'Wow, this has been here all along.' So I created the music from the words. There wasn't actually much direct interaction."

Allen did many of the interviews on the *Spectres* junket, communicating a sort of frank and jaded weariness that was refreshing to see from a seasoned rocker. In comparing *Agents of Fortune* to *Spectres*, he stated, "Well, what distinguished *Agents* from previous records was the production, and the fact that everybody played better than they used to. On this record we play better yet still. There were a lot of weaknesses on the last record that I don't find on this one at all. It feels real strong to me. I hate to say the word, but it's really professional. I don't know, maybe we're getting boring in that sense. It's not radical, except again personally. It's as radical as any kind of art can be, just because it's trying to be something good. But it's typical Blue Öyster Cult stuff. A bit of the fantastic, and also a lot like night. There's a nocturnal ambiance about the record. It seems that no matter what we do, that's what comes out. We've brainwashed ourselves over the years."

When asked about repeating the success of '(Don't Fear) The Reaper' Donald denied even thinking about it. "If there's anything I hate it's a follow-up single that sounds like the first one. That's what I liked about the Beatles. 'Please, Please Me', 'She Loves You' and 'I Want To Hold Your Hand'—none of them sounded alike." Albert: "My only reason for not liking the name *Spectres* is that it sounds like a follow-up to 'Reaper.' But we're not trying to deny 'The Reaper.' Because of that song, we got a bigger budget, and the record company's more excited about us. Financially, we did pretty well this year, and everything is because of 'The Reaper.'"

Years later, Sandy exposed the pitfalls of such thinking. "What happened was that they got desperate as a collective. Having made lots of money and having tasted the heady nectar of a Top 40 placing, they started writing songs with radio in mind. Eric wanted to follow models that had already been established but were not BÖC. They were gonna go for gold, but gold proved elusive."

For all the band's vehement denial, *Spectres* really did sound like *Agents of Fortune* Part II, and that is by no means an insult, the record remaining one of most fans' favourites of the catalogue. *Spectres* was rife with the same swoopy heavy peaks and lush valleys; it is a scintillating, mildly horrific masterpiece of pace and grace. However a formula had been set with *Spectres'* successful predecessor, a formula that denied the concept of formula, one of exploded diversity. But diversity between ten songs, multiplied over six more records pleads the listener to partition tracks into little piles; rockers, ballads, wannabe hits, experiments, monster songs, UFO songs, love songs, epics. But when individual tracks are usually masterpieces, formula can be excused. The band however, had all felt the growing effects of road burn and the making of the album was not nearly as fun or innocent as projects past.

Spectres opens with 'Godzilla', an uncharacteristically lunk-headed but lovable rocker from Donald, shades of BTO from BÖC. This decidedly heavy metal track (apparently partly inspired by a song called 'Go Go Gorilla') would become a semi-hit and a classic rock radio staple over the years, also serving as centrepiece to the band's live show. The band's biggest prop to date has been the 20-foot-high Godzilla with glowing red eyes, head turning from side to side, smoke blasting out of its mouth. The song's opening sequence comprised an amusing Eric rap over the thundering footsteps of the approaching oversized dinosaur, Eric later doing his impression of Japanese on the heels of Joe's bass solo (composed as a tribute to Stanley Clarke), with Albert donning a Godzilla head between strobe flashes during his drum solo.

Eric's Japanese rant translates roughly as follows: "Attention, emergency news! Attention, emergency news! Godzilla is going toward the Ginza area! Immediately escape, catch up, find shelter please!" Eric had actually undergone an intensive 60 hour course in Japanese prior to the band's '79 tour, to be able to do the song justice, and also to impress and show appreciation for the Japanese fans when touring the Far East. "I was a language major at college, and I can speak Spanish and French fluently. I've always wanted to learn Japanese. It meant I could talk between songs in Japanese and handle that long introduction to 'Godzilla.' The fans certainly loved it."

Years later, in an interview with myself concerning this topic, Eric filled in a few blanks. "When we were going to go on tour, '78, '79, I went to the Berlitz School and took 20 or 30 intensive Japanese lessons. So when I got there, the funny thing was, is I get to Japan and I sat down with a guy from Sony Records who was Japanese American, and I started practicing some stuff with him and he goes, 'Everyone's going to laugh at you for saying that stuff.' And I go 'What do you mean?' And he goes, 'Well, that's like school Japanese. Nobody talks like that.' So I wanted to wring their necks for teaching me all the wrong stuff (laughs). So I had to sit down with him and phonetically learn a few good things like, 'How y'all doing?!'"

For those not partial to trashy sci-fi movies, Godzilla or "Godjira", is the atomic bomb-mutated star of a series of sci-fi movies from the '50s and '60s, usually seen stomping all over Tokyo, battling the likes of King Kong, Mothra and various other giant monsters. The song is of course, especially popular in Japan. It's one of the band's few straightforward lyrics, ending with the telling warning about history repeatedly revealing the folly of man. Al summed up the song as "all about monsters and the atom bomb controversy; very sociological as well as humorous," with Patti Smith deeming it "a Japanese sci-fi monster thing which is going to be a revival of dirt."

"That was just a heavy riff that was created in a Dallas hotel room," recalls Donald. "What came to my mind was Godzilla because, what's heavier than Godzilla? (laughs). Nothing. The song was pretty much right in the pocket to what people wanted to hear. We're all huge fans of the original movie where they dubbed Raymond Burr into the movie for the American release. They put him in a narrative role. If you look closely in the scenes where he's interacting with the Japanese actors, they never face the camera because there were obviously other people standing in. His scenes were probably shot in Hollywood and edited in. With the lyrics what I did was just reprise the moral lesson that the movie did: that Godzilla was basically man's fault. In the movie it was messing around with nuclear energy that was blamed for Godzilla's unleashing. Ironically if it was nuclear testing in the Pacific that awakened Godzilla, it was Tokyo that suffered. I thought that was weird."

David Roter (now-deceased friend and lyric-writer for the band: see *Cultösaurus Erectus* chapter), counters and conjectures that, "Patti Smith started that song. It might have been Patti Smith's idea. Albert really knows the story. Donald started doing something with her, and then he didn't see her for about a month. Then next time he saw her, he said, 'Oh, I finished it. I did it.' And that was that. It's really funny, on some of these songs, the idea is 40 to 50% of the deal, like writing a song about Godzilla. But I gotta say, the lyrics to that are great. But it was a weird thing. He started out with her and then he did it. I personally don't think Patti Smith could write as well as Donald did in that song. What also makes that song great is that it's so succinct."

"I'll tell you exactly how that came about," begins Albert, with respect to his drum solo dressed as the large beloved reptile. "That was totally Donald's fault. We were going to do an in-store, in Chicago or something, somewhere in the Midwest, and we went to a novelty costume store in Manhattan, and we picked up a Godzilla outfit. It had a head and a suit and stuff, and we put it on our luggage, or maybe it was a carry-on. But we got to Chicago and we had to change planes. So we're waiting in Chicago, and Donald picks up the head, and puts it on and starts walking around the airport. And of course everybody is freaking out, pointing at each other, and it was very humorous, and I thought hey, I should do that in my drum solo. That would be really funny, because I was doing a drum solo in 'Godzilla.' So that's how that become part of my routine."

"And that Godzilla head, the same one, we ended up buying it from the company, from the store, where originally it was going to be a rental. I don't know what happened with the body; I think we threw it away. But if you look at it, it didn't really look that much like Godzilla. It looked like a horse's head, and it was kind of funny. It was made out of paper mache and was very hard, and somewhere along the nose was a screen that was painted the same colour. So that's how I could see out, even though, it was not where the eyes were; it was a whole different place. I didn't think it looked that realistic. It looked sort of corny, but actually, when I would use it in the drum solo, we'd have the lasers and we got the strobe lights and you couldn't see really see it that well."

"But once I left Blue Öyster Cult, I think Rick Downey wore it for a little while, although somehow… I don't know if Rick didn't like it, but somehow it got lost; it disappeared. So it didn't last through Downey's tenure on the drum throne. So it wasn't available when we first got the Brain Surgeons together. Actually, when Pete Bohovesky, our original guitar player… when he left the group, his mother had a puppet company, and they used to make full-bodied puppets, little ones too. Really awesome stuff. So I said, 'Would you make me a Godzilla head?' He said, 'I thought you'd never ask!' So he made me a Godzilla head out of foam, which would bend and everything and was much more lifelike, a lot of fun. He also said, 'I'm not going to make the scary Godzilla, the original Godzilla; I'm going to make the kind of mid-period… when Godzilla was really funny, with Godzilla baby and all of that' (laughs). The funny Godzilla. He says, 'I want to make a funny one. The song is funny.' I said, 'Yeah, yeah, it is.' So it's a funny Godzilla I've got now."

But was 'Godzilla' a song by a serious heavy metal band, or just some smart guys slumming? "You know, that's what Meltzer says," responds Albert. "'Oh, those guys, they weren't really a heavy metal band. They were jazzers that pretended to be heavy.' But I don't agree. We really did like that kind of music; we enjoyed playing it. I think there's this thing that Cliff Burnstein and Peter Mensch say about heavy metal, that it has to be made by young men who have no other option except to pump gas. I disagree. If you look at those Metallica guys, come on, those are not pumping any gas. You talk to Lars, and he's a very intelligent guy and he's reading Kierkegaard and all this stuff; I mean, come on. So are Mensch and Burnstein, so it's just a pose that heavy metal has to be dumb. I don't agree. You know you've got all kinds of interesting things happening now and even though metal, I don't think, is as popular now, there's a lot of very interesting metallic music coming out, tons that are putting out high quality music, in my opinion."

"'Godzilla' is a much bigger song today than it was back then," adds Joe. "We tried to get it on radio but I think there was a shift in Columbia Records. I think Clive was fired from Columbia. There were some nice people there, but they had other priorities and 'Godzilla' was not one of them. So we didn't get too much hit play on 'Godzilla'."

"'Godzilla' wasn't an AM hit," qualifies Sandy, "if you remember AM radio or have some vague recollection of it. But it was a huge AOR album-oriented radio hit, so it was an FM hit. I mean, I noticed that some of the fans despised 'Godzilla.' I don't know why, really. I haven't the slightest idea. But having said that, 'Godzilla' is a really heavy song, and in fact one of the reasons I wound up producing The Clash is they loved 'Godzilla' and 'The Reaper.' All of the bullshit about me being forced down their throats as a sellout to tailor them to the American market is nothing to do with anything. None of that's true. And they liked those records, and they also liked The Dictators, and that's when I wound up... they called up Patti Smith and she said, 'He's awesome.' They spoke to Andy Shernoff and Scott Kempner and they said, 'He's awesome' and they liked them, so let's go. What I'm trying to say is that 'Godzilla' was one of the biggest hits Blue Öyster Cult ever had. It was all over radio and by no means was it a lightweight song."

Next up on *Spectres* is the record's tour de force, 'Golden Age of Leather' oddly placed as track two, odd given its epic feel and ambitious lyric by Bruce Abbott. Al says the following, with respect to Abbott's connection with the band: "Bruce was Donald's college roommate. He was also in a lot of classes with me, because he was going to be a civil engineer, and Donald was an electrical engineer. So I was in all these classes with him and he said, 'You ought to meet my roommate! You guys would probably get along.' So he was the one who introduced me to Don Roeser."

This is the track Albert had called Queen-like. In the same shared vintage interview, Donald expressed skepticism, saying "I'd be very surprised if I heard that from Queen." Albert counters, "Sure, you hear all sorts of those harmonies, and it's sort of an opera, a mini-opera."

Sandy establishes the link with the 'Transmaniacon MC' thread. "Yes, it's definitely part of that storyline, although I didn't write it. Donald and Bruce Abbott did. And 'Shadow of California' can be seen as the final chapter. Whereas 'Transmaniacon MC' establishes the identity of a rogue sub-set of Hells Angels who are the catalyst for the evils perpetrated at Altamont, 'Golden Age of Leather' tells the tale of a motorcycle gang's final battle, a sort of violent, valiant, Viking suicide pact, in which the gang will choose a rag of either red or black, then fight unto death. 'Shadow of California' poses a symbolic visitation by bikers in a post-human, spiritual form."

Bolle adds, "Buck's friend Abbott co-wrote the song as the story of the dying legend of the motorcycles and their last fight, because in his mind, he thought the days of the Harleys were over. The Hells Angels as a 'race' era was dying completely. He started writing this poem during the oil embargo of 1974. He figured nobody would be driving a motorcycle after 1980. So that was his idea, his scheme, which he put into the context of a nice singable song for Donald."

In terms of the music, 'Golden Age of Leather' is a characteristically "light" metal BÖC saga, based on a couple of tidy riffs, neither very aggressive, one happy-go-lucky, one sinister but delicate, which lapse into nice harmony-laced passages and moderately prog rock sub-sections. It was also the usual selection during live shows to feature the band's trademark five-guitar assault, where every member of the band donned an axe for a big electric churn. All in all, it's a quintessentially late '70s-style commercial rocker reminiscent of the Kiss-Starz-Angel trinity.

One of the interesting features of the tune was the inclusion of the Newark Boys Choir. "Well, I have to give credit where credit is due," explains Al. "That was pretty much Murray Krugman's idea. He was always looking for ways to make the records extraordinary. That was his contribution, to put the Newark Boys Choir on. Donald had already had a vocal part that went there which was the same. But Murray thought using the choir would be a wilder thing. I guess there were about 20 kids. It was kind of funny. We did that particular part in the Record Plant, and all the studios were being used. At first they were going to put them in the mixing room, but obviously that was too small for all these kids, so they put them in this gigantic storage room they were going to make into a studio at some point which incidentally never happened. So they cleared it out; it was just cinder block walls, and they put them in there with some tie-lines. And only the conductor wore earphones, not the kids."

Brother Joe calls this a *Spectres* highlight. "Yes, probably the thing that made the biggest impression on me was bringing in the boys choir. I didn't think they were going to do it (laughs). It was just one of those things, because the Rolling Stones had the boys choir on 'You Can't Always Get What You Want,' and we thought we should have a choir on 'Golden Age of Leather'. It was a pretty involved record. And they had a bigger room in the back of the Record Plant, an unfinished room, and they had probably 25 young boys from Newark, New Jersey, all singing, 'Golden age!' It was really cool and interesting. Of course, it was a very expensive thing to do for about 14 notes, on an album, but we were rock stars, and we could afford it at the time. If I had known, probably, from the beginning, that we were going to do something like that, we might have set it up and got a better arrangement for it. But it does add a lot to the track."

Spectres' third track was a somber, stealth-like ballad called 'Death Valley Nights', lyrics by Richard Meltzer, music and vocals by Al Bouchard, who commented, "It's about loneliness. It covers a lot of ground, yet is really simple and trying to say something people can understand." Even though it's not, the song sounds more like a Joe or Allen composition, with its palpable air of the vampiric, and an (un)healthy dose of Allen's brooding keyboard work. It is one of three songs on *Spectres* superficially comparable with "The Reaper".

Al, discussing working with Meltzer, says, "That was done in a way that I did a lot of Richard's stuff. We worked on a lot of songs that have vanished into the sands of time. He would usually just send me an envelope with just some sort of funny letter. I've kept them all of course. He would tell me what's happening in his life, and he would include a bunch of lyrics. I had gotten those lyrics when he had already moved to California, and I knew from some other communications that he was having a hard time there. I mean, when he went out there it was like, 'New York sucks, and I hate this town and I'm glad to be moving out,' you know where he could be free blah blah blah. Then he gets out there and he hates it. I know for a fact that that was kind of a reaction to being lonely out there."

"I think that was my favourite of all the ones that I gave them," notes Richard. "I had moved to L.A., and had a girlfriend who fancied herself as a Manson girl. She had met some of the Manson people who hadn't been locked up just yet, like Squeaky Fromme and Sandra Good. She never met Charlie. And she was always insisting on taking me to Death Valley, where Charlie hung out. Let's go to Death Valley! I want to show you Charlie's hideouts, okay? But the lyric was more just a mood piece, a tone poem that I wrote at the time she took me to Death Valley. But there was a TV show called *Death Valley Days*, and it was a play on that also. I'm thinking that Ronald Reagan was on that show, actor Ronald Reagan, early '50s." Richard's right about Ronald Reagan, but on the show, which ran from 1952 to 1975, Reagan was the host in the mid-'60s.

Next up is the record's lone Allen Lanier track, 'Searching for Celine,' sort of a squalid-sounding, floundering, soft but perturbed funk number (lapsing opportunistically into disco) about arguably mad novelist Louis Ferdinand Celine. "That's another love song for lost poetry," comments Bolle. "Allen was quite clever there. It's a love song if you want. When Allen sings it on his demo, it's 'searching for his company,' because he's talking about the poet, but it's clever because Celine's also a French girl's name. When Eric sang it, he refused to sing about the poet, and it became primarily a type of love song."

Closing side two was Albert's breathless nightshade ballad 'Fireworks' which rivalled Donald's similar side two masterwerk 'I Love the Night' for mysterious, dark and ritualistic. This was the tune most compared to "Reaper" given its soft, guitar picking and its uptempo sense of determination and forward mass. The lyric encompasses all sorts of emotions resulting from what can be construed as forced marriage, forced love and/or forced sex, ranging from the traumatic to the orgasmic, to something supernatural. All in all, it's a chilling and intense Blue Öyster Cult classic.

Al clarifies, "To my knowledge, that's the only one of my lyrics that ever made it onto an album, or the only full song anyway, where it was all my lyrics. That was really about my relationship with this young lady who was particularly reserved. I was always writing songs to her, and it was my attempt to get her to loosen up a bit. The Record Plant, where we did both *Spectres* and *Agents of Fortune*, was big. They had four rooms, and it was right in the heart of Manhattan, so they were working all the time. We would be upstairs in Studio C, and Aerosmith would be in A, and Kiss would be in B. We would all be working at the same time. Or maybe it was Springsteen down in A or we would be mixing in D, and Bruce would be in C. So there was a lot of people, a lot of interaction. I remember Bruce and I hung out a lot, in those days. I remember he came to the mixing room and said, 'Oh, this song is a hit!' And this was 'Fireworks' which, of course as soon as he said that, I got obsessed with trying to make it radio-friendly. And I totally drove the mixing engineer crazy. Because he's like, 'Hey, this is what it sounds like. You know, you can't make it sound... it's what it is! I'm making it as good as it could be, for what it is. If you want more bass, the bass player's going to have to play it over. You know, put some more bass on. You're going to have to add something. Because I can't make something out of nothing.' Oh, we got into this big fight, and it never really got on the radio, really. But it was a good song, and a lot of people liked it."

What did you want to do with it?

"I just wanted to make it sound thicker. More like an Aerosmith song, something that just had that heft to it, instead of sounding thin and sort of aerated. It had this delicate kind of an Elektra Judy Collins sound (laughs)."

Side two of the original vinyl opened with a deceptively simple call to arms, 'R.U. Ready 2 Rock' becoming a live anthem on one level directly about the live experience, on another, a depiction of one of Sandy's shifts in history. "That's a very complex song actually, notwithstanding its title," explains Pearlman. "And the key there are some lines that weren't used for some reason. It was sort of my version of *Dune*. It was like in the future there would be a new religion, and the new religion would be born in the stars, born as a function of human beings reaching a state that would require trans-luminal morphed travel to reach. Once that had happened, there would be incredible insight as a function of being exposed to environments that couldn't be dreamed of before. New apocalyptic, messianic religions would arrive as a function of that experience. The ruler's son was basically seen as the Dune Messiah. Yeah, I guess it's the notion that new religions can arise as a function, not only of more conventional factors, but also as a function of technology. I guess I'm right, you know? (laughs). Looking at what's going on right now, I guess I'm right."

The song's initials R.U.R. were a reference to the K. Capek play, Rossum's Universal Robots, which was known to contain the first mention of the word "robot" in sci-fi literature. Al, alluding more to the early germination of the song, puts this slant on Sandy's thought process. "One Easter, Sandy was watching, I don't know, something like *The Greatest Story Ever Told* or *Jesus of Nazareth*, one of these stories about Jesus' life, and he somehow got this idea that the whole thing was about sex, for some reason. That song was his reaction. But the tune took about a year to write and it really went through a lot of changes, going through about five major revisions in the lyrics. It was one of those songs where I contributed a line here, a line there. 'Flaming Telepaths' was another one like that."

Next up was 'Celestial the Queen' a rousing, blustery pop tune from the quirky pens of Joe Bouchard and Helen Wheels, also sung by Joe. It was a typically opaque siren song from an ever-expanding chorus line of female temptress songs, Helen offering that "Those lyrics came to me one dawn walking home from CBGB's. It just came to me. I guess I sent those lyrics to Joe as poem. He sent me back an eight-track tape or something, and it became one of their numbers. I love that one."

"I just traced that down," laughs Joe on the mechanics of the track. "If you had asked me that question about a month ago, I wouldn't be able to tell you. It actually started as a demo. The original title I had was 'Seize the Time'. It sounded very much like a Byrds/Beatles-type of song; that's how it was presented to the band. But they definitely didn't like the lyric, so I stripped off the lyric for 'Seize the Time' and put on 'Celestial the Queen'. That still didn't work. Then I found a cassette that I had recorded on the road in a hotel somewhere, where I'd written this riff that became the chords of the song. I put that with Helen's 'Celestial the Queen' lyric and hey, it worked. The mix is a little muddy on that one, and there are parts of the form that don't jive too well. If I had really wanted to write a pop song, I wouldn't have written it that way. But at that time I didn't care; just write the song the best I could."

"I had a break from the tour," adds Joe, reminiscing on the chain of events a few years after the previous missives. "We were supposed to be playing in Canada, actually, and the Western Canada dates were cancelled, so I came home a couple days early, and came up with 'Celestial the Queen' and 'Nosferatu' in a couple of days. Helen Wheels sent me the lyrics and they were sitting on my piano, and I just sat down and worked out the songs in a couple of days. I don't remember actually getting the guys a demo. But there supposedly is a demo of the recording, but I don't recall giving them one—it came out pretty well, both of those."

"But yeah, basically, they needed two more songs to finish the two songs with Helen, 'Celestial the Queen' and 'Nosferatu' says Joe. "It was pretty good. I am not the kind of guy that has to be the focal point of the group. Usually it was a team effort. The writer usually sang the song that they brought to the table. I didn't usually collaborate with Donald because he would come in with fully formed songs. There was no need to say, 'You need to change that' as the songs were done. The '(Don't Fear) The Reaper' demo just blew us away. That raised the bar considerably. It was a blessing and a curse! At that point we wanted to make different kinds of albums and follow up on that kind of success. I am very content with my little corner of the band and I would say that *Spectres* is probably my favourite overall album that we did."

Allen, back in February of '78, alluded to the break in the band's schedule as well, saying, "The second time we got better sounds out of the studio. There seemed to be more energy coming right out of the road and back into the studio. It's too bad we're not good writers on the road. It would be a great way to use the time, but we're people who germinate the ideas best at home."

Offering a survey of the album and the environs of its recording, Joe figures, "'I Love the Night' was a nice song. I felt that that could've been a hit. We spent a lot of time getting the feel right on that. This was the first album where we would work on just one track, for more than one day. Normally we could get two or three tracks in, in a session—like the way people used to make records. But by the time we got to *Spectres*, we decided that we were going to be very certain that we had the basic tracks. So I think certainly 'Godzilla' took two days—we had 54 takes on 'Godzilla.' Like I say, 'Nosferatu' and 'Celestial the Queen' were written after most of the album was done. It was like a very quick thing."

Do you remember any guests coming by the studio, crazy parties, bands next door?

"Well, we shared a studio with Aerosmith. I think they were cutting a surroundsound version of 'Walk this Way' or something, during the day, and we were cutting 'Godzilla' at night. So we would run into them in the hallway. Maybe it was something else. I remember Steven would come out with this clipboard, saying, 'You know, I've got to fix these lyrics.' Of course, I didn't want to go there, but I should have made a comment (laughs). We didn't have a lot of crazy parties there; it was an expensive studio. One of our roadies had a little run-in with Gene Simmons. Kiss was using the studio downstairs. One of our roadies would be out front, and there would be all these Kiss fans lined up, to try to get an autograph. I think one time, he said to one of the fans, 'So what is Gene Simmons' real name?' These fans didn't know, and he said, 'Well, I could tell you.' Then Gene found out about that and got really mad. He was going to beat up this guy, Ronald Binder, and so, we almost got to fisticuffs (laughs). But then, David Lucas, who was helping us with the production on that record went down and said, 'Okay, stop being like little kids.' So in the end, I think we sent Kiss a big tray of oysters, and they sent us a big bushel basket of candy kisses. I'm pretty sure this was during *Spectres*, as it was definitely The Record Plant."

Same story. Different Bouchard. "I don't remember the oysters, but I do remember, what happened was, it wasn't really a roadie. He was sort of our mascot. He wrote lyrics; he was the road manager for Helen Wheels, and he wrote lyrics, and he wrote a song on, geez, he wrote songs for every record, but he wrote several songs for *Spectres*. I think he wrote a song for *Agents of Fortune* that never got recorded. I mean, demos, but it didn't make the record. Ronald Binder. Anyway, he was coming into the studio. We were up there working, and he was walking into the building, and Gene Simmons was there signing autographs, with a whole bunch of fans. Ronald came by, and Gene kind of sneered at Ronald. Because you know, Gene was big, and Ronald was very little, and Gene was like a rock god. Ronald was a little schlocky guy, and he gave Ronald a look that made him mad, and he did something that was probably not cool. He said, 'You guys, you think this Gene Simmons is so great. Well, he's just a schoolteacher from Queens. His real name is Chiam Klein.' With that, Gene was like, 'How dare you disrespect my fans!' He started running after Ronald, and Ronald ran into the elevator and closed the door. So Gene came up to the studio, and Ronald was running in... 'Gene Simmons is after me! Gene Simmons is after me!' (laughs), and Gene comes in, 'Where is he? Where is he?' It was pretty funny."

Back to the record, the pop continued unabated with a surprise Eric Bloom track co-written with Ian Hunter called 'Goin' Through the Motions,' which glimmers with glam. Eric explains: "That's an interesting collaboration because Mott and BÖC were playing together quite a bit in the '70s. Ian and I got to be friends, both of us ending up living in Connecticut. He came over to my house and I opened up a really good bottle of port and we shared the bottle and said why don't we write a tune? So we went down to the basement where we had our little band set-up and we wrote that tune. It was fun. That Mott influence is definitely there. Without him, that song wouldn't even exist. He'd always had an idea for a song called 'Goin' Through the Motions,' so that title's his. Some of the music came from me and some of the lyrics came from me, so it wound up being a 50-50 deal. What was neat about that was that the song wound up being covered by Bonnie Tyler on her *Faster than the Speed of Night* album."

"It sounds sort of like P.J. Proby. It's the story of a relationship built not on love, but merely on the physical," laughs Albert. "Really heavy. Eric felt bad that he didn't have any songs so they got together and knocked that one out in an afternoon. We almost had to force him not to sing in a British accent (laughs)." "'Goin' Through the Motions' is what it is," adds Sandy. "We put more work into making 'Goin' Through the Motions' than probably the whole of the rest of the record."

Eric got to brush up on his keyboard playing in the construction of the song. "Ian played keyboards on the first demo, but it didn't come out good enough, so I had to sit down and figure out what the hell he was playing by ear, 'cos I wasn't watching. I had to listen on the headphones for about three hours and pick it apart, note-by-note on the string synthesizer. It was tough on the bridge." Eric would eventually guest cameo on one of Ian's projects, adding background vocals to Hunter's hit record *You're Never Alone with a Schizophrenic* from 1979. He was credited as Eric Bloome.

"'Goin' Through the Motions' was actually the single," recalls Joe—and in fact, it was even used as an encore track, just before obvious closer '(Don't Fear) The Reaper'. "We tried to make 'R.U. Ready 2 Rock' a hit, but it didn't connect. I think to me, it's just one of those songs that has too many sections in it—a little too complex. So the single was 'Goin' Through the Motions,' where you have a co-written song with Ian Hunter. Great writer, nice to have Ian's vibe in one of our tunes, but that didn't connect either. They really pushed that, and I think at that point we thought, well, we have one smash hit and that's probably it. But you know, that's more than the Grateful Dead had."

Donald's 'I Love the Night' was far and away the record's crown jewel, very likely one of the most distilled and beautiful compositions of the entire BÖC canon. "I think 'I Love The Night' is one of the greatest songs ever written by anybody anywhere," agrees Sandy. "It's a tribute to how lame Columbia Records was, that they weren't able to do anything with the song. In fact they didn't even try to do anything with the song (laughs), so I shouldn't say. It was just, 'Wow guys, this is a smash.' And it's the kind of smash that if you do get it to go, will ensure that these guys will sell millions of records for the foreseeable future. I don't think they understood that. I don't think they understood how much it exemplified a really, pretty clear image of this vampire-like subconscious that everybody has. This is an eternal recurrent theme. And I thought that Buck had totally encapsulated the entire vampire-oid myth into some extraordinarily beautiful language, and then created an extraordinarily beautiful musical framework to launch the language out at you. It really is a sort of Moreau dreamscape, or Redon dreamscape. It's pretty amazing. And it didn't really go anywhere. Columbia didn't get it." According to Bolle, this song's original demo contains a third verse not used on the album, which nevertheless saw the artificial light of night during selected live renditions.

Sandy continues on the worthiness of *Spectres*, opining that, "Up until 1978, we got a very good result out of Columbia, then they changed some of the upper and middle management people. They thought they knew better than me or Murray or the band. Essentially, they buried *Spectres*. It still sold, but it should've sold a lot more copies." Continuing his praise for 'I Love the Night' Sandy offers that, "Donald has written five or six songs of genius, maybe more. Maybe seven, including 'Harvest Moon.' But I thought 'I Love the Night' was an incredibly great fusion of form and function; very convincing and very disturbing. One of the great vampire odes."

Spectres closes with the record's second mini-epic, namely 'Nosferatu', another Helen Wheels/Joe Bouchard collaboration, also sung by Joe. Allen's classical ivories are ever-present as Joe croons one of his signature vampire tales, thematically consolidating the record's ghostly themes within a storyline that is familiar to all, texturing the track with light and heavy passages, building it to a crescendo that emphasizes the old world, sci-fi drama of the trusty vampire legend. The lines 'Rats in the hold. My crew is dead—I fear the plague' are from the captain's log shown in the original *Nosferatu* silent film, which was logically enough Helen's inspiration for the lyric.

"I always specialized in a lot of vampire, gothic stuff at that time," relates Helen, "and they actually said that if you've got any of that stuff, send it over. And I had re-watched the original *Nosferatu* film. It's a silent movie, with those really long, long nails. So I watched it again and wrote the song that night."

"Allen did do a great piano part on 'Nosferatu'," recalls Joe. "And I did the

Chamberlain, which is the mellotron. So every once in awhile I would get a few licks in on the piano or one of the keyboards. Allen was always pretty protective of his parts in the band. I on the other hand, would do anything, whether it was just playing the bass or adding a guitar part or adding an odd keyboard part here and there. I have a degree in classical piano from Ithaca College, so there were times when something keyboard-wise did not fit Allen's style. Allen has a style that is kind of quirky, and one of the conventional things that he does do very well is play a sort of honky-tonk piano. He didn't do much of that, but he can do it very well, probably better than me. But in the more classical style of keyboards, you know, where melodic things have to be done, or just a certain background part, I would do a few of those. But it was always contentious. I did piano on 'Morning Final'. Actually, I think I did two piano parts; I did a grand piano and I did an electric piano part. But I would say to Allen, 'Okay, you do the organ part, and that will even things off'."

While putting the final touches on the record, Albert was optimistic about its chances. "By the time we return to the States, the album will be out, and it's definitely more rocking than *Agents*. We'll do even better than last year, which was a great year. I don't know if we'll knock The Who or Zeppelin off the top of the heap. We're not trying to conquer the world and we don't have a Cult Army. We're just trying to give our best." The Cult Army comment is a reference to Kiss and their overwhelming success with the Kiss Army fan club, first trumpeted with the release of *Destroyer* in 1976. BÖC in interviews would often compare themselves with both Kiss and Aerosmith, citing both as examples of how to succeed in rock 'n' roll, both as contemporaries with similar modest origins to their own.

And whether "best" was achieved is argued to this day, *Spectres* yielding no singles anywhere near the stature of "The Reaper," while creatively triumphing with songs like 'I Love the Night,' 'Death Valley Nights' and 'Fireworks'. Additionally, 'R.U. Ready 2 Rock' and 'Godzilla' became trusty concert highlights, essential in shaping and pacing the band's live set list. Sales were acceptable, the record fairly brisk in its attainment of gold status, hovering around 750,000 to 800,000 now years later. Chart-wise, the album achieved a No.60 placement in the US, and No.43 in the UK. Neither of the two US singles—'Goin' Through the Motions'/'Searching for Celine' or 'I Love the Night'/'Nosferatu'—made the charts, nor did any of the mix-and-match UK issues.

"After 'Reaper' and *Spectres* we started getting a little bit more retrospective about what we should be doing or what we shouldn't be doing," reflects Joe. "*Agents of Fortune* was pretty much, okay, let's just go with the best songs that we have. We'd probably given up on having a big, big hit. And 'Reaper' just came out of the pile as a miracle. And I don't think we thought about who was selling, although, I mean, we were always sort of jealous of Aerosmith's success. Because we would go platinum, they would go double platinum. They were always like twice ahead of us. But there's probably other reasons for that. You know, they made nice records and Steven happens to be an inspired singer."

"Ted Nugent, we understood where he was coming from but that wasn't our style. Maybe Deep Purple would be a closer sort of comparison. I know people have said to me recently, 'Oh, you know, my favourite bands are Deep Purple and

Blue Öyster Cult.' And I said it's funny you say that because out of all the bass players out there, I think that Roger Glover... I'm really close to his style of bass playing. And they're a little more, working class type. Which is great fun. We thought of ourselves more the sort of martini-drinking intellectuals as opposed to the beer-drinking middle class guys."

But a palpable seed of restlessness would be planted, with the band (after a quick live record) hitting the panic button in their quest for higher commercial plateaus. "We felt like *Spectres* was a failure," asserts Albert. "Of course while recording it, we felt that every song was a hit, which of course never happened. And even though it sold 750,000 copies, we just felt like, 'Oh, we're over, we're finished, we've had it, we'll never have another hit!' They didn't really lose any money on *Spectres*, but we felt bad about it."

The 2007 reissue of *Spectres* included four bonus tracks; highlight being slinky piano-tinkled rocker 'Night Flyer'. "I believe the original title was 'Night Rider'," remembers Joe. "That's pretty obscure. It was Donald's idea to change it to 'Night Flyer'. At the time that that was conceived of, Donald I think came up with a way to fix it. It was a time when there was a lot of drug smuggling at night in small planes, and that was basically the story there."

'Dial M for Murder' sung by Eric and Hammond-pulsed by Allen, rides a bit of a jumpy new wave vibe. Says Joe, "I know the idea was from Murray Krugman. There was a movie out at the time called that, and Murray pretty much came in and wrote the lyrics; I know it was an improvement when Murray wrote the lyrics."

"'Please Hold'—that is completely Allen Lanier's work," recalls Joe, on another quirky original, this one sounding retro like Stalk-Forrest Group. "I made some suggestions, to improve the bonus tracks—they were rejected (laughs). I mean, this is just recently. Because I thought that it was really incomplete. There are two ways to look at bonus tracks. You can just leave them raw, what they were, or you can sort of put yourself back in the frame of mind of that era, and say, you know, it really needed background vocals. And they decided not to put them on. Plus I also have a version where I played percussion on it. So it would've had percussion and background vocals."

Finally, there's '60s cover 'Be My Baby'. "Yes, that one, before I joined Blue Öyster Cult, they were going through their transition from having Les as a singer to having Eric as a singer. And so they were experimenting with different styles, and doing cover tunes to see how to get the best out of Eric's voice. And even before I joined the band, they were playing 'Be My Baby' and they did an absolutely note-perfect version. The version you hear on the reissue is not our best performance of that song. But Eric could really sing the most incredible vocal on that one. And so we kept playing it at sound checks, and what you hear there is a very raw rehearsal tape, of the song. That's another one that I had wished we had spruced up the bonus track, to give it a little more feeling of what I felt, when I used to hear the Soft White Underbelly play it—it was incredible. They had chosen some really odd covers to play, back before Les left the group. There were a couple of R&B things that Eric could do really well, stuff that Les couldn't do at all. So that's how 'Be My Baby' ended up being on the bonus tracks."

With respect to his stated "medium kind of way" involvement in the reissue program, Eric explains that, "They had to put them on these vintage playback machines and listen to everything, track by track. That's some chore. Maybe there are two songs per reel, so they had to go back and listen to all the multi-tracks and see what's there. I'm really glad they found those never-heard-before tracks, and the quickie take of 'Be My Baby,' which, to me, is the most fun thing on there. 'Dial M for Murder' and 'Please Hold' have the original vocals, but Buck did a new vocal on 'Night Flyer' because there was no vocal on it. When these songs go by the wayside as you're recording, it becomes obvious which songs are going to make it and which ones are not. So we drop all work on those and not waste our time. There might not be any background harmonies, lead guitar, or vocals when we stop working on songs. We put down bass and drums, and maybe a couple of guitar parts. The only thing we might keep is the bass and drums, and then layer everything up later. The last things to go on a record would be lead guitar and lead vocal. So these songs were dropped before that actually happened. I did not re-sing anything, and I know Allen didn't re-sing anything."

The lion's share of the tour dates for 1977 constituted, in fact, a victory lap for the success of *Agents of Fortune*. Normally, the band would present a record at the beginning of the year and then support it, but this cycle, the new album was not delivered to the masses until November, with the break in tour dates to execute recording taking place in the summer of '77. The first half of the year found BÖC continuing to hammer the US but also mounting a decent Canadian campaign, supported by band buddy Todd Rundgren and his starkly weird Utopia. Multiple dates were also logged with Rush, Piper, Atlanta Rhythm Section and Derringer. In October, the band consummated its most extensive pairing ever when they roamed the west supported by Black Oak Arkansas—BÖC with BOA. Closing the year in the Midwest found them playing with Edgar Winter, Detective and local Detroit favourites The Rockets, led by hard guitar pioneer Jim McCarty.

Naturally then, most of 1978 was also taken up with the *Spectres* tour, the band playing multiple dates with Rush, Angel, The Godz and Be-Bop Deluxe in the states before transitioning to Europe, where they played two English legs supported by art rockers Japan, and mainland Europe supported by John Cougar. Back in the US, the band played extensively with Cheap Trick, UFO, Thin Lizzy and Mott the Hoople offshoot band British Lions to close out the year, amidst a September release for the band's second live album.

On playing Europe, Joe notes that, "It was expensive to go there and you didn't know if you would be able to draw. It's just a whole different culture over there, and things that would catch on in the United States would not necessarily catch on over there. For starters, radio's kind of different over there. We concentrated on promoting our albums to radio in the States, and if there was anything happening over in Europe it was just like word-of-mouth, as far as I could tell. And then finally in 1978, 'Reaper' was a hit for the second time in England, and we did a tour of England where we sold out every seat in every hall—a great way to go on tour. You could feel that radio in England, it took them two years, but they finally came around and said, 'Oh, we gotta play this record.' We did take our lasers over there, and half the time they wouldn't let us use them. It was frustrating. I didn't worry about the production end, pretty much. I always felt that, you know, if we put on a good show, our songs would carry us through."

Marbled throughout such a hectic schedule, there are interviews to be done, within the parameters of which Buck took the opportunity to publicly express his reservations about Blue Öyster Cult's embarrassment of riches when it came to songwriting depth, noting that all the variety of personalities tended to dissipate some of the focus when it came to presenting a common front. "It was a strength and a problem too. Most bands have one singer and one attitude. With BÖC, you've got the Buck stuff, the Bloom stuff, you've got the heavy stuff. It's a little diffuse for most marketing people to grasp. They want some simple, coherent concept, which we didn't have. BÖC's always had a little more depth than that, while not having a really strong focus. That's probably been to our detriment, in terms of selling us."

Eric looks back somewhat agitated, "Who's to say why a hit's a hit? In my opinion it was a couple of untapped songs, for example 'I Love the Night,' which is similar to 'The Reaper' in tone. But then nobody asked me for my opinion."

Some Enchanted Evening

"Cranked-up in your souped-up hot rod"

Blue Öyster Cult's live show was getting bigger than the band's collective wallets. David Infante of Laser Physics Inc. had been hired, starting with the '76 tour, at great expense to crank BÖC's live show to the next level with the pioneering introduction of a choreographed laser show. By 1978, the ever-expanding system had become a bit of an albatross. Reports on cost varied from $200,000 for the original system, growing to twice that amount by the time the *Spectres* spectacle hit the road. Another report pegged the cost at $300,000, while still another UK piece stated that the system brought to the UK was worth £200,000.

Whatever the final bill, it was a lot of money for a still-breaking band. Comprising four computer-controlled lasers in its final incarnation (including a light source attached to Eric's wrists), the system had been getting bad press over a Food and Drug Administration study which was investigating possible eye damage. The band played it straight and obtained FDA approval for the system. But despite FDA blessing, on the band's LA stop, the Forum still placed limitations on the show, stating that no light from the band's huge mirror ball could hit the audience. Bloom at the time griped, "They are the only hall in the country making us do this, even though the FDA has completely approved our system."

"Pearlman actually found a laserist doing a laser show in a loft in Manhattan," explains Eric with respect to the idea's origins. "He said that we had to come down and see it. We were flush from all the money from 'Reaper' being a big hit. We said, 'Let's do it.' It cost us a fucking fortune! In those day, having a big stage show was what you did. After a year, year-and-a-half, we stopped; it was breaking our backs financially. Lasers may be road-able today, but in those days, they weren't at all. We were carrying around huge, scientific lasers that should not be moved. We were schlepping them in a semi and setting them up in a different city every day! The tube cost six grand every time it broke and it would break all the time. It cost two grand to ship it back to where it was from. It was nuts. We did it for a year-and-a-half and then sort of kissed it goodbye."

"To make a long story short, we had the bucks in the bank from *Agents*," reiterated Eric, years later in an interview with *Vintage Rock*'s Shawn Perry. "Pearlman said he'd found this guy who had this outrageous laser show. He charged admission and you'd go into his loft and watch him do laser light and different things that nobody is doing. I had seen lasers in a rock show twice. I saw Wings—which was about the best laser show I ever saw—and I saw Led Zeppelin and they had a pencil light go over Jimmy Page's head during the guitar lead. It was still very cool and no one had ever done it before, so this was the real beginning. When I saw what this guy did, I said, 'Wow.' Pearlman said, 'Well, it's going to be expensive. Do you really wanna do it?' And I said, 'Absolutely.' So we jumped on it. It was good and bad on some levels. It got us some notoriety and made our show quite outrageous. On the other hand, the expense was crushing. After a year-and-a-half or so, we stopped doing it. OSHA sent a representative to several shows for several weeks, measuring the light during sound check, making reports. At the end of our tour, our laserist went to Washington to meet with a panel and was presented with reports on why we couldn't use the lasers any more. So that was another reason to get rid of it. It was dangerous. There are apocryphal stories out there. Someone said to me, 'I heard you got sued for blinding some guy.' But that never happened."

In any event, the shine had worn off. "I wouldn't have rented these expensive lighting systems," says Murray Krugman in retrospect. "I didn't want to do the lasers. I wanted to save as much money from the road, and give them more time off to write better material. It was a radical difference of opinion, and it happened right after they made it big. Sandy rented the Led Zeppelin lighting system, got these huge lasers. I felt they could have justifiably gone out in jeans and t-shirts like the Rolling Stones had done, not do this super huge production."

Allen: "You just get sick and tired of having to worry about the endless hassle of technology as well as having to go out and play every night. Well, the albatross is off my neck. They're gone." Eric also conveyed weariness with the whole thing, "There were a number of reasons we stopped the lasers. Obviously cost was one. But we also felt we'd come to rely on them too much in our show. But the lasers had also been declared dangerous by the US government. They had scientists monitoring them for a month, checking on possible damage to the eyes. They were really overprotective. They'd presume we'd be stupid enough to direct a pencil-thin beam directly at the crowd. They even came up with this scenario that the controller might have a heart attack!"

"They were a big hassle," continues Albert. "I mean, number one, they would get so hot, and we used to have to run hoses from the mens room or the ladies room or whatever, to cool them off with water. They were water-cooled. And water would just come through the pipes, and just go out into the parking lot, so there was always a big puddle of water after the thing. And the mirrors had to vibrate so that the laser wouldn't stay on any particular spot too long—if it went in somebody's eye, it would only be there for a fraction of a second, a microsecond, and there would be no danger of anybody getting burned by the laser, because they totally could burn you if they stopped moving. So there were always these issues. They would have these motors and the mirrors would be mounted on a shaft and it would fly off, or the motor would seize, and it was sort of a cob job, you know? But they were really powerful. I have to say, when we started having the lasers, I would dream about them. Before the lasers, I don't ever remember having vivid colour dreams. Ever since then, I dream in colour, in vivid colour.

It's weird and very cool. Yeah, I don't know, it affected me in some way that I can't quite explain—it triggered a colour part of my brain that never changed."

Finally Albert opines, "Yeah, we paid for it, it cost us a fortune, and my son's college education went down the drain. But hey, live and learn. It's okay, he's going to go to college anyway! Both of them will!"

Bolle Gregmar offered a few particulars on the system's operation. "The hand laser was delivered via a thin plastic hose that was run up Eric's body and along his arm, but just for 'Astronomy.' The little shooters at the end of 'Flaming Telepaths' were simple flint shooters that were attached to his hand like a ring. A squeeze on the trigger would get the spark going. Simple!"

But notwithstanding the cost of touring, crowds had been good, no doubt in small part drawn by the band's brave new technology, which also included a full quad system at this point. Sandy had figured that given the relatively poor sales of *Spectres*, it might be good to take the offensive and unleash another live album, arguably prematurely, but in hindsight anything but. *Some Enchanted Evening*, released in September of 1978, only ten months after *Spectres*, remains the band's second biggest selling record, eventually going platinum, rising to No.18 on the US *Billboard* charts, although only No.44 in the UK.

Sandy: "*Some Enchanted Evening* is probably their biggest triumph for one reason or another. It just set loose a series of events that made them into one of the biggest live bands in the universe. It really sold well. They didn't believe in it by the way. They were really pissed off that I was forcing them to make this record, which I believed in. At the same time I was making The Clash's *Give 'Em Enough Rope* record, which of course, they couldn't care less about. That's when the disenchantment became really heavy. So that's it. They resented me working with The Clash, which is kind of beyond my comprehension, why that was a problem. I felt that it didn't really divert attention from Blue Öyster Cult."

Al vigorously confirms the band's resentment. "Yes! (laughs). In a word, yes. We felt like he was letting everything fall apart on our end. Also, he would go on and on about how great these guys were, and we thought they were just kind of jerky, and they were just doing all this pot, because by this time we were distancing ourselves from the drug scene."

"When the Sabbath thing came along in '80," Al continues, "we weren't as ticked off. Because to tell you the truth, by that time we had other people to take care of our business. We had Martin Birch, and it was fine, you know… get Sandy out of our hair."

Sandy also had continued his work with The Dictators, in addition to producing Pavlov's Dog and Shakin' Street, a female-fronted metal band that cranked two personable hard rock records, *Vampire Rock* and smoother sophomore *Shakin' Street*. "And as far I was concerned The Dictators gig was fine too, because I love those guys," notes Al. "I thought that they were a terrific band. I thought that all of them, or most of them, were very, really nice people, especially Andy and Blum (a.k.a. Handsome Dick Manitoba), and I've been friends with them for many years, so I didn't mind."

So *Some Enchanted Evening* was in part conceived as an answer to naysayers that felt *On Your Feet or on Your Knees* was either half-baked, too long, or merely the product of an inexperienced band with limited chops, dodgy material or both.

The band's confidence was certainly at a higher plateau, given that the band had been gigging solid since *Spectres* (apparently there are no overdubs on this record whatsoever). Taking role call, five tracks were recorded in the American south (Atlanta, Columbus and Little Rock) in April of '78, while two tracks were recorded in Britain two months later—which doesn't exactly sit right with this most American of bands, but there you go.

Without missing a beat, Eric had announced, "I'm not honking my own horn, but it is a totally amazing album." Perhaps supporting and reinforcing Murray Krugman's opinion that the band's deterioration was due to too much time on the road, and not enough time to write songs, Eric sighed, "We've been on the road straight since last October, and it will be a full year by the time we get back from our tour of Japan. But we'll spend as much time as we have to on the road. It's the only way we can pay ourselves."

Allen, however, speaks for most of the band in terms of their generally upbeat attitude towards live rock 'n' roll: "Obviously it's a lot of fun, or we wouldn't do it. I can't think of anything that's better. There's always that great illusion of power, being in rock 'n' roll. I still feel it, I do. When you get onstage, it's an enormous rush. I still think that rock 'n' roll bands, more than anything else that's happened in show business, actually do have political power and political influence. If nothing else, just in a cultural sense, the way one lives."

But Allen is also quick to lodge the usual road-weary complaints. "It's such an isolated life. You're on the airplane; at the hotel... you really need a more broad-based approach to what the world is. That's why I don't get along with a lot of people in rock 'n' roll. You just have to watch some people perform to know how closeted they are, how terribly protected people are in this life. And art doesn't come from that type of isolation." Speaking somewhat more cynically, Buck offers, "There are maybe five major cities in the United States that are really nice to play. The rest of them are just where people live."

Getting philosophical, Allen opines, "Well, no matter what, rock 'n' roll continues, you know what I mean? It will always have that preposterous aspect. It makes no sense. Like, everybody in rock 'n' roll is a gifted amateur, and you have to kick your ass all the time to do it. At least I do. I get the feeling that's the case with most of the bands I know. Sometimes it just seems the most ridiculous thing in the world. We did a stadium date for about 40,000 people, and I just thought, what in the world are these 40,000 people doing here? You're not like Caruso or something. I mean, you can go up there and not be sure why they came. But, you do as well as you can to prove to them that they should be there. Somehow, by the ambiance of their feedback, they prove that yes, there's a reason for them being there, and it's because they're actually having a good time. What else could be better?"

Expanding on the band's relative success, Allen offered this perspective. "One of the biggest things we've already won, is that we're the first band to prove you could be a big city, New York, East Coast band and be successful. I guess the Eagles are still selling records, but I think we made a place for that whole Anxious City depression thing, as opposed to the Eagles. I'm really proud of that."

"It's always been a matter of transcendence," mused Allen, in a separate chat. "No matter what idea you have, no matter what concept you have, when you perform on stage, the idea is to transcend it, because it's simply not a rational medium. I don't mean this to sound pretentious, but the only parallel I've ever found for it is like a religious ritual. It goes beyond the words that you're actually singing or beyond what you're playing." And later... "The road really wipes out all the bullshit. You can't go out on the stage every night thinking of this great concept. You simply have to do it, play and sing it."

Added Donald in the same Spring '78 interview, "I think we're just coming into our own now as singers. We're just starting; I mean the group. Eric has always had the best pipes in the group. But we all want to feel our oats, and I think we're starting to now."

Also, apropos of the times, Donald attempted to posit that, "*Tyranny and Mutation* would stand today as a good example of new wave music. And here it was recorded in 1972. Except the lyrical subject matter is a little more esoteric than the standard punk fare. But sonically I think it's right in the groove there, and it's a good example of what's happening now."

Back in the real world, *Some Enchanted Evening*'s cover art was another elegant illustration, done for the band by T.R. Shorr. It depicted a (very fearful) Reaper on horseback, BÖC symbol faithfully in place as part of the horse's bridle, this imposing duo in full gallop over a moonscape ('Astronomy?'), which is part of the painting on the front cover, and rendered as a photograph on the back: Another striking presentation.

The record opens with 'R.U. Ready 2 Rock' featuring an odd but warm, laid-back almost funky arrangement, Allen's ivory tinklings to the fore. Next comes 'E.T.I.' followed by the record's only oldie, 'Astronomy' which many feel is the definitive recording of the tune, live or studio. Side two opens with MC5 anthem 'Kick Out the Jams' which by nature, is a hard song to improve drastically or blow. BÖC does neither, marching through it in fine fashion. Next up is 'Godzilla' followed by the band's real monster hit '(Don't Fear) The Reaper'.

Closing the record is 'We Gotta Get Out of this Place', another paean to past influences, bottom line a boring tune, BÖC by virtue of their timeframe keeping up their tradition of going back into the '60s for their covers, this one an (appropriately) Doorsy pop hit from Eric Burdon and the Animals. Trivia note No.1: the version of this song on the original CD issue is from a different show (London vs. Newcastle) than that which occurs on the original vinyl and cassette; a simple error, the tapes somehow becoming switched. Trivia note No.2: flipside to the US single release of 'We Gotta Get Out of This Place' is a live version of 'Stairway to the Stars' while the UK issue gets 'E.T.I.'—neither charted in their respective territories.

Notes Albert, "We put out 'We Gotta Get Out of this Place' as a single and that really didn't do very much because, frankly, even though it was a great live tune and we always did it live ever since we started from our cover band days, it just was not better than the Animals' version. So if they wanted to hear that song, they'd play The Animals. But it did get some play for a little while. They gave it a shot."

"I think we had played that in a few clubs," notes Joe, of this well-known rock standard. "But one of the first big shows we did in California, in Long Beach, was a moment where I thought, 'Oh my God, we're really doing well.' Because the opening act was Eric Burdon. So we're doing a sound check for that show, and so we decide that we're going to, as a goof, in the sound check, play 'We Gotta Get Out of this Place,' and it really came out great. Eric Burdon's crew came out to us after we did the sound check and they said, 'Boy, you guys play that better than Eric Burdon!' So not only was it a thrill to feel like one of your idols is opening your show for you, but that Eric Burdon's crew thought we played really well. So I think we kept thinking about that, and we would play it every once in awhile, just as an extra encore or something, or sound check, and then we decided to record it. I think it was a good decision. Ted Nugent told me that he loves the bass sound on that. It's one of the few times I've had a really good conversation with Ted. He said, 'The bass on that song—pretty good!'"

Speaking of bass, the enhanced CD issue of *Some Enchanted Evening* from 2007 includes, among other things, a Joe Bouchard bass solo. "Yes, that's part of the bonus material. I'm glad that that came out. I've heard comments that bass solos are the bad predecessor to a bad drum solo (laughs). But I'm very proud of it. I used to play some incredible bass solos. I mean, not trying to pump myself up, but it was a moment in the show when maybe the material, the set list, was etched in stone, and it was my one moment where I could really improvise. So every bass solo was different, I had a few key things that I would bring in at critical moments of the solo, to make sure that the audience was with me, but a lot of that is improvised, and it was a lot of fun every night. I think once again, when we decided that it was getting tired and we didn't do the bass solo, I was getting very itchy that I should be doing other things."

The 2007 issue also includes a bonus live DVD, digipak packaging, a bunch of new photos, plus, on the CD, bonus tracks 'ME 262', 'Harvester of Eyes', 'Hot Rails to Hell', 'This Ain't the Summer of Love', '5 Guitars', 'Born to Be Wild', and 'We Gotta Get Out of this Place (Alternate Version)'. '5 Guitars' contains Joe's nearly four-minute solo, but the highlight here is 'Summer of Love' which gets an intimate and greasy treatment due to Albert's military snare beat, a new circular bass line from Joe, and funky organ out of Allen.

As additional trivia involving this album, the liner notes credit additional percussion to two of the road crew, Tony Cedrone and Rickey Reyer. As well, the record was to include yet another '60s cover, 'Be My Baby' by The Ronettes, which was scuttled a mere week before the record was finished.

Notes Bloom on the bonus DVD, "It's one show from Capitol Center, near Washington D.C. We headlined there several times. I'm guessing, but I think it's the feed from the Jumbotron in the arena. It looks like someone bounced that feed back to a Sony U-matic tape at the time, which was state-of the-art back in those days. That cartridge was found somewhere and it had the live show on it. It sounds like a board balance to me, in other words, whatever our soundman was feeding to the PA went directly to the tape. There are no nuances, there's no mixing, there's no editing. It's that night shown on the screen. That's why when you hear the audience applauding, it's very dim. There were probably no mics in the audience at all. It's a sold-out, 18,000 seat show, but it's hard to hear the audience. It's still good. It represents a certain era in our career."

"*At its most powerful, Blue Öyster Cult's second live album establishes the band's reputation as America's favourite technological dinosaur*," wrote *Rolling*

Stone's Mitchell Schneider, just into the next year after the issue of the live album. *"Armed with truckloads of skull-crushing chords and scalding lead guitar lines, the Cult at times here achieves a kind of intensity and rhythmic momentum that such wheelchair cases as Van Halen and Rush can only dream about. Though you could easily argue that* Some Enchanted Evening *is a premature and riskless venture (four of its seven selections are from the group's last two LPs) it's still a genuine pleasure to hear the band without the glossy production of* Spectres, *whose Alvin and the Chipmunks harmonies simply weren't very funny."*

As to the covers, Schneider suggests a tie. *"The Cult jumps headlong into the MC5's legendary 'Kick Out the Jams' with the same agility and passion that carry the buoyant melodies of its own 'R.U. Ready 2 Rock.' The band's reworking of the Animals' 'We Gotta Get Out of this Place' misfires completely. Whereas the Animals sang this life-or-death '60s classic as if they had to get out of the dirty old heart of the city, the Cult's members merely sound like they'd like to."*

Looking back, Albert sets in perspective the effortless quality of the band at this point in their career. "I really think that the best the band ever was, was in 1977. We still had that drive of people that had something to prove. I have a video from Jones Beach where it's nighttime and it's raining. There's just an electrifying feeling about what we're doing. It was almost as if the lasers would force us to operate on their plane, at their level. We became an efficient machine. I know I was trying to imitate Billy Cobham at times, and I was overplaying a lot. Sometimes I'd be amazing and sometimes I'd just lose the beat and get lost! I think other people in the group... we were all reaching a little too far, and would get 'out there' and not be able to get back. But the public would forget, as long as we had a good ending (laughs). But we had new songs and old favourites. Pretty well every show was great at that time."

This was also the era of touring with all the greats of '70s rock, Blue Öyster Cult right in there hangin' with pretty much every big name you can imagine. "Rush were a great bunch of fellows to play with," recalls Albert, "because we would party all the time. I mean, not Neil. Neil seemed to be a bit of a loner; after the shows, he would hang out and have a bite to eat, but Geddy and Alex... we would go over to Howie's, their road manager's room, and we would jam, if there was nobody next to him—we didn't want to upset the guests. But if we could, we would just hang out and jam, party. Not crazy stuff, crazy drugs or anything, but we would have a few drinks, tell a few jokes, lots of fun, play Led Zeppelin or Beatles songs, stuff that we played before we were famous."

We've heard about Rush's comedy sketches... "I don't remember anything like that, from when I was on tour with them, but after that, I remember they had made a whole little video that was pretty funny, where they were doing all these comedy routines. We were friends with the roadies, and they would bring back these videotapes and say, 'Hey, look at what these guys did.' Pretty funny. They were into a lot of different things; they would make demos with people you've never heard of—a very creative bunch."

How about Ted Nugent?

"Ted is always fun to hang out with, because he comes up with this ridiculous stuff. You can't really take him seriously, but he's funny. I don't know. He didn't drink, but he would come and say these funny things and then he would disappear with some girl—that was his thing."

"Technology has certainly been our history," noted Allen at the time, ever one to philosophize about rock 'n' roll's place in the world, and in this instance, live rock 'n' roll and BÖC as practitioners of it. "The technology of our show at the moment is just overwhelming. Lasers, huge sound systems and all that sort of thing. It can be frustrating to keep it all in harness, to try to make it look right, to try to utilize it, to twist a lot of knobs, crank up a lot of diodes, transistors and wires to make them do what you want to do. People used to ask, 'What's been the biggest influence on our sound as a band?' But everybody's influences are the same. Everybody listened to Elvis and the Beatles and Motown. The influences are so prevalent that nobody can escape them all, because it's popular music. It's not a matter of discovering some obscure deviation to form the basis of what you've done. We're no exception from any other band, in the sense that we have stolen as many licks from other bands as other bands have stolen from us. That's inherent in the form. No, you know what our biggest influence is? It's a big amplifier. It's a hard balance to swing between getting those seductive sounds and putting some life into the thing, because you can get trapped so easily. People come to concerts and they want to see the elements that they're used to, but they're also waiting for an overwhelming barrage of sound, that phenomena of being in a coliseum full of earthshaking sound. That in itself is an experience that they're coming for."

"The sounds we live in are loud," continues Lanier. "We're so conditioned to it. Like that line, 'I think I've never seen a thing so lovely as a tree.' That's okay if you're talking an environment which is just woods and trees, but the world isn't like that anymore. People go home and crank up their stereos. It's the sense of what comes out of it as part of the environment that elicits a response. Some people's blood never runs faster than when they hear the hum of a big car. All these inputs and stimuli are related. It's funny; it can get really depressing because it can have a sad aftermath. It's like more, more, more, and you still feel unsatisfied. It's all the more imperative then that you use it for some good purpose—that some magical reason somehow communicates itself through what you're doing, instead of 'mere-ness.' That word mere, forget it. People used to put that word in front of everything. Mere television, mere rock 'n' roll, mere this, mere that, which is possible to do in an artificial situation. It's a word that denotes artificiality in the sense that we did it and God didn't. A belittling term, because it's a belittling world. I find it that way and that's one of the reasons that rock 'n' roll is so popular, because it seems to be such an extravagant celebration."

"Yeah, it's the politics of living. There is a war to be won, which is to say just to look is to arrive somewhere. All these middle-class, middle-aged parents can't understand coming to a rock 'n' roll concert: 'Ooh, it's so obnoxious; it's beating you over the head,' they say. My reaction is yeah, it's terrifying because it's like a great horror movie because it's so monstrous. But it takes that kind of kick to break through that barrier of numbness and that's probably why people take drugs. The same sort of thing. I put drugs into two categories. There are the flamboyant ones and then there are the Zen ones. The Zen ones are those when you stare at a paperweight and it just looks great. I don't do drugs now, but I do have fond memories. It's funny that whenever you talk about rock 'n' roll, it always goes off on these tangents because it seems like they are all part and parcel of the environment…"

Less esoterically and year later, bassist Joe nonetheless expresses a similar appreciation for the magic of rock 'n' roll, and more specifically rock 'n' roll as barely contained on a live album. "I think that's pretty easy to figure out. Live shows were where it was at at the time, and people wanted a souvenir of that live show. If you could make live recordings that just brought people back to those shows, they would just go out and buy them in droves—and they did. People just like to remember. Nowadays everything's up on YouTube the next day; you can find anything. So I think the specialness of having a live recording has lost a lot. But back then, that's what you had, and that was your souvenir and you could play it in the car. It was great—and great on the 8-track. Cranked-up in your souped-up hot rod (laughs)."

"I don't think that hard rock bands were recorded in the studio very well until Metallica came along, and that's quite a bit later," adds Joe. "It's hard to say. I can say that just generally, they weren't recorded as well as they have been recently. Plus the songs got better: you had months and long tours to hone our skills. We didn't have that many skills when we first went in. When I recorded the first album, I had no idea what I was doing. But I felt like jumping up and down, that's all (laughs). I didn't know what I was doing, but every day was exciting. It was like wow, this is like Christmas and your birthday and Halloween all rolled into one. But people want to take a souvenir away from the show. And where *On Your Feet or on Your Knees* had a lot of rough edges, *Some Enchanted Evening* is a pretty refined album. We treated the recording of that album almost like we were in the studio. Every night after the show we would go into the recording truck and it would be just like sitting in the studio and listening to playback, and we would make mental notes like, 'Oh, that didn't work; let's fix that tomorrow night.' Instead of just doing take after take in a regular studio, you had the same feeling, but you had to wait a day to fix it; you would have to wait a day. But it was a very pleasant way to make a recording. I remember working with Corky Stasiak, and I think there were a few other engineers. But Corky, you know he worked with John Lennon, worked at the Record Plant, but a very sort of mellow kind of guy. Just, 'Oh, you know, I think the bass sound needs something here.' He says, 'okay, let's fix it.' So the next night we'd go in and we'd get a little bit better. So that was a process that was pretty good, and I think it's a very quality record. There's a lot of inspired moments on that record. But that's the thing: people want to have a souvenir."

"Speaking of live albums," continues Joe, "I really love when I heard the recent Rush live recordings, because their instruments have a little… you can feel the rattling and the cabinets and the floor kind of shakes a bit, and that puts a little more electricity in those songs. That's a thing that live is going to do for you, especially if it's a good band like Rush. So yeah, our version of 'Astronomy' is very good on there. The single off of there was 'We Gotta Get Out of this Place,' and it did okay; they pushed that in Europe a lot as a single."

"Live albums were popular back then," agrees Albert. "When Peter Frampton had that huge hit, I think everybody was like, oh, yeah, that would be a good thing to do—put out a live record. A lot of the bands toured a lot and had a pretty good live show. So I would say that there was the fact that people would see the show and they would want to get a record of that, and also the live album in some cases was better than the studio record. The studio records were more careful, but the live album would always have more energy. For a hard rock show, energy is a big part of it."

Explains Sandy, asked why live albums often sold better for hard rock bands over their studio counterparts, "That's because the studio albums are pale facsimiles of what happens in performance, and this is a people's music. It sounds like a cliché, but it's not. It is really, for reasons that we've laid out, it's folk music, and people are dedicated to extracting the most out of this experience, and the live records are the best possible recorded representations of the experience."

"You know, in classical music, Leonard Bernstein is allowed—was allowed— to record five versions of any Beethoven symphony, or how many he did. And Wilhelm Furtwängler, probably the greatest conductor we know of—who unfortunately spent most of his career in Nazi Germany, and was actually a Nazi, so he's less famous than he should have been, although he is quite famous— might have recorded let's say eight versions of Wagner's 'Eighth Symphony.' I'm just giving you an example, and I may be exaggerating but only very slightly. Nobody says, 'Why is he doing this old music again?' Because they realised his audience, the audience, these conductors realised that every one of these versions revealed some new, previously unrevealed truth about the work. The same thing with rock 'n' roll. You know, when I see complaints about multiple live albums, like, 'How many do they need?,' well, every night is different. If you have the resources to record 50 shows right on one tour, and you can listen to them all carefully and pick the greatest hits version out of those 50 performances, you've got another great document of what the band can do, which is not going to happen in the studio."

"Most of the things they record in the studio are new songs that have not been fully realised. For example 'The Reaper:' Richard Meltzer went to see Blue Öyster Cult play and introduced the show at Angel Stadium in Anaheim in 1976. Big show, whatever the place holds: 80,000? 50,000? They all hold more than they do for baseball because you can get out on the field. When they played 'The Reaper,' he said, God, that's just amazing because you appended the outro to 'Gil Blanco County,' as it was performed live, to 'The Reaper,' as performed live. Well they're both folk songs. To certain extents they're the same folk song. It shouldn't be that big a surprise. But we didn't think to do that in the studio. So just a few months later we had a much better version of the song, or different version of the song. I mean the studio performance of 'The Reaper' is kind of a miracle. Shelly Yakus turned to me and said, when the basic track was recorded—there's no editing on the basic track on the drum; it's all real, which is very unusual, believe me, much more unusual than one thinks—he said, 'That's the best track you'll ever hear. That's amazing.' I do listen to that song a lot because I teach that song as well and he was right. So we had this supernatural performance."

"It's like the Dead in their 'Golden Road (to Unlimited Devotion)' period, and the Byrds on their first three records—it's all there. All the greatest folk-derived rock 'n' roll, surreally supernatural awesome stuff of the mid-'60s is in that performance, plus a lot of insights developed from becoming a heavy metal band

and playing other music, which shared some basic elements with folk music, but also introduced some new totally electric insights. So that's what 'The Reaper' is. Then three months later another insight was uncovered, which doesn't really make the song better, necessarily, but was pretty awesome and shocking to Richard Meltzer who had not been following the evolving performance tradition. He just walked into a show at Anaheim and heard it live for the first time and was shocked at how it had developed in even a few months, and that's what happened live."

"Then of course there are other things that happen live, like Frampton where nothing is live (laughs), except for the bass drum, I was told, by the people at the place who'd worked on the record. That's all they kept. When you hear Blue Öyster Cult, the live records are about 99.99% live. They might drop in for a bad flub, fix a bad flub, but that's about it. What we did was record a ton of stuff. We were always recording, and in a lot of different environments. So recording at the Apollo in Glasgow or in Birmingham gives you an entirely different audience, louder for example, than other audiences in the world. With the upper balcony at the Apollo swaying—which it tends to do when the crowd is particularly enthusiastic—they had a bunch of those on *Some Enchanted Evening*. We had stuff recorded in Little Rock in front of a completely insane—or very different kind of insane—audience. Actually some of these performances probably were used not because they weren't necessarily better but because the audience was better, and it was just an entirely different kind of energy."

Indeed. So logically, if one follows Sandy's line of thinking, as well as Albert's, with the passage of time, fans and critics have pretty much decided that *Some Enchanted Evening* is the most personable and representative of the Cult's live records, most aficionados of the band finding its predecessor too raw and its follow-up four years later too sterile. *Some Enchanted Evening*, on the other hand, captured the band at its creative peak, its optimism at commercial possibility boundless, and its live show hammered into a thing of beauty.

"I thought that after 'Reaper' and *Some Enchanted Evening*, that they would probably be like, trans-enormous," sums up Pearlman. "Didn't happen. They became very big, but they didn't become what Aerosmith became. Actually, they were bigger than Aerosmith for awhile, but obviously didn't in the long run exceed Aerosmith's stature. Yes, the public is a funny thing."

Mirrors

"No, I'm not interested; there's no material here"

L ive records for hard rock bands in the '70s seemed to act as breathers, an opportunity to look around and take stock. Acts such as Rush, Kiss, Thin Lizzy, Judas Priest, UFO and Foghat have said as much to me in interviews, often giving variations on the sentiment that, "This was the end of an era for the band." Blue Öyster Cult also consciously saw things this way, making radical changes after *On Your Feet or on Your Knees* and also with *Mirrors*, the bright, shiny successor to *Some Enchanted Evening*.

So the stated purpose for *Mirrors*, issued July of '79, was to make a pop record, something a bit more in tune with average American tastes, something that would make some real cash. To this end, Tom Werman, hot off successful runs with Cheap Trick and Ted Nugent, was brought in to produce the album, a controversial move, given that this would be the first record of the band's seven thus far that would see the Krugman/Pearlman/Lucas team step aside. All three had been without a doubt BÖC's sixth, seventh and eighth members, and they were now leaving the picture after years of invaluable contribution, as crucial to the band's records as any given member, save for perhaps Buck.

"I think because 'Reaper' had gone to a million, then *Spectres* didn't, we were definitely searching around," explained Joe, characterizing the bands at a crossroads. "Also there's a sort of problem that Sandy might have been a little restrictive. We were always looking for another musical avenue. You know, Sandy is a great conceptualist, and I don't think anybody could argue that. But we still wanted musical input, because we were just regular guys, not really virtuoso players. So it wasn't anything personal against Sandy, finding another producer. It was like, hey, we want to do it better. It's a very competitive business and we wanted to do it better."

Allen echoed that sentiment. "We did eight albums with him. That's a long time to have one producer. Sandy was busy doing other things and producing other people and we said, 'What the hell, we'll just go off and do it differently and see what happens.' It was a tough thing though. We went through all this producer audition crap. I won't mention certain names, but they come in with their managers and everything. It was ridiculous! Producers have become bigger prima donnas than the artists in this business. But we weren't so much looking for a producer's aesthetic to inject in it. We just needed someone we could work with, because everybody in the band must be qualified to produce at this point. Although with five writers and five producers, it's a ridiculous proposition. We thought of doing it ourselves, but we realised it would take eight years to get done."

In reality, Allen says, the record took an amount of time typical for the BÖC. "About two months—a month and a half of recording and three weeks of mixing. From beginning to end, from rehearsing to recording, getting it packaged and putting it out, it took about three and a half months." While recording, the band knocked off a few incognito west coast-only club dates as the Soft White Underbelly, just to try out the new tunes and see which would click on stage. Allen sums up the attitude at the time. "There was very little worry about, 'Is this going to be a BÖC record?' Let's do it, make it sound good, and to hell with the consequences!"

Once all was said and done, however, the whole thing would be seen as a bit of a debacle, a sell-out of sorts—longtime fans sometimes call the record *Errors*—which to boot, didn't do anything for the boys' pocketbooks.

"There were a lot of problems by this point in the band," explains Albert, "including petty jealousies between the girlfriends and wives. But I'd still have to say it's one of the most together records we made, as far as a feeling of unity within the band, okay? Because we really came together, and really tried to rise above what we thought was a bad situation. I think we really sort of united behind Donald, because we thought, okay, here's this guy, he's Mr. Pop Man, he's the sound of the boy next door and we're going to make a real pop record and we're going to be set. Even though we had some hits, we thought this would establish us as a pop band, which of course, how wrong we were! (laughs). I think I'd have to say in the end that Tom Werman messed the whole record up, even though he delivered what he thought we wanted. Werman just has no jazz in his soul whatsoever. You can still be kind of jazzy and still speak rock. People do it all the time."

"I think he was stiff and completely misunderstood where the band was at," continues Al. "He was used to producing Ted Nugent and stuff, bands that had a crude element, and he had to pull out the melodic bits. With Blue Öyster Cult, we needed no encouragement on that front. Like I say, the way we worked, we were kind of a jazzy band, and he just didn't get that at all. So he took all the jazz out of everything, all the looseness, all the fun, for us. It was a miserable experience. So *Mirrors* is very sterile, but at the time we didn't realize it. See, that was a strength of ours, that we weren't sterile, that we had lots of depth that way. We also stopped being scary, which was something we'd really perfected. So we went and had a Top 40 hit with 'In Thee' and we didn't sell any records. Not only did we not sell any records, but all the reviewers said, 'What happened with you guys? This is lame. How come you went so soft?' And it was humiliating."

Summing up, Al conjectures (while including a glimpse into the early evolution of the *Imaginos* project) that, "we made more demos, auditioned more producers, and worked harder on every facet of that album than any other up to that point. We also had a feeling that we didn't have the goods. Many of the *Imaginos* songs were written by then, but they were not that similar to what ended up on the *Imaginos* album. 'Astronomy,' 'Warned,' 'Presence' and 'Imaginos' were written and similar, but the others were radically different. I think it does take time to make a great album, but we were not ready to make *Imaginos* then."

Brother Joe puts the following slant on the *Mirrors* sessions. "Well, yeah, the poppy-ness I think comes from the influence of Werman. But I don't have anything bad to say about Tom Werman. I think he's a great producer. He didn't get along with some of the guys, or put it this way, he got along with some people in the group better than others. He didn't get along with Allen and he didn't get along with Albert. With Albert that was a weird thing. It was another one of those cases where I had to sort of calm everybody down from killing Albert (laughs). You know, and it was done in California, so we were away from our home base. But I like the album a lot. It's a little poppy. It could have been a little more hard-edged."

In terms of personality clashes, Eric is quick to add that Tom didn't make him feel all that welcome either. "I really can't speak for him, but I just know he didn't want me around very much. So I did very, very little on that record, and I think that's the way he wanted it." Albert adds that, "Everything had to be perfect. He had a stopwatch out to make sure the tempos were right, and he wouldn't let Eric play on the track because 'Eric Bloom just wasn't good enough.' All of this stuff, and we were like, 'Come on, man! It's rock 'n' roll! What the hell!'"

"But the sound is really good," Joe concedes. "That's the first album where I overdubbed most of the bass. Most of the bass was done on the second try. On all the other albums I usually played at the beginning, so there's little flaws in the bass, which they had to try duck in mixing. But Tom made very certain that every bass note was placed perfectly in the song. So when it came to mixing it, he could mix the bass louder. I think there's a lot of songs that have different interesting layers. I like 'The Great Sun Jester.' I like 'Lonely Teardrops'. As an album, it's a little strange, and it never got the promotional push. But it was a strange time. It was the '70s, the disco era. *Saturday Night Fever* (laughs). What are they going to do with this? Hey, if it sounded like 'Staying Alive,' we could have sold it. Even Grateful Dead had a disco song."

The story from Werman himself, barely correlates with the above, but here are a few comments form the man himself, now in the Northeast fulfilling another dream, running a bed and breakfast. "Well, it's been so long since I listened to the record. The thing I remember most about my sessions with those guys was the unfortunate alienation of Eric Bloom, because I loved Donald's voice and I thought he was every bit as good a singer. I let him have a number of vocals on the album, at least half. Where Eric used to do almost all the vocals. So he was irritated by that. At the same time, I had a wonderful time working with Donald, because he's a funny guy, he's a great guitarist, he was just a complete joy to work with all around. He gave me a laugh. He played great guitar, he was a good singer, he was cooperative, he just made everything great. The Bouchard brothers were great, and Lanier was wonderful. I mean, everybody was great. I just felt bad about Eric being pissed-off as he was. That's too bad. I mean, that was the album I wanted to make, and it was the album they wanted to make."

When asked if there is indeed a Tom Werman sound or methodology (remember, the man later had huge success with Dokken, Mötley Crüe and

Poison as well), Tom thinks a bit and then offers that, "If there was, I would like to think that it was a fluid, locomotive rhythm. A prominence of rhythm guitar, doubled rhythm guitar licks, around which the song's based. That's the way I listen to music. The strongest thing to me about rock 'n' roll is the good, elementary, catchy, basic guitar lick, as in 'Girls Girls Girls,' as in 'Cat Scratch Fever,' and a number of songs that were big. Everyone knows what a hook is, but I prefer to build a song around a real driving guitar hook. Probably the best example of that is ZZ Top; I love their drive. I always try to add good solid drive to the song. Certainly by doubling the guitars, but by helping it to roll along through percussion, through reinforcement, through other instruments playing accents for beats; you know, there are a number of ways to do it, for example tailoring the drums to serve the guitar, rather than vice versa."

"Well, you know, if you ask one member of the group, they'll say one thing, and another member will say another thing," reflects Werman, with respect to Albert's charge that the album is just too poppy. "The producer is damned if he does and damned if he doesn't. There's no question about it. If it's a stiff, it's the producer's fault. If it's a hit, it was always in the music and the songs. You know, everyone hates the producer. So, you know, I don't remember... I thought the Bouchards were fine. Maybe I wanted him to play different rhythms or patterns. Maybe he just didn't want to do it. I don't remember him as being difficult or outstanding or anything; he was just there."

Werman also acknowledges that the album is anything but a fan favourite, landing way down the rankings by Cult watchers. "Oh, way down, I know. But I've heard that about almost every record I've ever made. I'm a pop producer; that's why I'm hired. To try and get the bands on the radio. *Mirrors* was one of the ones I missed. But that's the reason I worked with Ted Nugent, Cheap Trick, with Molly Hatchet, to get them on the radio. Mötley Crüe. I mean, who ever thought Mötley Crüe would ever have a hit single? There's a lot of stuff that goes down that I get blamed for. But the fact is, I think the primary purpose of my work is to get the band on the radio so that they can get an audience. And then they can do whatever they want. I thought 'Dr. Music' might be a single. Everything else... it was really good stuff. But again, it's one of the album I pay least attention to in retrospect. I just don't go back to it. It was a disappointment to all of us. That happens. I think I batted about 400 in terms of hit records, which is astonishing. But the ones that didn't make it, really didn't make it. A couple of albums I thought were the best albums I ever did, were almost complete stiffs, like The Producers or Mother's Finest. I mean, these were killer records. I don't know; nobody ever bought them. So I guess they were just killer to me."

The cover art for *Mirrors* is considered by many to be the least remarkable of the catalogue, indeed the BÖC symbol this time carelessly plopped on the front cover as if in hasty afterthought. But the story behind it is pretty interesting. First of all, the sky with rear-view mirror scene is not a photo but a painting of high realism.

"A friend of mine named Loren Salazar did the *Mirrors* album cover," divulges Eric. "He also did *Magazine* by Heart. A lot of people look at that—it's a rear-view mirror—and they think it's a photograph, but it's a painting. Another sidebar to that story is that Loren sent the original painting off to CBS to get photographed and it was lost by the express company. It was insured but it was a weird happenstance because it was used on our album cover and then the painting was lost. But if you look at the clouds in the sky, you can see off to the left, that he's painted in a couple of sperms. Not many people know about that. As a matter of fact, I have one of his paintings hanging right in front of me as we speak. He's given me or sold me about five or six of his paintings. Actually I have lithos of them because they are very expensive now."

Albert adds, "That one was a band decision. Loren was actually a guy I wanted to work with for a long time. I used to hang out in Seattle a lot in those days, and he was a friend and I was very impressed with his artwork. I have to say that the *Mirrors* cover is the worst piece of art that he's ever created. But I don't know; it was a band decision." Salazar is not credited in the liner notes.

It's odd that people call *Mirrors* the band's pop record, because in mathematical bottom-line terms, *Mirrors* delivers as many heavy rockers as either *Spectres* or *Agents of Fortune*, and that would be three, give or take an arguable fraction either way. Lead track 'Dr. Music' is one of them, featuring a sly Meltzer lyric which mixed rock 'n' roll with light-hearted S&M, propelled by a buoyant hard rock groove that quickly turned the tune into a crowd favourite. "Joe did that one with Meltzer," notes Al. "Donald might have come up with a couple chord variations, but it's basically Joe's song."

"That was another five-minute wonder," quips Richard. "That got some airplay on... you see, I made much more money from this band from airplay, from ASCAP, than I ever got from sales of the records. So I get these foreign statements every so often and 'Dr. Music' gets played in Germany once in a while. I actually got six cents from Russia for 'Burnin' For You'."

Next up was 'The Great Sun Jester' which is ushered in by beautifully recorded acoustic guitar. The tune then transforms into a pomp rock classic, a fantastical fantasy tale with an irresistible Styx-like hook and rosy look, co-written by Bloom, prolific science fiction writer Michael Moorcock, and longtime friend of Eric's, John Trivers, who helped prepare Eric's demo tapes, and is a bass player, with the Broadway musical *Grease* to his credit.

Eric explains his love of sci-fi and the Michael Moorcock connection. "I've always been a sci-fi and fantasy buff—always. Since I saw *Flash Gordon* and *Buck Rogers* on TV as a kid. My earliest drawings were pictures in a notebook of rocket ships and ray guns, stuff like that. I wrote Michael a fan letter 20 years ago, because I loved his books, and I always thought that those books should be made into films. So that's what I approached him about. He sent back a letter saying he was a fan of ours. He lived in England at the time, and when he came to New York on business, we sat and had lunch and became friends."

Rights to the publishing of Moorcock's handful of BÖC lyrics later became a bit of a legal dust-up. Eric: "He sold off his publishing rights to somebody, and then he basically told us why don't you guys go and publish it, because they had screwed him around. When we did, they came after us saying you can't do that. So it became a bit of a business mess, but it's all straightened out now." 'The Great Sun Jester' is mentioned in two of Moorcock's stories, *The Fireclown* and *The Transformation of Mavis Ming*.

Track three was a rare Allen Lanier tune, 'In Thee' becoming the focal point for the pop accusations, with its gorgeous acoustic guitar, general hi-fidelity arrangement, and of course, moderate hit status. The song was a tender break-up tale for his girlfriend Patti Smith, lamenting the wayward, travelling nature of the soul-destroying rock 'n' roll game. The song features, surprisingly, an actual string section.

"I wasn't sure about putting strings on it at all, and I had some debates with Tom Werman about it," says Allen. "We used the synthesized string section on several other cuts on the album, and we tried it here, since it was a ballad. But then we decided to see what the quality, the timbre and tonality would be with real strings. The arranger and I figured out the basic arrangement, sitting at a piano in New York, but then the band had to split to Japan before we got a mix on it. I thought there were too many strings, so we remixed it, got them down a little lower and evened out the voices."

Notes Albert, "*Mirrors* kind of bombed, but the irony was that 'In Thee' was a radio hit. It got into the Top 40 on mainstream radio, and yet we didn't sell many records. What it turned out was that people would hear it on the radio and have no idea who it was, and it was too innocuous for anybody to even care. But it wasn't the label. I think that maybe we put some pressure on ourselves to try this pop thing, while our fans put pressure on us to be heavier. But nothing from the label, no."

The track is still played live to this day, in a close, acoustic, "unplugged" format, after being dropped for a number of years. It was of course, reprised acoustic on record, to close out '98's *Heaven Forbid* album. The curious line about Jim and delivered destinies refers to Jim Carroll and his song 'Day and Night' (a collaboration with Lanier on Carroll's *Catholic Boy* album), which includes a similar line of text.

'In Thee' gave way to the band's first title track through six studio albums, 'Mirrors', like the song before it, glimmering with an undeniable pop sheen, Donald teaming up once again with Bruce Abbott (see 'Golden Age of Leather'). Bolle Gregmar sets a possible scene. "'Mirrors' is really fascinating, quite complex. I think it's his reflection on the media. Who are we, what do we look like, what should we be? On a personal level, every time you look at yourself, just by glancing in a mirror, what is your perception of yourself? Who are you at that very time? He tried to explain it logically through Einstein-esque theories, which is great. He was very much into deeper thought when he did this stuff."

Buck adds to the lyric's resonance. "'Mirrors' was written by Bruce Abbott, who is an old friend of mine, a college classmate who also wrote 'Golden Age of Leather.' And he's just fascinated by the whole female vanity thing. If you look at it, girls come by it honestly; it's societal, it's what you're supposed to do. It's funny, this was written like eight to ten years before the invention of the supermodel spokesperson, so I think he was a little ahead of the curve there."

The song's absolutely swinging chorus features backing vocals by semi-somebody scenesters Genya Ravan and Ellen Foley, who happened to be in New York at the time. The pair also show up as classic back-up singers on 'Dr. Music'. Al speaks kindly of 'Mirrors': "It was pretty cool; I think Donald's demo was really good. It's another one where I would have used the demo."

Joe Bouchard's eccentric 'Moon Crazy' closed side one of the original vinyl, the track mixing an icy hard rock verse with a pop, R&B, jazz, even disco-based chorus which becomes a whirling dervish of vivid memories for Bouchard as the song winds itself up and out. "Very simply, I read Norman Mailer's book, *A Fire on the Moon*," notes Joe. "I love Norman Mailer's stuff; I've read a few of his books, and that one brought back a lot of things that had to do with me and my life back in 1969. It's kind of a personal thing."

Side two opened with 'The Vigil', (arguably) the band's most powerful musical piece thus far, a track that featured headphone-heavenly production, the band's most sure-footed harmonies, dramatic breaks, shimmery, silky acoustic guitars and a verse riff that is one of the band's most wollopingly effective, perhaps only 'Tattoo Vampire' rivaling it for sheer heavy metal power, from this, a band who evoked the term mostly without playing directly to it.

Albert: "'The Vigil' was originally called 'The Devil's Nail,' which was a Patti Smith lyric. And it was deemed too obscene by some of the people in the band. It had the line, singing about the devil, right, blah blah blah, 'He was nursed on God's big dick.' You know, so people thought this was too much (laughs)—couldn't have that. So we censored ourselves. And you had a UFO song instead, which was written by Donald's wife Sandy."

The song quite poetically and opaquely tells the story of the Roswell Incident in 1947, one of the most famous and persistent stories in UFO lore, about a supposed UFO crash in the New Mexico desert, which included an elaborate military cover-up, even more so captivating by the supposed recovery of the alien craft and even one of its occupants, albeit killed by the crash. The USAF's only recently issued report explains away the UFO conjecture, stating that the spotted craft were part of a secret program known as Project Mogul. High-altitude balloons were equipped with special sensors and radar deflectors to detect Soviet atomic testing, but the project was cancelled, with the balloons being allowed to fall back to earth. The references in the song to 27 faces pointed at the sky may refer to the VLA (Very Large Array), an installation of 27 telescopes completed in New Mexico about the time *Mirrors* was released.

A technical note from Allen, who remarked at the time, "We do 'The Vigil' live. It was a lot of fun on that song to discover things that would work on keyboards and electronic instruments. On the record there's a build-up under the guitar solo that was done by recording another guitar backwards. I spent a day trying to imitate the tension and release of that on the Prophet, and I think I got it fairly close. I just programmed it into the memory, and at the right moment Eric hits the button and plays the few notes, and it's there."

Second track, side two was a heavy Joe Bouchard rocker, 'I Am the Storm' co-written with Ronald Binder. "Ronald Binder's actually a friend of ours, and worked with us, I guess you would say as a roadie," cites Joe (who's of course told us a bit about Ronald back in the *Spectres* chapter). "He was connected with the punk scene in New York and was on the cover of *Punk* magazine once as the superpunk. But he was also a lyricist too, and had given me a bunch of lyrics, and I took a liking to that one."

Closing out the record are an Al tune and an Allen tune. Al's track, 'You're Not the One (I Was Looking For)' was the second track (the other being 'The Vigil'), that would be co-written, strictly speaking, by a wife or girlfriend, a trend that would expand come *Cultösaurus Erectus.*

Al relates a pretty funny tale. "I would say if I had any mistakes on a Blue Öyster Cult record, it would have to be 'You're Not the One'. I fought them tooth and nail not to put it on the record. It was just a joke; I made a joke. It was supposed to be, you know, making fun of Tom Werman. It was written about him, the producer, and they were so dense. None of them had heard The Cars. And I said, 'No, no, this is like...' I took the Cars song, 'Just What I Needed,' and I put new lyrics to it, and they said, 'Is it exactly the same?' I said, 'No, it's a little different; it's like a parody.' They put it on the record! Then when the record came out, the Cars song broke big, and everybody went, 'Oh my God, it's exactly the same! I thought you said it was different?' It was like, I told you not to put it on there! They wouldn't listen to me, so there you have it. That's the one real mistake."

"But yeah, that was a Cars tribute song that was supposed to be a sarcastic joke," continues Albert, adding as background to the tale, the story of the band's search for a new producer. "See, we had decided that Sandy was invested in his own songs, and Eric didn't like that Sandy always wanted me to sing the songs rather than him. I felt like Sandy always wanted to mix the records and he just wasn't a very good mixer. So there was a lot of anti-Sandy feeling at that point. Also he was spending a lot more time with The Clash and Pavlov's Dog than he was with us, which we felt like, well, he's bailing on us, so we better get somebody else to shepherd this record through."

"So we auditioned... or actually, a bunch of producers auditioned us. We really wanted Keith Olsen, which was *the* person because he had just produced the Fleetwood Mac record. And of course his big claim to fame was he was in The Music Machine, which we all loved. All of us played 'Talk Talk' in various bands, that we weren't playing in all together. I mean Donald and I were playing together, but his college band played it, Eric played it in his college band. So we loved 'Talk Talk' and we thought Keith Olsen was the guy. He rejected us. He said, 'No, I'm not interested; there's no material here.'"

"So eventually Columbia assigned us Tom Werman, who came and he talked to us and he was like, 'Well somebody's gotta be the asshole.' We went out and we got really drunk, and I didn't like him. I was like oh, this guy is obnoxious. I also felt like how he worked was to take a band that wasn't very tight and make them tight. Or a band that didn't have a lot of structure and help them structure their songs. So he would simplify and tighten up things, and I felt like this was the wrong thing for us. That we were already a tight band and we didn't need any of that. What we needed was somebody to help us mix it and pick a good song."

"So like I say, I wrote this song, and basically it was a joke. At the time I was writing all these funny songs. I wrote 'Cities on Flame with Disco,' which was like 'Cities on Flame' except it was disco, and it had all these lyrics like in San Francisco they disco with Crisco. Stuff like that. So anyway, then I had like a Deep Purple song called 'Ritchie Blackmore's Dildo.' Which he didn't appreciate. So this was like another one of those stupid, silly songs, 'You're Not the One' which was supposed to be a parody of The Cars. Of course Tom Werman heard it and said, 'Oh, we've got to do that.' I'm like, 'Well it's kind of like The Cars. I mean we should probably change it or something.' He's like, 'No, don't change a thing;

we've got to do it just like this. It sounds like a hit.' I said, 'Well it is a hit!' (laughs). He's like, 'Oh come on, I've never heard it.' So we did the record, and of course by the time the record comes out everybody hears 'Just What I Needed,' and they're like, oh shit. I said I told you it was just like it! So anyway it's there; it was my contribution to that record. It is what it is.

'"But other than that," continues Bouchard, "the songs I was writing at the time were jazzy, far-out kind of things that the rest of the band wasn't interested in. Plus I had a whole series of irreverent take-offs on some of our other songs, like 'Cities.' It was difficult because I was trying to go in a different direction from the rest of the band, to break out of the mould. Of course the song of mine that they chose for the album was just a sarcastic comment on the choice of producer. It's probably my least favourite BÖC song that I wrote."

Brother Joe confirms the story. "Yes, he had been listening to The Cars, so he wrote this song, and we rehearsed it, and Tom Werman says, 'Oh, let's do that one; that sounds good.' The problem was, Tom Werman had never heard The Cars. So we kept doing it, and I thought well, he'll end up changing it or something. Because you never know what was going to make the album, and it won't be so much like The Cars. But by the end, it was a lot like The Cars, and kind of a goof, you know?"

So in some twisted, maybe even subconscious or semiconscious manner, the song was a direct play for a hit single, being a simple retro-pop ditty of love lost, love found based wholly on The Cars, the kings of skinny tie rock at the time. The "gremlin-like" babbling sample found in the track (after the set-up line about fancy ladies talking and talking) can be slowed down and deciphered as a repeating portion of 'The Lord's Prayer'. Released smack in the middle of the backmasking craze (scorn aimed primarily at Zeppelin, Queen, AC/DC and Kiss), religious zealots quoted the backwards line as "Furthermore, our father who art in heaven… Satan."

Allen's 'Lonely Teardrops'—typically frosty, detached—ends the record on a somber, highly creative note, putting much of the rest of the record to shame with its gritty, urgent lyric contrasting the track's smooth but strangely uncommercial musical arrangement, sent into the land of dreams by Wendy Webb's haunting backing vocal. On a purely musical level, the song pairs nicely with 'Moon Crazy' (and for that matter 'Searchin' For Celine', 'Morning Final' and 'Tenderloin'), representing in aggregate a recurring BÖC style one might call decadent, mysterious, soft disco.

Allen, addressing his creative process and his approach to working on *Mirrors*, figures, "The songs I wrote on *Mirrors* were very basic. I kind of wrote them at the last minute, but I also like the process of throwing out a basic skeleton and having the band see what they can do in terms of developing it. There's a wealth of imagination and ability to be exploited in this group. It's not like you have to paint by numbers for everyone."

Thirty years hence, Joe sums up the controversial *Mirrors* experience… "I used to love 'The Great Sun Jester,' another great Eric Bloom song, but for some reason it never connected with the fans in a big way—I don't understand it. I thought we recorded it really well, yet 'Moon Crazy,' on the other hand, was a throwaway, but a lot of people like that. Little kids like that song, for some reason—I don't know why. 'Mirrors,' the song, we spent a lot of time working on that song, because Donald had that track record, but that's never really come out as a stellar track, for some reason. Of course, you can never understand popular taste. 'I Am the Storm' was sort of a last-minute addition to the album, and as I listen to it now, I wish it was heavier. Someday I may do a really heavy version of 'I Am the Storm.' But you know, the impression I got from the record company was, 'Wow, this is nothing like we expected Blue Öyster Cult to be.' I was a little shocked, because I was pretty proud of the album. But the record company was disappointed."

Yet, says Joe, the record company wasn't really leaning on the band one way or the other. "No, there was a concerted effort to not say anything by people, at least in Columbia. I'm thinking Don DeVito was one guy. Don was a friend of mine, and of course his claim to fame is he produced a couple Bob Dylan albums just because he would babysit for the studio. But I'd ask him, and he said, 'I don't want to say; I don't want to say anything that appears like I'm trying to shape you into what the corporation wants.' It might have been more for us, because we, from the very beginning, were sort of the odd group. The odd man out at Columbia, for sure. So he might make a comment, but he says, 'Don't go by what I say, you know. I mean here's what's selling, but that shouldn't affect you. Do your own thing, make it as good as you can.' But somebody like Rick Derringer, I could see where... he's capable of writing very commercial hits, and I can see where he'd be pressured, maybe, 'Hey, why not do that?' I know that, say Joe Zawinul, talking about a jazz keyboard player who wrote a couple of pop hits. What did he write? 'Mercy, Mercy, Mercy'. He wrote a big hit for Weather Report called 'Birdland', and he used to have really big arguments with Columbia. They would want him to do more commercial kind of jazz things, and that wasn't his thing at all. He was not going to be told what to do. But we never had that as far as I know."

"As for Tom Werman, we bought into him because we really liked Cheap Trick—they made nice records. What we liked about him might be not as much Tom Werman as just the band. We liked the songs, we liked the band, we liked the singing. I personally learned a lot from Tom about making a traditional kind of record. It's good to know that, and you can always disregard that when you're recording. But that was his approach, and it didn't settle with most of the guys in the band. Eric wasn't happy.

Nor did the music of the day direct the sounds and styles that *Mirrors* had presented as the face of BÖC circa 1979. "Well, you had the Grateful Dead doing a disco song. You had the Rolling Stones doing a disco song. We refused (laughs). We liked dance beats and all of that, but there was no way we were going to do anything that had anything to do with disco. So I think there was like, well what do we do, guys? Well we'll do what we always did, but it's not very popular. I read a lot of those music books, too, about disco killing music and, you know, when you look at a producer's kind of record, you're never going to have any longevity out of a producer's record. As far as building a career—The Knack, Cars, Police... I don't know, they were all pretty cool. But I'd say The Police probably had the biggest influence. They influenced Rush for God's sake. The idea of putting a big chorus, a chorus box on a guitar, sort of came out of all that Police stuff. And then on the other hand you've got a very good writer in Sting. So that's going to sink into your thing even though it might not be the right thing for all those heavy bands."

"It's self-evident that somebody, not me, was listening to The Cars and thought they were the key to the future," reflects Sandy. "Somebody in Blue Öyster Cult, somebody was listening to somebody else, and thought it was the key to a profitable future. Did I like that? No. But you know, I soldiered on. The answer is yeah, lots of members of Blue Öyster Cult, many, and there are only five, decided that this was the way to go."

Again, to Columbia's credit, Sandy figures the label wasn't pushing the band for major changes.

"No, the pressure was all self-induced. I mean think about it. We had some measurable success with the first three albums. They go live and they were a recording act, in actuality. Then we had a big breakthrough with *On Your Feet or on Your Knees*. Then we had a bigger breakthrough with *Agents*. But you know, with On *Your Feet or on Your Knees*, it is conceivable they could have done respectable business at Madison Square Garden after that came out. Or let's say a year or eight months after it came out, because it did really well at radio, unbelievably. The live one that did even better at radio was *Some Enchanted Evening*, which ruled at radio."

"The next record out was *Agents of Fortune*, which, as I've said, with the portable multi-track devices being there, everybody kind of went into their own corner and started to write on their own, rather than writing on a collective basis. So we drifted from Albert and Richard to Albert and Caryn, or Donald and his wife Sandy etc.—a lot less joint compositional effort. I think that 'E.T.I.' is a joint compositional effort and that's because I brought it in relatively late in the game during rehearsals as opposed to the portable multi-track, the home multi-track. So I think they all decided that if you didn't have anybody in the room at the same time—including me at the compositional phase, or Murray in the compositional phase—I think these home multi-track devices caused one to make a good representation of what you had in mind. I think the heaviness was a function of the collectivity, but as individuals this is what they liked, and they had the freedom to arrange the stuff, right? They'd just bring it in. Joe did not have to come up with the fundamental bass line. The author of the song could come in with the fundamental bass line, etc. Not to single out Joe, but that's what happened, and that's the way they worked from then on."

Touring duties leading up to the June 19th, 1979 release date of *Mirrors* found the band doing a few warm-up club gigs billed as Soft White Underbelly, as well as mounting their first trip to Japan, hitting Hawaii on the way back where they retired their laser show. By mid-May, BÖC had settled into an exhaustive US tour that would take them through to the end of the year (with the author attending the July 19th show in Poughkeepsie, NY, supported by The Lisa Hartt Band and Roadmaster), broken into two legs by an English campaign in November, Magnum supporting. Regular support in August was Roadmaster and The Pat Travers Band with Ian Hunter taking over in early September. Late September into October found the band playing with Rainbow, while Head East, April Wine and Gamma helped BÖC close out the year.

Despite headlining arenas all year, BOC saw sales of *Mirrors* peak at a disastrous 300,000, less than half the figure afforded *Spectres*, itself considered a letdown. 'In Thee', although holding up over the years as a classy light popster, peaked at a lowly No.74 in the UK while neither it, nor 'Mirrors', also issued as a single, could crack the charts stateside. 'You're Not the One (I Was Looking For)' was also floated in the UK, backed with 'Moon Crazy' but it failed to crack the Top 100. Over to the full record, *Mirrors* reached No.46 stateside and No.44 in the UK, all of this quite an ironic and surprising disappointment indeed for a record so overtly commercial all over the place, a record way more hi-fidelity, hooky, and easy on the intellect than any Cult album that provoked with a fork before it.

Cultösaurus Erectus

"So at least we still had our pride"

With the relative commercial and fairly sweeping critical failure of *Mirrors*, Blue Öyster Cult were looking for answers. The one thing they had decided was to return to their roots, to make a heavier record again. "I think *Cultösaurus Erectus* was an obvious return to scary sounds," notes Albert. "I remember myself lobbying very hard to not make a commercial record, not worrying about it, just getting back to writing those weird songs again. That's when we thought, we've turned off all these people, and we have to get them turned on again. We have to show them that our hearts are pure and that we're going to stick with our image and that we can do a scary mysterioso, and just be odd and quirky, make the kind of music that would make you think. I guess after the disaster that was *Mirrors*, one of the first steps was getting somebody heavier in to produce."

It was a strange time for the band. Tensions with Albert were at an all-time high. Some chalked it up to his artistic temperament, his incessant arguing of any and every point, even if, as discussed, some concede that it had much to do with feuding between the wives and girlfriends within the band. There was also a malaise caused strangely enough by geography, which sets in motion Albert's second and third collaborations with his wife at the time, Caryn.

Albert comments on his move out of the city, which has its seeds back around the recording of *Spectres*. "As far as my writing with Caryn, I think that was a product of the fact that I had moved to Connecticut, actually to be close to my brother, Joe. He and Donald both lived in Stamford. They were there, and I was in the city and I wanted to be close to them, so I moved to Stamford in early '77. 'Reaper' was a hit and I had moved out of my apartment. Once I got there, man, there were all kinds of problems. The wives started fighting; there were all kinds of petty jealousies. It was just very strange. Well, put it this way, within a year I really didn't have too much to do with either of Joe or Donald, although Joe being my brother, I've always maintained a relationship with him. But anyway, they were at least there, and I needed lyrics. Joe didn't really do lyrics, and Donald was very stingy with his. He's not really a team player when it comes to writing. If you're working on something, he might throw an idea in. If he's working on it, forget it."

"But anyway, I wasn't around Helen Robbins—Helen Wheels—and I wasn't around Patti; they were still in the city. I think we were trying to break the hold Sandy Pearlman had on us at that point. The break came earlier than *Mirrors* and *Cultösaurus*, like around *Agents of Fortune*, but at that time there were all these people around, all these resources that I had, in particular, Patti and Helen. Once I moved to Stamford, I could work on old Patti songs but I had really gone deeply into it in '75, using a whole bunch of Patti Smith songs. Basically I had tracks, I had ideas, songs, I didn't have any lyrics. So I went to Caryn, 'Would you write something?' She was very much into music and had fancied herself a writer and came up with 'Monsters' and 'Hungry Boys'."

The first step towards making *Cultösaurus Erectus* a heavier record was the ushering in of Martin Birch as producer, who cut his teeth on such Deep Purple classics as *In Rock, Machine Head* and *Burn* (although officially only getting engineer credits), more recently conjuring great results on Black Sabbath's thrilling *Heaven and Hell* record (Sandy had recently signed a management deal with the band), which, with the help of ex-Rainbow belter Ronnie James Dio, produced a renaissance for BÖC's old rivals, and in some ways, heavy metal as a viable genre.

Sandy had this to say about his experience with the Birmingham bashers. "Management is horrible; it's a necessary evil. When I took on Black Sabbath, I thought I was gonna make a lot of money, but it didn't work out that way. It was no fun at all. It was very difficult to make money with Black Sabbath—they developed an ability to consume large amounts of money! My favourite thing is writing. I like producing, sometimes, but it can be really horrible because people can't sing anymore or they're psychologically crippled for a couple weeks for one reason for another."

"Martin certainly brought discipline to the table," notes Pearlman. "Martin Birch is really good on concentrating the minds of the people he worked with. I mean, look at the records he's made. The next production, of 'Burnin' for You,' was awesome. Now it's true, most of it existed before he showed up to rehearse with the Cult, but he nailed it and made it even better, and I'm very familiar with 'Burnin' for You' (laughs). So given the bands that he's worked with—Cult, Sabbath, and Maiden—yeah, I'm not a big Maiden fan, but I think Martin Birch has a tremendous amount of discipline, great engineer, he knows how to extract the most out of the raw materials. He extracts different things out of the raw materials than I would—that's okay, I can't argue with his success. The Cult has a whole different sound, all different number of ways, right? You know, the sound of Black Sabbath, *Heaven and Hell*, is way different from any Black Sabbath album that preceded it. I mean, with Sabbath, it really is a sea change, if you listen to back to back with the other stuff."

Plus it was back to the grit and history of Long Island for recording, the band first producing about a dozen demos with George Geranios, which then went to Birch for his comments and input, the songs slowly but surely metamorphosing into what is arguably the band's most self-assured record.

Joe on Martin Birch: "I loved Martin; he was a great guy. He had a different approach than Tom Werman, who makes nice records, but is very polished and planned-out. Martin's approach was the total opposite: spontaneity, feeling, emotion. Even though there may be parts with mistakes in them, he'd leave 'em on, just because he felt impulsive about it. Also he was a producer/engineer. He really became part of the console. He knew what he was putting on tape, in every aspect, and he would know what would come out the other end. It was actually quite simple, but inspiring."

"Some producers are very hard-edged, and you've got to do it my way," continues Joe. "But Martin was just the opposite. He would give us a lot of freedom. What I found was that he really knew, when we started doing the album, where everything was going to fit in the mix, as he was recording it. He had a pretty good sort of long range, 'Okay, this is where this is going.' A lot of times when we were struggling on a part, he would just let us struggle, and he wouldn't say anything for an hour, two hours, and then we would be throwing around ideas and throwing around ideas, and then you would hear the talkback from the control room, 'Oh, I like that! Do that!' That was it. So he was a great sort of laid-back producer. We were completely blown away by his work with Deep Purple. But because he wasn't a sort of aggressive producer, our records didn't really sound like Deep Purple at all."

The cover art also edged the band back to their original premise, offering a humorous sci-fi portrait of a "Cultösaurus Erectus," from what is actually a pre-existing, quite famous Richard Clifton-Dey painting (occasionally spotted as a jigsaw puzzle!) The ever-present BÖC symbol gets its smallest billing ever, crudely etched onto the hull of the rocket ship speeding past the unwieldy monster. The back cover offered further fun and fake archaeological info, making inside references to Stalk-Forrest, Diz-Bustology, Professor Victor Von Pearlman, Stony Brook, The Underbelly Institute, Oaxaca and the Horn-Swooped Bungo Pony. One might draw parallels between the absurdly built "Cultösaurus Erectus" itself and the odd band of tale-spinners writing and recording this record—perhaps both were doomed to extinction, or at least cursed to struggle in a world not primarily populated by eggheads.

But the music inside really signals a proud re-tooling of the band's vast, strange legacy. Contrary to stated goals, the record, released June 14th 1980, is not considerably heavier than past, post-*On Your Feet* documents, but it does make a healthy return to the land of the mysterious. The record is pretty much this author's favourite of the catalogue, and also the favourite of Bolle Gregmar, mad Swede, and our previously heard from foremost expert on the Cultsters.

But one has to concede some of the following points made by Sandy Pearlman. "I just hate *Mirrors*. That was really the first time I got the notion that they could really make a record like that. That was really disturbing. I had nothing to do with it. *Cultösaurus*, I don't like it; some people do. I just don't like it. It doesn't do much for me. *Fire of Unknown Origin* has some great songs on it and so does *Revolution by Night*. But none of these have this aggregate kind of overwhelming impression. Which may be one reason they didn't sell as well as they should have. Because at the end of the day, on the earlier records, there really is this cumulative aggregate impression which is synergetic in quality, yielding a lot more than the individual components would suggest it would yield. It sort of requires you to play the whole thing. So the record becomes a more addictive experience. With these other records you could just kind of random access it and you know, get away with it. It's really two or three songs deep and that's the end of it."

Pearlman has a point. Where you might disagree that records like *Cultösaurus* are only "two or three songs deep" (I tend to think it's more like six to eight, and maybe a bit less for its successors), the lack of synergy, or put another way, the loss of innocence and of confidence, is palpable. *Cultösaurus* is a series of great, individual songs, songs that demonstrate (betray?) a level of work, craft and showmanship not seen on past BÖC records, even if the intellectual levels are lopped short by a couple or few.

Perhaps opening track 'Black Blade' personifies all of the above. The song shoots into view with heart-stopping space ship sounds, then proceeds to showcase the band's writing polish, the tune mirroring 'The Vigil' as one of the band's modern day "everything but the kitchen sink" mini-epics. Again Bloom works with his technical partner John Trivers (Eric stakes claim to "melody and music"), adding another Michael Moorcock lyric which is signature swords and sorcery, perhaps too self-consciously and self-evidently BÖC-ready, exactly what Sandy was lamenting. Note: Moorcock's main lyrical (and vocal!) vehicle, Hawkwind, has an entire album called *The Chronicle of the Black Sword* based on the same theme as 'Black Blade', the Elric stories, Elric of Melnibone being a main character in many of Moorcock's books. Elric is an albino king who receives power from the supernatural black sword, a sword that actually rules its master, and eventually the universe. Hawkwind's album also contains a song called 'Sleep of a Thousand Tears' which was a Moorcock lyric originally intended for use by BÖC, aboard a musical track that eventually supported the song 'Feel the Thunder'.

But musically and production-wise the album is a tour de force, full of memorable passages that are not without humour, perhaps undercutting the *Dungeons and Dragons Trek*-iness of the lyrics.

Joe defends the album and its opening salvo. "*Cultösaurus*, I heard that recently and I thought that that was a damn good album. I forgot how good 'Black Blade' was. That's a song that has different layers. You can't get it all in one shot with that song. That took some work. I also liked *Mirrors* a lot. Our record company didn't. It probably could have been mixed better. With *Cultösaurus* we deliberately tried to revisit the early eccentricities of BÖC, but it was no *Machine Head*. I loved working with Martin Birch. He upped his track record with us with 'Burnin' for You' on the next album. He is forgiven (laughs)."

"The slow fade-out on 'Black Blade' contains the "voice of the Black Blade" muttering almost sub-audibly "you poor fucking humans." "I didn't write it, but I arranged a lot of it, including the whole sequencer part," says Albert, with respect to this eventful musical trip. "What happened was, Eric had the verse and chorus, and I said, 'Eric, first of all, this is a Michael Moorcock.' You know, I read the Elric books, and I had some Elric graphic novels, and so I felt, well, if you're going to have a song called 'Black Blade' written by Moorcock, it needs to be an epic—any Moorcock songs have to be an epic. So I said, what we need to do is, we need to have a couple more sections, where it goes somewhere, and then it finally comes back to the 'black blade' chorus. He just totally went with that, and so I created this other part, a galloping thing, and the sequencer, and the slow, grand section, all of that."

So although you had Allen, Joe and even Buck getting in on the whole keyboard/synth world, the drummer knew a thing or two as well?

"Oh yeah, I went to Clarkson, I took Fortran. I'm an engineer. Give me gear. They used to call me Gearboy. I read manuals for fun (laughs)."

Next up was another heavy rocker, one of the unsung and under-rated songs in the BÖC canon, 'Monsters', co-written by Albert and Caryn, valiantly vocalized by Eric. Indeed Albert stated at the time, "I wrote most of these songs with Eric in mind as the perfect vocalist." 'Monsters' stomped with a heavy two-note riff, countered by a hilarious transition into jazzy blues and then back out again, sax work courtesy of Mark Rivera. The staccato stop/start section near the end recalls a similar section in 'Cities on Flame' the latter, as discussed, partly inspired by '21st Century Schizoid Man' this one sounding even more like the King Crimson classic. It is of note that Albert had brought an entire record's worth of demos to the *Cultösaurus* sessions, most of them quite heavy, Albert perhaps most determined of the bunch to reverse the pop trend *Mirrors* had suggested.

Indeed Al was experimenting and learning much during the *Cultösaurus* era. With respect to 'Monsters' he says that, "Around that time, I managed to get a hold of a big book, the Steely Dan songbook, every song up until that point, transcribed, the chords, explanations. I had felt for many years that I was like a second class citizen as a musician, that guitar players spoke another language which I didn't understand. So I made a very concerted effort to learn a lot about guitar and one of the influences was Steely Dan where they play a lot of these impossible chords. That was a good education. And I also transcribed some Django Reinhardt stuff and a lot of mysterious guitar music that interested me. So I actually did like a zillion demos using all these chords and stuff. None of them have ever seen the light of day. You know they're sort of like predictable jazz tunes, because it's one thing to know it, and it's another to live it, to have it in your soul. But anyway, that was an outgrowth of that and I felt that the sax was always a burlesque-y kind of thing, and I always wanted to work with Mark Rivera. I think he's one of the greatest sax players around, really. I had just called him up and he said, sure!"

Track three was Buck's 'Divine Wind', "a response to our problems with Iran at that time, the Ayatollah Khomeini regime over there," says Buck. The track is a doom-laden blues which somehow befits the whole Ayatollah Khomeini controversy of the early '80s, this new fundamentalist leader reversing the previous Shah's friendship (some same puppetship) with the USA, in fact entering a war of words, calling America "the devil" and "the great Satan," breaking all ties with the US government and western society in general, and most importantly holding a group of American hostages for many months.

Bolle: "The difference between Buck's original demo and the final recording is night and day. Buck's vocal presentation made it more of a sincere 'Who the hell does he think he is?' type of song, not overreacting. He was very calm. Then Eric came in and sort of shout-sang it, the send him to Hell part. It's heavy and it's really cool. But what you sense in Buck's version is the indifference. He doesn't care. The same way the Ayatollah dismisses America is just reversed. It was quite clever." All in all the song was simple but effective, very gloomy but deflated, laid-back and well, indifferent. When performing the song live, roadie Joe Lauro would join the band on stage playing guitar, complete in rubber Ayatollah mask.

Adds Albert, "Donald would do these songs where he did the entire arrangement, just soup to nuts, where he had figured it all out, kind of like 'Reaper,' but even more so as we went along. So 'Divine Wind' was pretty much... Donald made the mould and we just poured ourselves into it. I got to put some crazy fills to it in the end, but you could tell exactly what the song was supposed to be. It was very dramatic and would have a build, then it would stop and there would be this dramatic, pregnant pause, and the whole thing would come crashing down. Great song and lots of fun to play. I'd say that's the only song that has that kind of blues feel, that we ever had."

Closing side one was 'Deadline' a terrifying true tale, concealed in a sort of effervescent but still mysterious pop. Again this could be construed as Donald operating somewhere between 'Reaper' and 'I Love the Night' although more uptempo. Albert explains that the song is about Phil King (also known as Phil Friedman—Joe also talks about him with respect to 'Hot Rails to Hell'), a booking agent who used to book gigs for the band in their pre-Columbia days. Phil was apparently trying to collect on a gambling debt and was shot. Allen once described Phil as "a big dude in a cheap vinyl leather jacket, two-tone blue '64 Lincoln Continental, who wore a Fu Manchu moustache, combing his hair at all times. He had a perfect *Shaft* hairdo and chrome shades he never took off, wore 'em to bed..." Rumours that it was a Mafia hit turned out to be unfounded.

"He was a kind of glad-handing asshole," recalls Meltzer, of King. "He was promising me that he was going to get me some kind of paid appearance, that I was going to get to do a reading, somewhere, I don't remember where. Everybody was going to reap this bounty from his connections. He got shot over a card game, I think."

"Every once in awhile I just want to write one of these horror tunes," quipped Buck with respect to 'Deadline' "and that's one of them."

Side two opens with one of those true Blue Öyster Cult oddities, strange on this record, and strange given the rest of the catalogue. 'The Marshall Plan' is a cleverly titled, humble little pop metal epic, somewhat reviled by BÖC fans as innocuous in the insipid spirit of 'Let Go' and 'Beat 'Em Up'. The Marshall Plan was an economic plan for the rejuvenation and reconstruction of post-World War II Europe, here resonating with a double meaning, referring to a young gentleman's plan to make it big in rock 'n' roll, i.e. as in Marshall amps, the young hopeful possibly envisioning his own economic renewal. The song sports an uncharacteristically plain and not so cryptic lyric, really piling on the cheesiness with a cameo from Don Kirshner himself announcing, 'Here's Johnny!' (Note: Don can be seen doing his bit on the infamous *Black and Blue* tour video, which documents the celebrated Sabbath and Cult co-headline jaunt). Credit goes to the entire band, no surprise given the friendly, collaborative feel of the thing, the tune sounding anything but the work of any one member. Even Martin Birch did a fair bit of heavy lifting, pulling much of this very "quilted" song together in the studio.

Al explains the unique process of assembling this light, likable ditty. "That was almost like an exercise. We decided we were going to write a song all together. I got this idea because there was so much squabbling about royalties. I figured we'd write a totally democratic tune, share the wealth, improve morale, bond artistically. It was like, after 'The Reaper,' it was kind of a difficult thing, in my opinion. I would have to say that I was responsible for organizing that disaster. But, I really wanted to see if we could write a song all together, everybody contributing something. And so that's probably the most democratically written song we ever did. I can't remember who contributed what, but that was it. I know that Allen did the lyrics, with input from Donald. Joe and I did most of the music and Eric did a little bit of everything."

Bolle: "While recording the song, Eric tried some alternate lyrics on the break where young Johnny talks to himself in the mirror. On one take, for example, instead of dreaming of stardom and getting his girl back, he speaks of this tough record executive telling him to get real guitars, real amps, growling, 'Hey kid, come back when you have a real band. Don't call me, I'll call you!'"

"We all knew that there wasn't anything commercial on the album, and that's the way we planned it," continues Albert. "So Columbia decided to make a video out of this song so it would be played on *Don Kirshner's Rock Concert*. It was fun making a video although I was disappointed with how it came out. It was a silly song that was as tongue-in-cheek as anything we ever did. Then the next year I heard 'Jukebox Hero' and two years later, 'Summer of 69,' and I thought wow, this idea might have been good if we had been sincere about it. I was thinking about if I had written the lyric, it wouldn't have been anything like that, but more open-ended. I like open-ended songs. I usually don't feel the need for closure in a song, whereas Donald always felt the need for closure. Most of his have a definite ending, like a short story, starting with 'Last Days,' but excepting maybe a few on *Flat Out* and the songs he wrote with Meltzer. Those are all open-ended."

Trying to figure out what would work on radio was turning out to be a fool's game, says Albert. "Well, oddly, we'd put out 'Godzilla' and that never did very well on the radio, even though if you listen to classic rock now you hear it all the time. But that one was one that didn't do so well on the radio. 'In Thee' was a radio hit even though the album bombed. Then I think we put out 'Marshall Plan' from *Cultösaurus* and that didn't do well. But we kind of… it was against our wishes. We did not want to put out anything. We didn't want to have a single on that record. Of course Columbia says, 'What?! You gotta have a single.' So they put it out and it didn't do anything. But you know, it didn't bother us because we're like, that's not the point. We were trying to make an album that… because what happened was after *Mirrors* didn't do well, we really took a step backwards. When we first started and we would hang out with these Alice Cooper guys, we were all into making something that was original—and if it sounded like anything else we changed it. Because it was all about being original and different, and we lost sight of that after we had the hit. So we had to get back to that attitude, as far as creating our music. As a matter of fact, Donald had written 'Burnin' for You' for *Cultösaurus* and we rejected it because we thought it was too ordinary. Which he never fails to rub it in: 'Oh, you didn't want to do it the first year.' Then we needed a hit. 'No, you fixed it up.' 'I did not.' It's exactly the same (laughs)."

In any event, the light-heartedness of 'The Marshall Plan' is quickly forgotten come track two, Albert and Caryn's fast-paced rocker 'Hungry Boys' (originally 'Hungry Boys in Brooklyn' sung by both Joe and Al), a song that takes a twisted black humourous look at, well, looking for and craving drugs.

"'Hungry Boys' was inspired by Kasim Sulton in the summer of 1977, when we were on tour with Utopia in Canada," explains Albert. "I believe we were in Winnipeg, and Kasim came to my room and said, 'I am starved! I can really use something to eat. Is there anything to eat?' I said, 'Well, I brought some apples back from the gig and I've got some beers.' He went, 'Ugh! But I'll take an apple.' So he did and he left. Caryn was there with me at the time. She was pregnant with my oldest son, and I said, you know that gives me an idea for a song, 'Hungry Boys'—listen to this! Originally it sounded more like Utopia and it was really dedicated to Kasim. But she said, 'This is a terrible idea, but we can make it into something else.' It was her idea to make it about a drug deal, people from Queens that she was familiar with." Side note: One of Buck's rare non-BÖC sessions was for Sulton's solo record, on which Buck can distinctly be heard on three tracks.

Following 'Hungry Boys' was another one of Joe's subversive pop tunes, 'Fallen Angel' (originally 'Fallen Angels') pomping along with one of the band's signature, buoyant light metal arrangements, topped with an oddly histrionic Joe vocal, loosely fitting lyrically within Joe's usual portfolio of good versus evil stories. The lyric mixes with considerable aplomb biker imagery, the story of Lucifer, and transformation at the hands of a captivating woman, the character resenting feelings of love as he pines for his outlaw days. There's a great sense of motion, due in large part to the succinct lyric provided by Helen Wheels, who recalls, "That was due to my many years of motorcycle experiences with Harley riders and various types of outlaws; just something that erupted out of the middle of all that."

Joe offers this chain of events. "That actually started as a Pepsi jingle (laughs). It's actually true. We were asked by David Lucas who was a jingle guy in New York, and he said, 'Hey! I want you to come in and do a Pepsi tune.' After we did it, we thought it was stupid. Luckily it didn't catch on, although you know, I'd probably be driving a nicer car today if it did catch on (laughs). So I came back from that session with the thought that hey, let me write something jingly. Also, I was thinking in terms of a Todd Rundgren song, so that's where that came out. I was thinking, well, what would Todd do in a situation like this? Helen rewrote the lyrics several times to that. But the real key was when I had gotten into the studio, I sang one line of the song, and Martin Birch said that was great. He said, 'Well, why don't you sing the whole song like that?' It was in this high voice. I ended up sounding like Roger Daltrey but actually in my mind, I was trying to sound more like Bon Scott, because I really liked his singing with AC/DC. I tried to nail it, but I don't know, maybe I didn't have enough whiskey in me (laughs). Then again, I probably wouldn't be alive today. But that was the idea with that."

Further on his vocal abilities, Joe says that he's, "sort of influenced by a lot of the classic vocalists. Brian Wilson... I just saw him a couple of weeks ago. I saw him twice, and for a guy who is 65, he's pretty good, you know? I sort of take my approach to harmony from him; he's the master of harmony. But there are other people. I think John Fogerty has done great work. He's older than I am, so those are my influences. So, if I can keep my thing going like that, I'm very happy. Albert says that my solo album has some of the best singing I've ever done on a record. A critic. You've got to impress your brother (laughs)."

That's Joe as a vocalist, but how about as a personality, within the chemistry of the band? "Wow, I don't know. I was always a pretty happy guy. I loved being on tour, I loved performing. I would be like… if there was a stress in the band, I would try to be the peacemaker. That was kind of my role. Maybe other people have different ideas. But I certainly loved the shows that we did. My solo album's got a song called 'Travelin' Freak Show,' a travelogue. I had been reading books about famous rock palaces and venues all over the world, and I'm thinking, wow, I played there. I would think this would make a good idea for a song. But as I was writing it, I started thinking about some of the tours that we did, like with Alice Cooper and after that we did a Rod Stewart and The Faces tour, which certainly was a freak show."

Back to *Cultösaurus,* Joe expresses considerable fondness for the record as a whole. "This is an album that has a lot of layers. You've got your 'Black Blade,' your 'Divine Wind;' that was a pretty intense song. I'm not crazy about 'The Marshall Plan,' but 'Hungry Boys' is a bizarre tune, 'Unknown Tongue.' That's a pretty good album and Martin was great, a real producer. You could tell that he just knew what sorts of sounds he would get on tape. It was a pretty simple process but it was inspiring."

Next up was 'Lips in the Hills' which stands today as one of the band's heaviest metals, amongst a catalogue which—let's face it—usually didn't cough up too much heavy metal on a purely musical level. But 'Lips in the Hills' is a quick-paced tune with a considerably aggressive riff (Albert says calls it "really fast and a little hard to do") and some nice textural soloing from Donald. Writing credits go to Donald, Eric and Richard Meltzer. Bolle: "Buck's third submission was called 'Hold Me Tight,' a great riff but certainly not a very Cult-sounding lyric. During rehearsals, this was mainly referred to as 'Track X' as they tried a few alternative lyrics, before settling on Meltzer's 'Lips in the Hills.'"

The lyric had a nicely enigmatic quality to it, fusing BÖC's two favourite worlds of sci-fi and the supernatural, delivered in their usual cryptic manner, with a great, dramatic vocal from Eric. "'Lips in the Hills' is another Meltzer song about feeling entrapped by people," explains Gregmar. "But I think it's another male/female love story. I can't quite remember what Richard told me. We talked about quite a lot of his lyrics and he just goes, 'You know, I was on acid when I wrote this.' But, he always has an explanation with it, which is cool. He was such a weird, wild guy. You have to know that Meltzer is no taller than Albert. He's 5'2" as well. Buck, Albert and Richard, the short midget guys in the band. 'Lips in the Hills' is definitely about sexual frustration, which he felt he could write in terms of Blue Öyster Cultology. Meltzer felt he could mix these messages with scientific aspects, even though they were the ones that had read all these HP Lovecraft books and Meltzer didn't. He was more into discovering everything for himself. So he tried everything. His latest book, *The Night (Alone)* has some fantastically funny anecdotes about Blue Öyster Cult, but it's hidden, veiled. You'll find them when you read it." 'Lips in the Hills' may also be interpreted as a second, more opaque reading on the Roswell incident (see 'The Vigil').

Richard himself offers a trivia note, then a tangent. "There was a book cover by some Texas writer (ed. James Crumley). This was in the '70s; he wrote a book called *The Last Good Kiss* and another book called *Dancing Bear*. Nice guy, I met him; he did a lot of scripts in Hollywood. But anyway, the cover of *The Last Good Kiss* has lips above mountains, and that's where I got that. Basically, after a certain point, the stuff that ended up on Stalk-Forrest was stuff I really felt that I had a real personal interest in, and I wrote those things with great care. By the time they were BÖC, they had rejected so many things I gave them that were any good, that I just went out of my way to write things as fast as I could, you know, with expedient rhymes, really, just images that, once they were doing videos, 'Oh, give us something we can do a video of,' and I think it affected all bands' videos. The lyrics of all bands became 'What can we shoot?' It certainly affected them. But in any case, I don't mind 'Burnin' for You.' That I wrote a bit before they used it. 'Lips in the Hills,' I'm sure I tossed off in five minutes."

Closing the record was 'Unknown Tongue', another metaphysical pop song, mysterious but served with hook, slightly tough in arrangement yet melodic and smooth, captivating lyric courtesy of David Roter, a friend of Albert's and Sandy's from way back.

"I went to Stony Brook and lived in a house with Pearlman and Meltzer and Andrew Winters," recalls David (since deceased from cancer). "Andrew's the guy they threw out, the most bitter man alive. Maybe Pete Best is more bitter. Donald was Andrew's best friend. Of course they hate each other now. So they started getting together. Andrew was playing lead guitar, but then Donald came around. You know the story; they picked up Allen hitchhiking. That's how they met. Albert was Donald's friend. So Albert was dropping out and they all found that house. I was just about to graduate, and I was like a folk singer there, and they actually backed me up for one show. But the year they actually started happening, I went off to grad school in California, sociology at Irvine. Then that next year, everybody was trying to get out of the draft and everything. Then I came back and they were living in a different house. They were just starting to gel. Pearlman was like a big deal writer, with *Crawdaddy*, and so was Meltzer, so they got the band gigs. They actually backed Jackson Browne."

Which begs the question: why aren't there any David Roter lyrics on earlier BÖC records? "I think they thought I sucked (laughs). I don't know exactly what they thought. No, they thought of me as a folk singer. Plus I wasn't really around. Pearlman and Meltzer were actually writing words then. But they didn't actually think that they could write. I think the whole thing was really run by Pearlman at the time. I think they were in awe of him intellectually. It's funny, because anything even close to becoming a hit was written by Donald. In my opinion, he wrote the best lyrics."

Albert gave this profile of Roter (when Roter was still among us), with an interesting digression into his daily routine these days: "We team up regularly. But actually, I have a day gig. I teach in a high school now, and this job was provided by him who encouraged me to take this gig when I was completely broke. Actually I was driving a cab to be honest and David was working as a teacher. I've known him for over 30 years now, and for most of that time he's been a school teacher. Now I'm a teacher. I teach music, and supervise the school newspaper. It's actually a lot of fun. My problem is that I just don't have enough hours in the day. It's terrible, because every time I go on vacation, I come back to work and I'm totally into the band, and I've got to do school. As the year progresses I get all these great ideas on how to make classes exciting. I've been doing it eight years now, so. But anyway I see David every day. Actually, what we have collaborated on without fail is every graduation we sing a song, and we always do a different one, never two the same. We do little songs for our friends and for our students." Of note, David co-wrote '(666) Devil Got Your Mother' on the first Brain Surgeons record, and Albert returned the favour, producing on David's own recordings.

David explains how the link-up with the band finally happened. "Well, Albert dug what I was doing, and at one point, Sandy Pearlman and Murray Krugman were going to sign me to Columbia. But it's the way they are, you know, how they dicked around with *Imaginos* and everything. It was like a year or so of, 'Oh, we've almost got it.' In truth I really had no idea how to put things together. So I started working with Albert, recording some things. Then actually it hit me: how do you get these guys to record a song? You offer them something. So I said to Albert, 'Hey man, I'll give you 50% of this 'Unknown Tongue'.' We made a demo of it, and I said, 'You get the Cult to do it, I'll give you 50% of it.' He said, 'Aw, I'll take 25%.' That's when I realised that's how rock 'n' roll is done. When you really think about it, that's all rock 'n' roll is—it's arrangement. Albert was really responsible for the arrangement. So anyway that's it. It came down to if Albert didn't do one of my tunes, he could get maybe one of his tunes in. Man, I remember one night, we were working on a song, about 3:00 in the morning. This is when he was living in Connecticut, when he was totally fucked-up! I said, 'Hey man, why are you doing this? Why are you working on my stuff so late?' He said, 'Because I think you should be heard, man.' Then I decided, man, that guy was going to be my friend for the rest of my life."

David sheds some light on the 'Unknown Tongue' lyric. "Well, see I'm a Jew, and it's about my fascination with gentile chicks. I was going with my first one, and when we'd have sex, she would say stuff like, 'Mary Mother Of God!' That just drove me nuts, man. I thought that was just great. So yeah, I wanted to write something like that Billy Joel thing, 'Only the Good Die Young.' I wanted to write something like that, but only a little darker. So it's really a Jew's misconception of what gentile chicks are all about. Because the thing I really dug about Catholicism was how the blood and the sex all came together. So that was that."

Bolle has this to say about the specific story line of Roter's mysterious lyric: "How do I explain 'Unknown Tongue?' This girl's trying to find out what life's all about, she's like 12, 13—her first menstruation comes about. She tries to discover what it was all about. She probably was shocked, because nobody had ever told her. She doesn't speak to her mum about it. But it becomes obscure, because the song begins in the middle of the story and ends several chapters later, in the middle of the story. We don't get the beginning; we don't get the end. David Roter is that kind of a character. So it's about awareness of life from a female point of view. The part about her cutting her palm and watching the blood, I think that's just his imagination, adding a fictional element."

Whatever one's interpretation, the song skillfully bridges the physical world with the spiritual, Roter wrapping an everyday occurrence in the language of mystery, telling the tale with enough obfuscation so as to allow a straight supernatural reading if one wishes.

It was refreshing to see that critics took Blue Öyster Cult seriously enough to be hard on the band, but give credit where it was earned. "*Since the glory of 'The Reaper,' it's been all downhill for Blue Öyster Cult,*" wrote *NME*'s Phil McNeill. "*Agents of Fortune, the album built around that classic track, took the metallic imagination and occult preoccupations of their previous records and added a lethal touch of sophistication: undoubtedly one of the best albums of '76. Together and in contrast with* Secret Treaties *and* On Your Feet or on Your Knees*, it established BÖC as the world's heaviest heavy rock band. Their deterioration since then has been as grim as the parallel decline of Britain's once finest, Thin Lizzy.* Spectres *took a distinct AOR tack, the live set* Some Enchanted Evening *portrayed the Cult as just another bloated American stadium supergroup, while last year's* Mirrors, *their first record without the guiding hand of Sandy Pearlman, was a pathetic mishmash of twee love songs and turgid harmonies.*"

"*But straight from the title,*" continues the clearly knowledgeable McNeill, "Cultösaurus Erectus—*a well ironic appellation for the shortest dinosaur rock band on the planet—sets them firmly on the right track. At last. For a start, it's LOUD—not because it features bare-chested men screaming their lungs out and strangling their Gibsons in the familiar sorry demonstrations of machismo that motivate 99% of heavy metal halfwits, but because the music drives the volume with its own power. Donald Roeser long ago proved himself the contemporary master of danger volume guitar (a position disputed in my mind by Aerosmith's Joe Perry until his dismal Joe Perry Project debut set), and here he is given full reign, though always in context.*"

"*Producer Martin Birch has ditched the flatulent 'fat' sound of recent Cult albums, and the pulverizing guitar work and violent climaxes finally have the streamlined context they require. The songs, too, are a vast improvement. For a while there they 'grew up,' seemingly embarrassed about their sometimes clumsy comic book scenarios, but confidence flows throughout* Cultösaurus Erectus, *rendering their fantasies suspension-of-beliefable. If it had just one song with the haunting power of '(Don't Fear) The Reaper,'* Erectus *would be the Cult's best record to date. As it is, 'Unknown Tongue' is the closest they get. Strange, morbid, perverse and rather absurd, it refreshes places other hard rock bands don't even know exist. All this and best cover of the year too? I think they may be onto something here...*"

Roy Trakin, writing for *New York Rocker* puts a similar amount of elbow grease into his assessment, declaring, "*The entire first side of BÖC's latest features a virtually unbroken suite, with lots of nods in the direction of new wave-ish polyrhythms, and (curses!), spacey fusion. No anthems, just inexorable armies of churning guitars shot through the inevitable Marshall amps, as seamless in its bloated way as The Cure's minimalist* Seventeen Seconds.*"

"*Trouble is, if I wanted to hear progressive riffing, I wouldn't be listening to Blue Öyster Cult, now would I? From their inception, Blue Öyster Cult were critic's darlings—after all, they still sport lyrics by the legendary R. Meltzer, for years they were produced by ex-scribe Sandy Pearlman, and they helped spearhead a New York rock 'n' roll revival that eventually spawned Kiss, the Dolls and the Dictators, let alone Patti Smith, Television and the Ramones. But the band has been drying up creatively since '(Don't Fear) The Reaper,' and both 1978's desultory live album,* Some Enchanted Evening, *and last year's* Tom Werman-produced Mirrors, *seemed the cul-de-sac of their regression."*

"*Seen in this light,*" continues Trakin, "Cultösaurus Erectus *aims for a regeneration of sorts. The band has opted for still another producer, Martin Birch; the sound is depressingly arid and almost, shall we say, tasteful (?!). Confronting their own extinction with the tongue-in-cheek cover art, Blue Öyster Cult is consciously trying to stretch their limits and it shows, for good (the attempt) as well as for ill (the execution). At its most effective, heavy metal leaps from white noise to heavenly choirs to irresistible choruses, fudging over the shifts with sheer god awful bravado. The best heavy metal exploits these dynamics to create moving anthems. Unfortunately* Cultösaurus Erectus *comes alive in this way, only once, for the last three minutes of the first side on a track called 'Deadline.' The implication is that the guys came up with a melody under intense pressure to find one amidst the rest of the LP's metal meanderings. Otherwise, that same pressure has turned BÖC's effort into just the beast they lampoon on the cover. Not dead yet, but certainly mired, for the time being, in a tar pit of their own device."*

Cultösaurus turned out to be a real frustration for the band sales-wise. All felt that it was a really strong album. Indeed a surfeit of material was provided, possible for inclusion, including 'Lover's Loan' and 'White Hot Star' from Helen Wheels (the latter originally a Patti Smith lyric called 'Soul Jive' and then 'Jungle Fever'). Ronald Binder had offered 'Operation Stardust', 'Undying Flame' and 'Alpha and Omega', none of which ever made the cut, leaving 'I Am the Storm' as the only Binder song ever to appear on a BÖC record. Two additional Meltzer/Al Bouchard songs, 'I Need a Flat Top' and 'Adopt Me' weren't used, along with 'Lucy (Love's Lost Legend)' (Al and Caryn), 'Hell Bustin' Loose' (an Al tune, about Cozy Powell drumming with a dildo thrown on stage during a BÖC tour with Rainbow), Joe Bouchard's 'Gun' (fully finished twice, for this record and with Tom Werman for *Mirrors*), 'Hot Desert Sand', 'Anyway You Want It' and 'Infinity Machine' also from Joe, and finally a novelty track by Eric called 'Showtime' which re-emerged for '01's *Curse of the Hidden Mirror*, losing its novelty feel and becoming a classy musical track with a rich BÖC-worthy lyric.

There is a noticeable lack of contribution from Allen Lanier, who indeed receives no writing credits on the album whatsoever. This can be chalked up partially to the fact that much of his writing and indeed keyboard work was going elsewhere. Sandy, when asked about Allen's diminishing songwriting role had this to say: "Well (long pause), not much of what he did came to the band, so I'm not one to judge. I'm not sure where they wound up, with Patti or Jim Carroll or whatever, which is fine. So that's an interesting question. But like I said, from 1979 on and precious little between '72 and '79, not much was coming to the band from Allen."

Lanier contributed to most of girlfriend Patti Smith's records, plus songs to two of Jim Carroll's records '80's *Catholic Boy* and '83's *I Write Your Name,* John Cale's brilliant *Music for a New Society* from '79, while also (ironically) helping out Sandy Pearlman's stable of bands over the years, including Pavlov's Dog, the Dictators, Shakin' Street and The Clash. Those honky tonk keys on 'Julie's Been Working for the Drug Squad' being Allen's time-everlasting contribution to that classic Clash tune.

So quite evidently, there was no shortage of good material. But commercially speaking, the record was considered a bit of a non-starter, given the lack of label promotion, especially overseas, save for a successful mini-jaunt through Britain in November '79, which included four nights at the venerable Hammersmith Odeon. *Cultösaurus* was the first BÖC record to break the Top 20 in the UK, entering the charts at No.14, reaching No.12 (highest UK position ever for a BÖC record), and staying within the Top 40 for six weeks. Significantly, Britain was in the throes of the New Wave of British Heavy Metal, hard rock surging like never before with such acts as Motörhead, Saxon, Iron Maiden, Def Leppard and a rejuvenated Judas Priest, all doing brisk business, causing the biggest spike in metal sales since the beginning of recorded time. So BÖC's heavier material seemed poised and positioned for success—if only the record had been properly marketed. In the US the album peaked at No.34 on the Billboard charts, staying there for only two weeks. Sales are estimated to be 200,000 to 250,000, a slight reduction from the 300,000 racked with *Mirrors*.

Albert adds this final note. "The record sold even less than *Mirrors*, but at least the fans and the critics were saying, 'This is more like it.' So at least we still had our pride."

With the record hitting the streets on June 14th 1980, the band embarked on a few warm-up dates before hooking up with Black Sabbath and assorted support acts for the infamous *Black and Blue* tour, from late summer through to the Autumn.

The connection went beyond the similarities in band names. Martin Birch was producing the current BÖC record and then the next one as well, just as he had been on board for *Heaven and Hell* and then *Mob Rules*, from 1981. Sandy Pearlman was managing both bands as well, soon to cause a conflict of interest that built friction as the tour played itself out.

In any event, the pairing would be named Tour of the Year by *Performance* magazine, with Sabbath and BÖC co-headlining across America, switching off lead status based on who was bigger in what markets, resulting in a somewhat shoddy video recording the occurrence for posterity. As alluded to, all was not well interpersonally between the bands. Eric remarked at the time, "All I'll do is quote Ronnie Dio who claimed that, 'The only people who got anything from the *Black and Blue* tour were Blue Öyster Cult, who got a chance to play in front of our fans.' Well, what can you say to that?"

Albert also confirms that the band had problems with Dio, who was "certainly acting the prima donna."

And the late Ronnie's take on things? "I believe it was more the road crews that had a problem with each other. I don't know why. We really never had a problem with them. I've known Eric just forever. When he was going to school at Hobart University, my band, which wasn't Dio then—we were probably Elf or Electric Elves at the time—were playing there, and he would always come to the shows. It was great, just wonderful. So he's been a friend for a long time and I've known him for a long time. I've known Joe and Al and Buck, but Eric more than anyone else. So personally, I never had a problem. I don't think Tony did, I don't think Geezer really did. I think it was much more the crews who had an opposing feeling about it. So I think that was the problem more than anything else."

"The problem was that we had the same manager," continued Ronnie. "I believe that he, because he began that band and was there from the inception, and in fact, the band was really patterned after Black Sabbath—therefore Blue Öyster Cult, Black Sabbath, whatever—and so I think his allegiance was much more to them than it was to us. That annoyed us of course, as it should. It reached a culmination point in Madison Square Garden, on that show that has been documented, I guess, because the *Black and Blue* tour was done there, and it became a full-length feature film of some kind, and they were given everything and we were given nothing. They had all their pyro, everything; we had nothing, not a thing. And I think that really defined what the problem was. 'Hey, you're our manager too. Shouldn't we be using those kinds of specifications?' Within the film itself, there was a video that they had done that was part of that, and ours was only the presentation at Madison Square Garden. So I think that was a lot of the problem."

Did Sandy also do good things for Black Sabbath's career?

"Oh yes he did. He had good ideas. I like Sandy. I don't think anyone else did, but I'm maybe a bit more of an understanding person. He was very alien to them because he's a guy from New York, and he was managing Blue Öyster Cult as well, and maybe there was some friction between what Geez and what Tony felt. I don't want to put words in their mouth; I'm not really sure. I really think that it was... he did have good ideas, he did some good things, but I think a lot of them were lent so much more to Blue Öyster Cult than they were to us."

Geezer Butler remembers the tour as, "chaos." I asked him to clear up just who was fighting whom. "Well, because their manager had always managed Blue Öyster Cult, knew they needed a boost, and he saw us as being... he managed that version of Sabbath, and came up with the idea of both bands doing the same tour. But both bands insisted on using their own PA and their own lighting system, and so instead of like where it's half an hour between sets, it was like two and three hours (laughs). Whoever was finishing the night off ended up going on at one or two o'clock in the morning. It was just horrible."

Were the crews also fighting during that thing?

"I have no idea. I'm sure there was a few swear words exchanged."

"It was like a war!" adds Joe, leaning more toward Geezer's blunt assessment rather than Ronnie's expected (pathological?) smoothing over of feathers. "No, that wasn't blown out of proportion at all. It was a war zone. Okay, I'm talking about all these other bands, and most of the time I wasn't really sure what was going on with other bands on the tour. Because I would be preparing myself for our performance and didn't want to get too worn out. But I would follow what was going on with Black Sabbath on the *Black and Blue* tour. And there was just... it was not good. I wanted to have a good time, because it was the biggest tour of the year. But I think that Tony felt that they weren't getting their... all that was deserved by them, and we were just copying their riffs. Even though we were two distinctively different bands. They would always go on late and be a problem. If we did well, they would take an hour-and-a-half before they would go out and play their set. All the shows ran over time. It would be interesting to hear what Ronnie had to say about it."

So what was Ronnie's role in there? How was he to deal with?

"Well, at the beginning of the tour I talked to him, and told him what a fan I was," answers Joe. "Because I knew him when he was in Ronnie & the Prophets. Way back, when I was still in high school, I would go see him play. I was always a big fan, and when I got to college, he was like the big college band in Ithaca. Here it is, it's 1980, and he is headlining his band and I'm in my band, and there was a lot to celebrate and be happy about. But no, they were nasty. There was probably some internal stuff going on. Bill Ward left in the middle of the tour. Just left all of a sudden. So, what could have been an enjoyable co-billing... it was war (laughs)."

And Ronnie's problem was...?

"You know, I really don't know. Because after that first show, we didn't talk. Maybe I would see him once in a while, but after that he became aloof, and never came near us. Like I said, I've been a fan of his since I was in junior high school. He's a very talented guy. Now Geezer, he was like okay. Geezer came out because he liked my bass sound. He asked me, can I play through your bass rig? I said sure, come on out. So I was at a sound check and he came out, and I'm letting him play through my bass gear, and he went out like a week later and bought the same stuff that I was using. I don't consider myself to be a real bass maven, someone who is really into the high-tech of it. But it did sound pretty good, and when he played through it, it sounded great. So Geezer was like, okay. But Tony was not good."

Clarifying the scheduling issue, Bouchard explains that, "Yeah, if they had to open they would go on late. They just didn't like that at all. Eventually we said, well, rather than throw the schedule off for the whole thing, let's go on first, and we'll let them close the show. Even though we were supposed to alternate night after night. We said no, this is just too frustrating. We'll go on first and then they can do their thing."

"So yeah, I would say most of them, we let them go on. But that was good for us, because we played very good, very tight on that tour. Even though there might have been some personal friction in the band, we put that all aside, because our main goal was to do a much better show than Black Sabbath. So it was good, because competition brings out the best in a lot of people. So some of the *Black and Blue* shows were some of the best we ever played. And not because, you know, we weren't doing it for the money, we just wanted to show those guys! (laughs)."

With respect to who exactly was warring, Joe figures, "It was the crew, yeah, all the way from... and the problem was, Sandy was caught in the middle, because he was managing both bands. He made a lot of money on the tour, but he said it was some of the hardest money he ever made. Probably if he had the chance to do it again, he wouldn't. He was in charge of getting those other guys on stage, and trying to keep the peace, when crowds were all hyped-up and ready to riot. As the shows went on, we had a major riot in Milwaukee. We were banned from Milwaukee for years after that. They would not let Blue Öyster Cult play in Milwaukee, even though we had nothing to do with the riot. I was back in my hotel. I'm sitting there watching Johnny Carson on late night TV, and I hear a siren, and I think, 'Oh, I wonder what's going on?' Then I hear like four sirens, and then 25 sirens. I'm thinking oh no. What happened is, Black Sabbath went on really late and somebody threw something on stage, so they walked off; somebody said something. But I wasn't there; I was at the hotel. But I heard 150 cop sirens going past the hotel heading to the venue – oh my God, what the hell is going on? They pretty much destroyed the whole hall, in Milwaukee."

Of course Sabbath was under additional pressure due to strife dealing with their out of control drummer, er, sorta like Blue Öyster Cult, come to think of it. "You know, I don't know if it was Bill or if it was Vinny," muses Joe. "I didn't talk to Bill; I rarely saw him. I would see him on stage and that's it. Then all of a sudden, he hopped in his motor home and took off, and nobody saw him after that. I mean, this is the biggest tour of the year."

Sure Blue Öyster Cult might have done a few things that might not have been entirely nice...

"No. I mean, not that I know of." says Joe. "I'm sure when there are two road crews and there is friction between the road crews there might be something. But I would say that on our end we were always very professional. Get on stage when you're supposed to, get off stage when you're supposed to. You know, there are only a few rules. Everything else you can just go crazy. We had our fireworks. We had a motorcycle. There was no problem with that. You know, I don't know. The motorcycle... Eric would ride it out at the end, through all the smoke, and it was a nice thing which we would do for 'Born to Be Wild' or something like that. But I thought our show was really tight and the band played great—we were out to show those Black Sabbath guys how it's done (laughs). But they had sort of a different vibe going on there. Who knows? They've done well over the years, and they are legends, and I'm still a fan even though we had a lot of disputes."

"It was just that the Black Sabbath band were in a bad mood," says Joe, as a closing comment. "It was a bad mood that didn't go away. Still to this day, Tony will not let the company that wants to release the *Black and Blue* movie... he will not let them put it out, in America. Ronnie went and did another interview talking about the *Black and Blue* tour, and Tony said, I don't want it out. We don't have the papers to get the release of that between all the artists, and the guy who produced it has passed away, and supposedly some of the papers probably went with him."

Albert weighs in as well, answering first as to whether the Sabbath guys were particularly grumpy. "Yeah, I mean, Tony was. Tony was, and especially Ronnie Dio. Although, I think Ronnie's issues had more to do with Wendy, his wife and manager, and that she was trying to stick up for Ronnie's integrity or status or rights or whatever. It seemed like Wendy was making a big stink about a lot of stuff. And what would happen is, the slightest thing, and the roadies get all incensed. So it's the Sabbath roadies versus the Cult roadies, and there are subtle sabotaging things. Also, if the set runs over a little bit... for us, I mean, it was good, because as a band, we would thrive on competition—if they did something, we would just try to retaliate with the music. So it was good in that it just pumped us up to do a great show and try to pull out all the stops, every time we could. But sometimes, you know, if they were opening the show, it would be harder, because they could do stuff like take forever to come on and take forever to come off. So by the time we came on, the audience was exhausted. So it was easier when we were opening the show, because we could just leave the audience devastated, in our allotted amount of time. They would have to get on and compete with what just preceded them. But yeah, as drummers, I thought that Bill Ward was a fine fellow. He was always nice to me, and I thought Vinny was even a finer fellow. Vinny is a great guy, and still a really good friend."

Comments Eric, specifically on the doomed commercial video, "It wasn't all that good and I don't think too many people saw it. It's a totally raw performance with nothing fixed up which doesn't happen too much nowadays. Usually there's post-production where they'll fix a flat note or use a different camera angle when something's played wrong, but we had none of that because it was too expensive! So as a singer, there are embarrassing moments."

"Well, there were no problems dealing with the Blue Öyster Cult," reflects the man in the middle, Sandy Pearlman. "I'm trying to think exactly what happened. There were some problems with the initial phases of the Black Sabbath tour, of 1980. It just wasn't doing that well. I suggested that we put them together with Blue Öyster Cult, and the shows did very well. Yes, I was right—it was the Tour of the Year, and every venue we played was sold-out, everywhere. We set records in some places for attendance. In Aloha Stadium in Honolulu (ed. August 31st, 1980, with Molly Hatchet and Shakin' Street, a third Pearlman charge)—I think it's been surpassed since then—but soldiers love Black Sabbath and Blue Öyster Cult, soldiers and sailors and Marines and Air Force dudes, who are all within a ten-mile radius of Honolulu. As well as a bunch of Hawaiians, who love heavy metal."

"So we got it all, and it was a fantastically successful tour. Black Sabbath resented having Blue Öyster Cult on the show, resented splitting the income. They regarded this as theirs. One day one of their long-time roadies pulled me aside and said that the problem here is this is Black Sabbath and Van Halen all over again. Van Halen had opened for Sabbath, as they did for Blue Öyster Cult, by the way, in the early '70s—Black Sabbath in the late '70s, Blue Öyster Cult in the early '70s. They really had trouble dealing with bands that were opening for them being better than them. So there was a tremendous amount of resentment. At some point, I can't remember when the tour reached Denver. Bill Ward, who was not in the best of health at the time, was having trouble making all the shows, playing them. He travelled by RV, separately, and sometimes they didn't get in as early as other times. But having said that, that really wasn't the problem. It's just that his health wasn't great, and it was always kind of dicey whether he was going to go on or not. When we got to Denver (ed. August 21st—Vinny was drumming for the band at the aforementioned Honolulu date), he either didn't get in early enough or he just couldn't go on. There's nothing deep, dark and mysterious about his ill health—it just wasn't good. We brought physicians in. We brought them in sometimes to the show, because he was having trouble actually performing."

"So in Denver he did not go on, and it was sold-out, and the gross was, for the time, 1980, enormous. Afterwards, some of the Sabbath retainers pulled me aside and said, 'Well, how many tickets did you have to give back?' I said, 'Oh, 15.' McNichols Arena held like 18,000 people, so they were thinking, oh, 15,000. 'No.' '1500?' 'No, 15.' Andy Blue Öyster Cult had just taken all of what was not a large amount of money these days but in 1980 it was an enormous sum of money. So yeah, they get to keep everything. So they decided that was it for Bill—I'm talking about Black Sabbath, not me. They fired him and Ronnie called up Vinny and there we are."

Fire of Unknown Origin

"But I never thought they would kick me out"

If *Cultösaurus Erectus* had caused warpage in the figures, radios appeared once again in 1981, playing BÖC's flashiest, most commercial and self-evident record of their career, *Fire of Unknown Origin*. Everything about this taut, immediate album played to the band's strengths. The cover art was a typically mystical sci-fi-ish illustration that possibly showed us once and for all, just what a Blue Öyster Cult might look like, Greg Scott's illustration portraying a secret society (a venerable BÖC preoccupation) in full regalia, with the band symbol on the lead druid's robe, and each mesmerized member holding in his hand, a blue oyster.

Greg's connection to the Cultsters is an interesting one, having first pitched the band as a cocky college kid. "It's funny. I had actually gone to New York during the summer in the midst of my being in college. It was '74, I guess. I was definitely a big, big Blue Öyster Cult fan. I think *Secret Treaties* was out at the time. But I took some of my artwork and basically snuck through security at Columbia, the big CBS building, and talked my way into getting past the receptionist, and got into the Blue Öyster Cult office and met Sandy and Murray. They didn't really know who I was. I was just a young guy from the Midwest with a burning desire to do album covers. Nevertheless, we had a brief meeting and that was it. They were kind of receptive to the little portfolio of work that I had."

"But you know, I had a ways to go before I was really ready to be an established artist in New York and so forth. I had gone to art college at the University of Nebraska, in Lincoln where I grew up. After I got out of college, I had gone to San Francisco to try and get a job at *Rolling Stone*. Some of my friends had moved out there the year before, and I had decided I really wanted to get out of Nebraska and start my career as an artist. I had this idea that I wanted to go interview at *Rolling Stone*, or see what other kind of job I could get in San Francisco, to get to the west coast. Basically I was hired right off the street, and I spent the next five years with them, and moved to New York with the magazine, when they moved. I basically started as an art assistant, and worked my way to assistant art director then associate art director."

"In New York, I was meeting all sorts of people," continues Greg, "and Paula Scher was one person I met at Columbia, and I had this idea for a Blue Öyster Cult cover that I'd been carrying around in my head. I mean, I had numerous ideas for them. Their name had always mystified me. I have a leaning towards the occult and mysticism myself anyway. I was born on Halloween, and a lot of my artwork has reflected this interest over the years, especially my more personal work. So I had this idea that I had presented to Paula, after I had met her. She had designed *Cultösaurus Erectus*, so I knew that she worked on BÖC covers. So I presented this idea of these masked monks standing as if like in a cult, and just basically translating the band's name into a visual image. She was very receptive to the idea. She basically said I can't promise you anything, but if you bring me a painting, I'll show it to their manager."

"I used an age-old painting technique called egg tempura, on a wood panel, although acrylic is my primary painting medium now," explains Scott. "But that was egg tempera on panel. It took basically a whole month working every day, although the original is quite small, about 15 inches square. I had left *Rolling Stone* in 1980, and one of my first projects after that was that painting for Paula. So I did the painting, brought it to her, and she showed it to Sandy. It actually sat around for nine months, because they had had a photo idea for *Fire of Unknown Origin*, which was based on a *National Geographic* photo, where there were kids, boys and girls, who were getting some kind of light therapy in Russia, and they were standing in a circle in their underwear. They attempted to recreate that photo for the cover, spending a lot of money photographing it, because they couldn't get the rights from *National Geographic*. They built a whole set and got all the kids to model in their underwear and so forth. They shot the photo, and then the powers-that-be at Columbia basically had one big meeting where they took my painting and the *National Geographic* spin-off photo and compared the two. They ended up choosing mine. They thought mine had more marketing possibilities, at that time for the band. Of course that image has been used in all kinds of ways for the band since."

On the subject of the mysterious mandala-like back cover illustration, Greg explains that, "That was a drawing I had already drawn for another illustration project. Basically Paula just had me re-draw the centre portion with the BÖC logo which they photo-mechanically inserted into the drawing for the back cover. The record finally came out in '81, and the painting was already a year old by that time."

As we dive into this surprise hit record for the band, I asked Albert about the "Special Thanks To Albert From Martin" designation on the inner sleeve of the package, the answer being an interesting glimpse into the sought after and guarded nature of production credits: "Well, after we finished the record I said to Martin, 'I did a lot of the producing on this record; do you think it would be too forward of me to ask you to put me as co-producer or something?' He declined, but offered to put 'Special Thanks To Albert,' saying, 'It's in my contract that I don't produce with anybody, but I'll put the special thanks to you, because you really did a lot of work on the record.' But Martin was great, a fantastic bloke and until recently, probably the best engineer and best producer I've ever worked with."

"When I first met him," continues Al, "I didn't know what to think because he didn't say much but once he got to know us he was very helpful in making those records. He spent a lot of time with the sounds and didn't mess with the arrangements too much. He told a lot of stories about working with Fleetwood Mac and Deep Purple. The night we mixed 'Burnin' For You' he called Christine McVie to chat."

"But having Martin on board," says Albert, didn't quell the problems the guys were having with each other. "I thought the group was going to break up because not one of them wanted to be in the studio while we were making it. Many tracks were just me, Joe and Donald on the basics. Martin Birch didn't even want to do it until I promised him that I would stay in the studio with him the entire time that he worked on the album and I did. I knew he could get us back to the things that we did well. I slept in the studio most nights. But I never thought they would kick me out. You have to mess up pretty bad to get kicked out of the thing you started, but look at Steve Jobs. It happened to him too. I was caught in a conundrum. I felt that part of our lack of success was because I hadn't asserted myself, but once I did and we got the success back, the guys couldn't stand to be around me, I guess."

Assessing Martin against the band's other knob-twiddlers, Joe figures, "Sandy and Murray were more conceptual while David Lucas was more practical. Tom Werman and Martin Birch were amazing and were totally different than the other guys. I learned from all of them. I actually went and took some engineering lessons. After I left Blue Öyster Cult I took a class on engineering to learn some tricks and that helped. Martin Birch was a guy who went for a lot of spontaneity, where Tom Werman wanted to do records that were well calculated. If a great accident happened in the studio with Martin then you knew it would stay in. They had different ways of doing it."

"I am obsessed with... you can go on YouTube and you can find songs with just parts of the song. You can find like Fleetwood Mac with just the bass and stuff like that. When you hear a song all together you are not sure how they did it. The big one for me was when they put out a box set of all of the sounds for *Pet Sounds*. They had all of the vocals and all of the other stuff. VH1 has *Classic Albums* and I love watching how the albums are made. I am obsessed with that show. If it's on, then I am watching it. I want to know how Jimmy Page got the echo on his guitar. I want to know how fat the kick drum is on Mick Fleetwood's drum. I am a geeky guy, I can't deny it. I like the tiny little details. I love that part of the recording process. I wasn't into it back in the day. I did my parts and I got out of there. Donald was the guy that was there for most of the recording. He would do lots of guitar parts over and over. I probably should have paid a little more attention to that. I knew the appeal of the group was Buck Dharma's amazing guitar. We had some good vocals and we could do some harmonies. Allen would squeeze his personality in there, but the main thrust was to get that Buck Dharma guitar in everybody's ears."

"I like that album a lot," continues Joe. "I feel we connected; I love that record. It was our second record with Martin after *Cultösaurus*. There are a lot of people who like that record but I don't think we had as much of a balance on that record as we did on *Fire of Unknown Origin*. We had different producers over the years. Mostly Sandy Pearlman, our manager. We went to Tom Werman who had produced Cheap Trick records. I love those but as I say, he was very structured in the studio. He had his way of doing it and that is the way we did it. Martin Birch was very laid-back. He would just let us experiment all we wanted in the studio. When the chaos reached a fever pitch Martin would say, 'Its time to record!' He would push the button at the right time in order to capture a real performance. We spent a lot of time rehearsing before we went into the studio. It was kind of like Martin Birch's attitude where he said, 'Figure out what it is you have to do and I will tell you when you have taken it too far over the edge.' He would rein it back just enough. He was exciting to work with. I would have stayed with Blue Öyster Cult if I could have done another record with Martin. He is a brilliant engineer/producer; he mans the controls. Some of the things he did with Deep Purple were great. He would let them get off into some heavy performances. There is not a lot of polish on those Deep Purple records but you can tell that each guy in the group is feeling it when it all comes together. A record like *Machine Head* is fabulous."

So, in the capable hands of Martin Birch, a stirring and inter-stellar record was hatched. The band's tenth such statement in nine years, issued in June of 1981, *Fire of Unknown Origin* opened in fine fashion with its long-gestating title track, utilizing a Patti Smith lyric over what is essentially an Al Bouchard song, although Joe, Eric and Donald also receive music credits. This tune was put forth as a possible song as far back as *Agents of Fortune*, mention of it even getting into magazine pieces at the time, with Al's demo, according to Bolle, being one of the finest BÖC rarities (I disagree—see comments in the *Agents* chapter).

Al reiterates the story of the track getting bumped from *Agents of Fortune*: "The choice among the three producers, Pearlman, Krugman and Lucas, was between 'Fire of Unknown Origin' and 'Tenderloin.' They told me that even though they felt that they liked 'Fire' better, that Eric would freak out if I sang more songs on the album than he did, so we went with 'Tenderloin.' It's funny that they didn't think of replacing 'Debbie Denise' with it. For some reason they thought 'Debbie Denise' was better. I didn't mind because I thought 'Fire' would be released eventually because it was a really good performance. I gave myself goose bumps when I sang it. It was method acting. Murray told me to think that it was my parents that had died in that fire and I really got into the pathos of the moment. Later on, I felt I'd gone over the top and so I rewrote it for Eric to sing in his mechanical style."

The song, as issued, is a minimalist, chilling pop salvo that evokes the synthesized new wave of similarly morbid band The Stranglers. Patti's lyric is succinct and beautiful, one of the most compact and imagistic of the band's entire catalogue. Patti actually had recorded a radically altered, very angry but sparse version of the song which saw release as the b-side to her single, 'Frederick'.

Next up was the song that, to put it bluntly, saved BÖC's collective hides. 'Burnin' for You' was a perfect pop song with a gushing hook, a radio-friendly, almost Cars-y chorus, and an arrangement that is an excellent example of the band's ability to craft enjoyment with spare tooling.

"That song wasn't even supposed to be on the album," explains Bolle, "and it's clear it has nothing to do with the rest of the record. As far as I'm concerned, those two songs 'Burnin' for You' and 'Joan Crawford' should never have been on the album. 'Burnin' for You' was a Richard Meltzer lyric which was given to the band in 1979, early '80. I believe there's three different versions of that song.

Albert wrote one as did Joe and Buck. Albert didn't like his version, heard Buck's version, thought it was great. That same week, Joe submitted his version to Albert who said Buck's version is way beyond this, but it's still not good enough, so let's fix it. So they worked on it. Buck did not want the song to be a Blue Öyster Cult song because he said that's too much me. Not lyrically, but musically. He said he wanted to keep it for his solo album, *Flat Out*. The band persuaded him to do it because they really, really needed a hit single again. They were really concerned that 'Burnin' for You' was the only thing that would allow the band to continue, otherwise they would have to quit. There was no money left and they owed so much money from three records that had bombed. I think *Fire of Unknown Origin* went platinum immediately, while perhaps even edging towards double platinum now." It is of note that Albert (in the late '90s, mind you) thought sales figures for *Fire of Unknown Origin* were around 800,000, still a considerable number.

"I lifted some of that from Jack Kerouac, somewhere in *On the Road* I think, or *Dharma Bums*," notes Meltzer on the 'Burnin' for You' lyric. A couple of those lines came out of that. And I don't remember if more than a couple lines came out of that or if just the inspiration was that. 'Home on the highway, home in the city,' all that kind of business. But I didn't think of it as a country song, which is kind of what they did with it. I mean, mainly I would just write lyrics and give them to Albert or Allen or whoever, or Buck, and if they did anything with it, great. But I would say they only used about 2% of what I gave them. I've got stacks of it, in a box somewhere. I mean, some of the things that they turned down, where they end up, I don't know. Some of them I gave to the Dictators who didn't do anything with them; I'm just not sure. The Dictators never used any of my lyrics, but they have that song on *Bloodbrothers*, 'Borneo Jimmy,' which is about me. Because that was my first pseudonym."

Meltzer had this to say in a 1982 interview, about working with the band, "My set-up with them is that every so often I send them a bunch of lyrics, like maybe ten songs. For *Fire of Unknown Origin*, I gave them seven, but they actually had 'Burnin' for You' from the album before. I've given them these kind of personal lyrics before, but they've never used them until now. The Cult very rarely show their soul. They've generally avoided using lyrics as a cutting edge. Instead they go for the arrangement or pompous guitar. They've been together 14 years. They're in their late 30s. It's not just them; bands that old tend to get a little rigid and there's not that much room left for irony."

"This was a song that we thought would be a hit as soon as we heard Donald's demo of it," notes Al. "It's funny because the year before, he'd played it on acoustic guitar and we rejected it because it didn't seem heavy enough. There were two mixing sessions, one that Donald mixed and one without him (for most of the time). We used the one without him for the record. The muted echo on the rhythm guitar during the verses was done completely by hand—no automation of mixes in those days."

Sandy also raved about the song, and Martin Birch's role in bringing it to perfection. "'Burnin' for You' could not have come out better. It's a great song, and Martin gave it a great sound."

It is of note that the song figures in what was to be the band's first television appearance, the Cultsters playing it live on *The Merv Griffin Show* on July 25, 1981, along with the required '(Don't Fear) The Reaper'. 'Burnin' for You' was also featured in a band appearance on *The Uncle Floyd Show* that same year, as well as *The Tomorrow Show*, where Eric and Buck were interviewed by none other than Charles Grodin.

"I thought 'Burnin' for You' really didn't fit," laughs Joe. "That's how stupid I was! 'Take that 'Burnin' for You' song off of that album!' Sometimes I make good suggestions; sometimes I make bad suggestions. Donald had this demo, and the bass part was very light. So when we recorded it, Albert and I locked into a very heavy thing. So it could have come out a lot lighter sounding, but the way Albert and I played it, it came out with that heaviness which was great for the song, and it's become a classic."

Which brings up a good point. Yes, 'Burnin' for You' has punch, but then again, so does the whole album, compared to its predecessor, also recorded by Martin Birch and not that long previous. What gives?

"That's a good question," muses Joe. "I don't think *Cultösaurus* was mixed that well. Here's Martin Birch's theory. When he did *Cultösaurus*, he had just finished *Heaven and Hell* with Sabbath, and he was really exhausted. So when he did *Fire of Unknown Origin*, he was fresh, and then when he finished *Fire of Unknown Origin*, he went to Black Sabbath and did *Mob Rules*. I talked to him about this after, that it was better when he was fresh (laughs). If he was doing back-to-back really heavy albums, his ears were shot. But I don't really know. I think it was just that Martin was not used to the studio when we did *Cultösaurus*. So it was a new studio for him, and you never know what you can get. It was the first time working with us, so by the second time he figured it out; he had gotten a bit better sound out of each of us."

Adds Albert, "Well, from my perspective, I worked a lot harder on *Fire of Unknown Origin*. With *Cultösaurus*, I was not really part of the mixing. With *Fire of Unknown Origin*, I really felt we had a hit record. *Cultösaurus*, I felt that I wanted it to be a little rougher; *Fire of Unknown Origin*, that was not to be the case. We were going to try grab the golden ring again. I was concerned that we not screw up, because there's a million ways... like there's lots of ways to make a hit, but it's not that hard to screw it up. It's like, how to make a hit is not subtle. But it's not obvious either. You know what I mean? In the beginning, when we first started mixing it, I felt like stuff was getting screwed-up. So I asked Martin if I could be there for all the mixes, which was fairly grueling. I mean we would work for 20, 30 hours on one song with no break. It was insane. But I'm pretty happy with how it came out."

What were Martin's strengths and weaknesses as a producer?

"Well, one of his strengths was his tenacity. I mean, he would just go in and focus on a sound, and try to get the perfect sound, and he would just go over and over and over it until he had it, exactly the way he wanted it. You might not see that he was doing little things, fiddling here and fiddling there, but then at the end, you would go, oh wow, that really sounds clear and full and fat. As far as *Fire of Unknown Origin* goes, I heard what I wanted to hear out of the band."

Next up was 'Veteran of the Psychic Wars' another Eric Bloom/Michael Moorcock collaboration, the record's epic, a song with a canny link to Queen's

'We Will Rock You' with shared signature pounding percussion riffs (even if we haven't heard 'Veteran' at too many hockey games lately!). It is appropriate to mention here that *Fire of Unknown Origin* as a whole record, rocks somewhat disjointedly. One cause of this might be that some of its tracks were written for the pioneering animated movie *Heavy Metal*, which was a simple sword and sorcery story, taking its lead from the themes that regularly showed in the unique magazine of the same name. The movie became somewhat of a cult classic, aided toward that status by its heavy rock double LP soundtrack album featuring a number of big bands offering exclusive tracks.

"The *Heavy Metal* people approached us for some tunes for the movie," explains Eric, "and they sent us the screenplay, the script. I think, Albert just took some words right out of the script and wrote a song. In all we gave them six or seven songs, but politically they could only choose one, because they had to feature a lot of other bands. 'Veteran,' which I wrote, was a song for our record, but they liked it best, and used it in the soundtrack, so it had nothing to do with the movie, but they liked it. The songs we wrote for the movie, they didn't want. So that's that story."

The flashy title was later used by Moorcock in '87's *The Dragon in the Sword*, but Moorcock's own 'Standing on the Edge,' a song from Hawkwind's '75 record *Warriors on the Edge Of Time* contains some very similar text. Lyrically, the song's an intelligent enough look at the state of mind in which a "veteran of a psychic war" might find himself, embattled, drained, wise but wholly without energy. Musically, the song's a definite atmospheric classic, full of mysterious twists and turns. It happens to be one of Joe Bouchard's favourite BÖC tracks. "I think that that's the best thing Eric's ever done," says Joe. "A great song. I like the songs that are very opaque, songs that are what they are, songs with different layers and sounds. 'Veteran''s a good example of this."

"This track was brought in by Eric and we knew right away it was a good song for him to sing," adds Al. "Donald did his solo in three different passes with the echo printed to tape and then we edited it together. If you listen carefully you can hear the echo trails change at the edit points. Possibly Eric's best vocal on record of all time."

"The drum part was an idea that I got from my brother," adds Joe, offering another explanation for the track's 'We Will Rock You' bottom end. "When we were little kids we used to do these parades with our high school bands. We would do this beat as we got closer to the cemetery. I said, 'Albert how about you do that beat that they would do when we went to the graveyard?' It is really ominous. Unfortunately, the bass guitar part is all but lost (laughs). But if the song really stands out as a production then that is really what counts."

Continues Joe, "I played the bass part on that, but as the song was developing, we said, 'You know what it really needs? A bow bass.' A big, you know, double bass, playing with a bow and playing these big roaring sounds, so Martin said, 'Okay, let's do it. Let's get this guy.' So they got a cellist and a bass player to come in and play the bass line on 'Psychic Wars.' It meant that my part was almost... you couldn't hear it at all. Then they added the drums, which were played live by four different people, which added incredible emotion to the track. Like I say, it's my favourite Eric Bloom song—it's a real credit to his talent."

"Another Mike Moorcock tune," continues Albert, "which, that one I didn't have to add that much to it, other than to try and get that really panoramic kind of drum sound. Like I say, I think Eric's vocal on it is fantastic, the best, I mean, I thought Eric had finally recorded a hit. But of course, it was a big song in the movie, but it was never… it was just outshined by 'Burnin' for You.' If I was in BÖC today, I would make them play that song every show—I would! I don't know why they don't do it. You know, Donald has a million places to shine, every show, but Eric, not so much, you know? Why they don't do that song now... I mean, they whip it out occasionally. I would do it all the time; I think it's a fantastic song. But anyway, that rhythm, I got the idea from the drum part in a Peter Gabriel song called 'The Intruder', which I was listening to a lot in those days, and we got that sound on the basic track, with the gated drums and all that stuff. Then Martin was like, 'This sounds a little bit too much like Peter Gabriel; wanna add something to it?' This is a good basic rhythm, why don't we just go crazy with it? We'll put a timpani on there and we'll get a bunch of other things; maybe we'll use some marching cymbals, and that's what we did. We had, I don't know, four or five people in the studio playing different tom toms and stuff, and anybody who knew how to play the drums, got up there and played that rhythm."

It doesn't sound too incredibly like Peter Gabriel though. Did the idea of using gating fall by the wayside?

"Yeah, it did. You know how you get these ideas, and then you go, 'Oh, I don't know. Maybe that's not so good. Maybe it's not that important.' Where you hear the gate is where I play the marching snare drum thing. It was really in your face (laughs), but yeah, I like that track, I'm really proud of it. I'm proud of that whole record."

Next to plate was 'Sole Survivor' a rare low-key Bloom composition, co-written with John Trivers and Liz Myers. Another in a long line of frosty, stand-offish pop songs, the tune's sci-fi lyric documents the thoughts of the last man on earth who, when offered what is believed to be his last chance of escape (via an arriving starship), skulks away and hides perhaps with thoughts of somehow reviving his species. It seems that Eric would have taken the alien invitation. "I guess it's kind of morbid, but I'll tell you something. If an alien walked in right now and said, 'We're waiting to take you away with us. You can never return but you'll be glad you went,' then I really think I'd go. It would be the biggest choice of my life, but the thought of that has been such a big part of my thinking, right from reading science fiction as a kid. I'd much rather talk about this stuff than rock 'n' roll any day!" For an expansion of this theme, see Eric's 'Take Me Away' lyric.

Al had this to say about 'Sole Survivor'. "That's another track that Eric wrote and although it has a pretty good vocal and a kind of story, I find it predictable and prosaic. If we had all the time in the world and were trying to make our *Sgt. Pepper* we probably would have made it better. This might have been the track that Martin mixed the day he flew back to England to start his next record."

Closing side one was one of BÖC's top five or so heaviest rockers, namely 'Heavy Metal: The Black and Silver', a tune that suffers somewhat of pandering to the cinematic, which Eric confirms. "We rewrote the lyrics of this song specifically for the movie, and we were surprised they didn't choose that one." Eric goes on to expand on his growing preoccupation (distraction) with the celluloid. "Film is almost more important than music to me now. I feel I've done the music business thing, while film still has magic for me. One of my major projects right now is an attempt to make a film based on Elric."

The lyric is an increasingly infrequent one from Sandy Pearlman, and it is one that has been criticized for being loose, fuzzy and perhaps unfinished. But Sandy defends it as his poetic, purposefully cryptic treatise on the alchemical origins of heavy metal, the engaging if somewhat un-useful supposition that heavy metal as a music, derives at least some of its inspiration from ancient alchemists' attempts at forging their own heavy metals. "The alchemical theme, 'Heavy Metal: The Black and Silver.' Right. It makes plenty sense. You take lead, the starting point for gold. Lead is the most catalytical of elements, identified with Saturn. The Blue Öyster Cult symbol is of course a symbol for lead in alchemy. And it's a symbol for Saturn in Greek mythology. It's also a symbol for chaos in Greek thought in general. So that pretty much wraps it up (laughs)."

But Al concurs that the lyric was somewhat haphazard. "That song was a real cut and paste job. The track was already recorded and I didn't feel that the lyric we had, 'Ear Damage' was 'mystical' enough for a BÖC album. I asked Pearlman to make a lyric for it, seeing as how he really had no financial reward from the album, not having produced it or any other songwriting credits whatsoever, and he was only to happy to oblige. 'Siege' (from *Imaginos*) was already written, so he just borrowed that line about 'world without end' to finish the phrase. Eric, Sandy and I went into a room with the tape of the track and worked on it until we had a finished lyric and melody line. Then Eric went into the studio and sang it, all in one night. We really rushed to get that record finished before Martin Birch had to go off and produce *Mob Rules* for Black Sabbath."

Al, in a separate interview, remarked that after the song was initiated as 'Ear Damage' it "then grew into 'Do it ('til it Hurts)' and was one of my joke songs, but Sandy Pearlman took a shine to the track and wrote the lyrics to order with Eric and me in the studio minutes before Eric did the vocal."

"'Heavy Metal' was a one-taker," recalls Joe. "I didn't play bass on that. I think Eric played bass on that. They just did it as sort of a goof, and it came out pretty good. Eric should've played more bass! (laughs). I don't know, I think Albert played the guitar. It was just crazy, what they were doing. It was like, let's just do one that is completely crazy. Because everybody had their little jobs to do, and every once in a while we wanted to throw everything out the window and see what we could come up with. That was an example of that."

Much of the specific imagery in 'Heavy Metal' derives from Adrian Berry's '77 book *The Iron Sun: Crossing the Universe Through Black Holes*, which sports the chapter headings "Where Matter Vanishes", "The Spinning Gateway", "Into the Whirlpool" and "The Forbidden Circle".

Side two opens with a second, 'Heavy Metal'-tailored epic, 'Vengeance (The Pact)' written and sung by the Bouchard brothers (Al came up with the riff), rocking out quite heavily, rife with what Joe likes to call "layers." Again, the song goes almost too self-evidently for the jugular, lyrically slotted into this new, too sword and sorcery-dependent realm the band found themselves embracing, almost as a crutch. The lyrics encapsulate the last story from the movie, featuring Taarna, a warrior woman who rides a giant bird. The song was cut from the film apparently because it wrapped up the entire 17-minute plot of the video in five minutes. It is another song that undermines the cohesion of *Fire of Unknown Origin*, helping to partition crudely the album between the movie songs and the non-movie songs.

Joe recalls that, "'Vengeance' is another song that we were trying to get on the *Heavy Metal* soundtrack. It should have gone in, if it hadn't been for the politics of the producers and stuff like that. But that was a song for which I had written other lyrics. We were actually out in North Dakota playing, and I had met this Eskimo who worked as one of the guys who sat in the nuclear silo. He was telling me his story, which became the original lyric, this thing about this Eskimo who was the guy that would be waiting there to pull the trigger if the Russians got out of hand (laughs). But musically at that time I was into writing epic-type things, songs with big riffs and lots of sections."

Next up is the second and best Bloom/Trivers/Myers collaboration, a sinister little cruise missile entitled 'After Dark', not a great lyric but an excellent verse arrangement and a deadly yet silky-smooth chorus. All in all, it's a composition with character and backbone. "This song I believe is under-rated," remarks Al. "It's a rocking track that has the popular vampire theme. Maybe the chorus is too repetitious but then that doesn't really hurt 'Smooth Criminal'. Go figure."

'After Dark' is followed by surprise concert favourite called 'Joan Crawford', a movie tune of a different colour, namely black and white. 'Joan Crawford' features a striking classical piano lead-in from Allen, which then collapses into a brisk, rhythmic pop metal verse and chorus combination, topped with brilliant, lucid but almost surreal lyrics from David Roter. Joe Bouchard had actually created the trademark piano intro at Albert's house one day, and had performed it on the demo. "I'm really proud of that little piano flourish. It's not really part of the song, but everybody hears it and remembers it. Albert did some skillful editing with the quarter-inch tape at the time. It came out pretty good."

"But yes, I did the demo for it. Basically, I went to Albert's house, created this part, just by improvising. Actually, I was doing some musical theatre at the time, as a rehearsal pianist, just as a side thing. My wife is an actress, so I was helping her out in a theatre project. And so I started doing this theatrical piano part, and then Albert spliced it together, spliced it and diced it, and came up with a really nice intro to his demo, and it became part of the song. In the studio, Allen played it all. He just copied my demo and did a great job. I think he plays a little bit better on the live version of 'Joan Crawford,' but that said, it's good."

Al relates the humourous germination of the song. "That was purely David Roter's idea. It was inspired by my ex-wife Caryn. David had come over to do a demo of a song called 'Russian Army on the March,' and while we were doing it she came in and screamed at me, and called me out of the room. When I went out of the room, David said to Jack Rigg who was also there, 'Christ, Joan Crawford has risen from the grave!' Jack Rigg—which is of course why he gets 25% of the song—said, 'That would be a great idea for a song.' That's all he did on the song! So David wrote it and came to me and said let's do this and that and a song was born. So yeah, that song was inspired both by the book *Mommie Dearest* and also the behaviour of my ex-wife while David, Jack and I were trying to record this demo. And yes, Joe wrote the intro but Allen played it."

David tells the torrid tale this way. "We were recording a song called 'Il Duce,' and this was very, very close to the end of Albert's marriage. Actually the vital part of the marriage was over. He was about to be tossed out of Connecticut. We were playing, about midnight and his wife came down to the basement as we were playing and she said, 'You guys have to get the fuck out of here right now!' Jack Rigg said to me, 'Did you see her face?' I said, 'You mean that twisted face, like Joan Crawford risen from the grave?' Then I wrote the thing in like about four or five minutes. Then a couple weeks later, I was helping Albert move his stuff (laughs), and that was the end."

For those who don't remember, Joan Crawford was a legendary but icy and abusive actress from the '50s, immortalized in chilling caricature by her daughter Christina in her tell-all book *Mommie Dearest*.

As a coda to the story, the song they were working on that fateful night, 'Il Duce' almost made it onto *Fire of Unknown Origin*. "'Il Duce', that song's on my *Bambo* album," says Roter. "What happened with that was that a friend of mine was making a copy of some tapes, and 'Il Duce' started to play, and Martin Birch said, 'That song's a hit, man.' So they did it, but they couldn't actually sing it. They couldn't get a handle on it. If you listen to my CD you'll hear that there are things that are funny but sad at the same time? This was like that and they just couldn't figure out a way to sing it. Then Pearlman came in and had that song 'Heavy Metal,' and said, no, I want to do my song. In those days he had a lot of influence with them. They were getting a song into the movie *Heavy Metal*. He thought it would be a lock if he wrote a song actually called 'Heavy Metal.' But they didn't use it anyway."

Fire of Unknown Origin sort of washed, ebbed and receded to a finish with a curious track called 'Don't Turn Your Back', a hypnotic but almost stalled composition credited to Albert, Donald and Allen Lanier (Allen's only credit on the entire record). The song was another one designed for use in the *Heavy Metal* movie, being the last to get cut from use, leaving only 'Veteran of the Psychic Wars' to represent the band.

"That lyric's straight out of the movie, about the cab driver picking up the girl," says Bolle. "It becomes a really nice, almost James Bond kind of lyric. My favourite line is the one about using the special option in the car. That's where he discards the people in the back. He just pushes the James Bond button and they just disintegrate, dispersed by gamma rays or something." Adds Al Bouchard, "Originally Allen wrote the music, like a long time before, and then I got the idea for the song, to do it around a certain aspect of the *Heavy Metal* movie, the taxi driver part. Donald and I just hammered up the lyrics."

Al has also remarked that, "Donald wrote these lyrics after we'd been working on the track—originally written by Allen—for a couple weeks. For awhile I was thinking that he wrote it for me but now I think that it was probably just a coincidence that it corresponded to my situation six months later."

All in all, 'Don't Turn Your Back' is one of the record's most pensive and anonymous songs. Confirms Buck: "That was one of the songs written for that *Heavy Metal* movie. When they came to us looking for material, we all got on that and we cranked out about three or four songs actually. Of course, that one didn't make it to the movie."

Rolling Stone magazine was still liking the band, although BOC still had not—nor ever would—be the recipient of a major feature in the venerable rock mag. "*Over the years,*" wrote Parke Puterbaugh, "*Blue Öyster Cult have inadvertently cultivated a schizophrenic reputation both as a bookish clan at home on esoteric intellectual turf and as pile-driving arena rockers setting cities on flame with rock 'n' roll. In effect, the Cult forged their popular identity as an incendiary touring band, while their skillful studio sorcery was favoured by a number of rock aesthetes who signed on from the beginning. Now, at last, comes a record that should please all factions.* Fire of Unknown Origin *is potent guitar rock informed by literate songwriting, assured ensemble playing and flawless production. Though their genre may be limited, Blue Öyster Cult just might be the best thinking man's hard rock band in America. On the basis of this album, I'd say they have scant competition.*"

Al sums up the chain of events that shaped this curiously commercial but also quite self-evident, comfortable and less ironic Blue Öyster Cult record. "Back during *Mirrors*, Columbia were acting like a concerned parent of a teenager. I knew what we were doing, even if some in the band didn't. *Mirrors* was taking the commercial thing as far as we could, to get to the same level as Fleetwood Mac, respected but big sellers."

So, as Al relates, another adjustment took place. "When that didn't happen, I took a look at who we really were. What we excelled at was the quirky and mysterious. The first thing we had to do was reestablish our credibility. I decided that we needed to make a record that was non-commercial and as heavy as we could make, that might not sell, but it would cement in people's minds who we still were. Some people (even some group members) were disappointed that *Cultösaurus* didn't even sell as well as *Mirrors*, but the reviews were great and the fans at the shows still raved about it. I knew it was a success."

Coming full circle, Al concludes that, "When we did *Fire of Unknown Origin*, we simply unleashed those commercial urges that we'd bottled up for *Cultösaurus*, and it worked. I said 'Told you so' to said band members, and got myself sacked!"

"What was particularly good about this album is that it came when BÖC was in decline," noted Al in a separate chat. "Each record was selling less and the critics were tearing us apart too. We were able to come back with a critically acclaimed and commercially successful album at a point when most people were ready to write us off. I believe that this record proved that BÖC were not one hit wonders and that we were capable of being contenders. The bad part was that the tension of doing this record literally tore the band apart. By the time it was over, none of us were having any fun. Despite the subsequent releases, this was the last record that I worked on with the other four guys. It was my last BÖC record. Not bad for a parting shot though."

The tour schedule for *Fire of Unknown Origin* first consisted of US and Canadian dates in June and August of 1981 with legs supported by Humble Pie, Pat Travers and UFO, with Johnny Van Zant on board for many of the Pat Travers and UFO shows. Over to Europe, and, as alluded to, Albert would get fired, after a show at Queensway Hall, Dunstable, England, August 20th, with Rick Downey performing his first show at the open air *Monsters of Rock* Festival at Castle

Donington two nights later. Back in the US, the band would finish out the year mostly with Foghat and Whitford St. Holmes as support, with shows recorded for use on the band's forthcoming live album.

Fact is, the band were delivering to their fans fresh material that sounded great live. *Fire of Unknown Origin*'s combination of shiny accessibility and paranormal exotica had effectively put the band back on the map, after two less than well-received records of different stripes. The album charted at No.41 in the US and stayed there for three-and-a-half months (going gold in the process), also reaching No.24 on the UK charts, with the 'Burnin' for You' video receiving much airplay on a new thing called MTV, despite the fact that the fledgling video company had more or less banned the band's celluloid representation for 'Joan Crawford'. On the singles chart, 'Burnin' for You' peaked at No.40, staying there for three weeks. *Fire of Unknown Origin* also prompted one of the band's most spirited and energetic tours, playing to packed houses, resulting in the unwieldy *Extraterrestrial Live*, which nevertheless slammed home the point that this was a band with a breath-taking back catalogue of choice rock 'n' roll nuggets.

Extraterrestrial Live

"People seem to like live albums from the Cult"

1 982 was a stocktaking year for Blue Öyster Cult. The band was fresh off their biggest general set of successes. *Fire of Unknown Origin* may not have chalked the biggest numbers for the band, but the overall package of tour, sales, market exposure and critical acclaim found the band taking their roiling, active place in the frenzied media pit that is rock 'n' roll.

Donald had decided to spread his wings and pursue his delicate pop side with *Flat Out*, a solo record that arrived and went without a whisper. The album fit the temperament at CBS at the time, where slick, unthreatening pop records were emerging from the world of metaldom, setting wheels in motion for the rise of the "hair bands" or AOR or melodic hard rock... whatever you want to call the platinum and teased metal of the subsequent full decade. In any event, *Flat Out* was a pioneering pop metal excursion that easily could have been a smash.

"I've been wanting to do it for a while," explained Buck to Steve Gett, just prior to the record's release, "But it's been difficult to find the time in the past. I actually started recording for about three weeks after the Cult's *Fire of Unknown Origin* LP had been done. But then, we were out on the road for the rest of the year and it wasn't until February of this year that I could start again—it was about half-finished at that stage. Now it's pretty well complete. I find it really hard to describe the music I've been working on. It's totally different from what I've done in the past and most of the stuff was never really suited to BÖC. There are songs that I've had laying around for some time and the oldest stretches back to 1973. The material's varied—there's some rock and some pop and a lot of guitars, but it's not a guitar album. There are a lot of vocals as well."

"I've actually used Dennis Dunaway and Neal Smith, who used to be in Alice Cooper's band," continued Donald. "And Cult's drummer and Foghat's bassist have also been helping out, together with some New York session guys. It's been really interesting to play with other people and sales willing, I'd like to be able to keep a solo career running alongside my work with the Cult. But there are no plans to tour at all—it's too much of a headache. Going on the road with the band is enough!"

As for the live album, Buck figured, "Basically, we did it because the record company wanted us to. And the thing is that people seem to like live albums from the Cult. It also gave us the chance to put out some product that features our drummer Rick. Besides which the Cult won't be releasing a new record until the fall. It's the first one we'll have done in the studio without Albert Bouchard, and he was a big influence in the band. In fact, I'd say that he and I were largely responsible for the way a lot of the songs turned out. Albert basically left because of personality clashes. I get along with him a lot better now that he's not in the band! Rick's worked out very well, and it'll be interesting to see how the next album turns out. It'll certainly be different, I can tell you that."

At the time, Eric felt more of Buck's solo material could have been viable for recording with the Cult. "At this time of my life, I don't have to salute the logo anymore. We can do any kind of songs we want, and if that represents the personality of certain band members, then so be it. I was out-voted, and therefore, these very accessible songs will be on Donald's record, and I'm sure it will be very successful. They would have meant one or two more hits on our last album, but were not really hard rock songs."

I asked Joe if there was any resentment on the part of the band for Donald going solo. "No, but I felt like I would have liked to have helped him on it. I asked him several times, 'Hey, call me if you need some help.' But he had adequate resources. I think he just felt he wanted to do something on his own, and I don't blame him. I probably would have done the same thing. But no, I don't think there was that much resentment, at least on my part. I was glad that he did it. I think there would have been more resentment if it had all of a sudden become the next *Thriller*, and I was pumping gas somewhere (laughs)."

Were there any potential BÖC songs on *Flat Out*? Joe: "We always wanted to do 'Wind Weather and Storm,' but it never came to pass. I guess it was just conceptually wrong. But that was one of my favourites, and I was glad the way he did it was very clever. We might have rehearsed 'All Tied Up' once or twice, but that's it. Most of it was written outside of Blue Öyster Cult and recorded the way he wanted it done."

Same question went to Al. Any resentment of Buck's solo venture? "No, not at all," he asserts. "We were very happy that he finally got to do it. It was just after *Fire of Unknown Origin*, and I was doing *Imaginos* simultaneous to that. I think the biggest problem with that record was that he just lost his energy towards the end. It's very difficult to shepherd. I can appreciate producing. I remember when I was being relieved of my duties, I said, 'You know, I co-produced this last record with Martin. I've really busted my buns to make this work.' They said, 'Oh, you did nothing. You didn't have anything else to do. Big deal.' But I felt it was a lot of work, and then he did his record, and he totally dropped the ball when it came to the mix. I think that it shows. I mean, a lot of his demos were actually better than the record. He just didn't have the energy. I think that the songs are actually very good. But I feel that the arrangements are kind of demo-ish. It's an unfinished record, and the mixes are poor."

For *Flat Out*, Donald enlisted the services of a dozen or so collaborators, although in true solo project fashion, almost all lyrics and music were credited to Roeser. Notable players included the aforementioned Neal Smith and Dennis Dunaway from Alice Cooper's band, Craig MacGregor from Foghat, not to mention new BÖC drummer Rick Downey (more on that later).

The soft commerciality of the record could have turned *Flat Out* into a huge,

BOC-back-breaking hit. But most onlookers felt the songs were not that strong, even the best like 'Born to Rock' and 'Your Loving Heart' being compromised by the aforementioned timid production values. 'Born to Rock' (music co-credit to Neal Smith) was the only balls-out heat-seeker on the record, a sort of high-strung beach metal hybrid with rousing layers and players of guitars competing to cross the finish line. 'Your Loving Heart' relates a chilling love story about death and the ultimate sacrifice, a donated heart. Musically, this is the most involved piece on the album, a mini-suite that takes the listener methodically up the ladder to a gauzy set of Pearly Gates. Both 'Born to Rock' and 'Your Loving Heart' received the full narrative video treatment, with Buck playing central roles, the latter becoming almost Pink Floyd-like given the enhanced visuals.

Elsewhere, 'Five Thirty-Five' was meekly trotted out to radio as a possible single, while 'Cold Wind', 'That Summer Night', and 'All Tied Up' tugged the same (ahem) heartstrings as the record's epic love tale. From the curio shop, there's Donald's wife Sandy doing '50s slushpiece 'Come Softly to Me', a somewhat heavy instrumental for Anwar Sadat called 'Anwar's Theme' (Sadat was the Nobel Peace Prize-winning Egyptian leader assassinated by fundamentalists on October 6, 1981), and a humourous campfire singalong rendition of 'Wind Weather and Storm' lyric courtesy of Richard Meltzer.

Concerning 'Anwar's Theme' Buck told Gett, "That one's an instrumental and basically it deals with the life and death of Anwar Sadat. His assassination really affected me, though I'm not a political person. It can be dangerous to bring politics into music, which to me is the most important thing."

"We just came off a very good year for us," mused Buck, hitting the press trail in the spring of '83. "Even though money is tight and the recession has hit us too, we did better this past year than we did the last few years. So considering how things are, at this point we're glad to have a gig. One of the neat things about doing a solo record was that I got to play most of the instruments and produced myself. I reworked tunes and scrapped songs entirely. I would create songs by splicing different bits of things together. That was very exciting. I got quite fearless after a while. There's one song that should get the Golden Splicing award. On that tape, there were splices about every 24 inches. It was the most fun I've ever had making a record. *Flat Out* came out of a desire to do something different after 11 Cult albums. I think it's more romantic and softer than BÖC albums, although there are some rock numbers on *Flat Out*. It was really hard work. I'd never been responsible for a whole album before. I'd like to do another in about two years. By then I'll be ready to go again."

"*Flat Out* is like the cream of a good Cult LP," said *Rolling Stone*'s Parke Puterbaugh, "relieved of the dross that can occur when their heavy metal sense of humour gets the better of them. Dharma is a hypnotic songsmith who uses a hearty backbeat and his own febrile guitar playing to weave a delicious trance. He's an able lyricist, too, putting an illuminating twist on romantic commonplaces. Always, there's his elemental guitar, gliding into the stratosphere on wings of steel. No simple hard rock LP, *Flat Out* confounds the categories: you're not supposed to float like a butterfly and sting like a bee."

Final word goes to Buck, who glances back at *Flat Out*, 20 years down the line. "You know, it was done because I had a backlog of stuff that wasn't really appropriate to what BOC was doing, so I wanted to do that. I think the record was ignored by Sony, but that's another story. It's regrettable that it didn't reach a wider audience, just for my own thing, you know, ego, as far as getting people to hear what I was up to. But that's the way it is. I mean, I could be doing solo stuff my entire life, if it would be worth doing. It's really demoralizing to put your soul into a project, a lot of time as well, and not have it received or distributed; that's tough, but it probably wouldn't stop me from doing it."

But back to the central river that is Blue Öyster Cult. The band had decided to step off the "write, record, tour" treadmill that was causing increasing friction between previous good mates. As touched upon last chapter, the tour in support of *Fire of Unknown Origin* was to blow up in the band's face, resulting in the ouster of Al Bouchard from the band. Sandy relates the now well-known story of the straw that broke the camel's back, of Al finally going too far, of a line crossed causing irreparable damage.

"I think that they got to hate him and found him oppressive to work with. Whether that was justified or not, that's how they felt about it. Then of course three years after sacking him, like in '85, Steve Schenck talked them into bringing him back as drummer. They enjoyed it no more than they did when they parted ways in '82. But the actual event was the episode in England. I wasn't there. I was going to go over for those shows. But it all happened so fast, the shows during which Albert was thrown out (laughs). I had Max Bell in the car to report it to me (laughs). He used to write for the *New Musical Express* and he's now the editor of some other English magazine. He's an old friend of the band. He happened to be riding around with Albert and Albert's girlfriend at the time, who the band did not like at all. But yeah, I think that was the immediate trigger. Albert, according to all the reports, was late a bunch of times and not in a good mood. He was travelling alone, and not with the band because nobody wanted to travel in the same car with this girl. This was a long time ago, so I don't know. I don't even know her. Seen her, maybe, possibly. Her presence may have been the immediate trigger, but I don't think it was decisive."

Indeed, "Albert meetings" had already been taking place within the band, pretty much all members in agreement that something had to be done.

Of note, Steve Schenck is still Blue Öyster Cult's manager (and he actually played some keyboards on the *Fire of Unknown Origin* tour). Richard Meltzer offers this vignette of the man behind the curtain. "Basically, the Cult is now managed by this guy called Steve Schenck, who, for years, was Pearlman's lieutenant, and he went to college with members of the Dictators, New Paltz, or whatever it's called. But he was there in '72; I visited them. I knew them because I ran into them at rock shows so I met them at a Stooges concert, and they were fun kids, so I went up there to New Paltz, and I had never met Schenck before. 'Oh, here's our friend Steve Schenck,' and he says, 'Oh, I got four Fs and a D. I guess they're going to throw me out of here, so I don't go to class anymore.' Ha ha ha. Then within two or three years he was working for Pearlman. Who knows where his loyalties were? But basically he ended up probably shortchanging everybody from his earlier days. Going to the Cult... I mean, he's probably a better businessman than Pearlman; could do things with more efficiency. But nobody ever knew who he was working for."

Back to Al's sacking, Bolle calls the game this way: "Rick Downey was hired before Albert was even fired, at the beginning of the English tour, 1981. They started the tour in Germany and played a few dates. The drumming story is really three-sided as it comes from three different people. In one sense Albert was becoming increasingly bored with his role as drummer, and he was always a wannabe guitarist, and as we know, never good enough. So he always argued everything that ever went on. That's why I think some of the albums became such good albums, because he was always arguing. The very last test was the European tour. He was more concerned with the actual music than the drumming. He was just going through the motions. So he actually showed up late for two shows in England, not two in a row but the 17th and 19th or something. On the first night it happened, Rick Downey was taking a nap in the car outside the venue and Steve Schenck comes up to him and says, 'Wake up, you're drumming tonight,' and he goes 'What!?' 'You're going on in five minutes; dip your head in a bucket of water or something, you know the songs, you're a drummer, you're going on.' He was in shock. No ifs and buts. Do the show. He played up to the fifth song, and Albert came on for the sixth."

As we know, Rick is now long gone as the band's drummer. "Rick now does catering for Emerson Fittipaldi," noted Gregmar at the time. "Quite the change. Makes about 16 times the income per month he did in rock 'n' roll lighting, production or drumming for BÖC. He makes more money than the whole band put together. Forget rock 'n' roll. It's really not a good thing. That's the sad part of it all." Albert was surprised by this news. "Really? Well, one wrong turn and that job's going to be over (laughs). No, Rick is a fine guy, no bad words about Rick." Twelve months later, the grapevine had Rick running a recording studio in Florida, while sometimes driving a crew bus for the Penske Racing Team out of Phoenix, Arizona.

Albert himself pulls no punches (except for naming names!) on the subject of group dissension: "Oh, it all comes down to that thing I was telling you about: the women. What happened was, I took up with this person who was maybe a little questionable (laughs) to put it kindly. She was friendly with quite a few people in the band as well as myself and I ended up with her. I decided that I was going to leave my wife for this person, and you know, it seemed like a good idea at the time. But anyway, it probably wasn't and I did eventually think better of it. But of course, that was after I wasn't in the band anymore. But I guess what it all came down to was that I couldn't just leave my wife for no reason, so I made up a reason to. So this person was hanging around with me, and was a source of a lot of unhappiness to not only other people in the band who were, shall we say, friendly with this person, but was also a great source of aggravation to their wives. So there was a lot of pressure."

Albert continues: "Timing-wise, I took up with this person, I would have to say, right after *Cultösaurus Erectus*. We hadn't even started *Fire of Unknown Origin*. What had happened was my wife had moved out, we had already sold the house, and this other person stayed with me. We rehearsed and we made the record. I would say that band morale was probably at an all-time low when we did that record. I would have to say that everybody including myself was pretty miserable and extremely stressed during that time period. But I would also say that Eric's vocals were the best vocals of his career in my opinion."

So now for Al's rendition of "the episode." "Well, it's pretty much common knowledge what happened, and I can't defend myself that much, because I was pretty much an idiot. I should have seen the writing on the wall. But what happened was, I had left my wife at the time, my ex-wife now, and I had taken up with this groupie, and I wanted to take this individual with me to England for our tour. The band was not in favour of it, and they said, 'Well if you bring her, we're not going to go on a bus. We're taking individual cars.' I said, 'Okay, whatever, I'll take a car.' There were only two times I arrived late. We had a bunch of gigs and I made it to most of the gigs on time, at least until I got fired. But that wasn't the reason I got fired. They might have said that, because I was late. But the reason I got fired is because I had a temper tantrum after the second time I was late, and I just said some stuff I shouldn't have said, and was verbally abusive to the band and their friends. So that's really what happened. The reason I was late was that the first time, I got lost. I mean, it's not so easy to drive around England. They all went with Steve Schenck, and so they were all in a convoy, and I wasn't and I got lost. The second time the rental car broke down, and I ended up going with Max Bell, the writer. He came and got me, but he was still working at *Melody Maker* or wherever it was. He had something to do and couldn't come right away so I had to wait until he got there. So that's why I came late. But I don't think that's why they fired me. It was because I didn't control myself. I was so frustrated. There's a lesson there."

Al made sure he took care of business after this incident, in the parking lot after the show thrashing the uncooperative car Basil Fawlty-style with a 2x4. After deciding Albert was basically loony, the band bought him and his girlfriend plane tickets and sent them home to New York. As mentioned, Al's last gig was Queensway Hall, Dunstable, which left Rick Downey to man the drums for the band's high exposure Castle Donington gig with AC/DC days later, after which Allen had recalled that on top of the Al situation, it had rained and the PA had blown up.

Sandy speaks well of Albert's contributions throughout the years. "I don't think his artistic streak made him detestable. Look, there is no doubt that the records are far less amazing post-Albert than with Albert. But you know, Albert also... I mean, I stand in admiration of Albert's arrangement contributions and compositional contributions to *Imaginos*, and a lot of his other stuff. His contribution to 'Cities on Flame' is decisive, even though it was written by a bunch of people. But with his leaving, on top of my leaving the production game for a long time, there wasn't really much anybody could do because there just wasn't any material. They had two songs, and they had only written one of those two (laughs). They just didn't have anything. That's what happened. So I don't know. It's hard for me to judge. I think *Imaginos* is their second best record after *Tyranny and Mutation*, or maybe their first best record. But the band was not just Albert. I mean, look at the songwriting credits. It's not just Albert. 'Shooting Shark' and 'Perfect Water' are great songs. But the general level of what the band was doing fell precipitously. But I also think they sort of ran out their interactive thread, because they weren't interested in hearing from me, and they weren't interested in hearing from Albert. The only reason I was asked back is that I was considered less oppressive than Albert, and I'm not insulting Albert. That's just my theory on the way they looked at things."

Al Lanier: "It was the kind of thing where it's tough, but it was necessary. It wasn't a situation where we weren't going to be able to work with him. We were going to miss his input—composing, arranging. More than anything else, just his energy. Albert was so focused; there literally wasn't anything else to him, except the music. He was the guy, when we were in the studio, all jammed up, and couldn't figure out what to do in 'this section' because it's not working. Albert would be the one to come in the next day with a bunch of ideas on how to solve it. He was terrific that way. That we knew we were going to miss. But on the other hand, there was no way things could continue like that. It had become just so emotionally crazy, we couldn't play with him."

Eric: "He was just terrific at arrangements and ways of digging into the meat of the arrangement and finding out what wasn't working, and find something that made it work. I'd say on that level, he was probably missed. But you can't look back. You have to take the good with the bad. And in this case, the personality thing outweighed the musical thing."

Finally a word from brother Joe, the Cultster who probably knew Al's state of mind best: "Yeah, I'd say he was bored, but it was difficult for us to be smart enough to give him another role, or find an outlet that would do it for him, you know? He was very jealous that... you want the dirt? (laughs). You want the gossip? Well, I think there was a bit of jealousy. He's gotten over it now, but I think there was a bit of jealousy that Donald came up with the hits and he didn't, even though he was working harder. Donald just has a knack for that kind of thing. So that might have been bounced off other people who were around those people. But that's a difficult question. I think Albert is Albert. He doesn't complain—well you've talked to him—about the songs he's written. He thinks he's done really good work. If they hit they hit, if they don't they don't. But like you said, the catalogue stands up quite well, and the catalogue includes a lot of his work."

In any event, Albert was booted from the band, and Rick Downey was quickly ushered in as drummer. A double album called *Extraterrestrial Live* is the proof. On the record, longtime band tech George Geranios gets engineering and mixing credits, along with co-production credit with Sandy Pearlman. Albert explains the musical chairs connection between Rick, George, Tony Cedrone and the band. "George was our sound man. Actually when we were the Soft White Underbelly, he used to mix us at Stony Brook College; he went to Stony Brook. I think he did some other tours with some other people and ended up working for Blue Öyster Cult in the early days, and mixed the sound for us all the time I was with them. Tony Cedrone was my drum roadie, who was actually found by Rick Downey, who was the drum roadie before Tony. When our lighting designer left, this guy Elliott Crowe, who sidelined as a manager, had Rick in one of his bands. He said this guy would be a great drum roadie, so Rick came on as a drum roadie. Then the lighting designer quit—well, he got a better job—so Rick became the lighting designer, taking the place of the guy who hired him, and Rick found a drummer, Tony, to be my drum roadie."

Eric shortened the resume in an interview promoting the new live record.

"Our new drummer is Rick Downey, who has worked on our crew for the last seven years. He started off as a drum roadie when he was about 19 years old, and worked his way up through the ranks until he was our road manager, lighting designer and crew chief. He's been part of us for a very long time, and knows all the material inside out."

So now Rick was unwittingly drumming on his first Blue Öyster Cult record. Albert's only performances on this 13-song double album, issued in April of '82, would be 'Black Blade' and 'Dominance and Submission'.

Artwork-wise, *Extraterrestrial Live* (original title: *Cult in the Act*) was a wily continuation of *Fire of Unknown Origin*'s storyline. Illustrator and conceptualist Greg Scott, on getting involved with the project: "I met the band members at a show in New Jersey, and we started talking about doing artwork for *Extraterrestrial Live*, which was the next album slated to be done. So I came up with the idea of them, knowing the title of the album, exiting the spaceship onto another planet. Sandy suggested things like the Doberman pinchers and having all of their equipment unloaded. He gave me access to go out to Long Island where their equipment was stored. I went out and photographed all their cases and everything. So that was all their cases and everything off to the right. This was all a pencil drawing by the way."

"It was like in the middle of the summer '81 that I was working on that illustration. We did a photo session at Columbia, where I asked all the band members to wear winter clothing, or to bring a winter coat, so it looked like it was really freezing on this other planet. But it was like July or August. It was really hot in New York, but of course it was air conditioned in the photo studio at Columbia. They brought all their winter coats and we staged that photo. Later, we did another session with Albert, who wasn't in the band at that time. They decided to put him in with Rick Downey anyway, and so there's actually six members in that photo. Albert also posed as the Oyster boy on the stairway, not his face of course, but we rented one of those monk's gowns and he got up on a ladder for me and posed as a monk. That was also probably about a month's long drawing. It's quite large. Donald has the original. I gave the drawing to Donald. It's two by four feet."

I've not seen the original of the final artwork, but a friend of mine in Chicago owns the preliminary pencil sketch and it is stunning. Of note, Greg has made the transition to gallery artist, and his hugely ambitious works are somewhat in this style, perhaps closer to the techniques used on the cover of *The Revolution by Night*.

"In comparison, *Fire of Unknown Origin* was quite small," Greg continues. "About 15 by 15 inches. Egg tempera is a medium that is very conducive to working tiny. But they had store posters that were three by three feet. I don't even have one of those, but I'd love to get one (laughs). They were nice."

Other amusing artistic touches include the record's only colour illustration on the inside of the gatefold, and the inclusion of all the lyrics, giving many fans their first glimpse into how intelligent these guys (and their cabal) were as wordsmiths on the page. Then again, at 14 years young, your neo-literary author (and many others, as it turns out—we are a club!), took up the band's offer on the back cover of *Spectres*, to send in 50 cents (for postage and handling), after which what should show up in the mail, but a complete set of Cult lyrics printed on old school continuous feed computer paper!

Back to the future, psychologically speaking, *Extraterrestrial Live* captured the band in their second and last career high, storming around small stadiums with an energy that was real, but somewhat diminished by the rollercoaster ride the band had experienced: a slow rise, a couple years of solid fame, two stiffing records and then this second (divine) wind. So quite appropriately, the record's sound is somewhat deflated, corporate and accurately representative of boomy, B-city hockey barns. What's more, it tries to please everybody, the tour set surveying each and every studio album, which, if hits are to be churned, necessarily causes large overlap with the band's other two live records thus far.

Eric's pre-release press wind-'em up went something like this. "We are a live group, and our expertise is onstage. A lot of people have said to me, 'Your studio records are good, but hey, when you hit the stage, all hell breaks loose.' We're trying to get that live performance right on the vinyl. You're hearing us play in 1980 and '81, and the recording techniques for live albums are much better now, so the fidelity of this record is highly improved. That's number one, that it actually sounds better. What's also unique is that at least half of this record includes material that no one has heard us play live before, on disc. Plus there's a lot of people who've realised who we are just since 'Burnin' for You.' There was one whole group of people who never heard of us before 'The Reaper,' and that was our sixth album. Now on No.10 we had another hit. Some people might think that was our first record!"

As mentioned, Albert only drums two tracks, 'Dominance and Submission' and 'Black Blade' recorded in late '80 (Poughkeepsie and Long Island respectively, 'Dominance' originally for a *King Biscuit* broadcast). The rest features Rick Downey and band recorded in Long Island, Philadelphia and Hollywood, with one performance lifted from The Country Club in Reseda, California, an elongated 'Roadhouse Blues' featuring Robbie Krieger on guitar (credited as Bobbie Krieger on the CD reissue). BÖC were most definitely Doors fans, Eric even throwing in references to other Doors songs during this track over the years ('Soul Kitchen', 'L.A. Woman', 'Crystal Ship"). In later years, the 'Roadhouse Blues' jam metamorphosed into a medley with 'Love Me Two Times'.

Performances of note include a snappy 'Joan Crawford', a power-packed 'Godzilla' complete with drum solo, Eric Bloom exuding solid presence on 'Dominance and Submission', the mirrored man singing (less successfully) Albert's signature track 'Cities on Flame', Joe handling 'Hot Rails to Hell', and the extensive Buck solo jam closing 'Veteran of the Psychic Wars'. 'Dr. Music' and 'Burnin' for You' both suffer from loose, guitar-sapped arrangements, perhaps personifying a general unwieldy malaise with the whole record, *Extraterrestrial Live* widely considered the least magical of the band's four live spreads, the most jaded, the band pretty much on automatic.

Out there in the journalistic world, *Trouser Press'* Jon Young, in his review of the record, said that, "*The Cult make better records onstage than in the studio*" and that the album "*matches its predecessors, offering hearty helpings of metal sci-fi and boogie madness*." Amusingly, he also mentions the "*beer-breath version of 'Roadhouse Blues'*."

Wrote Todd Everett from *Record Review*, "Heavy metal is a term that was invented to describe the kind of music put out by these very guys a decade or so ago; the phalanx of guitars was supposed to hit you like a wall of fire, melting (in one of BÖC's own phrases) your ears. These days, in what amounts to a concert presentation of much of their best stuff from the past years, the Cult sounds almost sophisticated compared to what heavy metal's become in the hands of the Brits and Krauts—not to forget the Yanks and Aussies. Old-fashioned, even. How old-fashioned? Enough so that the two numbers that stand out the most are their Byrds tribute (and only hit single), '(Don't Fear) The Reaper,' and the Doors' boogie 'Roadhouse Blues,' that became a standard throughout versions by bands like Status Quo. The rest of the album is prototype early metal, presented with just enough humour under the volume that the lyrics might even be worth an occasional listen."

The Revolution by Night

"Ukrainian social hall"

1983 marked the year when Blue Öyster Cult got to see what creative life would be like without Al Bouchard (it wasn't pretty). Rick Downey is featured on *The Revolution by Night*, marking BÖC's first studio record line-up change since the band saw birth back in 1972. Accentuating the positive, Eric remarked on the removal of what was arguably the band's chief songwriter: "This time the most salient feature of our move forward is that Albert Bouchard has been replaced by Rick Downey. Yeah, it's true that Albert's role was always significant. But in fact he was too dominant. The rest of us could never step to the fore because of his presence. Every album had to have some of his stuff on it. His leaving has been like a breath of fresh air. There's a new feeling in the band right now. Rick may not be as creative as Albert, but he's more solid and we're all right behind him. Albert's gone permanently. We wish him well on his solo thing (ed. *Imaginos!*), but he no longer figures in our plans."

One might think that given all the songwriting talent within the band, and the virtual army of lyricists available (including members of the band), the gap Albert had left would close and disappear faster than Tokyo's transit system at the hands of an aggravate large lizard. Not so. The decline in the quality of Blue Öyster Cult's material was astonishingly noticeable and unarguable, even given the very subjective and elusive nature of aesthetic appeal.

To add to the turmoil, the pressure was on to produce another hit record some time soon, and so great leveller and Vancouverite Bruce Fairbairn (AC/DC, Van Halen, Aerosmith, Bon Jovi, Yes; since deceased, May 20, 1999) was brought in to produce the band into palatable mediocrity. His knob job was predictably poor, but the songs came through, making *The Revolution by Night* (working title *Deadman's Curb*) a qualified, post-innocence, post-marketing age success.

"I like the record a lot," asserts Joe. "It probably took a little bit too long to record. I believe the mixes were finished by Sandy. Bruce Fairbairn was completely blown away (laughs), worn out by the project. So he supervised the mixes, but he wasn't really there for the final mixing. So that makes a big difference. Maybe rather than bringing Bruce to Long Island to do the record, if we had gone to his studio, where he's done all the big hits with Aerosmith since then, it might have been a different record. But you never know about things like that."

"He was more laid-back and was kind of like a businessman," continues Joe, adding to our understanding of Fairbairn. "He always had a written agenda. He would do his homework, and then the session started precisely at noon, and ended precisely at ten o'clock at night, ten hour days. I don't know, at the time, he had done those Loverboy records, and they are respectable records, in a sort of rock 'n' roll sense. But I don't think he got the rock 'n' roll aspect, into our record, that he should have. I didn't think he really knew what to do with this band. In the end, I said, 'I don't think this guy is a very good producer' (laughs). Boy was I wrong there! Because then he went on to do *Permanent Vacation*, *Slippery When Wet*, probably some of the biggest records of all time. We had pulled him out of his comfort zone in Vancouver where he was using a studio near his home, and put him on Long Island, at Boogie Hotel, which was in Port Jefferson, Long Island. I think it was owned by Foghat. I think they had different investors involved, but somehow they were part of it. It was an old Armenian... The Armenian Club or something like that. It was a big house, basically, with a ballroom in it. The ballroom was where the band recorded, and there were rooms upstairs so the band could stay over during the week. It was very convenient for me, because I would take the ferry from Connecticut to Long Island, and maybe less than a quarter mile up the street was the studio. I liked it, but it was a little strange. You're a little removed from the rest of the world. It works with some bands, but other bands, they want to be right in the middle of New York."

"Like I say, Sandy got into doing some of the mixes, and it was sort of that '80s mentality. You know, it's got to be bigger and better; it's got to sound as good as a Journey record, stuff like that. But I think we lost some of the really good Blue Öyster Cult ethic that our fans liked, that might have sounded better in the long run. Now, that being said, there are some amazing tracks on that record."

"I know they did *Revolution by Night* there, because I was working on *Imaginos* there at the same time," laughs Albert, at this point not in the band but embarking upon a richly related project. "I would be leaving and they would be coming in. Boogie Hotel was a place where you stayed, okay? They had rooms upstairs. They had lots of rooms all over the place. It was really like a Ukrainian social hall, and it had a balcony, and it was huge. They had some pretty nice equipment in there, but it was mainly the sound of the room. But you wouldn't have a lot of interaction with other people."

Indeed, even though the years of gold, near platinum and platinum albums seemed gone forever, *The Revolution by Night* saw acceptable sales of 400,000 copies, roughly double the mark of two still recent studio albums in *Mirrors* and *Cultösaurus*. Eric did his duty and cranked up the hype machine. "Every record we do, we think, 'Right, this is going to be it.' So far it hasn't happened. But this latest has certainly raised our expectations higher than for quite a while. We've done our best and are very confident about its chances. But now the songs are out of our hands."

The artwork this time around—courtesy again of Greg Scott, who, if you recall, also illustrated iconically on *Fire of Unknown Origin* and *Extraterrestrial Live*—was interesting if subdued. Greg explains the process. "Well, after *Fire of Unknown Origin*, I had plenty of time to make covers on my own, and make it dazzling, because I was basically freelance at this time, doing mostly magazine illustration. Through that time it was frustrating because I always asked Sandy on subsequent covers to give me some advance notice, give me a couple of months to work it into my schedule so I have a month to produce an image for them. That never really happened. They always came to me last minute. And *Revolution by Night* is a perfect example. The Egyptian drawing on the back cover was something I had already done back in California in the late '70s, when I was looking at a lot of Egyptian art, and had seen the King Tut exhibit that was travelling around the country at the time. That piece is actually entitled 'Akhenaten,' pronounced 'awk-knot-ten.' It's a portrait of King Tut's father. He had some kind of strange malady where his face got all out of proportion, and that's represented in various different carvings from when he lived. When Sandy came to me for *Revolution by Night*, they literally had no time. They gave me a week."

"So we looked through various artwork that I had, that had not been published, and he chose that Egyptian 'Akhenaten' piece, actually for the front cover. By the way, that was a pencil drawing. Then he asked me to come up with something for the back cover and the inner sleeve within a week, that went with the Egyptian theme. But for the back cover, Sandy had given me the idea that he basically wanted this sort of California highway complex, with this kind of speeding motorcycle, which I, rather than representing a motorcycle literally, just turned it into a streak of light, speeding along the highway. There was a lot of cosmic sky with lightning bolts and so forth coming down, leaving lots of room for the type and credits. Remember, this was supposed to be the back. But something happened along the way, and they ended up deciding to reverse them. Although later on the single releases, and all the advertising and t-shirts they used 'Akhenaten.' So ironically, that became the image most frequently associated with *Revolution by Night* anyway."

It is of note that the band's crooked cross is located in the bottom right-hand corner, etched into the concrete wall, next to a "12," appropriately signifying the band's 12th record. The cover art could be said to depict the cloverleaf junction from the first line of pivotal track 'Shadow of California'.

As noted, the back cover and inside sleeve are unified by an Egyptian theme. On the "Doberman on chest" drawing, or "Anubis" (defined in Webster's as the god who leads the dead to judgment; usually represented with the head of a jackal), Greg adds this note. "I subsequently found out the Anubis drawing was reused without my permission on the new box set, *Workshop of the Telescopes*, and my lawyer just negotiated a settlement with Sony Legacy, to pay me some money for reusing that drawing."

The title of the record may or may not be influenced by a Max Ernst painting entitled "Pieta, ou la revolution la nuit," which is actually inscribed directly on the painting. The Tate Gallery's translation reads: "Pieta or the Revolution by Night."

The music enclosed was a strange amalgam of lackadaisical pop plateaus, odd arrangements that assert irony or parody, and penetrating peerings into regular Blue Öyster Cult themes. The whole mess sounded uptight, due in no small part to a profusion of trendy electronic drums and Fairbairn's complementary shiny production values. Eric sounded apprehensive on Fairbairn's clueless production. "Well, we were really impressed with the sound

Bruce got on the Loverboy albums, and we all hit it off in the studio. He was a pleasure to work with and the band is basically happy with the job he did. I'll admit however, that some of the tracks (e.g. 'Veins') were extensively remixed by Donald after Bruce had finished with them. The problem there was that he was satisfied with something when we were not, so certain things had to be changed around. But overall, Bruce did a good job. It's too early to say whether we'd work with him again, but on a purely personal note, I'd like to retain links with him."

But *The Revolution by Night* opened with a bang, 'Take Me Away' announcing the wake with a crushing groove, a straightforward but acceptable lyric from Eric, music courtesy of Ontario guitarist Aldo Nova. Eric explains: "Actually I wrote the words and Aldo Nova wrote the rest. That's an interesting fan's story, and it's a Canadian story (laughs). Aldo was touring with us, and he actually moved to Long Island because we were managed by the same company. I used to go down to his house where he had home recording stuff. He gave me this tape one day, said here's a song that didn't make my last record, and a lot of people like the music, but they don't like the words, which were about some psycho killer. I think it was called 'Psycho Ward.' So he said maybe you can use it. I listened to it and said, 'Make me a tape with your lyrics taken off of it; just give me the track.' So I took it home, and the next day I had a tune. I just sat in my basement and came up with these new lyrics, which were 'Take Me Away'."

Eric's lyric contains faint echoes of his 'Sole Survivor' quandary, the two tracks addressing a lifetime of glamourizing space travel, aliens and sci-fi what-ifs. The narrator's emotions run the gamut from hope, yearning and optimism to an almost suicidal resignation, the nature of the pact even expanding to include the character's romantic interest. Eric continues, tongue firmly in cheek: "'Take Me Away' is a somewhat autobiographical tune about extraterrestrials that takes the viewpoint that wherever they are, I want to contact them, send that out at the speed of light, into the atmosphere, so they would know my address (laughs). So given that the song's been out four or five years now, at the speed of light, maybe they've got the message. It's out past Alpha Centauri now so who knows? Perhaps they'll pick up what I'm laying down (laughs)."

"That's the kind of genre I'm into," Eric offers, in a separate later interview, as further elucidation into his sci-fi fancy. "I'm a gamer; I play Internet games a lot, sword and sorcery games. I started drawing rocket ships and explosions when I was eight years old! I was big into the *Flash Gordon* serials. It's what I've always been into. BÖC is a little unusual. We have a diverse background. I have the whole comic book, fantasy and science fiction background. Buck was an engineering student. He is very bright and technically oriented. Especially on the sound side of BÖC. He has the latest software. The latest hot shit Macintosh at his house. I have been online since '94. I had a Commodore 64, I had an Atari 1040ST, I have had five different PCs since '93. It's the kind of stuff we are into. Where other guys might be chopping up lines and drinking a lot of beer, Blue Öyster Cult is on the Internet! In fact, I play this online game called *Gem Stone 3*. It's a scrolling text, role playing game; there are no graphics. It's kind of old fashioned. They have over 10,000 subscribers. Any time of the day, there are two or three thousand online. This genre is not dead; it is a little subculture. It's kind of interesting. I have been playing it since '95. It costs to play. It's not for everybody, but it is an interesting subculture. Eventually, I will tell people in the game who I am. I meet people from *Gem Stone* all over the country. I give them free tickets to the show; we hang out after the show. People look at us like, 'What the fuck are these people talking about?' We're talking about spells and sorcery and wizards."

A brief biographical note on the 'Take Me Away' co-writer: Aldo Nova's biggest hit was straight-line pop metal rocker 'Fantasy' from his self-titled debut album. Subsequent records *Twitch* and *Project* found him too enamoured with electronic rock, and a comeback record from '91 called *Blood on the Bricks* did little to revive his career. He is, however, quite respected as a multi-talented session musician, in fact playing both guitar and synthesizer on this track. Aldo Nova has also worked extensively with Bon Jovi and Celine Dion.

Adds Joe, "Our good friend, Aldo Nova—he had done a ton of shows for us, opening, and Eric and Aldo got together; I think it's mostly Eric's lyrics, and mostly Aldo's music—a nice combination there. The video was decent, but unfortunately it never caught on as a hit single."

'Eyes on Fire' was the band's first absolute surrender to outside songwriters, this track credited to Gregg Winter, who also adds back-up vocals. The music was poppy yet brash, electronic toms causing all sorts of distraction, quite possibly one of the most insipid songs of the BÖC canon, telling a standard heavy metal tale about woman's demonic hold on man, this particular siren holding the narrator in contemptuous indifference, seeing the hapless male with anything but "eyes on fire."

"'Eyes on Fire' is Journey," laughs Joe. "I mean, I like the song, and I like Gregg Winter; Gregg was a guy from Long Island that Eric met. He had, as would happen with Bob Halligan Jr. later, another hot cassette demo, and we said, 'Wait a minute.' Eric really enjoyed singing that song, I think, so that gave it a bit more validity, like, 'This can be a hit.'"

Track No.3 was a song many considered a possible heir to 'Reaper' and 'Burnin' for You', 'Shooting Shark' seen as a viable candidate to become the band's next smash hit. The tune sports a hypnotic and sparse arrangement, driven delicately by Randy Jackson's slap bass pattern and arguably too much synthesizer and synth drums. But the song benefits from Donald's pop expertise and smooth croon, which can't help but captivate, given Patti Smith's stunning lyric, which combines imagery and storytelling skill like the cream of the BÖC crop, prompting the oft-asked question: just what is a shooting shark? The song is another epic tale of love, man and woman locked in a battle of wills, circled by a mystical character that seem to have some prescience over future events. One immediately recalls the front cover graphic of *Agents of Fortune*.

Eric, describing the song at the time, said that, "Patti's now in retirement from the music business, but Donald had those lyrics knocking around for about five years before eventually setting them to music. That's the beauty of collaboration. It can generate stuff that might not get used immediately, but is stored up for the right moment."

Many consider 'Shooting Shark' the band's best lyric of the '80s. The sax solo is by Mark Baum, adding either atmosphere or AOR conformity to the song, depending on your sympathies for this new and shiny BÖC disposition. Adds Buck: "That's a Patti Smith lyric I had for years and years that I had forgotten about and came across it, and realised how cool it was. So I came up with that synth lick."

"'Shooting Shark' was the single, a beautiful track, very confusing song," explains Joe. "Lyrics by Patti Smith, which was really a dynamite thing. The main beat is a drum machine, but Rick played all the fills on those electronic drums of his. That was another situation where I was replaced, by, Mr. *American Idol*, Randy Jackson. He is a judge on *American Idol*. Also, he's one of the best players in the world—even though he is a judge on *American Idol*. He played some jazz in San Francisco, but he added the pop and slap, slap and pop technique, on the bass. Even though I had been playing bass for 15 years at that time, I had no idea what to do, in terms of that style. So Donald said, 'I think I want to have somebody do some slapping and popping,' and I said, 'I don't do that; I just don't do it. So do what you want to do with the song.' The original track, I played with a pick, and I thought the feel of it was quite good. And it might have been able to go on as that. But the dilemma with 'Shooting Shark' was—and this was Donald's thing—he was into timing, how long a record is. At the time—I remember we discussed this many times—how come a six minute song feels like it's only three? So his thing with getting a different bass player on 'Shooting Shark' was to make that song sound like it was three minutes long instead of six minutes long. I think Randy did a great job—an incredible job."

"We did that in San Francisco, because that's where Randy Jackson was living at the time," continues Joe. "So Randy took me into the studio, after a session, and he sat me down for two-and-a-half, three hours, and taught me how to play slap and pop bass. It was amazing, a revelation. It changed the way I play bass, in all aspects. He is an amazing musician, and it's kind of a goof that he is on *American Idol*. After he finished the 'Shooting Shark' thing, he did a lot of different things; he played on a Journey record, he played with Bob Dylan. He was Mariah Carey's bass player for a long time. He had a desk job at Columbia Records, you know, a high-profile desk job. Then he was just about to retire from the business, and then he got a call, 'Do you want to audition for this silly TV show?' (laughs). So he has reinvented himself several times, great guy. Absolutely great guy."

Next up was a clattery, edgy, and once more, over-produced number deliciously entitled 'Veins'. Again musically you could call it drama or melodrama, but this era of the Cult was not quite in charge of a chemistry that invites without strain or effort. Bolle on Meltzer's ghoulish lyric: "That is probably my favourite lyric from just a normal perspective. It's the ultimate opposite of 'Burnin' for You,' which is Richard Meltzer's dedication to real life. 'Veins' is his dedication to an outer, surreal life. You party so much, you lose yourself, you have no control. Then you wake up in the morning, you have vague, picturesque memories of violence, but you're not sure if you were involved. Was it a nightmare, a dream, or some kind of reality where you actually were in a fight and you killed somebody?"

"That's a Richard lyric," affirms Buck. "I think he was inspired by some literature; I don't know the reference. I'm not sure where that came from for him. But that's about being in a fugue state, probably from drink or something like that. Basically, I just wanted to support the lyric, and that's what came to mind. That was fairly soon after I bought a synthesizer, a Prophet 5 which I still have. I was messing with it and I got the riff from that."

"We worked hard on that one," adds Joe, "but I thought the subject matter was kind of non-commercial. Good lyric, but no 'Burnin' for You.'"

So far, 'Shooting Shark' was hands-down, the pinnacle of poetry on the record, but thematically it sits suspended without context, slightly beyond the half dozen or so major themes found throughout the band's work. Pearlman's 'Shadow of California', on the other hand, might be the record's anchor, linking this uncomfortably modern long-player to the band's rich legacy, touching many Cult pressure points, most vital being the link to the *Imaginos* saga. Indeed only this lyric and *Club Ninja*'s 'When the War Comes' tenuously keep in sight Sandy's captivating story, as we wait through the late '70s and early '80s for the return of the tale proper with '88's *Imaginos* concept masterwerk.

The interesting thing about the 'Shadow of California' lyric is that it weaves nicely two Pearlman storylines that may or may not intertwine in the future, and have or have not intertwined in the past, depending on one's propensity toward inclusiveness. 'Shadow of California' marks the return of the Transmaniacon MC, who figure prominently in Sandy's *History of Los Angeles* storyline, which Sandy expected to turn into a novel someday. But this dimension alone has little to do with the *Imaginos* saga. It is the return of the motorcycle club in spiritual form after their fantastic self-obliteration in 'Golden Age of Leather' that gives the song its extra depth. Note, this is an arguable link, given that the song is not a Pearlman composition, although Abbott might be consciously or subconsciously expanding on Sandy's tale, just as Derleth and dozens of others have carried on H.P. Lovecraft's Cthulhu mythos. Sandy (who, we learned earlier, is a big Lovecraft fan) supports this concept of continuing another's thread. "I didn't write 'Golden Age of Leather.' Bruce Abbot and Donald did. But 'Shadow of California' is kind of the final chapter. That's good you caught that. That's very good. I love 'Shadow of California.' It's a shame that nobody played it. I think I'll cover it with some other band!"

Add to this link a curious new ability by this rogue bike gang to time-travel and understand the implications thereof, and 'Shadow of California' resonates with life, possessing the ability to send the listener scrambling in many directions, most pertinently, into a re-examination of the BÖC catalogue as a whole.

Musically, the song was unremarkable, a half-hearted stab at writing a mini epic that came across as mere watery heavy metal, never really taking off from its sparse riff pattern, thumping into a sort of tech-minded march come chorus time, those electronic toms of Downey, front and centre and somewhat repugnant in their datedness.

"'Shadow of California' was a song I had with Sandy," explains Joe, "and I kicked it around, and it wasn't working and it wasn't working. And finally I had Neal Smith over to my house, the great Neal Smith from Alice Cooper. I said, 'Neal, would you play a little drum part along with this thing? I'm trying to get this thing.' He played a really cool drum part, and that's how that song started— I demoed it out with Neil on the drums."

Even if the rhythm is worthy, it is over-ruled distractingly by the choice of electronic drums. "They were Simmons drums," sighs Joe, "and they were just very popular at the time, but of course they sound completely dated now.

Nowadays, a drummer might use a Simmons drum for an effect, but you would never do a whole album with Simmons drums. I did the same thing with Neal, on a Deadringer record. In fact, I think I borrowed Rick Downey's Simmons drums, when we did that album."

And what did Larry Fast do on the record? "Okay, that was another thing where we needed some synthesizer stuff. Synthesizers were big at the time. And you know, I don't recall anything Allen did on the album. For instance, that's actually Donald playing the synthesizer on 'Shooting Shark.' Larry Fast had just finished something with Peter Gabriel, so there was somebody who knew a little more about synthesizers than we did. So we thought it would be wise to bring in somebody to make it sound a little more contemporary... which makes it sound dated! (laughs)."

The band showed a lot of gall (or a blazing lack of taste) following up such an important number with another, much simpler motorcycle tale, Eric's 'Feel the Thunder'. Never designing to be a pivotal catalogue track, Eric writes an entertaining enough tale, setting it forward with a characteristic, metal-lite BÖC bounce, recalling spooky proto-rock tunes from the '60s, oddly enough, 'Deadman's Curve' coming to mind. Eric offers this play-by-play: "Lyric-wise, it's sort of a Three Horsemen of the Apocalypse, Halloween song. I just got the idea from stories like the ghost ship, where they find the ship with all the food on the table, but nobody's there, just one of those kind of stories. It's basically about three bikers on Halloween that get too high, crack up and are forever doomed to ride."

It is of note that the track originally featured a Michael Moorcock lyric entitled 'Sleep of a Thousand Tears'. Eric offers that, "The other guys didn't like Moorcock's story line, so I changed it around."

Next up is one of those rare BÖC tracks that just makes you shake your head. It doesn't happen often, but when it does, you wonder if such massive stupidity is actually a demonstration of some sort of inverted genius. 'Let Go' is probably the most fan-reviled song of the vast BÖC catalogue, an insipid piece of party rock piffle that just seems to get dumber with an examination of the lyrics, which evoke a lifeless parody of all this band stands for, BÖC unsuccessfully attempting a connection between band and fan. Then there's the dreaded rah-rah chorus that just cracks up most students of the band with total disbelief. "It was going to be called 'BÖC' at first," says Eric, "but certain members of the band objected, as that smacked too much of 'Hey, hey, we're the Monkees.' So it was changed, although I'd like to have kept the original idea."

'Dragon Lady' was another in a long line of upscale "evil woman" songs, this one written by Donald and 'Broadway Blotto' a guy with a joke band called, simply enough, Blotto, who have a novelty song called 'Metalhead' that features Donald on guitar, plus a humourous cameo by Donald in the video. The song is another one of those arguably ironic pop tunes, oscillating between drama and melodrama, well within the "heavy metal version of the Beach Boys" parameters Sandy always felt to be a worthy goal for the band. It's a strangely pedestrian tale that seems painfully tailor-trimmed for the band, the dragon lady rendered in primary colours almost as garish and monochrome as those used for 'Godzilla'. "'Dragon Lady' is a collaboration with Broadway Blotto," cites Donald, simply. "We had met at the studio, doing *Flat Out*. And you know... we look at a lyric, as we always do. The bulk of our lyrics come from other people and I liked that one."

Ending the record on a note of drifted ennui is a Joe Bouchard/Helen Wheels conspiracy called invitingly enough, 'Light Years of Love' high-strung vocal by Joe. Musically, the song is a bit of an unwieldy ballad, with a lyric that speaks of love in terms of light's shine and its speed. "Boy, that came from like another period of my life," reminisces Helen. "Um, I guess you could say it was a love song. Joe and Albert would often ask me for whatever lyrics I had hanging around, so it might be a ten year span of pieces of paper, so I don't quite remember. That one had more of an early '80s influence."

Joe has fond memories of working with Helen. "'Light Years of Love,' that came from Helen Wheels, and Helen is an old, old friend. She was my brother's first girlfriend when he moved to New York and I always loved the lyric. She gave me about five different versions. She would work very hard on her lyrics. She would send me a version, and say I can do better, and send me another version, and I'd go 'Great!' I'd just sort of work with the lyric to come up with the music. Sometimes it works the other way around. That's one of my favourite songs ever of the ones I wrote for the band."

"That album was a little uneven," continues Joe, "and that was the last track. I played half of the guitar solo and Donald Roeser played the other half of the guitar solo. The key was really high. I was looking to do something that was kind of like 'Fallen Angel.' I thought, 'Hmm, that's a good one.' Recently, I found an acoustic demo of the song from probably ten years ago that I had thrown together. I may have posted it somewhere. I started putting the pieces together from the original version to the acoustic version that I did ten years ago and came up with the version I have on my solo album."

So *The Revolution by Night*'s artistic compromises were overshadowed by the record's somewhat acceptable results in the marketplace. 'Take Me Away' became a concert favourite, while 'Shooting Shark' made the odd appearance on radio, peaking at a lowly No.83 on the singles chart.

The lights weren't completely out however. Even *Rolling Stone*, long a reluctant supporter, threw the band a bone. Wrote Errol Somay, "*With The Revolution by Night, the Cult prove they can still pump it up, though they may be writing more on momentum than inspiration. Songs like 'Feel the Thunder' are heavy metal bone-crunchers meant to be played while you're breaking the land-speed record on your motorcycle. Air-guitar specialists on the other hand, will be sent into spasms by the dazzling sonic effects of 'Take Me Away.' Unfortunately, unlike such earlier Cult efforts as* Spectres *and* Agents *of Fortune, which carefully balanced more diverse mystically sober tunes with rude headbanging,* Revolution by Night *continues the band's trend towards heavy reliance on wrenching metalisms. Unfortunate indeed, because 'Light Years of Love,' with its stately synthesizer-guitar harmonies and elegiac melody, and the mesmerizing 'Shooting Shark,' enhanced oddly enough by a relatively restrained (for the genre) sax solo, remind us that Blue Öyster Cult are capable songwriters at both ends of the rock 'n' roll Richter scale. BÖC's latest is also a little too polished for its own good. Still, few bands mix aesthetics and ass-kicking rock to such good advantage.*"

The esteemed Malcolm Dome from *Kerrang!* focused smartly on an analysis of the record's production, obviously a sticking point of the band's as well. *"To me, it sounds as if everything in the BÖC camp is currently too hunky-dory, giving them no reason to be adventurous. The Revolution treads water. It maintains the style adopted on the last three, but is rather disjointed. Sure, most of the songs are good, but there is little Cult cohesion. They've fallen into the trap of actually trying to formularise and compartmentalize their approach. In doing so, they've lost their edge. Perhaps the choice of Bruce Fairbairn as producer has something to do with it. A man with a lighter touch than Martin Birch, he's certainly at home with the cherubic mainstream pomp/pop of 'Take Me Away,' not to mention 'Eyes on Fire,' and the balladic 'Light Years of Love.' In fact, I doubt if the band have ever sounded so good on AOR material. There's a clarity about Eric Bloom's vocals that, when blended with Buck Dharma's spearing guitar and Allen Lanier's synth washes, is almost too perfect. Maybe BÖC should've kept Fairbairn for the light stuff, brought in Sandy Pearlman for the more left-field, quirky material and Birch for the boomers. Then the band really would've put themselves back into a potential crisis situation, and perhaps The Revolution by Night would've been a cracker. As it is, what we're presented with is a package of occasionally strong medicine that's enhanced by the production and a lot of pills made difficult to swallow due to a misdirected production."*

The band wasn't always convincing in a live situation either. *"A clear night, cool breeze, sweet familiar aroma— what more could a person ask for?"* questioned *Metallion's* Mary Ann Gallipi, reviewing the band's June 23, 1984 *Revolution by Night* stop in Toronto, supported by Santers. *"A little excitement and energy on the part of BÖC, perhaps. After hearing their brilliant efforts on record, you'd think these fellows have an awesome stage show. This isn't to say they're not good at their craft: as musos, BÖC are right up there with the best. Valid tunes from 'Godzilla' to '(Don't Fear) The Reaper' caused some peaks during the concert, but most of the night was a plateau. The use of flares didn't even seem to spark the crowd. One thing that managed to catch my eye was Rick Downey's use of drum sticks. This man goes through more sticks than Dave Winfield does baseball bats! The band was desperate to stir some life into the crowd, obvious when an excerpt of Pink Floyd's 'Money' was thrown into the bass solo and finally when Eric Bloom drove on stage with his Harley for a finale of 'Born to Be Wild.' I don't know who gave birth to this prop scheme, but it has run its course. As a matter of fact, I'd say Blue Öyster Cult have run their course, performing live. Better they retire to a recording studio—soon."*

Touring in 1983, leading up to the record's release, found the band supported by Donald's friend Blotto and also Duke Jupiter, with a couple of New York dates supported by Uriah Heep. After the album's October release, BÖC continued to focus on the states, supported by Rainbow and then Aldo Nova and Dokken. Aldo Nova was also tapped for the band's extensive European tour in January and February of 1984. Back in the USA, Aldo Nova stayed on for a few additional dates with support also coming from Girlschool. Ratt and Pat Travers would also play with the band, who would conduct a club tour as Soft White Underbelly leading to Rick Downey's last show in late December, and, soon, the return of Albert Bouchard to his rightful and opinionated percussive role.

Club Ninja

"Albert, do you promise to behave?"

By the time 1986 lurched into view, Blue Öyster Cult were a mere shell of their former selves, having seen their fortunes decline precipitously, along with the battles and self-doubts that accompany such lows. But all felt it was time for a record, whether there was material or not, especially Columbia, who were itching nervously for some sort of life from this former commercially viable property.

The label did not believe in the band by this point. Their chips needed cashing. So the decision was made to attempt a band revival with an infusion of fresh blood. Heart, Cheap Trick, Alice Cooper and Aerosmith all received transfusions and the patients were doing remarkably well. But with BÖC, reigns were relinquished and chaos ensued. The resulting record, *Club Ninja*, released in North America in January 1986 (after a different mix was released in the UK two months previous, and yet a different mix in Scandinavia one month previous), was the band's most expensive, painful and protracted to make. And it was a commercial and creative flop, consistently showing up in fan polls as the worst record the Cult ever hatched.

Catching up on the personnel shuffles to date, Rick Downey was the band's drummer from August '81 through December '84. Beginning of February '85, Al Bouchard was back in the band informally (very informally, as these were Soft White Underbelly dates), which only lasted until February 11th. Buck and Eric had simply called him up and said that they had a tour booked for two weeks, and did Al want to come? Al had hoped it would be permanent, but it wasn't to be. He was forbidden to have a microphone, or ever come to the front of the stage.

"It was a situation where we found ourselves booked for a tour, without a drummer," says Al Lanier. "It was an emergency situation, and it was like, 'Albert, do you promise to behave?' 'Yes, I will.' It was a shame." Political innuendoes abounded, battles ensued and the reunion was over, Allen also packing it in around this time, effectively dissolving the band at the beginning of March '85, although the pieces would be picked up by mid-April with Jimmy Wilcox and Tommy Zvoncheck as replacement parts.

"There were a lot of reasons," continues Lanier. "Everything seemed to be losing focus somehow. It was always that damn bugaboo about the definition of, 'What exactly is BÖC music?' It got to be so neurotic, in terms of analysing. It was just nuts, you know? Then also, it was the kind of thing that everybody goes through. You start to see different types of trends happening in the music business and you say, 'Well, we've got to do some of that kind of stuff.' You know, the kind of thinking that is never, ever fruitful. Because you always come back to the truth of, 'What you can write is what you can write.' It doesn't matter what you try to do, it's ultimately going to come down to who you are in the end." Of note, alldgedly to this day, Al Bouchard has never been paid for his fateful reunion tour with the band.

By May '85, *Club Ninja* was beginning to look like a viable reality, and the band felt it necessary to revive the machine, play some dates and record some basic tracks. Rick Derringer had been an acquaintance of the band and had heard they needed a drummer temporarily, after which he had offered his, the aforementioned Jimmy Wilcox, who is the younger brother of Utopia's Willy Wilcox.

As mentioned, Tommy Zvoncheck had already been brought in as a replacement for Allen, in an unpleasant scene which was more a miscue than an actual forceful replacement. Joe recalls, "Well, Sandy had been doing the *Imaginos* record with Albert when it was going to be his solo record, using Tommy Zvoncheck. I guess Sandy wanted to use Tommy for *Club Ninja*. I guess it was a misunderstanding. Zvoncheck was at rehearsal and Allen showed up and got pissed off. So Allen just walked out and that was it. They didn't see him again for like two years. We worked with Zvoncheck, and the thing was that he was a great keyboard player, but he lacked Allen's personality. Sometimes the best player isn't necessarily the best guy for the group, especially for Blue Öyster Cult. We would just plug in all these virtuoso players and we'd be like, geez, sounds great and all that, but I think the record lacked a lot of personality. So I was glad to see Allen back later on, even though the bass player wasn't me when I saw them, but some guy doing me (laughs)."

"I'd say *Club Ninja* was the big catalyst for me leaving the group," continues Joe. "Not so much *The Revolution by Night*, which was a fairly pleasant experience. The basic tracks for *The Revolution by Night* were just wonderful to cut, because, like I said earlier, we were at Boogie Hotel. We lived there for a month. It was a fun time putting down those tracks. I mean, the tracks took 30 days, and the overdubs were going to end up taking 12 months! Unfortunately the record didn't sell so everybody panicked. The next thing you know, Rick Downey got the axe. That kind of burned me a bit, but I said, well, I'll just plug on. We hired this virtuoso drummer Tommy Price who's just wonderful. He was doing the *Imaginos* stuff with Albert and Sandy at the time. But then we started buying... the last straw was buying all those songs we didn't need to buy, 'White Flags' and stuff. I don't know what happened with that song. Could have been the mix. We spent a year to complete it, 12 months from beginning to end on that record. At the end of 12 months and a ridiculous amount of money, the most money we had ever spent up to that time, I just said this is terrible. I don't believe this; I'm leaving."

"I wasn't happy with my bass-playing at the time either," Joe continues. "I was working really hard at it, but it just seemed I was up against a mental block. I studied hard, and I thought I was moving ahead with my playing, but it just seemed sort of futile. Maybe it was because other things were starting to interest me. As soon as I left the group, I got my first computer. I had been doing MIDI music for about the last two or three years that I was in the band, and that's become my thing now. I've been doing a lot of MIDI music for the last eight years now. So when I started The Cult Brothers, I didn't want to play bass, but more guitar and keyboards. I was a piano major in college and I wanted to get back into that. So there were other interests."

"Anyway, we weren't making much money at the time either. I just said to myself, hey, if you're not making any money, and the music sucks, then there's no reason to stay. I mean if the music was good and you weren't making any money, all right, stick with it you know? My ideals were still there. I would have stayed for the love of the music alone."

"One of the reasons I left the band is that I was tired of being a bass player," Joe summed up in a later interview. "I wanted to get back into guitar. Even though I was learning more about the bass by the time I left Blue Öyster Cult, my guitar playing had improved while my bass playing had sort of stagnated. One thing led to another and they said, 'It's time to do something else.' I left the band. It has been an interesting ride for the last 15 years. I have tried different jobs but now I'm back in music. It never really goes away. I worked in publishing for a while and I wrote some instructional music books that did quite well. That was a good experience. I also worked as a teacher in a private school for a while. My first love is music and it just never goes away when you are a sick addict like me!"

"I have no idea what happened to us on *Club Ninja*," Joe muses. "You see, we had hired so much technology. We had auditions for mixing engineers. We had people on standby, we had session players, everything in the business, except brains. We should have just realised, hey, get rid of all that crap, go in cut a real band doing a real album, and you'd have something. But somehow it got out of control, and we lost faith in the idea that we could write our own songs. That was the worst. I recently did a lecture for Connecticut songwriters and talked about that. That was the big crisis in faith right there. I sort of laid out the songwriting process we had in place, right from the early days as the Soft White Underbelly. We had this songwriting team, then later introduced people like David Roter and Patti Smith, which were high points. Then the low point came where we were not really creating anything. Pretty disappointing. It was the wrong thing at the wrong time. I probably should have spoken up more at the time, and demanded a few more things that I like about records, to be on the record."

"I'd say that there were a lot of politics within the record company at that point," noted Joe in a separate interview. "They were changing a lot of the executives. Clive Davis, who signed us, pretty much had a hands-off approach to Blue Öyster Cult. He let us do whatever we wanted to do. Later on I think there was a lot more pressure from the record company to put out a commercially viable album. It is a thing where if you tell them to get lost then they probably would have gotten lost. We started out as this underground band who did these weird records and now we were in the position of having to sell very commercial records. What were we going to do? We did look for advice from different sources. Some of it was good and some of it was bad. The good part was that we got to do two records with Martin Birch. I think the record-making process got a little bit big at that time. You had to spend half a million dollars recording your record. Then there were legends where this band took three years making this big record so we should spend a comparable amount of time making a big record too. I don't know if it really worked with the personalities in our group. We would have been better off doing lower budget quicker records."

"I took every year as it came," reflects Eric wistfully. "I never really waxed too philosophically about it. I'm sure there were times for every single member where you said, 'I've had enough.' In your heart, you're going 'What am I doing here?' I know that would happen to me in the middle of a show. 'Why am I still doing this?' You just take it as it comes. I mean, I don't really know why Joe quit. Albert was fired; that was different. But there comes a time when things change in your life. I had no idea I'd still be doing this today. I joined this band when I was 24. It's been a long pull. It's weird. If you asked me back then, living in the band house in Great Neck, 'Would I still be doing this at 50?' I'd say, I doubt it."

So as things transpired, Blue Öyster Cult's official line-up for the release of *Club Ninja* would be Eric, Joe, Buck, Tommy Zvoncheck and Jimmy Wilcox, who as it turned out, would drum with the band from April '85 through September of '86, a total of about 16 months, although much of the actual drumming on the album would be by Billy Idol's Tommy Price, with some bass provided by Kenny Aaronson, another Rick Derringer team-mate. Insiders had called this line-up "3OC" and when Joe had left, "Two Oyster Cult."

Zvoncheck clarified his role in an email interview with superfan Robo. "I was asked to play on *Ninja* towards the end of pre-production, more or less in the role of 'additional musician.' I believe the reason being that I was 'on top of synthesizer technology.' The guys knew me through Sandy, and from playing in Aldo Nova's live band. Plus I was living in Linden, New Jersey at that time with former Ian Hunter guitarist Tom Morrongiello, who is responsible for introducing me to Albert and Kasim Sulton. I was only 40 minutes outside Manhattan where the band was rehearsing, and I knew that a good chunk of the material was from outside writers. Although the stuff that sounded best came from Donald's pen, e.g. 'Perfect Water,' 'Dancin' in the Ruins' and 'Madness to the Method.' You must understand that I was not really a major fan of the band before I played with them, so other than their hits, I didn't really know much about their material. I had seen them numerous times when I was with Aldo, but my wife knew their material better than I did! If the band feels they sold out on *Ninja*, then I guess they did. It didn't work though. My role with them was as a hired gun, so my input into their music was via the 14 synthesizers plus piano and B3 that I played; purely musical, not conceptual. I spent a lot of time recording my parts and it was a great experience, making that record. If people think it's the worst BÖC album, well, it's not my fault."

Sandy Pearlman, back to produce for the first time in nine years, offered this tombstone. "*Club Ninja* was the worst record I was ever involved with in my life. I still managed the group and I was still occasionally writing lyrics, but it was silly because there wasn't much motivation for me. The band was really desperate. They couldn't find anybody to produce them and there was no material, so I got brought back for *Club Ninja*, which I think is a failure. It's a low-pressure record and a lot of it is flirting with commerciality. I'm not proud of it; it's a horrible record. You know I'm really, really sorry. I guess there's two good songs on it. But in the aggregate it's horrible."

The first track on *Club Ninja* (incidentally, the first BÖC record to get simultaneous CD release, and the first BÖC record in 27 months), was the aforementioned Leggat composition, 'White Flags' which first appeared on a highly interesting double LP by the Toronto band (primarily Hugh and Gordon Leggat) called *Illuminations*. To my mind, this was a brilliant cover choice, a perfectly mystery-shrouded epic tune, from a mysterious source, an emotion-driven tune with a cryptic lyric about love and life's struggles, one of the band's recurring underlying themes. It was one of the rare songs on *Club Ninja* that captures the tonal essence of past Blue Öyster Cult songs and albums, other tracks here featuring better lyrics, but none surpassing this one musically.

"Somebody gave us a cassette, and the demo was pretty good," notes Joe. "We thought that we could make it sound like Blue Öyster Cult. I like that song, but nobody else... it's not a big song. Like I said, this was an '80s phenomenon, where the company gets in and we decide that we're going to have outside writers write our material. Just so we could become as big as Fleetwood Mac. I thought it was completely the wrong thing to do. I don't know why we spent a lot of time on 'White Flags,' and it maybe just didn't sound as much like Blue Öyster Cult than it should have. Record sales should have not been the criteria for choosing songs."

On the heels of this epic was one of the band's desperate shots at another hit single. 'Dancin' in the Ruins' is credited to Larry Gotlieb and Justin Scanlon, but is a direct descendant of 'Burnin' For You' full of Buck's pop wonderment, more hooks than a fishing tackle box. But it was hard to shake the fact that the band had to surrender their creativity to produce it, and that much of the rest of the record pales in comparison. The song was trotted out as a hit single (almost a year after the album's launch), made a few waves, then died a quick death. Says Joe, "'Dancin' in the Ruins' was good, but I think if Donald had written a song called 'Dancin' in the Ruins,' it might be another 'Reaper'—but we took somebody else's song. Probably didn't get the right promotion on that one."

After an insipid AOR limp through Bob Halligan Jr.'s 'Make Not Rock War' came 'Perfect Water' an excellent collaboration between Donald and Allen's friend Jim Carroll (New York poet and rock musician, most renowned for the book and movie *The Basketball Diaries*, not to mention his nasty heroin habit). The song sports a shimmery, enigmatic lyric that can effortlessly elicit all of the following interpretations. On the surface, the song is an elegant celebration of the mysteries below the surface, deep within the sea, the utter peace to be found at the depths of the ocean. On the other hand... well, Bolle had this to say: "Perfect water is what Hitler was working with, to make the atomic bomb. The song has nothing to do with clean water (laughs). Perfect water is the whole Norwegian experiment. You've probably seen at least one or two movies on TV about this. The best one was called *The Telemark*, which was a Norwegian/American thing about World War II. It's about developing the atom bomb, and as you know Oppenheimer won."

Sandy doesn't count out the possibility that there was an alchemical slant to the song, Jim maybe picking up on his theories on the alchemical origins of heavy metal. "Maybe, maybe not. Jim Carroll was hanging with the whole like...

how does one describe this? Not that these people ever really introspected personally, except through me. But he was like hanging with the whole Blue Öyster Cult, Patti Smith, Dictators, Shakin' Street crowd, you know, for awhile. Actually some of these people do know each other. Besides me there are others there who know everybody. Al Lanier knows everybody. So yeah, only in that sense though. It's kind of atypical for Jim Carroll. It isn't your average Jim Carroll song. I'd like to think that the pollution spewed forth by this whole scene, you know, crept into a wider and wider world (laughs)."

Buck however points more to the literal translation (in direct reference to the line about bells chiming in random order), adding hope that the song might see reworking someday. "I don't know exactly what Jim meant, but it's probably something Jim heard Cousteau say in some interview or something. Might not be a big deal or literal quote as far as Cousteau is concerned. The lyric to me is an interesting thought train, but I hate the *Club Ninja* recording of that tune. I think the song's much better than that rendition. I may re-record it someday."

"I think 'Perfect Water' is perfect genius," laughs Joe. "Awesome. When they re-did it on the DVD live, it's the best thing on that live DVD. It could have been a Top Ten smash. It's very heavy; it's very Blue Öyster Cult. They took my bass off of that one, and they had Kenny Aaronson play it. I think all the rest of the bass on the album is mine."

Why would they have brought Kenny in?

"We had finished the song and it sounded great—I do not have a copy of it, I wish I did; I did not have archives the way I do now. So we finished it, it sounded great, sounded like Blue Öyster Cult, and Sandy Pearlman and Donald Roeser said, you know, if this is going to go through to No.1 in the universe, we gotta do it better! I think that we should hire… Thommy Price, and Kenny Aaronson, a hit making rhythm section, to replace the original rhythm section! Which I think was me and Thommy Price. So I said, 'Okay, all right, I'll buy that. If we're going in for punchier and we really want to sell tons… Would it be alright if I played rhythm guitar, in the studio?' So I played rhythm guitar, and it was eventually erased and Donald re-did it. But I enjoyed it—at least I was part of that session."

Now where was Thommy Price from?

"Thommy Price had played with Billy Idol; he had played on several of the Billy Idol hit singles. A fabulous drummer; he's with Joan Jett now. One of those incredibly heavy drummers. He had played on Albert's *Imaginos*. Sandy liked working with Thommy."

Joe says that the musical chairs continued deep into the heart of the Blue Öyster Cult sound, i.e. the realm of guitars. "Phil Grande was in to sort of fill in. I think there is one whole side of that album on which Donald does not play one solo, and it's all Phil Grande playing the solos. Phil was a talented player. He was really brought into the situation to replace Eric Bloom, and to be able to play Eric Bloom-type parts live in the studio, but with a better player. Phil actually went on and played some of the later '80s hits with Joe Cocker. A talented guy, you know, kind of neurotic, but I thought it was crazy. Donald is one of the best guitar players on the planet, and he's leaving Phil Grande, who is a good player but is no Donald, playing the leads! 'Donald, get in there and play your leads! Do your stuff.' But they didn't listen to me."

And Eric? "I don't think he played at all on the whole album. Hey, we're talking about rock 'n' roll; we're talking rhythm guitar. It's not... but that was the mentality, the '80s mentality. It's got to be bigger and better, and it's got to have this sort of gloss that Journey had. So I think Phil did most of the rhythm guitar. Now with Donald's solos, maybe there were some done in an overdub situation when I wasn't there, but I'm pretty sure that Phil Grande had a big part to do with all the guitar on that album."

'Spy in the House of the Night' made a half-hearted attempt at heavier rock, Donald's music and an increasingly rare Richard Meltzer lyric combining for a curious little song about smoke, fire, might and combinations thereof. A qualified success, if mainly for the fact that it was an in-house job.

Side two opened with another ditzy Bob Halligan Jr. number, 'Beat 'Em Up' joining the ranks of 'Let Go' and 'Make Rock Not War' as the most lowbrow songs in the BÖC canon. Adding insult to injury, the song had already appeared on a medium profile record in '84, by Canuck schlock rocker Lee Aaron, and in heavier form. Owners of the *Career of Evil* compilation from 1990 will notice that the version of 'Beat 'Em Up' enclosed features a noticeably different, dirtier, more metalized mix.

"'Beat 'Em Up' was not one of my favourites," comments Joe. "Bob Halligan make great demos, and they sounded great on a cassette, and you know, when you're playing back choices for an album, you try to find something that sounds like Blue Öyster Cult, and you try something that will be possible, and that's how 'Beat 'Em Up' and 'Make Rock Not War' got on there. The demos had sounded great, and we tried to do them, and we actually did them worse than his demos. But anyway, they were not my favourite songs on the album."

Breaking the pattern of pedestrian rock thus far was another suspended, isolated *Imaginos* lyric from Sandy, 'When the War Comes' keeping 'Shadow of California' company until the deluge that is *Imaginos* arrives and spills all the beans. The song opens with a spoken word segment courtesy of New York shock jock Howard Stern, whose cousin is married to Eric. At least one of the European versions of this record omits Stern's cameo. Sandy on his lyric: "That's basically a song about political kundalini or political orgasm, about the incredible release inherent in the notion of revolution and then the unanticipated after-effects." Fans of the band cringe visibly when hearing the tacky "Ooka chaka ooka chaka" chorus break. Pretty silly.

Joe adds an interesting point with respect to Sandy's lyrics. "I did some editing on Sandy's lyrics. Most of the time Albert and Donald, when they used Sandy's lyrics tried to keep them as is, although 'Cities on Flame' was completely redone. But I would spend a lot of time rewriting Sandy's lyrics to make them more musical, more singable."

Next in line was the song that inspired the album title, 'Shadow Warrior' being penned by the ultimate Ninja specialist, top-selling author Eric Van Lustbader, whose Ninja adventure novels are a hit the world over. The lyric is Ninja-based but moves into other realms, Van Lustbader doing a pretty snappy job of penning a characteristic BÖC saga. "Eric Lustbader wrote those Ninja lyrics, and then Donald Roeser put in a few licks and that's how 'Shadow Warrior' came out," figures Joe. "I don't know how it could have been made any better than it was." The song has its origins in a composition called 'I'm a Rebel' (or just 'Rebel') that the band had fleshed out fully in demo form, complete with a nifty synth lick and double time rave section over which Buck solos.

Closing this dull, but not altogether failed record is 'Madness to the Method' co-written by Donald and Dick Trismen, who together create a laborious and unwieldy track about predatory life in the bars, addressing both male-to-male bravado and male-to-female lust, judgments clouded by night's evil influence. Relates Joe, "Dick Trisman is now Richard Trisman, and works for the software company that I make my albums for, Mark of the Unicorn in Cambridge. He does the software for film soundtracks, and a lot of rock 'n' roll records are made with it as well. A nice sort of epic track. We spent a lot of time working on that, but it just didn't connect. I wish the album was better. I might have stuck around for a couple more years."

Club Ninja, like *Fire of Unknown Origin*, also has a soundtrack connection, the band signed to do three songs for the movie *Teachers*. This never happened, but one of the songs, transformed, eventually reworked its way onto *Club Ninja*, the aforementioned 'I'm A Rebel' from Eric becoming 'Shadow Warrior,' while Buck's 'Summa Cum Loud' and Joe's 'Double Talk' were used for Joe's rare Deadringer side-band project.

Deadringer, incidentally, consisted of Joe on keyboards, Dennis Dunaway on bass, Neal Smith on drums (both of Alice Cooper), Ted Nugent's Charlie Huhn on vocals, and Jay "Jesse" Johnson on guitar, the band releasing an indie record (both vinyl and CD) on Grudge Records in 1989 called *Electrocution of the Heart*. The album was quite disappointing creatively, sounding like crisply recorded, stiff hairspray metal, sorta like Bon Jovi meets '80s Alice Cooper. 'Summa Cum Loud' had an interesting melody and a brilliant lyric, while the rest (outside of two power ballads) could be described as an attempt at the strip mall party metal at its commercial peak in that very year. It is of note that future Brain Surgeons Al Bouchard and Deb Frost contribute a track called 'When You're in You're in'.

Joe hadn't ruled out the possibility of doing a second Deadringer record at some point, having kept in touch with the guys over the years. "Well, Deadringer was really a project that Neal Smith cooked up. Neal and I have been friends and writing partners ever since 'Shadow of California.' I wasn't really crazy about the project, but Neal said to me, 'Hey, we're going to get a great sounding demo out of this' (laughs). Don't go in with the idea of making an album itself, and expect to get a good sounding demo. I didn't really have too much say about the production. In fact I was out on the road playing with Spencer Davis, like in the middle of recording the album. But I was very happy they used three songs of mine. So we made the one album, although I just got a call from Dennis about three weeks ago, and he said, 'Hey, it's time to make another Deadringer album!' I'm like, oh my god. But I helped Dennis set up his home studio. He's still very creative. Neal, I just talked to him, because Albert called me up, and they're doing something in the Rock and Roll Hall of Fame on famous drummers, and they wanted to include Neal in that. He's writing, he has a home studio, and I hope I can record with them again."

"The Deadringer thing, I don't know," continues Joe. "See, I'd have to work it out with Neal. We'd have to decide who was going to be the singer. I don't know.

Maybe Charlie would sing again. I really enjoyed working with Charlie (ed. since this interview, Charlie has worked with Humble Pie, a reformed Victory, and had settled in with Foghat, where he works magic to this day). But I think I'd like to make it more interesting artistically, and not have to tow the line to the commercial bent of everything. That was one of the problems. We had the owner of the record company in the studio with us every day. He was a nice enough guy, but he was more into the oldies thing. So every time we wanted to do something a little avant garde or wild or outside, he would squash it. That didn't make it much fun."

In terms of other projects, Joe had this to say circa March '96: "Right now I'm working on two records, one pop record and a sort of jazz/world record, with this band that I actually play live with. We even have a record deal with a company in Germany but I don't know if I want to take that deal, because it's another one of these commercial things. I have a day job, so I don't need to do it for commercial reasons. I'd like to do it for purely selfish artistic reasons (laughs). Plus there's a project with Andy Hilfiger's brother's company, Tommy Hilfiger, which has changed complexion many times (laughs). It started as covers of '70s classics and now it's going more original. Also I work with this group in New Haven with these three girl singers. I play bass with them, but the other groups, it's primarily guitar. I also substitute in a traditional big band, play with my students, who I did a complete reggae set with for the first time. Work-wise, I'll still be part of teaching, but I won't be full-time, because doing the guitar books, typesetting, proofing, editing, will be a 40 hour a week job. I teach bass guitar, piano, vocals, but looks like I'm going to be fairly busy starting July 1st. So yeah, it's certainly an interesting life—I do what I can."

Post-*Club Ninja* was a time of animosities, scuttled plans and declining fortunes (the record was said to have sold about 150,000 copies). The band broke up once again in late 1986, reforming again just before Christmas through the urgings of Albert, who proposed assembling the original line-up, touring the world and playing nothing but his and Sandy's *Imaginos* concept set, possibly even billing themselves as Imaginos. They originally agreed, and set out to find Allen Lanier, who was eventually located in Florida. Allen had originally declined the offer, stating that he really wanted to take a trip to Greece.

"In my two years away, I was bored to death," says Allen. "I'm not sure I would have come back, except for the insane karma of the way it happened. I had gone through this period of intense reading again. I was reading all the Greeks again, all my Aeschylus and Sophocles and Homer etc., and I was getting ready to make a trip to Greece, and visit Troy and ancient Messene and all that sort of stuff. Then the phone rang and it was Steve Schenck (the band's full-time manager at this point), who said 'How would you like to go to Greece?' I hadn't spoken to him in about a year. I said, 'What are you talking about?' Unbeknownst to me, the band had broken up. They had done a European tour, and then Joe left. They tried a lot of people for the band but it wasn't working. Steve Schenck was determined to not let it fall apart; it was still too viable. So he booked another tour, and that's when he called me and said 'Greece.' I said, 'You've got to be kidding. Yeah, I'll do that!' So sure enough, my wife and I went over almost a week early, and we did all the things I wanted to do. The band showed up and we played two days in an outdoor stadium in Athens, and it was terrific. I said, 'Hey, I enjoy this again.' Ever since then, it's been good."

Tour dates for *Club Ninja* essentially began back in November '85, when the album was issued in the UK in conjunction with an extensive tour there supported by Statetrooper and Girlschool. January and February '86 saw the band cross over onto the mainland, support coming from Morho and late-fer-dinner NWOBHMers Tokyo Bade. A February 23rd show in Berlin would constitute Joe's last show, with Jon Rogers picking up the pieces when the band began their US leg in California. April and May saw the band supporting Rush, followed by a short stint with Ozzy Osbourne and then essentially club shows through August and September of 1986. Allen's rejoining, serendipitously in Greece, isn't until long after a dormant period, with those two shows happening July 8th and 9th 1987. What followed were a few more European shows, in West Germany and Switzerland, and then only sporadic US dates to close out the year.

So Allen was back on board, but Joe still hedged due to the strains being in the band caused to his family life. Joe had relented and joined hesitantly, but eventually left after the completion of the European mini-tour. The sordid story continues next chapter, with Joe and Al both gone (as it turns out, for good), but Allen firmly within the fold.

"I had been in the band for 16 years," reflects Joe. "I had expected that the band would only last three to five years. I really had some other things that I wanted to do. There was a whole list of reasons as to why I left. I didn't know what I was doing, but sometimes you just have to move on. I have been very happy. I am also very happy to have been the bass player for Blue Öyster Cult for all of those years."

It is of note that *Club Ninja* was the only Blue Öyster Cult album not available on CD for many years, having been deleted by Columbia for some time. This has been rectified with a Koch release of the record, containing full graphics plus November '96 liner notes by Arthur Levy, the man responsible for the *Workshop of the Telescopes* essay. In his brief notes, he recognises the band's internet presence, the contributions of band expert and archivist Bolle, and two references to *Ezekiel's Wheel*, the then-considered title for a '97 Cult record that, lo and behold, eventually saw the cold gray light of dawn, heaven forbid.

Early Columbia Records promotional photo. Left to right: Joe Bouchard, Allen Lanier, Eric Bloom, Donald Roeser and a cheeky Albert Bouchard.

JOHN SCHER PRESENTS AT THE
CAPITOL THEATRE

April 26
CLIMAX BLUES BAND
☆☆☆
Renaissance

April 27
BLUE OYSTER CULT
☆☆☆
KISS

1974
CONCERTS

BackStagePass

Blue Oyster Cult

CONCERTS WEST
SEATTLE • DALLAS • LOS ANGELES • CHICAGO

Artful promo photo that plays up Eric's photogenic qualities.

Above: Buck, Joe and Eric, backstage at the Fairground Pavilion in Tulsa, Oklahoma, July 27, 1975. Also on the gig were Kansas, Ted Nugent and Diamond Reo. (*Richard Galbraith*)

Below: Classic outdoor scene for a '70s rock 'n' roll fest: hanging out by the limo with the ladies. Left to right: Joe, Eric, Allen. (*Richard Galbraith*)

Right: Albert doing his best to cultivate the band's biker image. (*Joe Bouchard archive*)

Below: Consummate front man Eric Bloom, Civic Centre Music Hall, Oklahoma City, Oklahoma, July 26, 1975. (*Richard Galbraith*)

BLUE OYSTER CULT
★★★★★★★★
MISSISSIPPI COLISEUM
AUG **31** 1 9 7 6 Jackson, Miss.
TUESDAY
8:00 P.M.

GEN. ADM.
AUG. 31, 1976
001251
SEC. ROW SEAT

Little Wing Presents BLUE OYSTER CULT TULSA 7-6-75 **STAGE**

Joe, Eric (note BÖC logo on guitar), and Buck, in signature white. (*Richard Galbraith*)

Albert Bouchard, Blue Öyster Cult drummer but much more, including singer and songwriter. (*Richard Galbraith*)

Right: Donald "Buck Dharma" Roeser offers Oklahoma more guitar. (*Richard Galbraith*)

Below:
The Cult's famed five-man guitar army formation. (*Richard Galbraith*)

Eric and Buck abusing the tools of their trade. (*Richard Galbraith*)

Rhythm guitar meets lead guitar, and all is well with the world. (*Richard Galbraith*)

Above: Allen and Joe in the '80s, playing the mature adults of the band. (*Richard Galbraith*)

Right: A cleaned-up Buck in the '80s looks askance at a still hirsute Eric and Joe. (*Rod Dysinger*)

Right: Roadie turned Albert replacement, Rick Downey. January 10, 1984, Columbus, Ohio.

Below: Eric shows Buck the future (*Richard Galbraith*)

Right: Allen, Buck, Joe, Ohio, 1984. (*Rod Dysinger*)

Below: Bassist Danny Miranda, who put in a decade with the band. (*David Lee Wilson*)

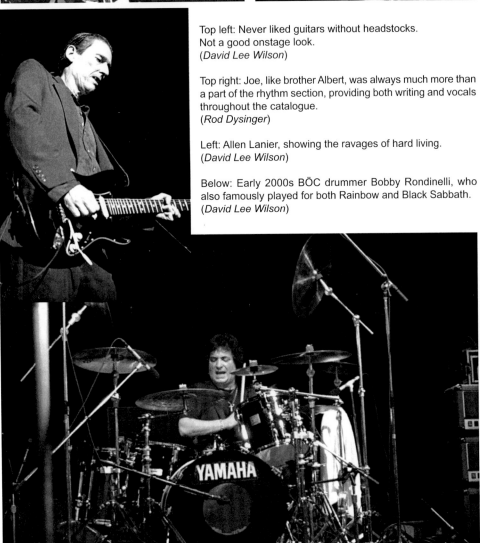

Top left: Never liked guitars without headstocks.
Not a good onstage look.
(*David Lee Wilson*)

Top right: Joe, like brother Albert, was always much more than
a part of the rhythm section, providing both writing and vocals
throughout the catalogue.
(*Rod Dysinger*)

Left: Allen Lanier, showing the ravages of hard living.
(*David Lee Wilson*)

Below: Early 2000s BÖC drummer Bobby Rondinelli, who
also famously played for both Rainbow and Black Sabbath.
(*David Lee Wilson*)

Imaginos

"Within the thrall of this neo-Wagnerian esthete"

S o we arrive at the last record from Blue Öyster Cult as we had known and admired them, the last record featuring a reasonable facsimile of the original line-up, the last record from the band for a decade, the silence to be broken emphatically with 1998's *Heaven Forbid*. Nothing about the existence, the assembly, the music or the literary train of thought of the band's baffling 14th record, *Imaginos*, is straightforward. It is the ultimate conspiracy, from a coterie of creators that thrived on all things conspiring.

As the saga goes, *Imaginos* begat life as a pile of poetic mumblings from one Sandy Pearlman, a collection of necessarily disconnected dribs and drabs that would be tinkered with many times since the mid-'60s, something Sandy called *The Soft Doctrines of Imaginos*. But as the '70s wore on, and when the muse attacked, Sandy would be there to receive piercings, transforming amorphous *Imaginos* thought into short, focused, commercially digestible peerings into the storyline, these exercises resulting in such integral *Imaginos* movements as 'Transmaniacon MC', 'Before the Kiss, a Redcap', 'Cities On Flame', 'Workshop of the Telescopes', 'Subhuman', 'Flaming Telepaths', 'Astronomy', 'Shadow of California', and 'When the War Comes'.

In the true nature of enigma, other Cult compositions could also fit the *Imaginos* concept quite comfortably, especially (and most logically) second-tier Pearlman compositions like '7 Screaming Diz-Busters', 'Redeemed', 'Dominance and Submission', 'ME 262', 'E.T.I.', 'R.U. Ready 2 Rock' and 'Heavy Metal: The Black and Silver'. But given the astonishing bandwidth of a story that includes time-travel, earthly evil, organic transformation and alien domination, the petty logic of story ownership can become wondrously suspended, allowing other lyricists to contribute to the river of time and space that is *Imaginos*. Thus 'Wings Wetted Down', 'Golden Age of Leather', 'The Vigil', 'Lips in the Hills', 'Veteran of the Psychic Wars' and 'Take Me Away' all could be seen as connecting the dots of *Imaginos* thought.

Indeed Al Bouchard, who was the second closest person to the project after Sandy, came up with his scenario for a second and third act of the tale, using existing material. After rearranging the order of the existing *Imaginos* tracks (more on this later), he posited the following: "*Act Two: Bombs Over Germany or (Half-Life Time)*: 'Workshop of the Telescopes,' 'Girl Love Made Blind' (left off

Imaginos), 'ME 262', 'The Red & the Black,' 'Cities on Flame' ('Motor City's Burnin'' version), 'Shadow of California,' 'Half-Life Time' (very few have heard this one), 'Veteran of the Psychic Wars'* and 'Career of Evil'*." Note: Sandy's preferred working title for act two was *Germany Minus Zero and Counting*.

Also imagining an act three called *The Mutant Reformation*, Al suggests "'Take Me Away'*, 'The Vigil'*, 'E.T.I.', 'R U Ready 2 Rock', 'Heavy Metal', 'Flaming Telepaths', 'Gil Blanco County' (left off *Imaginos*), and 'Redeemed'." Of the (*) tracks, Al states that these are "non-Pearlman songs, because I never plan to write another with him, and these tunes kind of fit the story," adding, "That's my idea of the *Imaginos* trilogy. Hopefully you can see how some of these old songs were supposed to fit into it, and maybe from all these songs you can get an idea of the whole story."

As one can surmise, *Imaginos* tied a torn and frayed, big, sloppy bow around the entire existence of the Blue Öyster Cult, hacking rough endpoints for a previously imagined infinite universe, while on this planet acting as metaphor for the flesh and blood infighting, charade and fraud that had become the band after so many years of stress.

Because of the exhaustive fragmentation with respect to no less than personnel, credits, execution, timelines, lyrics, production, botched launch and subsequent dismal sales, *Imaginos* is an unsatisfying record. Which is not to say people rally and throw stones as if *Club Ninja* had been much better. But considerable numbers of discerning fans (this writer not among them), find *Imaginos* to be the band's ultimate triumph, the culmination and unleashing of 20 years waiting to assemble the ultimate epic, written by the band's most difficult lyricist, Sandy Pearlman.

Certain facts cannot be denied. 1) Production-wise, *Imaginos* is lavish (if not lavishly flawed and uneven); 2) A certain bravery must be ascribed to BÖC launching a concept record, especially one so hard to decipher, especially so temporally distant from the heady days of Hitsville; and 3) By many measures, it is the band's most earnest stab at being heavy metal, offering lots of guitars, big, boomy drums, and an abundance of wattage.

So to flirt once again with the previously immutable concept of time, this 1988 record actually has its roots in the mid-'60s, its shards of storyline living in the air, emerging like water spouts, rains of frogs, alien abductions, spontaneous combustions and quick cattle decapitations throughout the '70s and '80s as Cult tunes we have grown to love. As the story goes, this 1988 record also entered earnestly into production seven years before release, in 1981, with the ouster of Albert from the band, post-*Fire of Unknown Origin*.

Press at the time recounted the story of Albert's final explosion and expulsion while on tour in Britain, Eric always added diplomatically that Albert was now working on a solo album, and that the split was best for all involved. Go solo he did, teaming up once more with Sandy on the great *Imaginos* epic, a journey through the futility of making music as inverted and labyrinthine as the *Imaginos* tale itself.

Albert adds some clarity to the tale. "Sandy came up with this *Imaginos* thing way before any of that. This was in late '67 that he had this idea. Although at the time he said, 'This is my version of *Giles Goat-Boy*,' something that I had no idea what it is (ed. a 1966 novel by popular American writer John Barth). But Meltzer seemed to know about it. This was a literary guy and had nothing to do with King Crimson. They seemed to all know about this *Giles Goat-Boy*, yet I've never seen it. This was Sandy's version of this epic, the *Imaginos* series. He had written a bunch of songs and he had kept working on it. Even as we were working on it later, he was still coming up with stuff. I would really bug him about it and say, 'Well, what will happen after this album? It doesn't really seem to have an end, so what's the next chapter?' He kept up with stuff. This is one of the big disappointments in my life, that it didn't progress beyond the original thing that I was hired to do."

I asked Al how broad in scope *Imaginos* was supposed to become. "Actually my original concept for it... I felt like it was an open enough concept that I felt that we could have done three double albums, and each double album would be about an hour's worth of music or 80 minutes tops. I think that the album that came out was about 50 minutes. With the parts they left out included, it would have been about 70 minutes. I have the whole thing. I have a version on tape. I took the best mixes I could find, excluding the Blue Öyster Cult mixes. I believe there's one song that is absolutely the best that it ever was, the version on the record of 'Frankenstein,' which is just a superb mix. Nothing I did had topped that."

Al offers a rare glimpse into just what went down with Sandy and himself during the course of the early '80s. "Well, I've always had a strange relationship with Sandy. He's always been nice to me but I've always been wary of him. I've always felt like he was trying to get over, but actually, I can tell you when the break came. It was when we were making the record, and we had all gotten together for the second set of basic tracks. We'd cut I think six songs, the first batch, and then we got together a month later and cut the other songs. I guess it was six more, to make 12 altogether. Like the first or second day we were doing the second batch, I think we took a week each time, Sandy said listen, 'You're the artist on this thing; I want to get full production credit.' I said, 'That wasn't the deal. We were going to be co-producers, equal billing. It was going to be produced by Al Bouchard and Sandy Pearlman, my name first.' He said, 'No, because you're the artist and I'm not the artist. Is this going to be an Al Bouchard album?' I said, 'No, it's going to be an Imaginos album.' He said 'Do whatever you want.' I said, 'Well, I don't want an Al Bouchard album; I want Imaginos. That's it; the band could be Imaginos, the record *Imaginos*, all Imaginos, and I want a production credit. I want to be a producer, and get a production royalty.' I said 'Sandy, we agreed to this already.' He said, 'Well, I want to change the deal.' I said, 'No deal.' He said, 'Well, I'm the one who got the deal with Columbia.' Then I said, 'Listen, you either agree to this right now or that's it, I'm walking out.' So I went out and the guys in the studio said, 'What's going on?' I said, 'Well, Sandy wants to change the deal and I don't want to do it. Are you with me?' They said yes. So I went back and said, 'Sandy, you've got to make up your mind whether you're going to stick by our original agreement or it's over, it's off. The deal's off. We're just going to scratch it.' Then you know, after about a half an hour he said, 'Okay, you've got me. I can't do anything without you.' I said, 'Well, thanks.'"

"But I knew it was sort of over then," Al continues with a sigh, "because from then on in, I felt that he was trying to squeeze me out, and in effect that's what he did in the end. Of course we kept cordial relations through the making of the record, and in the end, you know he managed to… he put me down as Associate Producer, whatever the hell that means. But you know, I didn't have anything to do with the final product, nothing, nothing, and that was after suing them, and suing Columbia. I tried to be nice about it, and they wouldn't hear of it. So I eventually had to sue them. But Sandy was determined to change the deal, and change the deal he did."

"So you know, I don't know," continues Albert, divulging other snags. "By the time we were making *Imaginos*, and Sandy had got this deal for *Imaginos* and they gave us all this money, we went into the studio. I hired all the guys to make the record with me and we worked really hard on it. I felt really good about it until one day when we had just about used up our budget and we needed more money to finish it, so four guys from Columbia came out, okay? It was one of my friends who I won't be mentioning. But the head of Columbia at that point was this guy Mickey Eichner, and I'd be happy to talk about him because his attitude was, 'Where's the single? I gotta have the single. If it's not a single it's not worth putting out.' I'm like, 'Well I'm sorry but this is… it's supposed to be a concept record. It's a whole big thing; you have to listen to it all at once. It's not really the singles. Singles are three minutes. We don't even have a three-minute song on here.' 'Well you gotta edit it.' 'Well I know you guys are supposed to sell it, but I'm the guy that's making it, and if you want a single then we'll write a single.' So he was disappointed. He said, 'Well, 'Astronomy'—we'll edit it down to three minutes' and I'm like, uh, okay."

Sandy, (in his Imaginosed manner!) gives his take on the mess of making the record, specifically its convoluted timelines. "In terms of *Imaginos*, a lot of those songs were written a long time ago and just not used. I'd been wanting to do this for a long time and the band really didn't want to do it, because it would have put them kind of within the thrall of this neo-Wagnerian esthete, you know? It would have been that. So for reasons that I don't quite understand—actually I do understand them and I don't think they're valid—they avoided doing it for a long time. But a lot of the material that was written for this project sort of eked its way out on individual records until we did *Imaginos*. So I think that nothing as good as the best of *Fire of Unknown Origin* happened until *Imaginos*. Oh I don't know, maybe that's not true!"

Eric provides the missing pieces. "Well, I'll give you the reader's digest version. When Albert was fired in '81, there was a lot of material he had presented to the band that was written with Sandy Pearlman, that was part of the *Imaginos* epic. A few of the *Imaginos* songs… Sandy wrote *Imaginos* in the '60s, the lyrics, and they were always floating around. There's this whole bunch of lyrics about Imaginos. 'Astronomy' was one of them; 'Subhuman' was one of them. So those two came out of *Imaginos* and made it onto BÖC records."

"Now over the years Albert kept writing one or two *Imaginos* tunes and no one else in the band wanted to use them," continues Eric. "So when Albert was fired, Sandy approached… we had a demo of 'In the Presence of Another World,' which I sang. Using that demo, Sandy persuaded CBS to put out *Imaginos* as a project for him and Albert, because Sandy wrote *Imaginos* and it was very, very important to Sandy that *Imaginos* see the light of day. It was his, you know, masterpiece. So Albert and Sandy got to work with this huge advance from CBS. They worked on it and worked on it, using all these different musicians and different singers and different players and it went on and on and on for years. It was like a Meat Loaf record (laughs). It got to the point where—it was a double record by the way—where they finished it. I'd say '81 'til about '84, about three years after they had started, they called it done. CBS heard it and hated it. Mostly the vocals, which Albert sang lead. So they shelved it and refused to release it, so it sat. So Sandy, being our manager, and together with his partner Steve Schenck, approached CBS saying, 'Give us some more money and we'll have Eric and Donald come in and sing it.' CBS bit on that, so Donald came in to play some guitar on it, and I went and sang on it, and they reduced it to one album, and put it out. That's the story."

Sandy speaks proudly of the final product, while expressing frustration at all the politics that scuttled the thing. "At the end of the day, on the earlier records, there really is this cumulative aggregate impression which is synergetic in quality and yields a lot more than the individual components would suggest it would yield. It sort of requires you to play the whole thing. So the whole thing becomes a more addictive experience. With these other middle records you could just kind of random access it and, you know, get away with it. It's really two or three songs deep and that's the end of it. But with *Imaginos*, we obviously tried to get back to that. But there was actually no intention on the part of Columbia Records at all to promote it. That's what everybody says when they have a failed record, but in some cases it's even true. In this case it was true. Basically the people wanted to work it, and they were told not to work it."

"But the band didn't want to make *Imaginos* in the '70s when it really would have worked," Sandy surmises. "Too bad actually. There's a summary of the entire career with *Imaginos*. If they'd done it in the late '70s, yeah, I think they would've gone very, very far. A record like *Imaginos*, given that AOR radio was still really big then, and the concept records really ruled AOR radio, it was an incredible mistake not to do it, just to get out from under me."

Contrary to Albert's opinion that the final product was not significantly changed from his early demos, Sandy states that, "We did a tremendous amount of work. Yeah, a lot of that is Buck on 'Astronomy' II. That's all Buck; it's actually all Buck and Joe Satriani. I guess it's not much Joe Satriani (laughs), but it's probably the only time they'll ever play together, so (laughs) I thought I'd mention it. So, yeah, no not at all. We did a lot of work on it. Does Albert basically think it's what it was when he was singing the songs? It isn't; it just isn't. It's a lot of stuff on that. The rhythm tracks are the same. I shouldn't even say that. The drums are the same, but a lot of things have changed. There's a tremendous amount of Buck's guitar on it."

"When I listen to *Imaginos* and all the stuff that Buck played," continues Sandy, "which, like I say, is a lot more than the revisionist opinions are giving credit for... I don't know, I don't even understand, the whole revisionist controversy around *Imaginos*, but the solo on 'Astronomy'—is there a better solo that anybody has ever played?! I mean really, is there a better solo in rock 'n' roll, than Buck played on 'Astronomy,' whether it's the short single version, or the version that is on the video, on YouTube, the UK video, you know, the long version? I mean, when I played the stuff in class... because we do a comparison of the three phases of 'Astronomy,' 'Astronomy' early, Metallica, and *Imaginos*, in my class, in several of my classes, and you know, people are just flattened by this solo, how great it is."

"But *Imaginos*, the reason that it's so heavy, was that Albert put together the best band in the world, and then I brought in some even better musicians, or whatever. In functional terms, the band that Albert and Tommy Morrongiello put together through the basic tracks was as good as it's going to get. It's an amazing band. I mean I'm sure there were better bands, but it was a really good band. Then I had the freedom to bring in some other people and we got what we got, and it was kind of like I could do what I want with my studio. For example getting Joe Satriani to play was simply a function of trading in studio time to make *Surfing with the Alien*, and him playing some parts. It's fewer parts that people think, actually. I read some of this stuff and I don't know what they're talking about. By the time it's done, people think the only musicians on it would have been Marc Biedermann and Joe Satriani. If you believe that, friend, that's not true. Not remotely true. But anyway, so once again I was there for the early arrangements of that and of course I was there for 98% of the recordings. So I got to make it as heavy as I wanted."

"That's how *Imaginos* eventually got made, right? Eventually... nobody was going to do what I wanted to do any longer, but Albert did want to do what I wanted to do, and what happened with Albert is the singing was no good—it was beyond horrible. But that's just the case, and this thing was going to sit on the shelf, which I was not terribly interested in having happen. So Columbia offered us, I think, actually, an imaginative solution to the problem. They didn't sell that many of the thing, though it's out again. The funny thing is they probably could sell a lot now because of the YouTube activity revolving around this record, which is enormous."

Bottom line is, through all of the "hurry up and wait" involved, Albert provided a framework of over 90 minutes of music, which then was handed over and finished without him. So even though he is credited as a member of the band, he was far from it at the time. But it looked good in the credits to see everybody cozily back in the fold. It goes without saying that there was no reunion to tour the said opus.

Which snaps us back to 1988, and the impending release of the mystery lump that is *Imaginos*, miles of tape, and even more brain matter, innuendo, very real legal hassles, and gnashing of teeth compressed onto one unassuming piece of black vinyl.

Underscoring the ridiculous state of affairs that marked the record's release, Joe deadpans: "I was working as a teacher, and a new record came out with my name on it. I kind of liked it. *Rolling Stone* gave it a very nice review. It's certainly a challenging artistic piece. I guess people don't do those kinds of things that much these days. That's one of those quirky, artsy records that Albert likes to make."

Joe modestly clarifies his minimal role. "I only worked on the record for about two days. The record took almost four years to do. Other than the two songs that

I wrote, 'Astronomy' and 'In the Presence of Another World,' my only input was playing a piano part which I think was erased and played by a studio musician! So I don't think it's even on the record. I hate to burst your bubble! (laughs). My background vocals are minimal, just here and there. So it kind of bothered me that I got such a big credit on the record, when I didn't have much to do with it. The bass playing is mostly Kenny Aaronson. They had gangs of people singing back-up vocals, and they had dozens of keyboard players too. It was a very long, involved project."

Artwork-wise, *Imaginos* offered an intrinsically Cult-like image, a stormy, black and white shot of the infamous Cliff House, a restaurant off Highway 1 near San Francisco (the band also recorded and mixed the record in San Francisco). Because of its dramatic locale, the house has been photographed for postcards and posters over the years.

Band cover artist Greg Scott (*Fire of Unknown Origin*, *Extraterrestrial Live* and *The Revolution by Night*), had suggested a continuation of the *ETL* theme. "Sandy and I worked together for some time when they were originally going to release *Imaginos*. I did a lot of artwork for it and then they shelved it. Of course *Imaginos* was supposed to be the original BÖC record back in the early '70s. But there was a period in '84, '85 where *Imaginos* was going to come out. I had done a full drawing for the front and back covers. Of course most records were still on vinyl then, and I was working with another artist on a gatefold as it was going to be a double album. So I was working on it for months, and spending a lot of time with Sandy, who was collaborating with me on the whole philosophy and the whole story behind the album. None of that was ever seen, because it was shelved. Then I moved here to New Mexico in '89, and they had lost their contract with Columbia just before that. Of course they haven't been on a major label since. They did end up releasing *Imaginos* in '88, but just ended up using the photograph of the Cliff House in San Francisco, which is okay. But it was disappointing to me because I had spent so much time doing my style."

So what might have *Imaginos* become graphically? "Well, the front cover was Imaginos himself, a very kind of apocalyptic image of him, standing in front of a stormy sky with the ship and the pyramid in the background, holding a mirror out towards you. His Doberman pinscher, which appeared in various versions of all my other artwork, was in front of him. That was a very intense and spooky kind of image. The back cover was basically all the same elements rearranged. It was Imaginos as a young boy, and he's standing waist-deep in the water with a model boat, and the dog is behind him in a constellation. So there's the drawing of the dog, where the constellation Sirius is coming through him. So it was basically all the elements; there was a kind of a farmhouse, in place of the pyramid. So each of the elements of the front cover were translated in the back cover in different places and in different ways."

The Siruis or Dog Star imagery fits well with Imaginos' origins in the stars, Sirius being a bright, "fixed and consequent" star used for navigational purposes because of its stable positioning in the sky.

One thing is for certain, more descriptive artwork might have aided in unraveling the convolution that passes for the *Imaginos* plot. Without getting into track by track particulars (this begins following his comments), Keeper of the Cult, Bolle Gregmar offers this fascinating overview, proving that the tale can be experienced on many levels.

"I'll tell you. The wonderful scenario that everybody's really been puzzled about is simple to solve," he begins. "Because it's dealt with in the description of what *Imaginos* is. It's also printed on the back of the original t-shirts for the *Imaginos* tour. It reads: 'a bedtime story for the children of the damned.' This also reverberates within Stephen King's *The Stand*. There's a rare video-only version of the song 'Astronomy' where you hear the intro to the song. Over the intro, Stephen King reads the following: 'A bedtime story for the children of the damned, from a dreamworld paralleling our earth time and space, the invisible ones,' les invisibles in French. In my wording, I'd just call them Les Invisibles, because anything else that's invisible, these are even less invisible. That's my joke, (laughs). So The Invisible Ones, to quote the back cover notes, 'have sent an agent who will dream the dream of history. With limitless power he becomes the greatest actor of the 19th century. Taking on many ingenious disguises, he places himself at pivotal junctures in history, continually altering its course and testing our ability to respond to the challenge of evil. His name is Imaginos'."

"The Les Invisibles part is so cool for me, because that's where you get the whole grip on the story," continues Bolle. "Because that's where Sandy talks about, 'Yeah there's a peoploid out there, the invisible ones.' The invisible ones? Well, once you start thinking about it, there's one single concept that reveals the entire thing. He is actually dreaming the world, dreaming about all this. Since he's now dreaming this, he's dreaming the whole dream of history. In your dreams, if you have a vivid imagination and good ideas, you have great dreams. So the whole *Imaginos* story is basically a dream by somebody. If you want, it could be a religion, which is really sick. Then Imaginos would be God (laughs). Or if you wanted to make more practical sense, it's any of us dreaming just a story about World War I and World War II. We find all these characters in there. Probably the faces we put to these characters will be people we know. But we're still dreaming the dream of reality as we know it, and of how we've been introduced to it through historical teachings. So I think that's fascinating as is. *Imaginos* is wonderful to me because it's a dream within a dream. Edgar Allan Poe. I can go along with that. That's our life. We are a dream within a dream. Maybe we don't even exist (laughs). Maybe we're just a figment of somebody's imagination. I love all this. I love it. I don't know anybody who's come close to this."

Despite this otherworldly interpretation, *Imaginos* does have a more material plot line. But this plot line does not follow the track listing of the record, although the correct chain of events can be gleaned from the record's liner notes. Why are the tracks jumbled? Hard to say. It could be a sly ruse played by Pearlman, the actualization of the dream as random access, or it may simply be a practicality based on splitting the vinyl into two sides of carefully sequenced tracks, sequenced more for commercial viability than coherence of the story. Cynics suggest the mystical, rationalizing notes about the random nature of the story were added simply as a rebuttal or disclaimer vis-à-vis botching the order.

The correct order therefore becomes: 'Les Invisibles', 'Imaginos', 'Del Rio's Song', 'Blue Öyster Cult', 'I Am the One You Warned Me of', 'The Siege and Investiture of Baron Von Frankenstein's Castle at Weisseria', 'In the Presence of

Another World', 'Astronomy' and finally 'Magna of Illusion'. It is interesting to note that Albert's perceived correct order begins with the same four placings as above, then offering 'Astronomy', 'I Am the One You Warned Me of', 'In the Presence of Another World' (with the added note that these two could be reversed), 'Siege', and then back to the same closer with 'Magna of Illusion'. In any event, it is agreed by almost all that the actual running order is greatly flawed, obscuring understanding, or as I say, perhaps forcing the listener to understand the tale's structure on a philosophically tougher level.

Sandy's succinct summarization of the story goes something like this: "Basically, it's an interpretation of history—an explanation for the onset of World War I, or a revelation of the occult origins of it. Imaginos is the main character and is what I call 'an actor in history.' He plays different roles in history and was born as a modified child, modified by an alien influence, and his mission is to present the human race with the challenge of evil. The aliens are playing with our history as if it's a game, and he motivates the game and presents the choices to the human race. They react as they will. The story also reveals who the Blue Öyster Cult are. They are aliens. When Imaginos is dying on a beach, they announce their presence to him and give him a choice—side with them or die as a human. He chooses the former and realizes he was one of them after all. In 'Astronomy,' he realizes he is descended from the stars."

But the tale is much more. The ever-unfolding story of *Imaginos* draws together many paranormal, alchemical, extraterrestrial, universal, religious, moral and ancient disciplines. In this respect it is a metaphor for all, a porous touchstone for the study of many streams of thought. But our story begins in Haiti of all places, where a clash between an older spiritual world and a newer material one is about to take place, with the arrival of Spanish explorers. Combining the explanatory liner notes with the much more cryptic and sparse actual lyric to 'Les Invisibles', we are led to believe that the native Indians of this region were under the throes and thrall of Les Invisibles, a fused paranormal and extraterrestrial force that manifests a persona through various voodoo rituals and through the concept of ghost-dancing, which was a common method of summoning the dead throughout many Indian cultures of the western hemisphere. Given Pearlman's respect for H.P. Lovecraft, it is no surprise that the very nature of Les Invisibles mirrors quite closely Lovecraft's concept of the Old Ones, from the aquatic imagery to the detached, amoral, almost purely and comically inquisitive disposition of the beings.

Recognizing the evil of the place, the Spaniards nevertheless succumb to it, first fearing the temptations of the gold found in abundance in this New World, then becoming slave to its riches. Numerous voodoo references can be found within the song's lyric, including a repeated mantra of the number seven, coupled with the presence of Les Mesteres, or the Loa, seven spiritual beings revered in voodoo. Baron Samedi is reputed to be lord of the graveyards, and other hints of magic can be found in Pearlman's references to drumming, rainmakers, sages, night dances, the rose cross and alchemy.

The mention of alchemy is an interesting one, recalling the fusion of magic and science that gave rise to that discipline in ancient times. Here the Spanish are wary and ambivalent about discovering gold, perhaps drawn to it through magic they can't begin to harness, even if they are willing to take the journey nevertheless. Undercurrents of corruption flow both ways here, the idea of the New World soon to be intoxicated by gold and silver, and the idea of a two-tiered hex brought upon the more spiritually pliable inhabitants of the old world, through the arrival of both Les Invisibles, and the white man (the ironic similarity of those two terms cannot go unheeded).

The reference to polar mountains and rose crosses, followed later by a reference to a magic casement, recalls another important and legendary landmark for alchemists, the supposed Treasure of Rennes-le-Chateau, the Swiss or French-based "treasure" reputed to be one or many of the following: the secretly moved and buried body of Christ, the Holy Grail, a huge actual treasure of gold and silver, or cryptic parchments that unlock the mystery of alchemy, or perhaps even immortality, which was often thought to be attainable through the application of alchemical processes to the human body.

Whatever the circumstance, so it follows that both the alchemist and the Spanish explorer have found ways to "create" precious metals, but not without damnation.

It seems that the portal of destruction, and the spread of Les Invisibles' power, happens to be a mirror of gold and obsidian, a mirror being an apt instrument of evil, given its ability to cause reflection, both moral and merely physical. Fashioned in Mexico, this mirror is said to be integral to the work of Dr. John Dee, an espionage agent, astrologer, cartographer and scientist in the employment of Queen Elizabeth I (1582 to 1589). It is said that through paranormal means, Dee and his assistant Edward Kelly were able to summons the Enochian Angels, who aided the English in wars against its neighbours, particularly Spain. These entities are Les Invisibles, unleashed and returned to the Old World by the Spanish, now used against those who fell to their second test of morality, the first fall from grace going to the Haitians, the second to these aggressive gold-mongerers, who committed lusty genocides in the course of ransacking the material world for their own benefit, genocides that greatly diminished the religion devoted to Les Invisibles.

Thus begins a new phase of history, the history of European civilization, and its uncivilized centuries of turmoil, leading through World War I, World War II, and arguably beyond. This avalanche of accelerated events is the dream of history, Les Invisibles becoming an otherworldly and secondary "first mover," second to the big bang of God, but closer to Western man, possibly more meddling, bent on conducting experiments in morality through the coming decades.

The scene then shifts to the record's title track, Pearlman once more saluting Lovecraft by placing his lead character and the reverberations of his own "Old Ones" in Victorian New England. With one of *Imaginos'* strongest parallels to the Christian story a child is born (albeit in New Hampshire), a child with special powers he cannot understand, a child who will live out his life in the service of The Invisible Ones. Perhaps this parallel plotline is demonstration of Les Invisibles mocking God. Certainly their wiping of Imaginos out in a shipwreck, and revealing themselves most potently to him at that time, plays cruelly on the image of Jesus on the Cross.

In any event, the image of Imaginos, born in August, singing songs that were not yet written, telling stories that were not yet told, is an arresting one. Clairvoyant images of fish rotting in the sun pervade the track, foreshadowing Imaginos' eventual death and resurrection. This once more parallels Lovecraft's image of the Old Ones, who often are portrayed as rising from the ocean floor, coming ashore, and performing their will.

Imaginos then becomes an adventurer, travelling through Vermont and Texas to New Orleans, circa 1829, ending the track at this "last exit to Texas." From here he intensifies his role, turning from traveller to explorer, 'Del Rio's Song' celebrating Imaginos' 20 years on "the edge of chance," visiting here, visiting there, always suspecting there all goals for his life of which he has not been told as of yet. His final destination will find the story coming full circle to the hot climes of Central America, Mexico, the Yucatan, where a mirror, or the deadly mirror manifested as elemental, an evil seed, awaits (this final destiny is not reached until the tale's last track). Throughout the track, Imaginos marvels at his transformational abilities, speaking of buzzardos, bungo ponies, and even such wild beast as rockers and rollers!

But with the advent of 'Blue Öyster Cult' (a re-working of 'Subhuman'), Les Invisibles demonstrate their violent nature and cause trauma, shipwrecking Imaginos, leaving him to die, hallucinate and generally suffer. Here, in bereaved contemplation, he receives his ambiguous instructions and powers with which to execute them. In a twisted baptism ceremony, he merges with tide, seaweed and oyster, and is reborn (dreams of Luxor is a reference to rebirth and fertility) as spiral architect. Les Invisibles show a rare glimpse of emotion in being excited about their new pawn (or should that be prawn?)

Alchemical inference is rife once again, many elements flickering and transforming, wind, weather and storm shifting by the minute, body convulsing between mammal and fish, and reality dropping the chains of time, space and gravity. Motion is all-encompassing, and Imaginos finds himself thrust into a new role.

Imaginos, now deemed Desdinova (translation: eternal light, new day or new destiny. Note: Desdinova was also mentioned in that fake book reference in *Secret Treaties*' liner notes), becomes quite forcefully, "the one you warned me of," this fourth tale fleshing out the psychological profile of this new confident member of the Blue Öyster Cult, while describing his dapper new threads. It is a colourful John Dee archetype, with graphic allusions to a set of wild, colourful eyes providing an arresting impression, while his fingers control the masses, perhaps through a sort of metaphoric puppeteering, played out with a church organ.

Al has commented that a certain prowess over the ladies was indeed intended through the reference to "meat," providing the image of a self-assured, power-steeped super-being dressed in tails to the nines, bed-hopping and crystal-balling to his black heart's content. Al has also conjectured that The Invisible Ones originally arrived from space, which certainly would account for all the astrological references concentrated here. Another interview has Imaginos himself an ex-patriot of space, moving to New Hampshire, and fathering the son in his image.

The tale continues with an acceleration into modern society and the ills thereof, Imaginos (whether he has become the Baron is unclear), delivering to

Europe new play-God knowledge, resulting in technology taking over the masses. The lyric to 'The Siege and Investiture' is one of the most obscured but also one of the most crucial to the story of *Imaginos*, questioning the desirability of immortality (this idea of world without end), or even a lesser meddling in the true course of nature. This exalted view of technology becomes Imaginos' crowning piece of work, delivering to the people the means to pollute and destroy with renewed vigour, respectively through the industrial revolution and modern warfare.

The lyric of 'In the Presence of Another World' serves much the same purpose as its predecessor, containing more profile than plot, the reader meant to rely on the liner notes to explain Imaginos' latest escapades. It expands on the theme of science gone too far, and predicts Nostradamus-like the results of merging such knowledge with malicious intent. A character sketch is made of a charismatic leader, a master who is a monster. It is easy to see how Albert considered these last two tracks reversible. Neither are particularly chained to time frame, both being obscure but universal warnings within this dream.

'Astronomy', great lyric that it is, is hard to peg to the flow of the *Imaginos* saga. One might find glimpses of the grandfather character preparing for the voyage 'Magna of Illusion' recounts, or one might see merely another character sketch of Desdinova. The image of the clock striking 12 might signal that a turning point is at hand, that things are about to get ugly. There is also the suggestion of upheaval of a more meteorological nature. There is also suggestion of a more visible form for The Invisibles, that this sharpening of tone is the signal of a vortex of violence. One point that Sandy makes is that 'Astronomy' maps out Imaginos' connection with the stars, a type of adoption revelation that Imaginos undergoes. Whatever the intention, 'Astronomy' is a loose fit to the tale, perhaps suffering from having been written and cast in stone 13 years before the release of this ill-fated "last" BÖC record.

Compared to what precedes it, *Imaginos'* final scene, 'Magna of Illusion' offers a mountain of plot. Imaginos, now a senior man of the sea, embarks on another expedition, arriving in regions previously steeped in the dominating presence of The Invisible Ones, the now no longer new world, Mexico, Mayaland, the Yucatan. It is August again, only now it's August 1892, and granddad has sailed to this exotic land, where he comes upon a pyramid. Here, after much labyrinthine exploring, he discovers the Magna of Illusion, the mirror of black and gold. Under circumstance of crime, he removes the mirror and returns it to Europe as a present to his granddaughter, whereupon its powerful presence, locked in hibernation for many years, poisons the soil. The imagery here is stunning, the mirror somehow being thrust "in vivo" into the good earth, becoming a germ or organism that calls on people to envision and make possible the darkest dark and the brightest, most blinding light.

So the story ends on a note of foreboding evil (indeed one as intense as Melville, most notably *The Confidence Man*), and it can only be ascertained through discussions with Sandy and Albert that the vision for the *Imaginos* story was to take it into the realm of the unavoidable: World War I, and then the violent throes of World War II. The project did, after all, begin life as a trilogy and a double record. Given the time-straddling nature of Imaginos' power, we might have even seen a story from the future, or the present, or the very distant past. One can only conclude that this is a project that should have no conclusion.

One of the two tracks Al mentions as having been songs slated for *Imaginos*, but deleted was 'The Girl That Love Made Blind'. Sandy offers this explanation of where she would have fit in the story. "'The Girl That Love Made Blind' is a kind of dream meditation. Imaginos is dancing with this girl at a ball in 1905, which is the other transit point into future history. And she can't... you know that line in 'I Am the One You Warned Me of' about his hilly eyes and too green rings? So she can't figure out what colour his eyes are. 'I looked at your eyes, blue she says to him. Oh no they're green as we danced in time and the dance was time.' That's the key line basically, the key sequence of nouns and verbs. That one is really the drama of temporal interpenetration. He is this time-walker, and in it, he's sort of dancing through all timelines. It's sort of like that movie *Celine and Julie Go Boating* or *Celine et Julie vent en bateau*. I don't know if you've ever seen it. It's a metaphor for time. Time is a river. They can sort of see all of time when they're out on the river of time. But when they're on the riverbanks, when they're off the river... which is also a metaphor that's used on *Imaginos*. The reference to time slowing and rivers freezing... that's 'Del Rio's Song.' Anyway, so in this song, Imaginos is in a position where he can dance across all time. He's not stuck in any one time. Fuelled by sexual energy, and as well the conaissance analogies picked up, he's now able to dance the dance of time, in and through time. So that's one of the ones that never made it."

The other key track slated for the project but scrapped was 'Gil Blanco County', which was considered, for a time, as an inclusion on the band's next record. This song was actually the first recorded *Imaginos* tune, showing up on the Stalk-Forrest Group record scuttled by Elektra. Curiously, it was credited at the time to Allen Lanier. Another track called 'Port Jefferson' was written by Buck during that same formative era, but it also never saw the light of day. Other lesser constructions considered by Albert were 'Blue Öyster Cult Reprise' and 'Imaginos Overture' plus an a cappella revisitation of the first verse of 'Magna of Illusion'. The song 'Imaginos' was also virtually completed in the early '70s, along with the two cornerstone tracks that did get released ('Astronomy' and 'Subhuman'). It wasn't until the *Spectres* sessions in '77 that more *Imaginos* pieces would rear their heads. At this time, Albert demoed 'I Am the One You Warned Me of', 'The Siege and Investiture', 'Del Rio's Song' and 'The Girl That Love Made Blind', while Joe offered a skeletal version of 'In the Presence of Another World'. The aforementioned 'Half-Life Time' was another track considered as part of the story, the song reported to be a re-working of 'Shadow of California'.

The assembly of *Imaginos* began in earnest when both Albert and the band were free of the Albert problem. To reiterate, in '81, Albert teamed up with Pearlman, and by '82 most of the basic tracks were completed, the duo (plus the expanded Imaginos band) finalizing much of their detailing by '84, a year which saw the strange circumstance of Albert constructing *Imaginos* right next door to a band called Blue Öyster Cult, working on their *The Revolution by Night* record.

So to summarize, Albert's version of *Imaginos* hit a snag when CBS voiced two concerns: 1) that Albert's vocals were unacceptable, and 2) that they would like to see the record with the Blue Öyster Cult name on it. The messy transition, we have discussed, deposited us in 1986. At this low ebb in the history of the Cult, the band had actually broken up. Discussing reforming to do *Imaginos*, there was the possibility of the original line-up flying once more. Joe seemed to be the most against it, and having Albert back in seemed improbable. A line-up which included '3OC' plus Jon Rogers on bass and Ron Riddle on drums was assembled (although they would not figure on the record).

Who actually did figure on the playing and subsequent credits to the record is semi-clear, semi-clouded in mystery. There is some debate as to how much doctoring was done to Albert's original demos. Indeed, Albert had managed to get Buck, Allen and brother Joe to contribute when it was still his baby. The most material changes are of course in the vocal department. Albert's lead was kept only on 'Blue Öyster Cult,' where he duets with Buck. Otherwise, Eric handles leads on 'I Am the One', 'In the Presence', and most of 'Del Rio's Song', while Buck takes 'Les Invisibles', 'Astronomy' and 'Magna of Illusion'. 'Siege and Investiture' was (quite histrionically) sung by New Jersey musician Joey Cerisano, who had worked with Albert on the original sessions. Cerisano has since become very successful as a vocalist on high profile commercial jingles. Another non-BÖCer by the name of Jon Rogers also contributes lead vocals, ripping through 'Imaginos', while also (according to Al) helping out on 'I Am the One You Warned Me of'. Rogers may also have contributed to 'Siege and Investiture', as well as 'In the Presence of Another World'.

In terms of instrumental credits, Albert believes much of what guitarists Tommy Morrongiello, Jack Rigg, and Phil Grande contributed had been kept for the final output, also citing Tommy Mandel as the record's main keyboard player. But Mandel isn't even credited on the record, previous session keyboard player for the Cult Tommy Zvoncheck stating that his parts had replaced most of Mandel's by the time the record finally saw daylight.

Other credits go to Kenny Aaronson (bass), Tommy Price (drums), Jack Secret (additional vocals), and The Guitar Orchestra of the State of Imaginos, namely Marc Biedermann, Kevin Carlson, Robbie Krieger, Tommy Morrongiello, Aldo Nova, Jack Rigg and Joe Satriani. Bolle Gregmar has stated that The Doors' Robbie Krieger contributed the lead to 'Blue Öyster Cult', while Satriani played lead on 'The Siege and Investiture'. Also, as noted, Sandy says Satriani can be heard on 'Astronomy'. Al says that on his early '80s version of the record, Krieger also plays on 'Magna of Illusion', 'In the Presence', and 'The Girl That Love Made Blind'.

The over-full stew of what emerged from such a bewildering cast of characters is necessarily fragmented. Just as *Club Ninja* suffered from too many cooks, so does *Imaginos*. As previously remarked, *Imaginos* is superficially a "heavy" record, perhaps the band's loudest, certainly its most bombastic. Alas however, its loudness is screeching, braying, steel on steel, and on top of that, strangely variable to the point of sounding in error, uncontrolled and uncontrollable. Quite simply, the guitars howl in pain from start to finish.

Following the established logical order of the thing, the record kicks off with 'Les Invisibles'. Immediately, the band has crossed the metal-lite threshold, somewhat brutishly stomping the dynamic, writing within a previously balanced format, but loading the track up with thick, stiff, boomy drums. The song's chorus indeed, is one of this cold record's more connecting moments, Buck finding the Dictators with a metalized dust-off of the classic 'Louie Louie' riff, causing a collapse into groove that is rare for this considerably emotionless BÖC swansong.

'Imaginos' comes next, kicking off as a sterile funk like something outta showbiz Alice Cooper. But the band loads it up with breaks, segues and lots of very electric non-Cult-ish guitar leads, underscoring the layered, almost prog rock tone of the record, hopefully making you, the discerning listener, forget those "Ooh Imaginos" croons that cause cringe like 'Let Go'. 'Del Rio's Song' corrects nicely, the boys turning in a melodic rocker that is both heavy and enjoyable, finding that metal/Beach Boys alloy that was often the original stated goal.

'Blue Öyster Cult' is of course the remake of 'Subhuman' with added and subtracted lyrics, a furrowed state of affairs that can be debated for hours (or at least 15 minutes!). But true to the nature of *Imaginos*, the track is loaded up beyond repair, tipping ditch-ward with keyboards that don't sound like Allen and guitars that don't sound like Buck. It also has its own 'Let Go' albatross, locked within the cheeseball strains of its infamous 'Blue Öyster Cult' chant.

'I Am the One You Warned Me of' is one of those songs that attempts to answer a headbanger's request to "show us the metal," a wish often voiced of fence-sitting metal acts of which the Cult are one of the greatest practitioners. It is a somewhat successful song, with a verse riff that enters the zone of Sabbath (albeit stupidly), and a break riff that is sheer brilliance, a riff that takes the song by force, providing a vehicle for ripping leads, setting the ominous tone of the record. On the whole, not particularly Cult-ish, but heavy and considerably creative. Also, Eric's vocals are downright soulful on this track, as is the case on much of the rest of his performances, Eric really giving these songs personality far and above what the music attempts.

'The Siege and Investiture of Baron Von Frankenstein's Castle at Weisseria' sounds as overblown as it looks. Imagine mid-'80s Sabbath crossed with mid-'70s Queen, throw in a little Meat Loaf courtesy of Joey Cerisano's thespian vocal performance, and you're close to the glam-bam sugar fix the Cultsters achieve (with a little help from their friends). It is a rousing success really, the band demonstrating courage with something so loud and prog at once.

'In the Presence of Another World' bookends 'Siege' perfectly, both featuring guitars and keyboards in full-throttle battle, both pomp rocking, glitzy and muscular, once more the Cult achieving a sort of *Welcome to My Nightmare*-style commercial shock rock.

'Astronomy' of course pumps up the classic of the same name, convoluting the arrangement, turning the track into a curiously upbeat gallop, silken vocal courtesy of Donald. Unfortunately, those "hey-heys" do their best to destroy the ambience, and the clusters of overplaying render the track considerably loud and, well, brutish. I'll take the original. Note: there are two significantly altered version of this song on various promo CD and 12" vinyl singles. One is a dancy remix called *The Wild Mix*, also distinguished in that it includes more of Albert's original vocals, and one contains a Stephen King intro, where King simply recites from the back cover's brief description of the *Imaginos* saga. There is also a version that combines the two, and a version that is a truncated rendition of the song. Eric, on hooking up with Maine's master of mayhem, says, "Stephen King quoted the song '(Don't Fear) The Reaper' in his book *The Stand*. Ever since then we've had a sort of loose relationship with him. He's certainly our type of writer, his type of macabre material crossing over nicely with our music. So we feel like kin, and when he was asked to do the spoken introduction to 'Astronomy,' he gladly agreed. It's great for radio. I just wish it could have gotten on the album."

Of the song's staccato guitar stutter, Albert offers that, "We were going for a Stevie Nicks' 'Edge of Seventeen' feel because I thought it was relevant to the emotional content of the track. The only problem was that the take Sandy liked was a little fast to sing. I guess the speed made it dance-oriented as well. At least it was different. It was consciously made commercial by Pearlman and Columbia brass. I thought it was kinda cool myself."

'Magna of Illusion' carries us out, returning to the record's recurring big drum thump, hair band power chords and elegant keyboard flourishes. But again, the progressive aspirations work well, 'Magna' providing complex melodies and a general theatrical drama that will triumph once again when and if Sandy comes through and turns *Imaginos* into a book or movie!

All told, *Imaginos* is a brash, unsubtle, abused affair, uneven of production (including, as I say, volume levels!), and somewhat of a sell-out of the band's flair for irony. In other words, its creativity is too obvious, leveled by virtue of the confused, quiltwork collaboration of it all. Lyrically, the trip is shockingly rich, but musically, one is left cold.

"Sandy, especially, had very strong ideas about how he wanted to produce the band," noted Buck in 2002, summing up the anti-climactic *Imaginos* experience. "We agreed most of the time, but not always. *Imaginos* was our parting of the ways. That was something that Eric and I agreed to do, sort of, out of respect for Sandy. His effort that he made with *Imaginos*. *Imaginos* was never going to come out, unless we agreed to get involved, so we did. It turned out to be very disadvantageous, financially, for us. It cost us a lot of money. We wound up repaying the entire *Imaginos* record advance, the one that we had, and also the one that Sandy and Albert Bouchard had received. *Imaginos* was begun shortly after Albert left the band, as a one-off project by Sandy and Albert. Albert wrote most of the music. It wasn't our thing. Sandy always wanted the Blue Öyster Cult to do *Imaginos* as a set piece, but none of the band members really wanted to do a whole album of Sandy's material. The band wound up shouldering the whole debt. It did very poorly, virtually nothing, sales-wise. There is a cause and effect there."

Indeed for all of CBS' bailing the band out, the label, through omission or active decision, did little to promote the project, *Imaginos* finally clocking in at around 50,000 confused customers served. At the time, Eric tried to mask his disappointment. "We're doing a pretty extensive tour of Europe, three weeks in France, because we're really big in France right now. Then we'll go home for ten days, and then we'll go back and do the rest of the continent and all of the UK. CBS in the states isn't really supporting the record, preferring a sort of sink or swim kind of attitude, and we have no idea why. There are certain things that have to be done to make a record happen. Certain people within the company are eager to do good stuff for us and certain people are not. So it's kind of frustrating. But the international branch is doing a terrific job for us. For example there's no video available in the US, but the international branch has had one for eight weeks, so in Europe you might actually be able to see us! (laughs). But in the states, there are pockets where the record is doing really well, and in others, they don't even know it's out."

Surveying the journey at the juncture of the '90s, Eric mused, "We just do what we like; we always have. Once in a while we cross over into something that's commercially successful, and many times not. But we're just happy to be playing. There's pluses and minuses to the big shows. It's quite the ego trip to play to 18,000 people; it's a lot of fun, but there was also a big overhead to it, and headaches and problems. This tour's like a low cholesterol kind of thing, lean and mean fighting machine kind of tour (laughs). We're just going out there and playing our asses off. We usually pack out every place, so it's kind of fun. It's a two-hour show and sometimes even longer than that if we stretch out the encores. We're playing all the ones people seem to want to hear the most."

Perhaps envisioning the demonstrative lull that would come over the band, Eric summed up the future thusly. "Well, we'll have some material that will come up, and it remains to be seen what we'll do with it. I hope we're around. If I don't do a solo record, I intend to do another BÖC record. And Buck's thinking about doing another solo record. But we're trying not to look too far ahead, just tour the record, then in May and June, slow down and take some time off."

Imaginos would mark the last fresh material from our Cultsters for fully ten years, Columbia releasing a few compilations, the band recording the *Cult Classic* re-hash record, but otherwise little action other than the boys' usual exhaustive touring itinerary.

The Great Drought

"We need some lyrics; ask him"

s *Imaginos* died a lingering death, Blue Öyster Cult continued to tour relentlessly throughout Europe and the US. The line-up had remained quite stable, basically the core unit of "3OC" with a revolving door of bassists and drummers.

A recap of the post and immediately pre-*Club Ninja* turmoil goes something like this. In terms of drummers, Albert was back in the band very briefly, before Jimmy Wilcox was in and back out due to previous commitments with a band that played hardball, unwilling to let Jimmy take a two month sabbatical and tour with BÖC. Buck's neighbour Ron Riddle assumed the throne, after Buck had seen him play around town. For a brief time in 1990, Buck, Riddle and Jon Rogers played as a trio called The Red and the Black. Erstwhile, Allen had been enticed back on keyboards, bassist Joe had left for good, to be replaced by Jon Rogers.

Ron Riddle then drummed for the band from July '87 through May '91, only to be replaced by journeyman Chuck Bürgi, who held the post from June '91 to September '95, with one month's work (June-ish '92) going to Meat Loaf drummer John Miceli. During this month, Chuck Bürgi went to record with David Rosenthal's and Greg Smith's Rainbow offshoot called Red Dawn. Rainbow's John O. Reilly replaced Chuck in October '95, John having played on the weak *Stranger in Us All* comeback record for Rainbow. After further vacillations between Chuck and John, John became the band's working drummer, with Danny Miranda completing the line-up on bass.

With respect to where the band went through all this—or at least in terms of the highlights—February and March of 1988 found the band on an extensive West German tour, supported by Irish meat-and-potatoes rockers Mama's Boys, followed by the release of *Imaginos* in July. Endless US dates ensued before another nice European tour commenced February of '89, supported by Patrick Rondat in France, Miss Daisy in England and Kansas and Steve Morse in West Germany. Then it was back into Canada and the US for mostly headlining club gigs to round out the year. It wasn't until September of 1992 that BÖC returned to Europe, and then November of '93 where the band was part of a consistent package again, playing Canada and the US with Nazareth, Uriah Heep and Wishbone Ash, swapping out Nazareth for Girlschool and Molly Hatchet for another return to Europe, mostly West Germany. Europe wouldn't figure in the band's plan again until June of '98, which isn't to say the guys weren't busy, touring hard all over the US and Canada in the interim years.

While Blue Öyster Cult were busy still burnin', Joe and Albert also refused to keep still. There was a nasty battle between Joe and the band, when Joe decided to tour as "The Cult Brothers" (Albert had originally been part of the line-up). Problems arose when less than honest promoters would fashion together ads and posters that could cause one to believe that the product on stage was essentially Blue Öyster Cult. Joe acknowledged in court that this happened repeatedly, while maintaining that he personally had no hand in this function of the tour. He speaks regrettably about the whole episode, and is glad the dust-up is over, while also speaking fondly of dates where Buck joined the band on stage for a little rip through a few well-chosen Cult tunes. Joe also found time to do the Deadringer album amongst a plethora of other music projects (see *Club Ninja* chapter), moving on to become a music teacher, avid music creator and fan, and then a music book publisher.

"Actually, I'm retired from teaching," said Joe in March '96. "I have a new job starting in July, working for a publishing company, and I will be publishing and editing music books. I'm really looking forward to the change. I've been teaching for eight years now. It's been good, but strenuous because I've been teaching children with learning disabilities, dyslexic students, kids with attention deficit disorders, so it was time for a change. I was going to write a book for the company anyway on bass guitar. I'm writing it now. They happened to re-do their deal with their distributor, so it was quite interesting. I'm going to be Assistant Vice-President (laughs). It's mostly instructional stuff. It's part of the National Guitar Summer Workshop. They have a deal with their distributor to do 30 books this year, and they basically had one guy working on it before, so they had to take on somebody else. Which is good for me because I learned to do the program which is called Finale when I was doing my master's thesis, and it just happened to come in handy because that's what they use. I'm sort of interested in teaching methods and stuff for my teaching job."

I asked Joe what his musical tastes were these days. "Let's see, I've got a bunch of rap stuff here (laughs). My friend Andy Hilfiger says he wants me to make a record that sounds like Coolio (laughs). I've been listening to Enya a lot. I haven't got too much heavy stuff here at all. Deep Forest. And I go back and put on my Beach Boys box set. A lot of classical music. A lot of this cutting edge… you know, all of these rock guys who grew up and got too much education and are now making classical music? There's groups like The Ensemble Moderne from France that does Frank Zappa, which is interesting. There are several sort of classical groups that are trying to get into a rock groove, Icebreaker from England, Terminal Velocity. I listen to John Adams a lot, his ballets. Sort of the bang-on-a-can people who do festivals in New York. Some of the players in that are friends of mine. I just got a stack of records from Paul Winter who lives around here. He's had his Paul Winter Consort for years. I'm probably still going to do a couple of rock records this year. I don't know if they're going to be released independently or not, but I've got a bunch of stuff that sort of relates to Blue Öyster Cult."

Joe's favourites from those heady days as Cult bassist sound like a roll-call of bands with which BÖC competed and shared stages. "Cheap Trick. I used to like the Heart band. I just love all kinds of music. Foghat and Pat Travers were probably, for my taste, a little too bluesy. I liked more of the pop metal edge kind of bands, although I play blues now. I enjoy it, but I still think it's more of an indulgence on the part of the player than what a good pop band like Cheap Trick or Aerosmith could do. Aerosmith were friends of ours. They always did a lot of business (laughs). We were always behind them. But who knows? They had their rough times too. I saw it; I witnessed it (laughs)."

There have been recordings. Joe and his Bouchard Dunaway & Smith band re-did 'Fallen Angel' for a Helen Wheels tribute album called *To Helen with Love!* for Al's and Deb Frost's Cellsum Records label. The Brain Surgeons, various Dictators, Buck and even Sandy Roeser are on the Helen tribute as well. BDS also released an album called *Back from Hell* ('Fallen Angel' included) and in '03 put out *BDS Live in Paris*, which includes renditions of 'Reaper' and 'Astronomy'. Finally, in '97, Joe released *Solid Citizen* as The X Brothers, which included an absolute gem of a Bouchard/Meltzer composition called 'Run for the Sun', a track that could easily have followed up 'Burnin' for You' as the band's third smash hit. Gorgeous song. BÖC should cover it. This was followed by *Hot Time in Hell*, *Beyond the Valley of the X*, and a Joe Bouchard solo album in 2009 called *Jukebox in My Head*.

Meanwhile, back in the BÖC camp, Sony proved their good taste by releasing a couple of half-baked CD-era compilation records, *Career of Evil: The Metal Years*, and *On Flame with Rock and Roll*, both in 1990, plus a cassette-only curio dubbed *(Don't Fear) The Reaper* in 1989. *Career of Evil* indeed leaned marginally towards the heavy side, although it covered most eras (not like the band ever had well-defined metal years). Liner notes were provided by Arthur Levy. Eight of the thirteen tracks were from the live albums. These low-key releases kept the band in the public eye, allowing for more viable touring, in an era when metal was still king and old-timers like Blue Öyster Cult were tacitly revered as influences.

In 1992, a small serving of new music hit the streets in the form of two tracks on the soundtrack album for cheesy and ignored science fiction flick *Bad Channels*. Emblazoned with the heading "Music composed and performed by Blue Öyster Cult." The CD actually featured the following: two spanking new Cult rock tracks, 'Demon's Kiss' and 'The Horsemen Arrive', followed by standard metal fodder by four unknown acts, DMT (recommended by BÖC's management), Sykotik Sinfoney (jokecore?), Joker (not jokecore, but bad glam), and Fair Game, which turned out to be Ron Keel backed by four female musicians. Closing out the album was approximately 25 minutes of instrumental BÖC, recorded in the slick, electronic fashion of *Club Ninja*, full of bluesy, Floydian Buck solos, lots of spooky keyboards, sound effects, and the occasional full band head of steam (although all drums are poor imitation synth percussion, and the full band in question is something closer to boisterous Duran Duran).

The new tracks are both credited to Eric, Donald and John Shirley, who begins to figure prominently in the Cult saga. John Shirley is a prolific science fiction/horror/cyberpunk writer with a huge cult following and over 40 books to his name. He was also the first screenwriter for *The Crow* and regularly works on screenplays. In addition, he records with his own band, The Panther Moderns, whose first record *Red Star* contains a version of *Heaven Forbid* track 'See You in Black'. Shirley also once blurped noise vocals for Portland's venerable Smegma, which oddly now sports Richard Meltzer as lead vocalist, and has also fronted punk bands SadoNation and Obsession. In any event, Shirley was to become—unarguably—the key lyricist for Blue Öyster Cult in their late period, penning words for most of '98's *Heaven Forbid* and '01's *Curse of the Hidden Mirror*.

John recounts the story of his hooking up with the Cultsters. "They knew of me, because my first book is called *Transmaniacon*—my first novel, from 1979—and was inspired by their songs. They had seen it, and it was dedicated to them. I think I've mentioned their lyrics in several of my books, like *City Come A-Walkin'*, which is still in print, that book. But really, the main connection came through this lady called Gracie. I know her by her first name, because that is her writing name, and she was connected with *Mondo 2000*, the cyberpunk futurist magazine. I wrote some of the first cyberpunk novels, so she knew me from that. I was interviewed in that magazine, and I knew her from that context. She was friends with the band and close friends with Pearlman. She knew they were looking for a lyricist. I think she suggested me and they said, 'Oh yeah, we know of that guy, and we need some lyrics; ask him.' So I jumped at the chance, because I was a fan of the band."

"Those songs, they were cool songs," recalls Shirley with respect to the *Bad Channels* tracks. "'Demon's Kiss,' that song, handled well, could have been, in my opinion, a hit single. They were perhaps a little hastily produced. But those were the first things I did for them. That was shortly after I sent them some lyrics. Then I didn't hear from them again for a long time. Then all of a sudden, I learned that they were doing a bunch of my tunes. There are eight of my lyrics on each of the last two albums, 16 in total. But I think those two are fun, dark lyrics. 'Demon's Kiss'... you know, I've just had a lot of relationships in my life. I've been married five times. I'm on my fifth marriage. I've lived with a lot of women besides that, sometimes two at once. There was a lot of strange women in my life (laughs), a lot of crazy women. I have this other song on an album I wrote called 'Panther Pit.' Some women are like falling into a panther pit (laughs), and that's sort of a similar theme. Certain women can be deadly. I think I suggest in the song that it's actually a supernatural event but it's really just a stand-in for how real women can be... there are crazy, dangerous, scary women out there (laughs). 'The Horsemen Arrive' is kind of a political allegory, as I recall, suggesting that the political direction of the country, for years overridden by conservatives, is probably self-destructing. But it's said indirectly; I don't say it too obviously."

Neither *Bad Channels* track is either musically up to snuff, sad to say. 'Demon's Kiss' is a smart enough piece of middle metal, mixing pop melodies with considerable heft, a solid Eric vocal, axe-colour commentary by Donald, and a pumping bass line courtesy of Jon Rogers (Allen and Chuck Bürgi round out the band during this era). 'The Horsemen Arrive' is more metallic and lumbering, but once again, unimaginative musically. Buck and Eric trade vocals over standard corporate thunder metal, while singing ominously about the coming of the apocalypse, civilization doomed by its own industry, corruption and greed. Too slick production for both tracks is courtesy of Eric, Donald and manager

Steve Schenck, recording at Alpha & Omega Studios in San Rafael, California.

Next up for the band was one of those ironic, inverted legal ploys, the band assembling something called *Cult Classic*, which was essentially the new BÖC re-recording the hits of the old BÖC, something of an appealing prospect given the generally weak production values on most of the band's output.

Computer-generated artwork was provided by longtime band supporter Melne, the band declining to apply a Kronos symbol for legal reasons. But even if the whole ruse was an attempt to make money off of songs the band now owned to a lesser extent (publishing sold to Sony), artistically *Cult Classic* somewhat succeeds. 'E.T.I.' is languished and powerful. 'This Ain't the Summer of Love' grooves highly with Chuck Bürgi's crashed cymbals leading the spirited charge, as does odd necro-boogie choice 'O.D'd on Life Itself'. In total, it's refreshing to finally hear these songs with enough bass and treble, even if many versions are performed so faithfully to the originals as to be virtually indistinguishable. The record closes out with three oddities, a studio version of 'Buck's Boogie,' and "TV mixes" of 'Reaper' and 'Godzilla,' both rendered as composed instrumentals halfway between karaoke and sound check jams. Complaints about the record were many and varied, fans citing boring vocals, lack of keyboards, sterile mixes and poor song selection, along with confusion as to why me might need these "TV mixes."

While all these silly Blue Öyster Cult records were being released, the band slogged on with their tour schedule, becoming working musicians whose main source of income was to be biker bars, country fairs and the odd larger festival date. Meanwhile, as mentioned, Al Bouchard had hooked up with his wife Deborah Frost and assorted close buddies as prolific recording act, The Brain Surgeons. Seven full-length albums were made, kicking off in '94 with *Eponymous*, followed by *Trepanation*, *Box of Hammers*, assorted cassette only live curios, *Malpractise*, *Piece of Work*, *Beach Party* and '06's *Denial of Death*, featuring Ross the Boss. As well, the band's label Cellsum Records is their own imprint, one which also includes records by BÖC lyricist David Roter, solo stuff by other Brain Surgeons, a compilation of Helen Wheels' output, a record by Joe Bouchard's son, one by the Bouchard brothers' other brother Jim, and even a record by original BÖC vocalist Les Braunstein.

The Brain Surgeons sound cannot be summed up simply, the band visiting most rock idioms throughout their catalogue. There's blues, pop, metal, balladry, and everything in between, written and crafted with the weight of rock history behind them. Most songs are collaborations between Bouchard and Frost, Deb also being the main vocalist, whose collection of voices ranges from whisper to roar, Patti Smith being the closest comparative than comes to mind.

Tracks with strong links to the Blue Öyster Cult saga, include *Eponymous'* 'Most Romantic Place in the World' due really to the song's sound, a vocal by Albert, and the fact that the tune is a Bouchard/Meltzer composition. Other co-writers on *Eponymous* include Patti Smith, David Roter, and two more with Richard Meltzer, Bouchard having with him a cache of Meltzer's old lyrics which he dips into from time to time. *Trepanation* continues these tentative connections. 'Hansel & Gretel', a Frost/Bouchard/Meltzer composition, was slated for possible recording by BÖC. The song is co-sung by Albert and Deb and sounds very Cult-ish, the band breaking into a gorgeous chorus that could have turned this one into a hit. It is of note that *Trepanation* also includes Bouchard co-writes with Patti Smith, one with Helen Wheels, and one more with Meltzer.

Box of Hammers contains two tracks which were demo-ed with Blue Öyster Cult. 'Gun' (credited to Albert, Joe, Deb and Helen Wheels) was put forth on numerous occasions. The track is a bit of a dull metal plod; perhaps best that it never made the Cult cut. Bouchard and Meltzer's 'Laura's Plastic Swords' on the other hand, also plods, but smartly, Albert singing this eccentric track with understated cool, Deb countering with a slightly more elevated blues treatment over a verse melody that rings a bit like Tull's 'Locomotive Breath.' This could have made a great Blue Öyster Cult track. The record closes out with a curio called 'Overture,' credited to Albert and brother Joe, the tune being a prog rock pastiche/jam that approximates an instrumental sampling of *Imaginos*.

Elsewhere, 'Tender Was the Night' funk metals with authority, this Bouchard/Meltzer track sung by Albert, again sounding like something that could have fit the Cult canon. Helen Wheels also shows up as co-writer on album opener 'Saint Vitus Dance.' *Malpractise* from '97 is a rip roarin' odds and sods album with a cover of Hawkwind's best song 'Hassan I Sahba' (and maybe their second best: 'Needle Gun') along with a number of BÖC standards covered forcefully, elegantly and not without humour. Most importantly, the album contained clearly crucial *Imaginos* puzzle piece 'The Girl that Love Made Blind', a vampy, vampiric shuffle of a spaghetti-westernized ballad.

While Al and Deb were cranking out their records, lo and behold, Sony decided to repackage and regurgitate their Cult archives once more, offering in '95, the two CD set *Workshop of the Telescopes*.

Buck and Eric, mostly from the road (what else is new?) signed on for the obligatory phone interviews. "This is the only compilation we ever spent any effort on," notes Buck, making a good point, in fact. "They just repackaged stuff really slovenly before that. So this is good. It's got a pretty fair compendium of the span of our Sony years. It couldn't be everything because then it would have to be more than two CDs. But we had to agonize over leaving stuff off that we didn't have room for. It's got a lot of obscure graphics and stuff so it's cool." Referring to the liner notes by Arthur Levy, Buck acknowledges that they are really just an expanded version of the notes in *Career of Evil*. "I think writers may recognise some of that text as stuff that's been previously published. But for people seeing it for the first time, it's a pretty cool story."

"Yeah I like it, but we didn't really have any say," offers Eric, offhandedly. "We're not signed to Sony anymore. It's just something they wanted to do. The artwork is neat. I think it's a decent selection of tunes. I'm online a lot with America Online, and I talk to a lot of the fans around the country and there's some feedback like, 'You left this out; you left that out.' What are you going to do? You have about 120 songs to choose from, and you pick 32 of them, so you're always leaving out stuff somebody likes."

Workshop of the Telescopes fails miserably in the rarities department. For a band that recorded many fairly fleshed-out demos of songs that never made the cut, the scraps thrown to the fans here are scant indeed (Sony of course rectified this considerably with their reissue program). There are four such scraps, one being 'Buck's Boogie' from '72's *Guitars that Destroyed the World* compilation, another being a studio version b-side of 'Born to Be Wild' from 1974. Otherwise, all we get are a couple of scrappy promo versions of old chestnuts, 'Workshop of the Telescopes' and 'The Red & the Black'.

The 16-page CD booklet is quite impressive however, offering a few shots of rare album and single covers, a tour poster, four buttons, a pre-concert shot featuring a big Kronos logo on the side of a building, and a big billboard announcing the arrival of *Spectres*. Oh, how the mighty have fallen. The liner notes are not all that revelatory to even the casual student of the band, but most of the major points are covered in solid fashion. One nice touch is the inclusion of a quote from Mike Watt, perennial Cult fan, and friend of Al Bouchard. Back tray card: a sinister array of ten backstage passes.

In typical 'On the Road Forever' fashion, Buck refused to call *Workshop of the Telescopes* any sort of final statement on the band's career. With ongoing rumours of a new record called *Ezekiel's Wheel* (this of course surfaced as *Heaven Forbid* instead) unfulfilled at the time despite much protracted talk, Buck was asked, somewhat impertinently by me, whether the collection could be deemed a gravestone.

"Well, gee even if it was, I'd hesitate to call it a gravestone (laughs). But I would say BÖC is somewhere between our heyday and the Rock and Roll Hall of Fame. But the fact is, is that we haven't put out any important recorded work for awhile. Probably at the bottom of that has been a lack of will to really do anything stupendous, as far as new material. Now that's not to say that it won't happen, because we've got a lot of good stuff that's boiling under right now. We'd like to make another record that really means something, and I think we're working towards that. But to be frank, after doing it for 15 years, and the band being together for 20, there wasn't really a lot left to say, quite frankly. So rather than just churn out mediocre stuff, why not just not do anything? So, it hasn't hurt us, to not to go ahead and not put out a bad record. So I guess the plan is to get something stunning before we do it again. In the short term, definitely, I've got plans. I own the rights to my acoustic version of 'The Reaper,' and the one that was on the first *Guitar for the Practicing Musician* record. They will be coming out somewhere at some time. If I get eight more, I'll have a record (laughs). I'd like to do a solo record again."

Looking back on the years during that same interview, Buck agreed that the band upheld a certain standard, and should have been more of a success commercially. "Yeah, you're right, and I think it's helped us as far as how history's regarded us, because it's pretty much agreed that we were under-appreciated. So that's good as far as now. You know, a lot of bands came out of that era and were either over-heard or over-exposed, and are just not as good as people thought they were at the time when people were buying their records in huge amounts. Whereas our stuff, I think it's really held up. But I've always felt that we were just too quirky for mass acceptance. I mean, there are underground bands that get mass accepted because all of a sudden there are three million people that want to hear them. But we were just always a little bit too quirky, the combination of personnel and ideas and whatever, just kept us away from the real big time. We had recognition, but we just missed out on the fortunes, is what really happened (laughs). But I'm not complaining. My career to date has been something that when I started, I never thought would have gone so far. So, no problem."

With *Workshop of the Telescopes* being somewhat the direct result of Sony's newfound ownership of the band's publishing, Buck states that, "Yes, we just recently sold the catalogue to Sony. But as far as what can be put out on records, yes I still control it. I mean, I don't know of anybody who doesn't have their record company owning their material, unless you are rich enough to fund your own records, and you sell them the masters, then maybe you can retain the rights. I think Billy Joel does that now. I know he's always done that with his videos. He's always paid for them himself so he can do what he wants with them. I don't think Sony's ever really known how to sell us, from the beginning. I think we've always embarrassed them or something. It was Clive Davis who signed us, and he left the company about three years later. Columbia's a weird company; it was a very conservative company. It didn't have a lot of rock 'n' roll, and what it did have... I never felt that they knew how to market us. Then in the middle years, I think we didn't know how to market ourselves. If you look at any band, you can point to a period of time where their best stuff was and their prolific period was. If they last a long time, you have to compare that to everything else. So that's all it is— we're just a band who's been around 20 years."

Eric, who is known to be more of a driving force with respect to perpetuating the Cult than Buck is, naturally came across as hopeful. "Sure, it would have been nice to have gotten more recognition. But, no, this is what I've wanted to do since I've been a kid. It's the best job I've ever had. I have no regrets. Sure, if there would have been more commercial success, it would have been neat. But we never really had that angle of trying to be commercially successful. We got lucky a couple of times with 'The Reaper' and 'Burnin' for You,' but I think a lot of the songs could have gone over better if it was promoted better. You can look back a few times. But I'd say we got a pretty fair shake. I wouldn't have done anything different. In terms of the future, we're negotiating with a couple of record companies, hopefully to get a new record out before the summer of '96, is what we're hoping for. 'Cos we got a lot of new material; we're writing all kinds of stuff. There's typical Eric songs, there's typical Buck songs. You know, we've got 'em. There's stuff to make a pretty good record, and we're playing two or three of them live every night." Does the writing come easy? "Oh yeah! As a matter of fact, some of the writing of the last two years are some of the best collaborations that Buck and I have ever had. We're trying to get a record deal to get these out ASAP."

As every diehard BÖC fan can tell you, such talk had been going on since the early '90s. Hearing those words from Eric in '95 conjured, for this writer, images of the proverbial stuck record. It would be another three years still until *Heaven Forbid* dropped. At the time however, it was speculated in the press that the provisionally titled *Ezekiel's Wheel* would include, presumably, the two new tracks the band had been playing live, 'Harvest Moon', a curious sort of blues pop by Donald, and the aforementioned 'See You in Black', an uncharacteristically vicious high octane metal rumbler. But after talks with Germany's SPV broke down, as well as negotiations with a shaky Castle Communications (since absorbed and retired by Sanctuary), things were in limbo, the band's ever-gruelling touring schedule even lightening to mortal pace.

While the band tended to family matters, and while Buck's enthusiasm for the band waned, yet another teasing snippet of new BÖC happened, in the form of three tracks on CMC's *Summerdaze* live album, the dodgy document of an even dodgier disaster of a tour that featured the Cultsters, Steppenwolf, Foghat and Pat Travers. Along with a mix of poor quality live and studio tracks from their tour mates, BÖC offered yet another live version of both 'Reaper' and 'Godzilla', both recorded five years earlier in '92, with John Miceli on drums, both muddy and loose. But a surprise addition was a sparkly new studio track called 'Power Underneath Despair' also a few years old, featuring Chuck Bürgi on drums, and credited to Eric, Donald and John Shirley. While still not as artful and proud as the band's best, this track was a welcome improvement over the *Bad Channels* material, both lyrically and musically.

In terms of *Ezekiel's Wheel*, there was a handful of material that fans speculated could help comprise a new record. Occasional live tune 'Wings of Mercury', crusty old *Imaginos* track 'Gil Blanco County' and Buck's 'Gamera's Missing', 'Live for Me' and 'Real World' had been batted around as possible inclusions. As time went on, Cult-watchers were enthusiastic that new bass player Danny Miranda would offer songwriting input, although at the time, Eric and Donald were only considering songs that they had composed previous to Miranda joining. Another encouraging sign was that the band's drum throne had been decided, John Miceli being the last seen there, as late as '97, until Bobby Rondinelli (Rainbow, Black Sabbath) took over.

In the meantime, Donald had performed in Atlanta as The Buck Dharma Band, charitably for the Zilla Fund, which had been assembled to benefit a terminally ill boy named Ricky Browning. Tracks played included 'Live for Me', 'Real World', 'Harvest Moon', 'Born to Rock', '5:35' and 'Deadline'. Donald's band included both Danny Miranda and John Miceli, as well as wife Sandy. But lo and behold, the first Blue Öyster Cult album proper in nigh on a decade was just around the cagey corner...

Heaven Forbid

"You know, Buck, we gotta hear you!"

So where are you now?

"Right now I'm in front of a supermarket in Gulfport, Mississippi."

So congratulations on getting the new record out!

"Yeah, ten years in the making."

So began my chat with Buck in celebration of *Heaven Forbid,* the strapping, assured new studio album the band had recorded as the first for their deal with CMC International, a label with a stigma for reviving the careers of old bands, a label known as Cheese Metal Cemetery by rock journos and classic rock followers alike. Whatever. Fact of the matter is that we Cultists had new material to digest, upon stomachs empty for too long.

"Most of it was recorded in the last year and a half," begins Buck, charting the circuitous course of the record, "and there's three cuts that were recorded in 1993, 'Power Underneath Despair', 'Still Burnin'' and 'Harvest Moon'. Production-wise, it's pretty much a straight-ahead, really clean, punchy tone. The overblown production that was popular in the '80s is pretty much over. I felt no reason to replicate that."

Evidencing a somewhat surprising vitality, the record turned out to be very guitar oriented. "Yeah, well, you know, I never stopped. I continue to work really hard at progressing as a guitarist." When asked about solo highlights, Buck says the following. "I like the one on 'X-Ray Eyes' a lot, the one in 'Hammer Back'. "My criteria as producer was to not accept anything that was less than perfect (laughs). I mean, I like every note I played on the record, put it that way. The solos are spontaneous, but I also like to edit after the fact."

"Eric and I more or less co-wrote half the record," continues Buck. "I wrote about four tunes myself with John Shirley, our lyricist; I wrote 'Harvest Moon' by myself. There were a lot of the tunes from that Red and the Black era (ed. the aforementioned casual band situation from the interim years) that may or may not turn into BÖC stuff or Buck Dharma solo stuff, and obviously it's good stuff, and I'd like to see it come out some day. Red and the Black did a pretty comprehensive demo that we shopped around to mainstream record companies; not all of it is BÖC material. I think the BÖC constituency expects a certain tone of material, you know? BÖC had a pretty hard time getting a record deal over the last ten years. It was kind of demoralizing, so we didn't really have that much of a backlog of material. When we got some financial backing to make a record after all these years, then we got really psyched-up, then we got some material. But it's not like we had 50 songs in the can. In terms of old songs, I have a hankering to go back and do a Soft White Underbelly song called 'Ragamuffin's Dumpling' which is a great tune. But whether that fits into what we're doing, I don't know."

I asked Buck if there was ever a point through the '90s at which he thought he might call it a day and terminate the concept of Blue Öyster Cult for good. "Not to the point where I wanted to open up a video store or anything," laughed Buck. "I mean, I consider myself fortunate to make a living playing and singing, so I wouldn't quit doing that. But like I say, I'm not really too invested in terms of where this goes, in terms of new fame or anything like that. I'd like to get more respect because I think I deserve it. I think the band does too. Other than that, I'm quite happy that I can do it now. I'm not poor, so it's okay. You know, the reality of it was that there weren't a whole lot of people who wanted to spend any money on us. We found SPV, and we found CMC in America, and we're happy with them."

Heaven Forbid's calling card is its ghoulish—some say camp, some say crap camp—cover art. "This was sort of like graphics by committee," laughs Buck. "I'll take the blame for the actual hideous image of the semi-decayed guy on the cover. I was just thinking about the CD as a graphic medium; it's quite inferior to the 12 inch LP. You can't really see anything when you walk down an aisle of CDs. So I was looking for something that would sort of pop out at you, you know? (laughs). Something that would really grab your eye. The inner tray painting, that was Eric's idea. What it is, is actually a sort of tribute reference to a Salvador Dali painting, to a section of a Dali painting. This artist, Eric found him. Eric was sort of bulldogging the graphical process while I was doing the record."

Past the cover and into the music, the album, as issued March 24, 1998, opens with an elegant jamming flourish on 'See You in Black' with the initial salvo approximating a fierce sound check jam before the track finds its undeniably addictive heavy metal gallop. Back in black indeed. Buck and drummer John Miceli create a sonic maelstrom that pricks the ears efficiently and forcefully for the record to come.

As previously mentioned John Shirley had, by this point, become the band's lyricist of choice. "I never hear music first," begins John, articulating the process of marrying his words to the band's music. "I write lyrics and they read them, but they have said that those lyrics suggest songs. I put them together that way, so that they suggest songs. On a couple of occasions, for a couple of the songs I've written, the tune that emerged was one that I basically heard in my head when I was writing the lyrics, which is curious and interesting."

"Sure, I get into Blue Öyster Cult character," continues Shirley. "I started listening to them very early, just as the first album came out. I heard them in Central Park at kind of a free concert they were doing there as part of a show with various bands, a sort of rock festival. I was into their first album, and I've been steeped in them ever since—the first five albums essentially—but I've liked them all. As a consequence, I think Blue Öyster Cult pretty easily (laughs). They have a number of modes that are recognizable as theirs. They have a mysterious, sinister, slightly ironic heavy metal... especially as you hear on the first two albums. Then they have a sort of thing you hear on 'Reaper,' which is more of a lyrical, dark ballad feel. Then they have tunes that are slightly satirical, like 'Joan Crawford' or 'Godzilla.' So those are recognizable Blue Öyster Cult modes and I can get into any one of those."

"As time has passed, I've started to write more for one or the other," laughs Shirley, intimating that there are indeed Buck songs and Eric songs. "Because it has definitely emerged that there are songs that are more Eric-driven, that he directs in the development of the song, and songs that are more Buck-driven. Buck does kind of power ballads and Eric does the grittier pieces. I sometimes have sent things by email to Eric that were more what he would want. Like I sent him one called 'Testosterone Poisoning' that he was working on, that I thought was kind of a funny song that he would like; 'The Old Gods Return,' I think I sent directly to Eric."

"Oddly enough, 'See You in Black' I wrote for them, and then I didn't hear from them. I didn't know if they were going to use it," says Shirley on the album's explosive opening track. "I had sent them a bunch of lyrics through an intermediary, who had asked for some. I thought that they weren't going to use it, so I wrote my own version of it and recorded it, and it was on kind of an obscure album I did, on Weathered Leather Records. It can be found at the John Shirley website, on the audio page, if people want to compare. It's somewhat different. I actually like my version better (laughs). But it's good; they do a great song there. But I just didn't think it was going to make it is a single, because it's too much of a speed metal sort of take for the broad base of FM radio to accept."

'See You in Black' is a perfect way to open the album. Its mesmerizing stop/start riff is propelled by what is possibly the greatest drumming performance on any Blue Öyster Cult studio track, especially come the resounding flame-out of the tune's final throes. "Yeah, the rhythm section is just astounding on this record," agrees Buck. "Danny's great and Chuck Bürgi is great. I mean, if we had had the deal when we recorded 'Harvest Moon,' it would have been Jon Rogers and Chuck Bürgi, and you know, the record should have been out five years ago, but that's another story."

"Back in high school it was a really big deal that one of the biggest bands in the world was from basically down the block," laughs bass monster Danny Miranda, at the fateful circumstance of his hiring into the ranks of the Blue Öyster Cult. "It was something that Long Island was tremendously proud of. I think the biggest band from there before them was The Rascals. But they didn't get nearly as big as they should have, because they were a groundbreaking band. It's great that Blue Öyster Cult not only hailed from Long Island, they were proud to wave the flag. A lot of bands from Long Island say they are from New York City and I'm like, 'Bullshit, you grew up in suburbia like the rest of us. You weren't from the mean streets.' So it was a really big deal to join that band. John Miceli, who is now drumming for Meat Loaf, was instrumental in me getting that gig. BÖC was in-between drummers and he subbed for them. They were talking and said they were going to need a bass player, and he said they should check out his friend Danny. I had met Eric before; we did a couple of cover gigs. I just went down and auditioned. I never officially was told that I was in the band. They just had me stick around for ten years. Maybe I never was in the band? I just wouldn't go away. I am just like a fucking cockroach with that band."

"It was a lot of fun," continues Miranda, asked by Jeb Wright about appearing on both of the band's latest (last?) albums. "I was really flattered to do that. I was in the touring band but they could have done whatever they wanted in the studio. I was flattered they asked me to do that. It was a great honour and a great learning experience. I think I was in the band a year or a year and a half, before they went in to do the record. They had written a few things like 'See You in Black' and 'Harvest Moon' and we were playing them in the set. I was like, 'Fuck, these songs have to be on a record. Why has this not been recorded?' We eventually got a deal and we did the record. I am really pleased that we did because it would have been a shame if it had not been documented. They were in their 50s and they were writing great music and people needed to know about it."

Post-BÖC Miranda actually went on to play with a modern version of Queen... "I've always been open-minded and I love different kinds of music," adds Danny, as context. "The other night I went to see a 12-piece salsa band—I love that music. I am going to see Pat Metheny tonight. In the course of an hour I can listen to everything from Joni Mitchell to Slayer. I really try to listen to—and play—as many kinds of music as is possible. Prior to my tour with Queen, I came to Vegas to play in the *We Will Rock You* musical, so I was already in that John Deacon mindset. It is different than being in a cover band. In a cover band you don't need to play it 100%; as long as you're playing it in the style, then it is cool. When you're playing a whole show based on that music, then it really needs to feel and sound authentic out of respect to the band."

"Once a year I get a call from BÖC even though I quit the band nine years ago," continues Miranda, bringing the story up to date. "I seem to play with them for a few weeks a year. I really enjoy it when I am there, but that is only a month's work. The way they travel is different. They are what we call 'weekend warriors.' A lot more bands are doing this nowadays. I will tell you a lot of really big country groups do that. You leave on Wednesday or Thursday, and you come back on Sunday. On paper, that sounds like an ideal lifestyle, because you're not gone for months at a time. The back end of it is that you're not home long enough to get anything started, other than doing your laundry. It is a bit rough. Those guys are older now. I think Eric Bloom is something like 69 years old now. I bitch and moan a lot less when I think of that. Eric has 20 years on me and does it, so I'm like, 'I better keep my mouth shut.'"

Back off the road and onto the record at hand, the 'See You in Black' lyric is a succinct but imagistic tale of a man wishing that the husband of his mistress was dead. A quality touch, all too expected with Blue Öyster Cult lyrics, is the added detail. We learn that the husband is physically abusive, we learn the name of the woman, we see her standing "bravely" graveside, and finally, the two run off to Greece for a celebration of the husband's welcome demise. Interestingly however, all of this is expressed as mere wishful thinking.

'Harvest Moon' follows, the band switching gears for a gorgeous tale from Buck about a Lovecraft-ian landscape, a country locale with a violent past that delicately comes back to haunt the place with the change of the seasons. "It's sort of inspired by Stephen King's writing," says Buck. "The concept is that the ground itself is kind of haunted, in a cyclical fashion, much the same way that the town of Derry in Stephen King's *It* happens. The setting that I had in mind was California, one of the interior valleys." For the family names explicitly used in the tune, Buck says that he "just picked some names of folks who were passing through my life at that time."

As discussed, 'Power Underneath Despair' was debuted on the *Summerdaze* album. It's a metal stomper of substantial quality passionately vocalized by Eric. The cult-like chorus is distinguished by an odd time signature and the tune as a whole contains a number of sophisticated melodic shifts.

"That's another story song," notes Shirley. "It's about a guy who, you know, has been brooding in prison and he's going to get revenge on the people who betrayed him and put him there. In the process of it... it's kind of a *Twilight Zone/Outer Limits* sort of feel. In the process of this brooding, he discovers that there's this hidden, interior power we can get in touch with. It's kind of a supernatural power he can used to destroy people. It allows you to become an instrument of vengeance. It's the power underneath despair. When he was in solitary, he found this thing within himself. It's also connected obscurely to my interest in spirituality and the supernatural."

"Probably the silliest tune," quips Buck on 'Power Underneath Despair', "if you could call John's lyric silly. I don't think you can, because I don't think that's where he's coming from. But that one almost approaches humour to me."

On the subject of the album's fairly metallic tone, as evidenced forthrightly by 'Power Underneath Despair' and others, Buck commented at the time that, "I don't know what *Heaven Forbid* will do for our heavy metal credentials. I think we consciously put a couple of uppers on there, you know, Eric's tunes. Personally, my taste goes all over the map. I am not restricted to any kind of vibe or groove. I really wanted to try a lot of different things and have a lot of guitar playing on the album, because people kept coming up to me and telling me, 'You know, Buck, we gotta hear you!'"

'X-Ray Eyes' is a funky, acoustic strummer with engaging fast breaks. Call it an upbeat, particularly percussive Buck ballad. "There's a mistake in those lyrics, you know," divulges Shirley. "You know what the mistake is? I hate to reveal it. But cinephiles will know. I accidentally wrote, that in the '50s, Ray Milland... because it's about the movie, *The Man with the X-Ray Eyes*. But the movie came out in the '60s (laughs). So every time I hear it, I wince a little bit. 'No, the '60s, you idiot' (laughs)."

"The way we and John Shirley work is mostly through faxes and email," explains Buck, when asked about the track. "We talked in person a few times, but he's on the west coast and we're in the east. So he sends us stuff periodically. I usually write some lyrics, but this is generally the way it works. We don't send the lyricist tracks and say, 'Here, make up some words for this.' It's usually the other way around. Sometimes we edit it. Mostly it's for content, in terms of how it fits the music. Sometimes it's for spin; we spin it to fit differently. But basically, when John sends us a tune—and he's very prolific—either the idea grabs me or Eric, or it doesn't. And 'X-Ray Eyes' was just a lyric that intrigued me. I'm a big fan of the original movie. Just the concept that you can know too much. Like, maybe you don't really want to know too much, that you don't really want to be omniscient."

Next up was 'Hammer Back', probably the album's most gleefully headbanging composition, the band finding a hard and heavy yet melodically sweet balance not unlike the totality of the 'Dr. Music' or 'Tattoo Vampire' vibes. What I mean by that is that the band seamlessly counter sinister riffs with party rock riffs.

"It's a kind of a noir thing," explains Shirley on his literary motivation for the track. "I sometimes write suspense stories. There's a suspense feeling in the song, a sort of overriding paranoia that somebody is out to get you, and you have to have your gun handy, the hammer back on it at all times, because you may have to fire it at any moment. It's probably based on another influence on me, which is Westerns; I'm a fan of Westerns. So there's a kind of blended imagery from the better Westerns like *Tombstone* and *The Outlaw Josey Wales* and detective movies. I'm trying to get that feel from those things, you know, being right on the point of having to fight."

"That's a tale of modern paranoia," adds Buck. "It's probably not totally unfounded. I don't view it as any sort of glorification or recommendation of arming yourself, but it certainly is the tenor of the times. I'm really happy with the way that one came out."

'Damaged' is by far the album's funkiest track, even if it moves at a brisk 4/4 rock speed, with blistering, almost shredding, guitar solos by Buck and a classy old school keyboard solo by Allen. "That one has a lot of personal resonance for me," says Shirley, "because I'm in recovery from drug addiction from years ago. I was a drug addict, and now I'm clean and sober. But the song is about somebody who is destroying his relationships because of drugs. He's trying to get somebody to stay with him, even though he knows he's a complete screw-up. I was in that position at different times. At the same time, it's about somebody who knows that their identity is partly created by the damage they experienced when they were somehow traumatized in their lives. So even though when they stop using drugs, they are still marked by being damaged. I think all of us have to find an identity that accepts who we are, scars and all."

Buck's trademark circular and effortlessly musical soloing can be heard on 'Cold Gray Light of Dawn', a slow and sombre metal rocker with a vocal that demonstrates that Eric is only getting better with age. Buck's resolving and bluesy guitar playing can be heard full force. "That's sort of like a cosmic morality play," notes Buck, John adding that, "It's kind of self-explanatory in a way. I'm middle-aged, the band is middle-aged, and it's about two things: recognizing that you're growing older and you're seeing, as you get older, the mistakes of your past life. The patterns of your life, shall we say, are emerging more and more clearly if you look at yourself and your life. You have to admit to yourself what your mistakes are and where you've been dishonourable and where you've done things you regret. You have to face them more and more as you grow up because you tend to spend more time contemplating these things. So there's a kind of crisis of self-knowledge in middle age. It's sort of poetically about that crisis, looking around and saying this is who I really am and what am I going to do about it? That's probably related to my having been in recovery too."

Buck calls John's 'Real World' lyric his favourite of the album. Musically, the song adds even more funkiness to *Heaven Forbid*'s overall persona. Buck applies taut acoustic guitar and a wry deadpan vocal to this tale.

"For years, I've been interested in parapsychology," explains John, on the lyric's deeper meaning. "Also I was interested if there is anything in UFOs. The band did a lot of songs about UFOs; they have a lot of fun with it. I don't know what they believe. I eventually came to the conclusion that there's no good evidence that aliens have visited us. So, I became sceptical about most of the supernatural. Most of it, like John Edward, all that stuff, most of those people are charlatans. That kind of leads to the lyrics, the idea that the real world is weird enough anyway (laughs). If you want to look for the bizarre, you don't have to look for UFOs. You can just look at the real world and say look at the strange condition we live in. Just ordinary suburban life is, in a way, very strange. That's part of the theme. But then, I used all the images from years of trying to find if there were any supernatural or UFO truths out there to create a kind of Fortean backdrop for the song. You know Charles Fort? There is a magazine called *The Fortean Times*, which I still enjoy looking at. It's a cool thing I've always liked. I like the way he collated information that people ignored—rains of frogs, mysterious disappearances, some guy vanishes on a street corner, reports of angelic beings and so on. So I was trying to create a kind of Fortean song, using all this information from all my years associated with trying to find out if there was any truth in those things. UFO people actually know me as a hidebound sceptic these days."

In terms of picking a timeless classic from *Heaven Forbid*—excepting sentimental favourite 'See You in Black', an irresistible classic of the gut, the loins, the pit of the stomach, the moshpit—one is left with 'Harvest Moon' and 'Live for Me'. 'Live for Me' is crafted in the spirit of 'Your Loving Heart' from *Flat Out*, less so 'The Reaper'. All three traverse poetically the silvery line between life and death then back again. All three smolder with Buck's platinum sense of melody.

"I was wishing that 'Live for Me' had been a single," offers Shirley, with regret. "I thought it might have been a hit, because to me it was a really strong piece and I think it could have been like The Eagles. It had a resonance with something like '(Don't Fear) The Reaper.' It's about death and life after death from a different direction. It's just a very rich song, the way they've written it. It has an overall mood that is very moving to people; a lot of people really love that song. That's one I would've wished... if it would have been a single, I think it would have had a better shot than the one they chose, which was 'See You in Black.'" Indeed that was the case, with Buck indicating at the time that 'Harvest Moon' would likely be the next single, that or 'Live for Me'.

The 'Live for Me' lyric also has resonance with old classic 'Deadman's Curve' and BÖC's own 'Shadow of California'; it is classic Blue Öyster Cult, and shockingly Buck, shocking in that John Shirley wrote it. Suffice to say it is a tale of death, the wisdom of the dying, and the inspiration of the suddenly wise.

As a final note, 'Live for Me' is the only song on the album that features the band's new drummer Bobby Rondinelli at the kit. "Bobby's our live drummer and has been for about eight or ten months now," said Buck at the time. "When we finished the record, sort of last October to December, we had Bobby and we thought we could beat the track we had with Chuck. So we re-recorded it with Bobby."

"The whole album was done," affirms Bobby, with extra vague bits added! "All the rhythm tracks were done before I joined the band. Something happened with the record company where they got half the money and then the record company disappeared or something (laughs), so all the rhythm tracks were done. Then they wound up getting their deal going again or they found where the rest of the money was, and they ended up finishing stuff. They wanted to redo 'Live for Me' and they wanted to get me on the record because I had been in the band already a year now. They really couldn't go in and redo the whole record; that would be crazy. So I played on one song."

Bobby recounts the tale of his joining the band. "Well, I was in Sabbath, and I was on vacation with Sabbath, and BÖC needed someone to fill in for a gig that their drummer couldn't make, an outdoor gig in Rhode Island, so they asked me if I could do it. I'd never played any of their stuff, and until you play the stuff, you don't know it. So I learned all the stuff, did the show. They kind of asked me if I wanted to join the band and I said it really didn't pay, because I was probably going to be going back out with Sabbath in a couple months. Then Sabbath wound up getting their original line-up back together for some *Ozzfest* stuff, so I wound up taking the gig."

"I kind of hit 'em hard," says Bobby of his style. "I just like to make it fun for me. I like to have a good time when I'm playing. You know, sometimes I play simple and sometimes I play a little over-the-top to make it interesting and fun. Usually, if it makes me smile, it's okay."

Back to the album at hand, nothing that follows could possibly live up to 'Live for Me' and indeed, nothing does. 'Still Burnin'' is a bit of a plodding rocker, propelled by Miceli's double bass and a vicious metal riff. The music is Buck's and the lyric is from Jon Rogers (Buck also credits Jon with much of the music as well), who turns in a standard, pedestrian tale surrounding the seductive intensity of womankind.

Closing out the album is an acoustic live version of the hit that almost was, 'In Thee' from *Mirrors*, first introduced way back in '79. Surprisingly, it is the only Allen Lanier credit on the album. "We're trying to get him to write some new stuff, but he hasn't done much lately," said a tight-lipped Buck at the time. "I mean, if you ask him, I'm sure he'd say, 'Yeah, I've done this and that.' He collaborates with other artists too. But as far as him... you know, I wish he'd had a stronger participation in writing for this record."

Where do you think his head is at? "I don't know. You know, you do this for 30 years, and it's not like it hasn't been done."

"That was Eric's idea," adds Buck, with respect to re-doing the oldie but softie. "I think it was good, just a bonus track for the fans. Also, we'd been doing it live getting a great reaction. So I thought it was a good idea. I also like the fact—just in terms of the pace of the album—it's nice that it ends with that. It cools you out before you pull it out of the CD player. My problem with CDs in general, especially long ones, is that I cannot listen to an hour-and-a-half of somebody's music, 74 minutes, whatever; I just can't do it. I pine for the old vinyl days when you had basically 20 minutes a side to do something. You know, you really tried to create. I really don't think bands are doing that any more."

"I don't see us working any less," offered Buck, looking ahead to getting out there yet again, but this time with a new record to promote. "We really think we have something that's worth hearing here, so we want to popularize it as much as we can. I don't think any of us really expect to do what we did in the '80s. That was then. I don't really view that as a favourable outcome. I'd hate to do what I did then, as far as like how hard it was, how strenuous it was. The biggest obstacle is convincing people that you're worth listening to, you know? Just because there's that prejudice with all bands. I think if you listen to this record, you'll agree that it's not so."

An innocent enough question, I thought, concerning the strength of Eric's singing voice got a bit of a strange response. "You know, I don't know if that's for me to speak about," offered Buck cryptically. "You know, he's been singing for 25 years, and he had a period where he wasn't anywhere near as strong as he used to be. Right now he's quite good, and he's come back quite a bit from where he was a year ago. But that's really not for me to speak about, especially for a publication."

How's your voice holding up? "Very good. I've been working very hard on vocals for the last several years, and it's bearing fruit, and I wish I would have done this 20 years ago. Yeah, I'm singing like a bird these days (laughs)."

"I think it's great but not enough people heard it," offered Eric down the line a bit after the album had come out and blown out. "It's a little frustrating to us, because we really spent a long time making that record. We put a lot of effort into it because we wanted to make it as good as we good. It's not CMC's fault. People had not heard from us for ten years. It's tough to get radio to go for that; I can't blame them. Every person that I have laid the record on is shocked at how good it is. Making a record is a cathartic kind of thing. It's like giving birth to something. It's like animals in the wild. You give birth to them, and then they are on their own! We do our best to help it along. We do interviews and let people know that we are alive and well. I wish more people would have heard *Heaven Forbid*. We would have been pleased if more people had heard about it. It is a damn good record and we are proud of everything we did on it. But we are not knocking Britney Spears off the charts."

Curse of the Hidden Mirror

"Railroaded into jail, ratted out and in prison"

Subsequent to the release of *Heaven Forbid*, Blue Öyster Cult executed a spirited few rounds of touring. The band's status as a classic rock act that held up more than well was solidifying. Its reputation among bikers was also growing in stature as the band continued to play biker rallies where tales of smoke and steel of all sorts went over a storm. But as a shock to almost everybody, the band were back a short three years after *Heaven Forbid* with a new album in 2001 called *Curse of the Hidden Mirror*. It was a brave record in that it didn't pander to the metal crowd. It was non-obvious, tasteful, and despite its stylistic diversity, oddly more holistic and—as Sandy would say—synergistic or "aggregate."

"This is a band record to me," begins Buck, attempting to nail the album's personality. "The current line-up with Bobby Rondinelli and Danny Miranda… I think we're so integrated that its sounds very cohesive and probably as much if not more band-like than any line-up we've ever had. So that pleases me greatly, listening to how this record came out, how we really sound like a well-oiled machine. I think we have an identity, a strong identity. You know, it's funny. If I was to kind of place this record, this record could have probably been made between *Spectres* and *Cultösaurus*. To me it is in that range, the way it sounds. As far as pop or heavy metal goes, to me it's classic Blue Öyster Cult in that you really can't pin it down. We encouraged Danny and Bobby, on this record especially, to be involved with the writing and they did a great job. I think their playing on this record is just stellar. We're just really proud of the whole thing."

Yet it persists that Allen Lanier's pen has not been lifted. "You know, we've all been goading Allen to write more, because he's obviously got a really thoughtful voice with the stuff he has written over the years," says Buck. "But for whatever reason, he's been reluctant to really jump in. But he's certainly been involved in the arranging and the playing of it. All I can say is that I used to feel that way in the early days. You know, I didn't write any of the Soft White Underbelly stuff and wrote very little music for the band's first few records. It wasn't until later on that I really assumed the responsibility of coming up with the stuff that I have now. Still, maybe Allen will do it again."

In conversation with esteemed rock journo Ken Sharp, Buck summed up the new record as a case of "going with your strengths. For us to reinvent ourselves, it's not really necessary or desirable. Certainly I think our best work is when we stay true to what our soul is, musically and stylistic-wise. I like to think of it as closing your eyes and creating or closing your eyes and playing - that's what came out when we did that metaphorically. It was joyful. Rather than worrying about 'What am I gonna do in 2001? How's it going to fit in with the popular culture of the day?' I'm just not worrying about that at all at this point."

Asked to characterize the band's sound and to account for its longevity, Buck goes with, "Guitars, rhythm, choruses. Real super-competent playing, a clever lyrical concept, some kind of content there that is not devoid of meaning. I think the endurance is a factor. It is stubbornness (laughs). Playing guitar and singing is what I do so I keep doing it and I think the rest of the band feels the same way. As far as the length of our career I'm kind of surprised that rock as we know it and as we do it has endured. I wouldn't have thought that going in. I'm just surprised at the way it's gone, as far as the support from the public that we've got. When I was a kid my dad's music hasn't endured like that."

"First and foremost, there's a really strong coherent band identity on this new record," said Buck in a separate chat, filling in a few blanks, and reiterating some of the above points. "The personnel is the Blue Öyster Cult from the last five, six years, in-tact. We're really pretty comfortable, and well-integrated with our playing. We spent many months writing and rehearsing the record, so we were very well prepared when we recorded it. The main difference between this one and *Heaven Forbid* is that we really consciously tried to make a classic rock record. What came out of that effort is that I think we made a record that could really be put alongside our classic work from the height of our career."

"The band is totally self-directed at this point. I still do what I've always done; I just get credit for it now. Between myself and Eric and the rest of the guys, we basically do what we want, from start to finish. I mainly oversee the audio end of it, as far as getting it onto a disc. But we all contribute. When people hear this new record, they're just so amazed that we have so much vitality. When Albert was the drummer, the band had a distinctive sound that's different from what it is with other drummers. That's more a function of Albert's unique and idiosyncratic style than it is of drummers in general. Also you can't discount Albert's obvious creative input. He was the most prolific writer of all of us. You know, and there are still those that are really fans of the Albert axis of the band, and that's fine. But you can't live in the past. You can revere those records, but that's about all you can do. I don't think we owe the original BÖC sound anything, any more than The Byrds had to always be The Byrds with the original line-up. Or another example would be The Doobie Brothers. There's different eras of The Doobie Brothers, and they're all good, but they're not the same. It's unusual for a band to stay together for this long."

"That's a song title from the Soft White Underbelly days," explains Buck, with respect to the album title. "Other than that, there's probably not much to it. Coincidentally, Rhino Handmade has released the Stalk-Forrest recordings, which are the Elektra recordings with Eric singing. So you can actually hear the song from which the title of the new record comes from." Turns out the use of that for a title arose outside of, but not from, a fan poll. "Yeah, Eric invited the fans to submit names and we got pages and pages of names, none of which were used (laughs). I'm not sure what was even close. My impression was that none of them were worthy."

"No, it baffles me completely," answers Shirley, on whether he had a hand in the record's naming. "It's some old thing they had. They had some Blue Öyster Cult song or theme of that nature, from some point in the past and they decided to dredge it up and use it. And I have no objection to it." As previously mentioned, the phrase does indeed originate from back in the annals of Sandy's *Imaginos* machinations.

The original song (which has mirrors in the plural) is a brisk, lightly psychedelic, almost easy listening number, at least with respect to how it appears on the *St. Cecilia* reissue. Meltzer's lyric (the music is Al's) could indeed be applied to the album's cover art with at least a modicum of intellectualized connection-making taking place.

Buck comments on the cover art: "We were conscious, for the graphics of this record… our most conscious thought was to make a package that was way more pleasing than the *Heaven Forbid* one which was not warmly received (laughs). It is generally thought of as the most hideous album cover the band had ever done. That was the prime objective. The cover was designed by a design house called Vivid Images and of the proposals they made, we said yes, that's it. But the Egyptian imagery, that's something we've called on before, with the scarab and the hooded monks and the graphics on the back of *The Revolution by Night*. It's a place we've gone to before. But it's easier to create a mystique at the end of a project than at the beginning of a project, so that's what we did."

The cover art, as Buck has indicated, was done by Ioannis, of Vivid Images Design, based in Connecticut. Ioannis (pronounced Yo-han-ess; his full Greek name is… really full!) got his start with a substantial amount of work for Metal Blade Records, then MCA/Mechanic, and later did much of the art for Sanctuary Records, hence the connection with the Cult.

But the crossing of paths goes back much further. "Actually, the first time I met the Blue Öyster Cult was in 1980," explains Ioannis. "Sandy Pearlman used to manage them; I remember them and Black Sabbath touring together. I never knew that both bands hated each other; I had no idea. So Black Sabbath had already talked to me about doing their next album. I showed my stuff to Sandy Pearlman and he wanted me to do something for the Cult but they didn't want to use the guy who was going to do Black Sabbath. In the end, I lost out on both (laughs). Then like 15 years later, whatever it was… it was really kind of cool."

"Steve Schenck was their manager, and I told him my trials and tribulations about Sandy Pearlman and we started discussing stuff," continues Ioannis. "There was a whole bunch of ideas about, you know, what does that mean? Lanier loves cats and Egyptian themes; I mean, they've always liked Egyptian themes. Some of the ideas submitted included cats and stuff. But as the story graduated, I started thinking that *Curse of the Hidden Mirror* sounded like one of those serials from the 1920s, one of those detective story thrillers that you got. You know, 'Man goes to the middle of China and discovers this hidden thing.' So just totally by coincidence, a few months before that… usually on Saturdays or Sundays, I take a long drive and hit antique shops and things like that, and my kid sister had bought me as a gift, close to about 200 photographs. Somebody had sold her a series of black and white photos that were taken in 1918 to 1921, somewhere around there, and it was his grandfather's trip to China. These images were just unbelievable, what China looked like in 1921, Peking and all that stuff. It was just wild. One particular image that struck me was this picture of this guy in a rickshaw, so I scanned that photograph in and then I composed the painting. I was getting very heavily in the mid-'90s into digital painting. It's just easier to correct mistakes, or if the band wants to change something."

"So the band just loved it. Eric Bloom just thought it was the funniest thing he had ever seen. They call him Rickshaw Hitler (laughs). So the guy is holding a mirror and it's reflecting the Cult image, the symbol. So if you look at the packaging, there's sort of a serial story going on. There's this character, out in the desert somewhere, doing excavations; again, the idea of a loose story."

"I tell you, man, I have gotten a mountain of emails from their fans. I just made available actually, a limited edition print, and it's selling like gangbusters. Their fans are a riot. I got an email from the guy who helps them write their lyrics; he loved it. I got an email from this girl from Michigan, who I guess is a hardcore fan, and she came up with a whole story about how all the covers of the Blue Öyster Cult make this story line that relates, right up to *Curse of the Hidden Mirror*. Somebody else sent me a letter saying I was a mental vampire and I had drained his ideas (laughs). Some things you pull out and respond to, and other things... no, I'm not going to correspond with this guy, because you never know where it's going to lead. One kid sent me an email and said he had the whole cover tattooed on his back. I just said, 'Send me a picture,' you know?"

"This is our first digital record," continues Buck on the album's rich production. "We used an Atari Radar hard disk recorder and an all-tube console, so what I was going for recording-wise was just beef and girth and the kind of full satisfying sounds you used to get with analogue. You know, we didn't want to lose anything for not using two-inch tape. Fortunately, that's pretty easy to do because there's a lot of outboard gear that you can use. Basically, you just ask your ears as it's going down, 'Does this sound happening or not?' There wasn't too much strangeness on the record. It's pretty straight-ahead. I did some stuff in my Macintosh computer as far as the effects. On 'The Old Gods Return,' all of those effects were created in the computer. Certainly we used absolutely state-of-the-art technology on this record, and yet it sounds to me like a record that might have been made in the complete heyday of classic rock."

"We worked great together," recalls Bobby Rondinelli. "We rehearsed on and off for a month or two putting the material together, and we worked really hard. Then we went up to Millbrook Studios and demoed the stuff and it sounded good. We went back to rehearsal, tightened up a few things and went up and did the record." Bobby is credited on a couple of tracks but says, "Yeah, I might have said let's try this riff or that riff. I don't remember (laughs). I just remember I had a lot to say during the sessions. I don't remember who came up with what part, but it was very much like a group effort. They were very open. I like those songs I'm on, plus 'Stilts,' 'Pocket'... I don't know, I like the record; it was a good record."

Opening the album was a curiously laid-back number called 'Dance on Stilts'. I actually consider this a bit of a dud, especially as an opener. It doesn't go. In any event, it does speak to a sort of bravery, if only one around career suicide.

Somewhere between prog and pop, 'Dance on Stilts' is most definitely stilted, the track stopping and starting, perhaps most often sputtering, yet blooming come Buck's fiery, swirling solo work. "Yes, I guess it's a little nervy to do jamming in this culture," comments Buck, on my impression that the record is indeed guitary, yet not in a metal sense. "There aren't too many records that actually have a lot of playing on them. Yet it just doesn't make sense to me not to do it. It's one of the band's strengths, so why not do it?"

"We took a chance with that one," continues Buck, realizing the oddity of a track like 'Dance on Stilts' as an opener. "The obvious arguments you make against starting an album with a long song, I just thought that that was... of all the places it could be on the record, that's where it worked for the best. One of the reasons I did it was just to be contrary. It was just something we had never done before. So far the reaction of it has been pretty good. I'm actually curious to see what people think of the programming. I almost see it as two sides. I almost think of this record as being classically oriented, a record that you can turn over. If you look on the disc and see how the tracks were laid out, there are actually two sides. So you can start on side B, and that's like another record to me."

"It was a little nervy putting a six-and-a-half minute song as the first cut on the CD but it did work. When I wrote that song it was almost like two songs. I've always liked the segue thing where one song turns into another. The band did a really great job on it. We've been playing that live and audiences who have never heard it before really dig it."

"As a listener I really like melody," continues Donald, asked about his approach to guitar playing. "One thing I notice is that the older I get, the more melodic I like to be as a listener and as a player. The energy and the angst of heavy music is appealing to youth but it seems like the older I get, the more melody I want to hear. If that makes me a fuddy duddy, so be it. Melodically I have to have that to satisfy myself and my playing in general. I always want to please myself and entertain myself. Okay, you can play fast or play a lot of notes, but for me everything you do has got to have a reason."

"That's an inspirational song, basically," notes Buck on John Shirley's 'Dance on Stilts' lyric. "It's acknowledging a relationship that is really supportive through good times and bad times. I mean, I like stuff like that. I'm actually a sucker for encouraging songs (laughs) rather than gloom and doom songs."

"I wrote it for Donald," adds John himself, "as a sort of power ballad kind of thing; that's how it emerged. It's a song about somebody who has a double life. It's about having an interior life that is very different from the life you live in your career, let's say, in your ordinary dealings with people. Like you have to drag yourself to some high-tone professional career, this guy, but he just feels like, while on the one hand he is working in these pristine office environments at a high level, in another way he's dragging himself through the gutter (laughs), because the corporation is actually run by scum (laughs). It's implied; I don't say it straight out. The only thing that saves him from despair and recognition is that he's in love with somebody. When he's with that person, they kind of rise above the murk and the debris and the dust of ordinary life, by dancing on stilts, which is a deliberately absurd image."

Yet one has to listen closely to gather all this: the lyrics, curiously, are not printed in the booklet. "I always prefer the lyrics to be printed because I wrote some of them, and I have the normal vanity about it," comments John on the absence of the words. "Also, you can't always hear what somebody is singing. Musicians don't regard the lyrics as all that important (laughs). To them it's just a sound. I mean, they do like them and they like good, meaningful lyrics, but it's not as important as a sound to them. They tend not to care that much about having them printed. There is a problem. I've heard it in one or two Blue Öyster Cult cuts, and almost everybody does this at some time. The musicians don't realize how inaudible the lyrics sometimes are. Because they hear them in their mind, and they get involved in a mix, and then in the process of mixing, the lyrics just become more like notes. They forget that other people weren't there when they were being devised and when they were recording the vocal tracks, and that other people don't hear them in their minds. They forget that they aren't as audible, in a sense, to people who haven't heard the songs, and those who weren't familiar with it. Therefore, the lyrics end up being too far down, too low, and you can't hear what they're saying. You lose some of the power of the song commercially and otherwise. So that's a syndrome that people should work on and I wish that the BÖC would remember it because once or twice, it seems to me, that it has happened."

Incidentally, Shirley is all over *Curse of the Hidden Mirror*, penning the words for eight out of 11 tracks. "It's easier for me to use other people's lyrics song-wise," explains Buck, on his personal shift away from that department over the years. "I mean, I do write lyrics but I'm very self-critical and kind of shy about it, so therefore I'm not very prolific. I think both Eric and I are very hands-on in terms of editing existing lyrics and creating some stuff. Yeah, we create the odd line ourselves. Or we get the idea of the concept and we'll go back to John and we say, 'I like this and this, but I don't like this; I'd like this song to go here.' John is very good with coming back with an additional lyric. Certainly we are involved, but as far as crediting goes, I really don't want to take credit for that. My job really is to create music and arrange the song."

"John's very prolific and always very much rooted in his novel writing," continues Buck. "He's very entertaining in his way. He writes tons of lyrics and sends them to Eric and I. Eric and I tend to like different styles of John's lyrics. I look for the ones that suit my sensibility and Eric goes for the ones that suit his. There are songs of John's that I'm working on that the band hasn't released yet that are different from the ones that you are hearing. I've written lyrics but I'm terribly self-critical and take a long time. I'm very shy about exposing my words. I would rather use someone else's words but they have to resonate with me for me to do it. I'm very happy to work with John. John was actually introduced to us by Sandy. William Gibson actually credits John with the whole cyberspace thing. He actually created it and William Gibson kind of cadged it from him."

I asked John if, given his involvement, he's ever been right there in the studio with the band as they stitched an album together. "No, they do it all way back east. I would love to do that, but you know, I don't think writers of lyrics are that much welcome in the studio any more than they're welcome on movie sets. I've written movies too, and you know, I haven't been invited over there much either (laughs). I wrote *The Crow* and I had very little connection with the actual production."

The album's second track, 'Showtime' reads amusingly along the same theme as 'Power Underneath Despair'—jail and the aftermath. Musically, it bobs like a cobra, when it's not bobbing heads like a Bob Marley reggae. The song positively oozes venom without the cheap ploy of rocking out.

"'Showtime' is a song that Eric wrote with his college band partner John Trivers, who is a big commercial music guy in LA now," says Buck. "That was a song that was written probably around the time of *Agents of Fortune*, and the band at that time never came up with a satisfactory arrangement so it got forgotten about. I think it was Bolle, who is the head of our fan club, who said, 'Why don't you take a look at this one?' The current band was able to come up with what I thought was a real steamin' arrangement for it. That's sort of like a 'railroaded into jail, ratted out and in prison revenge' song. It's funny, somebody pointed out that we had another one of those. 'Power Underneath Despair' is sort of the same thing. But it's funny, because it was created under totally different circumstances and a different mindset and a different time."

'The Old Gods Return' is a standard Blue Öyster Cult hard rocker—not too heavy, dark with a shade of ennui, a further shade of progressive rock, the Deep Purple definition thereof, most often voiced by Gillan and sometimes Glover.

"Well, that's kind of a humorous one," notes lyricist Shirley. "I mean, it isn't humorous but it is at the same time, like so many things. It's kind of a classic metal theme. I grew up reading H. P. Lovecraft and people like that, so there's a little bit of reference to him and that kind of thing, and I do think that the human race is very arrogant when it thinks it understands what's going on in the universe. I don't know if I understand, but I know there is a lot of mystery; so it does have that theme where, yeah, you think you know what's going on and then one day the curtain will be ripped back like that song, 'X-Ray Eyes,' a similar theme, a curtain over reality. On the other side of it, you would just be blown away if all was revealed, so don't look. So it does have that serious theme, but it also has some fun with the imagery, i.e. the references to the blind monkeys in Oz and so forth."

Does it also speak to this concept of all the old gods of rock 'n' roll returning to tour and make albums? Or just one height-challenged set of them in particular? "Oh well, it does contain a reference to the Blue Öyster Cult as the old gods; that is there, but I didn't want to say that because I don't know if they want to be thought of as the old gods (laughs). But in fact, that was in my mind too, yes, that Blue Öyster Cult may be the old gods who are returning."

Buck acknowledges John's nod, no offence taken. "That one is a fanciful tale, sort of like the Norse outlook on theology. John Shirley thought that was metaphorical for us, you know, the band: the old grandfathers are coming back to kick some butt in the new millennium."

Curse of the Hidden Mirror's closest thing to a swellegant Buck popster comes wrapped in the sunny, slashing chords of 'Pocket'. Buck croons it well, and his band sparkles and fades artfully all over the track. Its chorus is smooth personified, the highlight of the entire album.

"'Pocket' can be interpreted as just nostalgia for your ordinary life and feeling good at home with your family and how that can kind of lift you above things," muses John. "But it also has spiritual meaning for me, and can be interpreted as just a guy who... nothing is going to affect him. He's just going to be totally alive. That's kind of his warrior way of being in the world. But it also has deeper meaning for me having to do with the process of non-identification as a spiritual step, which is kind of a Buddhist... I'm interested in the teachings of G.I. Gurdjieff, and it's very much part of the Gurdjieffian teachings. But it's also very much of Buddhism, Zen; non-identification is being in life but not of it, so that you can develop kind of a spiritual self that doesn't get swept up in ordinary passions, and exists for something higher."

"'Pocket' was a lyrics of John's that I enjoyed," adds Buck. "That was written last year during the rehearsals when we were preparing for this record. To me, it's a song about being in the moment, sort of the Eastern philosophical way, be here now, be in the moment, enjoy life as it unfolds, be aware. It's a joyful tune to me. The record company has gone with it as the first single. It's been out about a week now and they've got about 40 stations playing it."

Jarring after such a triumph is the brutish, nay, sluggish metal bash of 'One Step Ahead of the Devil', a track with a plethora of parts, few of them all that successful, selected postures reminiscent of Led Zeppelin. "Well, that song is just about the feeling of being on the run and also just mortality itself," notes John. "I created a sort of short story, where you sense the character is in some kind of desperate situation, maybe a post-Holocaust situation like *Road Warrior*. But really it's just about everybody who feels that they are one step ahead of something that can destroy them, whether it's the IRS or cancer or just the dangers of life."

Of the humourous (but musically uneventful) 'I Just Like to Be Bad', Shirley relates that, "I think my wife said that once, and I just thought it was a funny line; she was just joking around about something and I made up a sort of short story about it. Again it's the story form. It's about a guy who has fallen in love with this girl who likes anonymity. She basically likes anonymous sex once in awhile—I hope she uses a condom—with guys that she meets somewhere, and doesn't like to get involved with anybody in a personal way. She's very flinty and removed where this guy knows her: at work. But he sees beyond that and sees that she needs something deeper. By the end... he just hangs in there, and by the end of the song, or the end of the story, he persuades her and she's going to be the same way, but just for him."

'Here Comes that Feeling' is another pop track, along the lines of 'Pocket' but oddly less successful, evoking more of a detached *Club Ninja*-type vibe.

"That's the other song on the record that was actually written some time ago," notes Buck. "I wrote that intended for my second solo record which I never got around to making. Again, I'd forgotten about it until I went back to all my old tapes. It was written with a guy named Dick Trismen who went on to try have a pop career at that time in the early '80s and gave up on that and now he's a high up computer programmer. He does music sequencing software. Oddly enough, you know, compositionally I respect Paul Simon, Don Henley and people like that, rather than more heavy genre bands or artists. I'm just coming from that place more."

'Out of the Darkness' is the only true ballad on the album and it is a classy one, driven nicely by Danny Miranda's bass work, which incidentally beautifies many of this record's songs, Miranda comfortably in sync with Bobby Rondinelli's hard sense of funk no matter what the genre addressed and blessed. Eric turns in a forceful, thespian, utterly convincing vocal, which, as it turns out, wasn't exactly destined to be.

"Eric sometimes takes things in a direction I wouldn't expect," notes John. "'Out of the Darkness,' I had written for Buck. Eric does a different vocal interpretation of it than Buck would and I had to get used to it. But you know, Eric is a really good singer and he makes it work and it's a strong song so it works anyway. But I was a little surprised to hear him do it. That one's a sort of short story. Some songs are like short stories. I mean, I'm a writer of short stories; I have books of short stories. I think even all lyricists, people like Dylan or Lou Reed, who was an influence on me, sometimes write songs that are telling stories. Johnny Cash is another great example of storytelling songs. You get a sense of a beginning and an end; Kris Kristofferson does that. That is a story about this guy who's in love with this girl, and her parents dislike him, don't trust him. He's trying to persuade her to trust her own instincts and go with him. He perceives that what is keeping her there with them and away from him is the parents' own sublimated hatred of one another. They are destroying their daughter because they're angry at one another. They're trapping her there; she is caught in their little neurotic web. It doesn't get resolved, but it is as much a story, really, as it is a love song. It's kind of an unrequited love song in a way. That I think has some of my best lines."

"In fact, that song was written about 1982," offers Buck on 'Stone of Love', a catchy dark melodic number, one of the album's more enigmatic tracks. "The reason that song was fresh in my mind is because recently, in the last year, I've digitized most of my home demos that I made from the 'Reaper' era right up to recent times. So I found that song again and thought the band could do a version of it and did a great version of it. I'm very happy the way that came out."

Says Meltzer, "'Stone of Love', music by Buck... that was basically lifted from a poem I wrote for Lester Bangs when he died. A lot of what's in there is word for word. I wrote about this thing; it's also in my book *Autumn Rhythm*, a poem for Lester. I would have written that in '82, '83."

Second to last... y'know, four of this album's coolest songs are in fact, the closing four. Get there. Experience. So yeah, second to last on plate is a lethal stealth rocker called 'Eye of the Hurricane' which Shirley calls "another one related to my personal and spiritual practices, but it can be interpreted in different ways."

"Yes, it probably is the heaviest song on there," muses Buck. "I think we have to give a nod to our reputation and our image, you know? We have to keep our hand... no matter what other styles we dabble in, we have to come back and make sure we cover that base. So I think that's what's going on there. Brian Neumeister, co-writer on that, is a friend of Eric's, who is a film composer and commercial composer in Arizona who Eric has collaborated with on a couple tunes."

Closing out the album is a jazzy, almost miniscule and eccentric thing called 'Good to Feel Hungry', a tune that starts weak and finishes strong with a number of parts evoking moves last heard in the black and white period. "'Good to Feel

Hungry' is a song I really like," laughs Buck. "I almost thought of starting the record with that one. It's got an odd time signature and it's a quirky tune and it's the kind of thing that BÖC used to do in its earlier stages when we had no fear, when we would just do any type of song. It's one of my favourite songs on the record. 'Good to Feel Hungry' and 'Out of the Darkness'... the core musical idea for those came from Danny."

"As I said, some of the songs are influenced by my spirituality," begins Shirley, when asked about this lyric. "I don't know if the band is even aware of that at all. Like 'Pocket,' for example, is about my interest in meditation and consciousness and mindfulness, and so is 'Good to Feel Hungry.' It's about a sense of self-awareness and the process of getting to know yourself and being honest with yourself about who you are and what makes you tick and what saves you from despair. 'Pocket' is about living in the moment. They both have that connection to spirituality that I'm interested in."

Curse of the Hidden Mirror, just like *Heaven Forbid*, did little for the band's collective pocketbook. The band was still a nice draw live, but there was an undeniable stigma and resulting downgrade not being signed to a major. CMC in turn became swallowed up by Sanctuary, and indeed without those Iron Maiden dollars driving the aggressive company, perhaps we might not have seen a DVD, a live album, and a best of (*Then and Now*), so quickly upon the backs of two bonafide studio spreads. Be thankful for the profusion of product, but also be resigned to the fact that rock 'n' roll is a young man's game, and that the band's fate was likely pre-doomed by this unalterable.

"Well, I think there are a lot of good songs on them," mused Eric, three years removed from *Curse of the Hidden Mirror*. "Maybe sonically they're not the greatest thing in the world. I really don't know. The problem with... I can't go back and listen to them. You hear that from other musicians. Because it takes such an effort to write the songs and rehearse the songs, and then record the songs, and then sing the vocal every day for three days in a row, and after a while, you can't even face it again. So it's hard for me to have any perspective now a few years later. But I think there are some very good songs on those records. I think making it digitally, the last one, was a revelation in technology—that was a lot of fun. It might be the road we go down the next time too. I think the technology thing might be interesting on the next project, whenever it is. Where Buck can take a record home and play the files at his house and MP3 them to me and I can listen to them here and then make a suggestion. We can cut and paste this over here or over there. I mean, that might be the way we do the next thing..."

A Long Day's Night

"We never suck"

Post-*Curse*, Blue Öyster Cult saw a comprehensive live CD and DVD set released. *A Long Day's Night*, recorded in Chicago, June 21, 2002, was commendable in that it included crazy old obscurities like 'Stairway to the Stars', 'Quicklime Girl' and 'OD'd on Life Itself'. The band also had the good taste to rescue 'Perfect Water' from the murk that was *Club Ninja*, and to rock out proudly with a scampered rendition of 'Lips in the Hills'. 'Harvest Moon' and 'Dance on Stilts' were picked to represent the here and now. Oh well, one out of two ain't bad when one of 'em is 'Harvest Moon', a track that gets an admirably muscular lift in the live environment. At 78 minutes, the thing's long enough that in the old days, we would have called this a double album. Ergo compare, more than favourably, with *On Your Feet* and *ETL*. And yeah, Miranda and Rondinelli are one helluva rhythm section.

On the subject of Bobby Rondinelli, we'd be remiss in not mentioning that besides his early work on two Rainbow albums (*Difficult to Cure* and *Straight Between the Eyes*), Black Sabbath's *Cross Purposes*, and the BÖC material, he has also guested on a Riot album (*Through the Storm*) and briefly worked with Doro, Sun Red Sun, McCoy and Quiet Riot (I'm still scratching my head over that one). As well, Bobby has been an integral part of two bands, Rondinelli and The Lizards, who have now cranked five stirring "new classic rock" albums helmed by groovy bass maven and rock historian Randy Pratt.

Bobby offers a few comments on doing the DVD gig. "Those kinds of days are always stressful, because we didn't do a safety shoot where you could do a couple of days. Everything was done in one day. So, from that point of view, I was pretty happy because we played pretty good. If you have a bad day, and that's the only day you're filming, you're screwed. But it was a long day, a stressful day, because it's a long sound check and line check, making sure all the audio equipment and all the video equipment is working. The one thing I really remember, is that I was glad when it was over (laughs). That was a decent show, you know? I was very happy about that. No problems really, just a few times, getting startled when you'd turn your head and there's a camera in your face. But other than that, no problems. That was a long show, probably about two-and-a-half hours."

It's a good performance though, and, says Bobby, there's a reason for that.

"Me and Buck have a motto: 'We never suck.' You know what I mean? Some nights we're better than others, but we never suck. We'll always make it work. It has to do with being a professional. You can't always be amazing but you should have a line that you just don't cross. You can't go on stage saying, 'Oh, we're going to suck tonight because we're tired'—fuck that! You see a lot of old bands and to them it's just a payday, and they suck a lot. There's a lot of bands out there that shouldn't be working. When I get to that point, I'll just stay home and teach, or do something else and make a living. I like people to come up and say, 'Hey man, you were killin'!' I like that. That's one of the reasons I play. I've got an ego, you know? I want to be good. I want to be better next year than I am this year. I always want to get better. I've got a saying that I tell all my students: 'When you stop getting better, you start getting worse.' Luckily, in music, you can keep it going. If you stay away from booze and drugs, you can play indefinitely. Who knows when it ends? The Rolling Stones are 150 years old and they're still out there doing it. I'll keep doing it, till nobody wants to play with me no more!"

"Now I understand why some of my favourite records, like The Allman Brothers *At Fillmore East* or the Rush live records sound so good," adds Danny. "Because that's what happens when you play 200 gigs a year, and then you take it in the studio. That's also why Steely Dan records don't sound like that. When you have a band that does so many gigs, you're a well-oiled machine, and you can do this in your sleep. I sometimes get sick of playing songs after six months. I don't how these guys can play songs for 25 years and find a way to tap into inspiration. But it's inspiring to me. Donald, especially, never plays like he's bored. That's very impressive to me. I mean they were always good, but those three guys are playing way better now. That's why they'll never be a nostalgia act, because they don't sound like a shadow of their former selves. I think Donald was always a great guitar player, but I think he's ten times better today than he was 20 years ago."

"Usually the biggest surprise is that we're great," chuckles Buck. "Because they don't expect that. They expect you to be, you know, wheezing shells of your former selves."

There you have it. What came next? Well, no progress whatsoever on discussions around possibly thinking about calling each other to see if there's a new studio album somewhere in the cards.

"Well, yes, I've sent them new stuff," says John Shirley on the subject. "I believe there is going to be another album from the current record label. The rumour is that there is a deal in the works. For a while it wasn't sure. But I've heard a rumour that there will be. I'm sending them material for it. I'm sure there will be other writers too. I know Buck has read my lyrics."

"We were in Palo Alto, and Sandy came by and saw the show," mentions Buck. "We haven't had much to say to each other after we parted company in a business sense, but I think we're getting over that now, so relations are moving toward cordial again. I would love to see some input if he's interested in doing it. Certainly from a creative standpoint, his input is appreciated."

"They're an underrated band at the present time," opines Shirley. "They're still doing great stuff. Except for a few rare exceptions, it's hard to get a middle-aged band's material on the air, even if it's great. It's really quite unfair. That may change. Demographics are swinging around and record companies are starting to realize that old people are a huge part of the record-buying public. There might be a lot more emphasis on bands with older people in them. Everything may actually change in the next ten years, to my surprise; this is something I read anyway. BÖC… the critics just ignore them; critics can be excruciatingly trendy and quite dismissive."

Man, do you hear the crickets? Not critics… crickets. As I pen a few extra words for close of day, last call, whatever ya wanna call it, there's basically nothing to report on of substance since the release of *A Long Day's Night* back in 2002. Danny and Bobby left and some young (but extremely capable) unknowns came in. Allen eventually faded from the scene, eventually passing from heart disease on August 14, 2103—it wasn't particularly surprising that he would be the first to go.

"We had a drum-off," said Eric in late 2004, concerning the shifting line-up of the band up into these wilderness years. "Bobby gave us plenty of notice, and we put out the word, you know? We called ex-drummers and got a lot of recommendations. A lot of people knew people who might be interested. So we had six people for a drum-off. One guy was a no-show. But five other guys showed up. Since then, several other people have been in touch (laughs). But it's too late now. Out of everybody who drummed, there were two really good players. We had to make a really tough decision, because each guy was very, very good. But we chose Jules Radino."

And were any of the other guys semi-famous?

"Well, I can't go into all that because maybe they will feel bad (laughs). But no, there were a few no-names and a few who were professionals. We just liked Jules' feel. It occurred to me the next day, why we liked his feel so much. He was a student of John Miceli, who is one of my favourite drummers. Miceli was Meatloaf's drummer, so he recommended Jules, and that's why I realised we liked his style so much, because we loved Miceli's style. So, being his student… as a matter of fact, Jules took over all of Miceli's students, when Miceli went on tour. So he's a very good drummer. I don't really know all his history. But I know for part of the past short time, he was in Popa Chubby, a blues act, I believe."

Jules is Blue Öyster Cult's drummer still now, 11 years hence. Not so with the bass player Eric and Buck were hiring at the same time…

"The bass player was… we got no notice, and had to come up with a bass player in less than two or three days," explains Eric. "That's too long a story to explain. But basically, this is one of those rock 'n' roll stories, where Woody, our soundman, he's with us like 90% of the time, but sometimes he's got other things he's got to do. One of those times, we had a tour in Europe, where he couldn't come. He recommended a family friend, Richie Castellano, who is a young man who has two degrees in digital engineering; he's only 24. But graduated college in three years, got his masters in a year and a half, and was actually teaching college in audio engineering. His father owns two music stores in Staten Island, NY. He's my son's age. Also he's a hardcore gamer, so Richie Castellano and I really hit it off. I can tell you like a dozen anecdotes. I don't get to meet a lot of people in their 20s that much, except backstage at a gig, 'Hey man, give me a pick.' But this is a very brilliant young man and a driven musician. We're both online gamers, so we compared a lot of notes. We actually play the same teams online on occasion and so does his father (laughs)."

"Which is really interesting—his dad is a great guy too. It was just a total coincidence. We knew his father, because he was the guitarist in the backing band for The Chambers Brothers, 30 years ago. I remember him from his six-inch platform shoes (laughs). But when I met him, he said, 'You know, I know you.' We started talking and we realised we had been on tour together in '73 or something. So when Danny took a hike, we said, 'Well, who can we get?' We had to get somebody right away. It was either that or blow off some big gigs. So it just occurred to me, you know, maybe Richie can play bass. Because I had been to see him. He has his own band that plays Staten Island and around. He did like all of *Rubber Soul*, you know, with seven guitar changes. He's just a shredding lead guitar player. I figured, anybody who is that good, you know, probably also plays bass. So I called him, woke him up at 10:00 in the morning and I said, 'Do you play bass?' He goes, yes. I said, 'Well, we need somebody for this weekend. How would you like to play bass?' He goes, 'Who is this?' (laughs). So he says, 'Wait a minute; now I'm up. What are you talking about?!' He had already mixed us for a whole tour of Europe, so he knew the show very, very well. He knew the songs, I mean, never studied the songs, but knew them from mixing them. He was totally thrilled and got his chops together very quickly. Donald lives in Florida now, so he did not come up in time to rehearse. So we had to have Richie join the band with no rehearsal. That's pretty bizarre."

"And the first gig, there were two gigs in a row. The first gig was a rain-out. So that gave us a little time. So what we did was we all went into somebody's hotel room. I mean, we were all there prepared to play, but it was outdoors and got rained out. So we went into one hotel room and we all got out guitars and stuff. Bobby was still in the band at the time so Bobby played on like a pad on the bed and we played through the whole show, and a few extra songs, and not only did Richie know them, he did not make one mistake. That's with no rehearsal, no nothing. That's just in learning on his own, off the DVD and off the record."

Why did Danny bail? "He got an offer he couldn't refuse, to join Miceli in that Queen show. Bobby… had a very good reason. He got an offer he couldn't refuse from a band called The Lizards. I think he wants to get a very big fat paycheck. I can't blame him. You know, he's got family and sometimes the bottom line is the most important thing. Bobby called me this morning from Sweden. Bobby is like, one of my best friends. In the seven years or so he was in the band, we got very close. He said it was the hardest decision he ever had to make, to leave BÖC to join that band."

I suppose the next development of significance was the replacement of Castellano on bass by none other than fat string legend Rudy Sarzo—for his on-stage introduction, the band broke into a little Ozzy, a little Quiet Riot, and a little 'Still of the Night'. How appropriate.

"Yes, and there even was some light discussion about making new music," says Rudy, who has since been replaced by Utopia's Kasim Sulton. "I was in the band for about four years, five years, maybe? It never came to fruition. But that doesn't mean that they would not record in the near future. You know, I've been busy. In less than a year, I've recorded five albums, so yeah, I'm out there recording as often as I can (laughs). But Buck's always coming up with stuff. When I was there, they did collaborate and they wrote music for videogames. No, no, they're very creative individuals. Eric likes to play video games, online. Buck's always playing his guitar. He travels with one of those little... it's like a thin little guitar, and I think Gibson makes them—it's a travelling guitar, and he's always playing it."

Anyhow, on the other side of the divide, there's a little more action. Albert divorced Deborah and he's playing again with Joe, plus Alice Cooper bassist Dennis Dunaway, in a fun little unit called Blue Coupe, who have stabbed into Canada on numerous occasions to play—on inaugural visits anyway—with a loose-knit group called The Outrageous Canadians, the whole she-bang put together by Hamilton, Ontario music legend (and massive Cult fan), Lou Molinaro. Blue Coupe has since knocked together a nice little discography and are a thriving and established outfit spreading the classic rock gospel everywhere.

Mentioned earlier, before the Brain Surgeons called it kaput, they enlisted none other than the Dictators' Ross the Boss on guitar for a record called *Denial of Death*. Plus, also as previously mentioned, Joe issued a fine new solo album for 2009 called *Jukebox in My Head*, followed by 2012's *Tales from the Island* and an EP in 2014 called *New Solid Black*.

"I wanted to do a record that sort of reflects where I'm at right now," explained Bouchard, on the first of those. "And so it's a collection of things that I had collected over the last four or five years, and a couple of new things, but mostly some things that developed. I wanted to have a sense of fun there, but I think it's a more serious record than I've done with The X Brothers or Bouchard, Dunaway and Smith, reflecting on what's going on with me and my musical ambitions. I don't know, I think it's pretty good. I figured I really had to get out and write more songs, so I started working with Dennis Dunaway more, and I worked with Ian Hunter, and then when it came down to this, I had a co-writer who co-wrote six of the songs on this record, Patti Gesmondi, Patti G, as she is known, and we started writing songs. We hit a real stride with some of these, and next thing you know there were a stack of songs, and from that stack of songs came the core of what this album was. I wrote a few more and picked a couple of interesting covers that nobody has ever heard, so it looks to be a great package that people will enjoy."

What are those covers?

"The covers are a song called 'Kickin' a Can,' which is a song my brother Jim wrote. He's an excellent songwriter from Boston; does a lot of acoustic music. Right now he does a lot of Internet collaborations—he's big into garage bands and pop rock. He doesn't perform as much as he used to. But I think he is the most talented songwriter in the family; he's written a lot of great songs. So I'm really proud of re-doing that song. The other one is called 'Dark Boat,' the last song on the album. Which gets a great reaction. That was written by my neighbour, when I was growing up, this guy John Cook, who is another acoustic musician, artist, antique dealer, guitar dealer—does everything. He always says he's going to do an album, but he's never gotten it together to do it. I would go to his house which was right next to our house up in the Thousand Islands, on the St. Lawrence river, and we would jam on his porch, and one of the songs that

I was quite impressed with was this 'Dark Boat.' It had kind of a 'Reaper' vibe about it."

Jukebox in My Head features a killer veteran drummer in Michael Cartellone of Damn Yankees and Lynyrd Skynyrd fame...

"Okay, yes Michael... I went to a Lynyrd Skynyrd show, and it was really hard to pick a drummer. I could've gotten a lot of different people; a lot of great drummers. I'm sitting there in the audience, just like anybody else, and I'm thinking boy, that is some of the best drumming I've ever heard. I just like the way he works with the bass, and certain things that he does, subtle things. He's a good solid player, but he does a lot of subtleties. I actually saw him like a couple months later in a club, and I said, 'I'm working on an album; I need a drummer.' He says, 'Oh, call me.' I didn't call him, and then he finally emailed me and said, 'When are we going to do that album?' He lives in New York City, and I thought, you know, that's one reason I didn't call, because I thought he was living in Nashville, or down in Florida where the Lynyrd Skynyrd guys live. But no, he lives in New York, so we had a couple rehearsals and talked on the phone a lot and passed demos back and forth, and he's just a monster in the studio. Most of the songs there are one take. There's a lot of creativity in what he did. He did a lot of great things in 'Dark Boat,' with the tom toms. What can I say? I was impressed. Most of the drummers that I was favouring were like jazz drummers. I really wanted somebody who could rock hard and Michael is the guy."

Asked about lyrical concerns, Joe brings up opening track 'Shadows on the Streets of New York'. "The idea was that I've had a lot of friends from New York who are now gone. Specifically, I'm talking about Billy Hilfiger, who passed away from brain cancer, and then Helen Wheels, who died from an elective back surgery problem; it was very tragic. So I said, well, these have been my friends... and also in that list is David Roter too, who I played with and performed with. He wrote 'Joan Crawford' and some great songs for Blue Öyster Cult, and all these guys had passed away. So I wanted to do a song that rocks hard, because they would be happy with a song that really had a good rock punch to it. So there's a lot of Billy Hilfiger in that song; he was a great friend of mine. I went through four different versions of the song. I actually wrote a jazz version of it (laughs), but from that jazz version came some good lyric ideas, and then I went back to the more hard rock version, with a hard funk in it. There's a lot of variety of styles on this record, but I hope that my personality and production style sort of brings it all together. I do a lot of different things—from metal to acoustic. My original idea was that this record was going to be 50% electric and 50% acoustic, but after I did the tracks with Michael, I thought I really gotta make this rock. So there's a lot more rock than acoustic. But there is little bit of both, and hopefully it's tied in together, and it's going to find an audience."

How are the other guys doing? How is Albert doing? What about rest the band?

"Albert is doing good. I just played with his new band, Underbelly, with Les Braunstein singing. I hadn't played a gig with Les Braunstein since the Soft White Underbelly days. We had this great gig playing for Tapscon, which is the Atlantic Paranormal Society. What it is, I don't know if you've ever watched the Sci-fi channel, on cable, but there is a program called *Ghost Hunters*. So this was a convention of the ghost hunters and they had about 3000 people at this hotel in Florida, and of course they love the Blue Öyster Cult songs, so we played a bunch of those and had a good times. It was a great gig. I'm not going to become a member of The Underbelly per se, but certainly if good convention type things come up, I would certainly like to do that again. We actually went on a ghost hunt, after we did the gig. These people, you would think, going to a convention of ghost hunters, are going to be pretty weird. But they were the most normal people! Except at midnight, they say, 'Let's go on a ghost hunt.' So we went up to the attic of this hotel, and I had the night vision camera. They are very serious about it. But it was really a lot of fun. Also, our good friend Helen Wheel's brother, Peter Robbins, who wrote a book on alien encounters that happened in England, he was one of the guests. So it was ghost hunters and alien watchers. So I can't say that the summer has been dull (laughs). That was definitely a great weekend."

"And Les is doing great. He does a version of 'Astronomy' that I thought was just fabulous. But he has his own stuff. He's been working on a lot of theatre music, and he's written kind of a musical that involves space travel. I can say no more than that. But he's got a lot of good songs in it; he's still a good songwriter. I'm not sure exactly what's going to happen next for that band, but that is what Albert is working on."

As concerns keeping in touch with the original Cultsters, Joe says that he "gets some nice emails from Donald every once in a while. They are very busy. They are just playing all over the place. They seem to be doing well in Europe. So they're going back to France in September. But generally, they are playing more gigs than they have in a long time."

Joe had had no contact with Allen Lanier. Speaking in '09, before Allen's death, he thought that brother Al had, but the drummer Bouchard says no such luck. "I've got a number that doesn't work. I get an answering machine with his voice on it, and it says, 'This is a number that we never answer and we never call back.' That's it. So I mean, if you talked on there and said, 'Hey Allen, it's your sister,' you know? Betsy or whatever. He might answer, if he recognises Betsy's voice."

A few years later, speaking to Kevin Julie about his second solo album, *Tales from the Island*, Joe remarked that, "Having the experience of the first solo album, *Jukebox in My Head*, behind me made this one easier and quicker too. It took about two-and-a-half years to get it all together. I'm already planning a third solo album; it might be a departure from the first two, but it's a nice feeling clearing the slate of old material. Positive comments and reviews make me want to do yet another album soon. *Jukebox* was unique enough that it wouldn't be mistaken for a BÖC album, but certainly has some elements to attract old fans and new ones. The new album seems to go a step further in being something different. A few comments seemed to lean that way, but for the most part I do my own thing. My voice and bass playing are prominent on the solo albums, so fans could hear that in the old BÖC style. Occasionally I'll think of how Donald might have played a guitar part, but I usually bring in influences from other favourite bands when I'm recording. I love '60s bands like the Beach Boys, the Stones, and so on. They influence me more than the BÖC style.

"The whole album was recorded in my home studio," continues Joe. "I was planning for Michael Cartellone to play drums again. We discussed arrangements and approaches to the songs for months. But he is on tour for the entire summer, and recording drums would have to wait 'til late in the fall. Also I was under pressure to finish the new Blue Coupe album and the new X Brothers albums. I could have waited and added more outside musicians, but since all the songs were the way I wanted them, I said right now was best time to release the album. It was an easy decision. I may do remixes and alternate arrangements for bonus tracks and repackages in the future, which could involve a number of outside musicians."

As for instrumentation... "The guitar is what I do most, and piano is probably secondary. But I love the mandolin and 12-string guitar. They were the backbone of several songs on the album. I added banjo to the Katrina song, because I couldn't find a suitable guitar part and the banjo was perfect. I used to play trumpet in the '60s, so I played trumpet on 'Katrina' too. Was going to replace the trumpet with a real player, but I like the idea of walking down the street in New Orleans and hearing a ragtag band coming out of a doorway with just those instruments, wailing away—that appealed to me. You don't have to be a virtuoso to make up cool arrangements. Some people say that track sounds like The Band from *Big Pink*, who often traded old instruments for effect. Bass is what I did with BÖC for 16 years. One of the reasons I did both solo albums was to show old fans that I could still pick up the four—or five—string bass and make it work."

"This is kind of an experiment, as I put the album out in April, but it only had six tracks on it," noted Joe, speaking with Jeb Wright on the subject of making his third record an EP. "I have talked to a lot of producers and they tell me that I should put out EPs. I have never done that and I think it's kind of crazy, but I know a lot of young bands are doing it. It felt incomplete to me. I hesitated and thought, 'What should I do with this?' I let it simmer for a while as I had just released it digitally, which is something that is new to me as well. You know who buys music just digitally? Well, not my fans. They don't even want to know about that. They want to hold it in their hands and they want to smell it. It has got to be a physical thing. They don't care about MP3s and stuff like that. There is something to be said for being able to hold it in your hands, as it makes it more tangible, and I think that makes it a better thing. I figured I should put a couple of bonus tracks on there, so I put the two that I have that are on there, and that made it a total of eight tracks and that made it feel more complete. I think a shorter album is easier to deal with if you're doing it all yourself. When we do Blue Coupe albums, there are three very opinionated people involved. It makes it a very slow process and everyone gets their say. When I make it by myself, it's different."

Double the Blue Öyster Cult content, and you've got Joe joined by Al for Blue Coupe. Asked in 2013 to contrast his old post-BÖC band with his new one, Albert says, "Brain Surgeons came about because I had been producing a number of young bands and each time they would start to get successful something would happen and they would break up. It got too frustrating for me so I figured I would just do it myself. The Brain Surgeons got good reviews most of the time and we could draw a crowd most of the time but we never made any money. I lost money on it from the beginning to the end. With Blue Coupe, we always have a blast and we always make money. This is the ideal group for me at this point. I can't think of anybody I'd rather play with. We laugh a lot. The only time we argue is when we're making the records and that's as it should be. Creation is a difficult process. Boredom, chaos, confusion, ego and self-doubt all play an important part in it."

Citing a connection between the band's second album, *Million More Miles* (follow-up to 2010's *Tornado on the Tracks*), Bouchard explains that, "'Ride' was originally a song for the *Cultösaurus* record called 'Tough and Tender,' co-written with Ronald Binder. It was rejected by BÖC so I retooled it with Mark Barkan and it sat around for 30 years. I showed it to Joe and Dennis and they wanted to do it. It fit the theme of the record perfectly."

As for balancing rock 'n' roll with real life, Albert says, "I am still the music teacher in a public high school in Manhattan. I love the job and take it very seriously. I've been doing it for over 20 years and have many grateful former students who show me how I have made a difference in their lives. I am now considering how I can get more involved in music education on a larger level."

Back in the world of the official Blue Öyster Cult, well, in late '08, Buck Dharma had slipped on his stairs in Florida, carrying a bag of groceries, injuring his shoulder, prompting some gig cancellations. Mr. Gregmar wondered if this could facilitate the end of the band as we know it, given that, a) the guys are more bitter and cynical than ever about their chances for much more of a career, and b) that type of injury is pretty serious if your trade is trading licks. Defying the odds, Buck recovered and the band continued on with their year after year of low profile touring whilst demurring on the idea of making another record. Sure, Buck and Eric will offer any excuse not to record, but the death of physical product and the virtual free distribution of new music has offered them the best reason imaginable to pack that side of their business in ice and shove it to the back of the metal locker.

Allen, of course, was long done, well before his official demise, Bolle saying in 2009 that, "He has aged four times as rapidly as the other guys," adding as an example, that he wouldn't even go to Europe with them because he couldn't endure the travel without air conditioning. Bolle also says that guys like Rudy Sarzo and the "very ambitious" Jules Radino wouldn't be on retainer, although if you think about it, this wouldn't serve as much of a problem one way or the other.

Anyway, a few musings before we close… remember I said I had dirt? Sure, got a bunch, but it falls into a category you might call life and its mundane problems. Mundane to those not living it perhaps, but a pain in the ass to those inside. Suffice to say that some folks in the band got road burn, hassles at home, various levels and intensities of bitterness about having to bust ass nearly 30 years after the band's last hit. As alluded to by Bolle, maintaining enthusiasm and more importantly, maintaining the quality levels expected of BÖC can be draining… more responsibility than one can bear at times. Then there's getting old, there's remembering, with a wince, all the rip-offs. Never a fun spot in the book of life's flashbacks, whether one is doing the ripping or one is getting ripped.

"I had a little skin cancer. Because when I lived in LA, you can't avoid the sun," says Uncle Meltzer, adding a medical twist to the end of our protracted tale, perhaps fitting, given the advancing ages of these legends, not to mention the slow fade and ultimate end to Allen. "So about 12 years ago I had a little skin cancer on my neck, you know, stage one, basal cell, got that removed. Now I put on sunscreen whenever I leave the house. I think my health's okay. My blood pressure is probably high. I think I'm due for a checkup and I keep delaying it. I had hemorrhoid surgery about three years ago. I'm 58; I feel like I'm probably about 45. I probably should stop drinking as much as I do, but this is a beer town."

A Selected Blue Öyster Cult Discography

Those who have my other bio-type books know the drill—I don't get too carried away with these discographies, showing every permutation and compilation from every nation. I like to keep it pretty much official, although I've offered a brief "Notes" section after each album if there was anything pop-fruity and full of zest I thought best to mention. Also, I've retained the ol' side 1/side 2 designation for albums released in the vinyl era. Also, minor point, many BÖC song titles were truncated or otherwise grammatically altered over the years by lazy graphics people, or perhaps through intention for some reason. Anyway, I've gone with the originals and kept them that way for uniformity. Yeah yeah, I left out the *Bad Channels* soundtrack and the *Summer Daze* compilation.

Official Albums

Blue Öyster Cult (Columbia '72)
Side 1: Transmaniacon MC, I'm on the Lamb But I Ain't no Sheep, Then Came the Last Days of May, Stairway to the Stars, Before the Kiss, a Redcap
Side 2: Screams, She's as Beautiful as a Foot, Cities on Flame with Rock and Roll, Workshop of the Telescopes, Redeemed
Notes: Sony Legacy expanded edition from 2001 includes the bonus tracks What is Quicksand?, A Fact About Sneakers, Donovan's Monkey and Betty Lou Got a New Pair of Shoes.

Tyranny and Mutation (Columbia '73)
Side 1: The Black - The Red & the Black, O.D.'d on Life Itself, Hot Rails to Hell, 7 Screaming Diz-Busters
Side 2: The Red - Baby Ice Dog, Wings Wetted Down, Teen Archer, Mistress of the Salmon Salt (Quicklime Girl)
Notes: Issued in the US as Quad LP, including special gold Columbia record label. Sony Legacy expanded edition from 2001 includes the bonus tracks Cities on Flame with Rock and Roll (from the Original Bootleg EP), 7 Screaming Diz-Busters (from BÖC Live in the West 1975), O.D.'d on Life Itself (from BÖC Live in the West 1975) and Buck's Boogie (original studio version from 1973).

Secret Treaties (Columbia '74)
Side 1: Career of Evil, Subhuman, Dominance and Submission, ME 262
Side 2: Cagey Cretins, Harvester of Eyes, Flaming Telepaths, Astronomy
Notes: Issued in the US as Quad LP, including special gold Columbia record label. Sony Legacy expanded edition from 2001 includes the bonus tracks Boorman the Chauffeur, Mommy, Mes Dames Sarat, Born to Be Wild and Career of Evil (single version).

On Your Feet or on Your Knees (Columbia '75)

Side 1: Subhuman, Harvester of Eyes, Hot Rails to Hell
Side 2: The Red & the Black, 7 Screaming Diz-Busters, Buck's Boogie
Side 3: Then Came the Last Days of May, Cities on Flame with Rock and Roll, ME 262
Side 4: Before the Kiss, a Redcap, Maserati GT (I Ain't Got You), Born to Be Wild

Notes: First official live album; gatefold.

Agents of Fortune (Columbia '76)

Side 1: This Ain't the Summer of Love, True Confessions, (Don't Fear) The Reaper, E.T.I. (Extra Terrestrial Intelligence), The Revenge of Vera Gemini
Side 2: Sinful Love, Tattoo Vampire, Morning Final, Tenderloin, Debbie Denise
Notes: Reissued on Audiophile gold CD in the US. Sony Legacy expanded edition from 2001 includes the bonus tracks Fire of Unknown Origin, Sally, (Don't Fear) The Reaper (Buck's original home demo) and Dance the Night Away.

Spectres (Columbia '77)

Side 1: Godzilla, Golden Age of Leather, Death Valley Nights, Searchin' for Celine, Fireworks
Side 2: R. U. Ready 2 Rock, Celestial the Queen, Goin' Through the Motions, I Love the Night, Nosferatu
Notes: Sony Legacy expanded edition from 2007 includes the bonus tracks Night Flyer, Dial M for Murder, Please Hold and Be My Baby.

Some Enchanted Evening (Columbia '78)

Side 1: R.U. Ready 2 Rock, E.T.I. (Extra Terrestrial Intelligence), Astronomy
Side 2: Kick Out the Jams, Godzilla, (Don't Fear) The Reaper, We Gotta Get Out of this Place
Notes: Second official live album. Sony Legacy expanded edition from 2007 includes the bonus tracks ME 262, Harvester of Eyes, Hot Rails to Hell, This Ain't the Summer of Love, 5 Guitars, Born to be Wild and We Gotta Get Out of this Place (alternate version). An 11 track DVD is also included.

Mirrors (Columbia '79)

Side 1: Dr. Music, The Great Sun Jester, In Thee, Mirrors, Moon Crazy
Side 2: The Vigil, I Am the Storm, You're not the One (I Was Looking for), Lonely Teardrops

Cultösaurus Erectus (Columbia '80)

Side 1: Black Blade, Monsters, Divine Wind, Deadline
Side 2: The Marshall Plan, Hungry Boys, Fallen Angel, Lips in the Hills, Unknown Tongue
Notes: Remastered and reissued in the UK on CD in 1999.

Fire of Unknown Origin (Columbia '81)

Side 1: Fire of Unknown Origin, Burnin' for You, Veteran of the Psychic Wars, Sole Survivor, Heavy Metal: The Black and Silver
Side 2: Vengeance (The Pact), After Dark, Joan Crawford, Don't Turn Your Back

Extraterrestrial Live (Columbia '82)

Side 1: Dominance and Submission, Cities on Flame with Rock and Roll, Dr. Music, The Red & the Black
Side 2: Joan Crawford, Burnin' for You, Roadhouse Blues
Side 3: Black Blade, Hot Rails to Hell, Godzilla
Side 4: Veteran of the Psychic Wars, E.T.I. (Extra Terrestrial Intelligence), (Don't Fear) The Reaper
Notes: First line-up change: Albert Bouchard is replaced by Rick Downey. Third official live album. Gatefold sleeve; nice touch including the lyrics.

The Revolution by Night (Columbia '83)

Side 1: Take Me Away, Eyes on Fire, Shooting Shark, Veins
Side 2: Shadow of California, Feel the Thunder, Let Go, Dragon Lady, Light Years of Love

Club Ninja (Columbia '86)

Side 1: White Flags, Dancin' in the Ruins, Make Rock not War, Perfect Water, Spy in the House of the Night
Side 2: Beat 'Em Up, When the War Comes, Shadow Warrior, Madness to the Method
Notes: Reissued on CD by Koch in 1997. A collaboration between many players, although officially, there's Eric, Buck and Joe, plus Jimmy Wilcox on drums and Tommy Zvoncheck on keyboards.

Imaginos (Columbia '88)

Side 1: I Am the One You Warned Me of, Les Invisibles, In the Presence of Another World, Del Rio's Song, The Siege and Investiture of Baron Von Frankenstein's Castle at Weisseria
Side 2: Astronomy, Magna of Illusion, Blue Öyster Cult, Imaginos
Notes: Issued on limited blue vinyl in the UK. A collaboration between many players, but officially, it's all of them, the original line-up.

Heaven Forbid (CMC/BMG '98)

See You in Black, Harvest Moon, Power Underneath Despair, X-Ray Eyes, Hammer Back, Damaged, Cold Gray Light of Dawn, Real World, Live for Me, Still Burnin', In Thee
Notes: Buck, Eric and Allen, with Danny Miranda on bass and Chuck Bürgi on drums. Most lyrics by sci-fi writer John Shirley. Japanese issue replaced "melting man" cover with the inner "woman with staff" graphic.

Curse of the Hidden Mirror (CMC/Sanctuary '01)

Dance on Stilts, Showtime, The Old Gods Return, Pocket, One Step Ahead of the Devil, I Just Like to Be Bad, Here Comes that Feeling, Out of the Darkness, Stone of Love, Eye of the Hurricane, Good to Feel Hungry

A Long Day's Night (CMC/Sanctuary '02)

Stairway to the Stars, Burnin' for You, O.D.'d on Life Itself, Dance on Stilts, Buck's Boogie, Mistress of the Salmon Salt (Quicklime Girl), Harvest Moon, Astronomy, Cities on Flame with Rock and Roll, Perfect Water, Lips in the Hills, Godzilla, (Don't Fear) The Reaper
Notes: Also issued on DVD (which adds six tracks). Fourth official live album.

The Key Official Compilations

Career of Evil: The Metal Years (Columbia 1989)

Cities on Flame with Rock and Roll, The Red & the Black, Hot Rails to Hell, Dominance and Submission, 7 Screaming Diz-Busters, ME 262, E.T.I. (Extra Terrestrial Intelligence), Beat 'Em Up, Black Blade, Harvester of Eyes, Flaming Telepaths, Godzilla, (Don't Fear) The Reaper
Notes: A compilation comprising a mix of live and studio versions, all from the official releases.

Workshop of the Telescopes (Columbia Legacy 1995)

Cities on Flame with Rock and Roll, Transmaniacon MC, Before the Kiss, a Redcap, Stairway to the Stars, Buck's Boogie, Workshop of the Telescopes, The Red & the Black, 7 Screaming Diz-Busters, Career of Evil, Flaming Telepaths, Astronomy, Subhuman, Harvester of Eyes, ME 262, Born to Be Wild, (Don't Fear) The Reaper, This Ain't the Summer of Love, E.T.I. (Extra Terrestrial Intelligence), Godzilla, Goin' Through the Motions, Golden Age of Leather, Kick Out the Jams, We Gotta Get Out of this Place, In Thee, The Marshall Plan, Veteran of the Psychic Wars, Burnin' For You, Dominance and Submission, Take Me Away, Shooting Shark, Dancin' in the Ruins, Perfect Water
Notes: The definitive compilation.

Don't Fear the Reaper—The Best of (Sony 2000)

Cities on Flame with Rock and Roll, The Red & the Black, Flaming Telepaths, Astronomy, This Ain't the Summer of Love, (Don't Fear) The Reaper, I Love the Night, Goin' Through the Motions, Godzilla, In Thee, The Marshall Plan, Black Blade, Joan Crawford, Burnin' for You, Shooting Shark, Take Me Away

Cult Classic (Herald/Caroline '94)

(Don't Fear) The Reaper, E.T.I. (Extra Terrestrial Intelligence), ME 262, This Ain't the Summer of Love, Burnin' for You, O.D.'d on Life Itself, Flaming Telepaths, Godzilla, Astronomy, Cities on Flame with Rock and Roll, Harvester of Eyes, Buck's Boogie, (Don't Fear) The Reaper (TV mix), Godzilla (TV mix)

Notes: Issued in Europe in 2001 with a new cover as Champions of Rock (or part of a series called that). There also exists a likely bootleg or grey market version of this odd "re-recorded classics" release, this time called (and also with new cover), E.T.I. Revisited.

The Essential Blue Öyster Cult (Columbia Legacy 2003)

Cities on Flame with Rock and Roll, 7 Screaming Diz-Busters, Harvester of Eyes, Astronomy, (Don't Fear) The Reaper, E.T.I. (Extra Terrestrial Intelligence), Godzilla, I Love the Night, In Thee, Black Blade, Burnin' for You, Veteran of the Psychic Wars, Shooting Shark, Take Me Away

Notes: Part of the prolific "Essential" series, with uniform design and budget pricing.

Then and Now (CMC/Sanctuary 2003)

Burnin' for You, Cities on Flame with Rock and Roll, Godzilla, (Don't Fear) The Reaper, Harvest Moon, Cold Gray Light of Dawn, Damaged, See You in Black, One Step Ahead of the Devil, Dance on Stilts, The Old Gods Return, Pocket

Notes: A compilation culled from the band's three albums (and one DVD) with CMC/Sanctuary. The vintage material is from the live album A Long Day's Night. From the uniformly designed Then and Now series.

Credits

Interviews With The Author
Bloom, Eric. 1997
Bloom, Eric. November 30, 2001
Bloom, Eric. October 7, 2004
Bouchard, Albert. March 7, 1996
Bouchard, Albert. May 6, 1996
Bouchard, Albert. 1997
Bouchard, Albert. April 22, 2006
Bouchard, Albert. March 11, 2009
Bouchard, Joe. March 13, 1996
Bouchard, Joe. 1997
Bouchard, Joe. August 4, 2007
Bouchard, Joe. August 13, 2008
Bouchard, Joe. March 2, 2008
Butler, Geezer. August 13, 2008
Dio, Ronnie James. August 13, 2008
Gregmar, Bolle. 1997
Gregmar, Bolle. 2001
Ioannis. April 20, 2004
Krugman, Murray. 1997
Lanier, Allen. November 30, 2001
Meltzer, Richard. January 8, 2004
Miranda, Danny. November 30, 2001
Pearlman, Sandy. 1997
Roeser, Donald. 1996
Roeser, Donald. May 26, 1998
Roeser, Donald. November 30, 2001
Roeser, Donald. June 4, 2001
Rondinelli, Bobby. November 30, 2001
Rondinelli, Bobby. 2001
Rondinelli, Bobby. January 30, 2004
Roter, David. 1997
Scott, Greg. 1997
Shirley, John. January 5, 2004
Werman, Tom. 2003
Wheels, Helen. 1997

Additional Citations
Blast. Reaping Fortune with Blue Öyster Cult by Buck Dharma as told to Robert Alexander. December 1976.
Circus. The Cult Change Their Stripes by John Swenson. Circus Enterprises Corporation,
Circus. Five Easy Oysters by Billy Altman. Circus Enterprises Corporation, July 1976.
Circus. A Summer of Work for the Blue Öyster Cult by Rob Patterson. Circus, 1977.
Circus. Cult-de-sac by David Fricke. Circus Enterprises Corporation, October 10, 1978.
Classic Rock Revisited (classicrockrevisted.com). Interviews with Eric Bloom, Danny Miranda and Joe Bouchard by Jeb Wright.
Columbia Records. Biography from Columbia Records: Blue Öyster Cult. 1972.

Contemporary Keyboard. Rocking the Keyboards with Blue Öyster Cult by Michael Davis. Feb '80.

Creem. Blue Öyster Cult is God! by Robert Duncan. January 1978.

Discoveries. Blue Öyster Cult: The Past 20 Years by Paul Gabriel & Larry Araha. No. 167. April '02.

Goldmine. "Don't Report This": The Saga of Blue Öyster Cult by Steve Roeser and Bolle Gregmar. *Vol. 22, No. 12, Issue 414.* June 7, 1996.

Hit Parader. Blue Öyster Cult's Allen Lanier: The Hit Parader Interview by Lisa Robinson. Charlton Publications, *No. 163.* February 1978.

Hit Parader. Blue Öyster Cult: On the Road with Phase Three by Joseph Rose. Charlton Publications, No. 166. May 1978.

Hit Parader. Great Balls of Fire by Toby Goldstein. Charlton Publications, No. 214. July 1982.

Hit Parader. Blue Öyster Cult: Exclusive Buck Dharma Interview by Charlie Crespo. Charlton Publications, No. 223. April 1983.

Kerrang!. Instant Dharma by Steve Gett. No. 19. July 1-15.

Kerrang!. The Revolution by Night record review by Malcolm Dome. No. 55. November 17-30, 1983.

Kerrang!. Songs Sung Blue by Malcolm Dome. Spotlight Publications. No. 56. December 1-14, 1984.

Melody Maker. Hot Rails to Hell by Michael Oldfield. July 27, 1974.

Melody Maker. R.U. Ready to Rock? by Ian Birch. February 4, 1978.

Metallion. Blue Öyster Cult concert review by Mary Ann Gallippi. No. 1, Vol. 1. Sept. 1984.

Music Express. Blue Öyster Cult by Kerry Doole. Wembley Productions, Issue No.50.

New Musical Express. Behind the girl with the rhinestone studded whip by Dan Nooger. March 30 1974.

New Musical Express. Blue Öyster Cult: Tyranny, Mutation, Flaming Telepaths, Heavy Metal Sorcery... by Tony Parsons. June 17, 1978.

New Musical Express. Cultösaurus Erectus record review by Phil McNeill. July 5, 1980.

New York Rocker. Cultösaurus Erectus record review by Roy Trakin. November 1980.

Pop Entertainment. Blue Öyster Cult: Don't Fear the Cult by Ken Sharp. 2001.

Record Review. Extraterrestrial Live record review by Todd Everett. Vol. 6, No. 4. August 1982.

Rolling Stone. Agents of Fortune record review by Ken Tucker. Issue No.217. July 15, 1976.

Rolling Stone. Some Enchanted Evening record review by Mitchell Schneider. Issue No.285. February 22, 1979.

Rolling Stone. Fire of Unknown Origin record review by Parke Puterbaugh. Issue No.355. October 29, 1981.

Rolling Stone. Flat Out record review by Parke Puterbaugh. Issue No.384. December 9, 1982.

Rolling Stone. The Revolution by Night record review by Errol Somay. Issue No.416. March 1, 1984.

Rosen, Steve. "Blue Oyster's" BUCK DHARMA. 1975.

Sounds. The Night William Burroughs Took All My Cake by Giovanni Dadomo. July 28, 1979.

Travellers in Time (travellersintime.com). Interviews with Joe & Al Bouchard by Kevin Julie.

Trouser Press. Review of Extraterrestrial Live by Jon Young. Trans-Oceanic Trouser Press Inc., No. 76. August 1982.

Trouser Press. Why You Should Care About Blue Öyster Cult by Jim Green. Trans-Oceanic Trouser Press Inc., No. 70. February 1982.

Vintage Rock (vintagerock.com). The Eric Bloom Interview by Shawn Perry. 1997, 2009.

Photo Credits

Most of the photos within this book were taken by a buddy of mine named Rich Galbraith. He has an incredible collection from the '70s and early '80s to his name—his is quite the story. His work is available for sale, either negs with rights, or just as prints. He can be reached at: egyptsknight@suddenlink.net. Or just ask me about him—I'll set ya up. Rich rules.

Additionally, Rod Dysinger stepped up to the plate with some key and capable shots from the mid to late '80s. Without his generous support, we wouldn't have pictures of these swell hairstyles and clothes on the guys. Rod can be reached at rdysinger1@hotmail.com and is always eager to pick up some work writing and shooting in the rock journo field.

Plyer of the fat strings Joe Bouchard himself supplied a bunch of cool things as well—his contribution is throughout the book, not the least of which is his words of wisdom and good humour.

Finally, David Lee Wilson supplied shots coving the recent years. Also a capable journalist and rock historian, he can be reached at isentertainment@juno.com

About The Author

At approximately 7900 (with over 7000 appearing in his books), Martin has unofficially written more record reviews than anybody in the history of music writing across all genres. Additionally, Martin has penned 52 books on hard rock, heavy metal, classic rock and record collecting. He was Editor In Chief of the now retired *Brave Words & Bloody Knuckles*, Canada's foremost metal publication for 14 years, and has also contributed to *Revolver*, *Guitar World*, *Goldmine*, *Record Collector*, *bravewords.com*, *lollipop.com* and *hardradio.com*, with many record label band bios and liner notes to his credit as well. Additionally, Martin has been a regular contractor to Banger Films, having worked for two years as researcher on the award-wining documentary *Rush: Beyond The Lighted Stage*, on the writing and research team for the 11-episode *Metal Evolution* and on the 10-episode *Rock Icons*, both for VH1 Classic. Additionally, Martin is the writer of the original metal genre chart used in *Metal: A Headbanger's Journey* and throughout the *Metal Evolution* episodes. Martin currently resides in Toronto and can be reached through martinp@inforamp.net or www.martinpopoff.com.

Martin Popoff – A Complete Bibliography

This Means War: The Sunset Years of the NWOBHM (2015)
Wheels of Steel: The Explosive Early Years of the NWOBHM (2015)
Swords And Tequila: Riot's Classic First Decade (2015)
Who Invented Heavy Metal? (2015)
Sail Away: Whitesnake's Fantastic Voyage (2015)
Live Magnetic Air: The Unlikely Saga Of The Superlative Max Webster (2014)
Steal Away The Night: An Ozzy Osbourne Day-By-Day (2014)
The Big Book Of Hair Metal (2014)
Sweating Bullets: The Deth And Rebirth Of Megadeth (2014)
Smokin' Valves: A Headbanger's Guiide to 900 NWOBHM Records (2014)
The Art Of Metal (co-edit with Malcolm Dome; 2013)
2 Minutes To Midnight: An Iron Maiden Day-By-Day (2013)
Metallica: The Complete Illustrated History (2013)
Rush: The Illustrated History (2013)
Ye Olde Metal: 1979 (2013)
Scorpions: Top Of The Bill (2013)
Epic Ted Nugent (2012)
Fade To Black: Hard Rock Cover Art Of The Vinyl Age (2012)
It's Getting Dangerous: Thin Lizzy 81-12 (2012)
We Will Be Strong: Thin Lizzy 76-81 (2012)
Fighting My Way Back: Thin Lizzy 69-76 (2011)
The Deep Purple Royal Family: Chain Of Events '80 – '11 (2011)
The Deep Purple Royal Family: Chain Of Events Through '79 (2011)
Black Sabbath FAQ (2011)
The Collector's Guide To Heavy Metal: Volume 4: The '00s (2011; co-authored with David Perri)
Goldmine Standard Catalog Of American Records 1948 – 1991, 7th Edition (2010)
Goldmine Record Album Price Guide, 6th Edition (2009)
Goldmine 45 RPM Price Guide, 7th Edition (2009)
A Castle Full Of Rascals: Deep Purple '83 – '09 (2009)
Worlds Away: Voivod And The Art Of Michel Langevin (2009)
Ye Olde Metal: 1978 (2009)
Gettin' Tighter: Deep Purple '68 – '76 (2008)
All Access: The Art Of The Backstage Pass (2008)
Ye Olde Metal: 1977 (2008)
Ye Olde Metal: 1976 (2008)
Judas Priest: Heavy Metal Painkillers (2007)
Ye Olde Metal: 1973 To 1975 (2007)
The Collector's Guide To Heavy Metal: Volume 3: The Nineties (2007)
Ye Olde Metal: 1968 To 1972 (2007)
Run For Cover: The Art Of Derek Riggs (2006)
Black Sabbath: Doom Let Loose (2006)
Dio: Light Beyond The Black (2006)
The Collector's Guide To Heavy Metal: Volume 2: The Eighties (2005)
Rainbow: English Castle Magic (2005)
UFO: Shoot Out The Lights (2005)
The New Wave Of British Heavy Metal Singles (2005)
Blue Öyster Cult: Secrets Revealed! (2004)
Contents Under Pressure: 30 Years Of Rush At Home & Away (2004)
The Top 500 Heavy Metal Albums Of All Time (2004)
The Collector's Guide To Heavy Metal: Volume 1: The Seventies (2003)
The Top 500 Heavy Metal Songs Of All Time (2003)
Southern Rock Review (2001)
Heavy Metal: 20th Century Rock And Roll (2000)
The Goldmine Price Guide To Heavy Metal Records (2000)
The Collector's Guide To Heavy Metal (1997)
Riff Kills Man! 25 Years Of Recorded Hard Rock & Heavy Metal (1993)

See martinpopoff.com for complete details and ordering information.